Beastly
LONDON

Beastly LONDON

A HISTORY OF ANIMALS IN THE CITY

HANNAH VELTEN

REAKTION BOOKS

Published by
REAKTION BOOKS LTD
33 Great Sutton Street
London EC1V 0DX
www.reaktionbooks.co.uk

First published 2013
Copyright © Hannah Velten 2013

Printed and bound in China
by C&C Offset Printing Co., Ltd

A catalogue record for this book is available from the British Library.

ISBN 978 1 78023 167 9

Contents

Horse-drawn chaos outside 'The Bank', 1886, engraving after a picture by W. Logsdail exhibited at the Royal Academy.

Introduction: Revealing the Beasts

Ask anyone living outside London, and even Londoners themselves, to name animals associated with the city and they are likely to list those associated with tourist sights or recent news items: the Queen's state horses, used at the wedding of William and Kate in 2011; the ravens at the Tower of London; the members of the Household Cavalry on duty at Horse Guards; London Zoo; the waterfowl in the royal London parks; the cat that lives at 10 Downing Street; the Queen's corgis; disorientated mammals swimming up the Thames; Battersea Dogs and Cats Home; urban foxes; and the exploding rat population.[1]

These potent symbols of London society and culture provide a snapshot of the rich heritage of the animal inhabitants of London from Roman times to the present. But dig a little deeper into the history of 'beastly London', and it becomes obvious that today's scant animal population pales into insignificance compared with the heaving mass of animals that once lived on the streets, in the Thames and in Londoners' homes. Instead of the roar of traffic, London's soundtrack was, until relatively recently, a cacophony of man-made noise, neighing, barking, mooing, bleating, quacking, braying, hissing, oinking, roaring, screeching, clucking, tweeting, trumpeting, meowing, snarling, squeaking and snuffling. It is only recently – within the last few decades – that animals aside from pets, and those mentioned above, have more or less become extinct in the city: the last brewery dray horses have left, the pigeons of Trafalgar Square have

been removed, the large animals of London Zoo have been evacuated, Club Row animal market is banned and the Smithfield Show and Crufts exhibitions have been relocated away from London. It can be argued that animals no longer have a place on the streets of twenty-first-century London because of the filth and nuisance they would cause. So far as the animals are concerned, it could be said that it is a good thing that they no longer have to endure urban life – especially its pollutants, its man-made habitat and its hectic nature. However, London has lost some of its rich character with the withdrawal of animals.

The interaction between animals and Londoners of all classes was an integral part of everyday life and experience. It is difficult today to appreciate how closely they lived side by side, sometimes in the strangest of circumstances. In the 1850s barbers sold bear's grease as a hair-growth stimulant and some 'particular and conscientious' barbers even pretended to kill their own bears and boil them down to render the fat.[2] However, Alfred Rosling Bennett (1850–1928) recalled as a child seeing a 'poor lean greyish bear' kept in a cellar; it was advertised as being due for slaughter that coming Saturday, but he saw the same bear again in another barber's cellar the following week.[3]

The animals of London were certainly used for all sorts of purposes. They were used to feed Londoners, to transport them and their goods, to entertain them, to provide a livelihood for them, to give opportunities for research and study, to provide sport and gambling opportunities, to soothe their urban souls, to provide secondary products and to act as fashionable accoutrements and companions. Wild animals and scavengers chose to live in London because the man-made environment met their every need. Even the dust in the streets that caused distress to all in the dry months was created by animals, especially the vast number of horses constantly passing over the thoroughfares.

However, it is rare to find more than a passing mention of the animal populations of London in general histories. It is as though the creatures did not make an important contribution to the life of the city. This book hopes to redress this omission and give the animals their 'voice', showing the role they played in shaping the economic, social and cultural history of London.

The more obvious visual reminders of London's past animal inhabitants are the animal-related street names that bear testimony to those parts of the city that have long-held animal associations. A short list includes Bear Gardens, SE1; Bird Street, W1; Birdcage Walk, SW1; Bull's Gardens, SW3; Cowcross Street, EC1; Duck Lane, W1; Falcon Court, EC4; Houndsditch, EC3; Nightingale Walk, SW4; Poultry, EC2; Puma Court, E1; Swan Lane, EC4; and Whalebone Court, EC2. There are also animal sculptures littering London, such as the statue of a tiger and young boy at Tobacco Dock in Wapping, which depicts an escapee tiger from Jamrach's Exotic Animal Depository. The two stone mice that fight over a piece of cheese above the heads of passers-by in Philpot Lane, EC3, commemorate two workmen who fought on the roof over a missing lunch, leading to the death of one – mice had been responsible. Some historic animal-related traditions are still enacted, albeit on an irregular or smaller scale, such as driving livestock across London Bridge or swan-upping on the Thames. Various plaques tell tales of the animals that lived and worked in urban environments long since swept away by new

developments; and artefacts on view at the Museum of London paint vivid images of the variety and uses of the animals that lived permanently in or passed through the metropolis.

While there is still evidence today of London's past association with animals, it is contemporary sources that reveal the most about the intimate bonds which existed between Londoners and the domestic, exotic and wild animals with which they shared the city. Accounts of these animals can be gleaned from early sources, such as the chronicles of London by William Fitzstephen (*d. c.* 1191) and John Stow (*c.* 1525–1605), and the diaries of Samuel Pepys (1633–1703) and John Evelyn (1620–1706). However, it seems that animals were so much a part of life in the early modern period that they were rarely mentioned unless they were causing a nuisance, being subjected to excessive cruelty or being viewed as a bad omen: in 1593 it was feared that the plague would worsen because a heron perched on top of St Peter's, Cornhill, for the whole afternoon, and in 1604 the House of Commons rejected a bill after a jackdaw flew through the Chamber while it was being proposed.[4] Meanwhile, early modern illustrations of London are rarely without the ubiquitous dog or horse gracing the street scene: a true indication of the animals' presence on the streets.

It becomes easier to 'see' animals in the nineteenth century, when an explosion of interest in their uses, welfare and lives led to writings by naturalists, social commentators, journalists, poets and animal-welfare organizations. Newspapers and journals also contained copious letters, features, and court and police reports concerning London animals. This interest stemmed from a change in attitudes towards 'brute creation', and subsequently campaigns were led to either rid the city of animals or improve their welfare.

Beastly London may be a difficult read for today's reader (and researching it was an emotional task for the author) because of the seemingly endless exploitation of London's animals and the questionable ways in which they were treated, certainly before the mid-nineteenth century. Some of the cruelty stems from ignorance of the animals' needs, which is particularly evident in the management of exotics, such as the elephant that was fed on wine and the zebra on tobacco. Working animals, performing animals and livestock were pushed to their limits because of economic necessity; pets were either overindulged or abandoned; sporting animals were exploited to satisfy bloodlust and gambling needs; and wildlife was systematically destroyed – all without much trauma to Londoners' collective conscience.

Of course, there are instances of animals being treated well – especially those that lived and worked with their owners and were depended upon – but the general neglect of animal welfare was a result of the way animals were viewed between 1500 and 1800, according to Keith Thomas's *Man and the Natural World* (1983). Early religious attitudes towards animals were shaped by the doctrine of anthropocentrism,

meaning that man was at the centre of the God-made world. All animals had been created for man's sake and were subordinate to his wishes and needs.[5] Therefore animals could provide labour, and be hunted and generally exploited, without a thought for any suffering they might be subjected to. However, from the fifteenth century several non-conformist groups raised concerns about the morality of unnecessary cruelty to animals, arguing that there was no need to tyrannize or ill-treat them unnecessarily by, for example, killing them using inhumane slaughter practices, hunting them for pleasure or baiting them for entertainment's sake.[6] But it was not until the later seventeenth century that it became part of Christian doctrine to treat all animals civilly.[7]

The other guiding religious principle that upheld the exploitation of animals was the Great Chain of Being, which placed the whole of the natural world in a hierarchical scale with men and the angels at the top, and animals, ordered by degrees of imperfection, below them.[8] This scale justified man's treatment of

City mice: a small monument to a human tragedy in Philpot Lane, EC3.

A horse cavalcade bringing the new bell 'Victoria' to the Clock Tower, Palace of Westminster, 1858.

subordinate animals and created a rigid barrier between man and beast. However, alongside the increasing concern about man's moral duty towards animals, the distinction between the two was battered during the course of the eighteenth century by advances in anatomy, astronomy, biology, zoology and geology. Animals were observed objectively for the first time and it began to dawn on people – first on intellectuals, then generally on the middle classes – that animals had their own habits and characters and that some were as capable of reasoning and feeling as humans: something that pet owners and anyone who worked closely with animals already knew.[9]

These revelations, along with cries from the naturally tender-hearted and philosophical teachings of sentimentalists and humanitarians, were eventually taken up by London's eighteenth-century educated middle classes, who called for 'an ideal of cultivated refinement' that targeted such uncivilized cruelties as animal baiting and cockfighting.[10] These people's concern for animals was heightened, according to Thomas, because the urbanization and industrialization of London had led to their isolation from the countryside. This created a longing for a rural idyll in which animals were neither dominated nor suppressed. They also became inclined to view animals as pets rather than as working livestock.[11] The middle classes had another (ulterior) motive when calling for behaviour to change towards animals – they were looking to discipline the behaviour of their social inferiors. The idea that cruelty towards animals led to cruelty towards humans was not new: one thinks of William

Hogarth's *The Four Stages of Cruelty* (1750–51), which portrays the Londoner Tom Nero torturing animals as a youth, progressing to beating his horse as a coachman, then ultimately murdering his mistress. But blood sports, seen in the eighteenth century as a mainly working-class pursuit, were also believed to lead to low standards of public order and less than industrious habits, which the middle classes abhorred.[12]

It also needs to be said that the slew of writings concerning cruelty to animals throughout the eighteenth and nineteenth centuries, particularly from the 1740s onwards, was connected to the growth of London. Although this pushed some animals out of the city, it also brought Londoners into closer contact with the animals that remained: working horses (whose numbers increased as London became more industrialized), the beasts found in urban dairies and those driven between Smithfield and the slaughterhouses, for example. Cruelty became more visible and the first campaigns focused on the plight of the livestock and working animals on the streets. Frances Maria Thompson, a patron of the Animal Friends' Society (AFS), stated in 1830: 'The increasing instances of cruelty in our streets have now risen to such a height that it is impossible to go any distance from home without encountering something to wound our feelings.'[13] Certain types of animal, and industries related to dead animals, also came to be increasingly regarded as unhygienic and dangerous nuisances in a civilized and expanding city such as London. Its inhabitants did not want to be living so closely to animals any longer and health inspectors tried their hardest to clear out the problem creatures. All of the above agitation against cruelty culminated in the foundation in 1824 of the Society for the Prevention of Cruelty to Animals (SPCA; in 1840 it became the *Royal* Society) and the passing – after unsuccessful bills from 1800 onwards – of a series of early legislative acts: against cruelty to horses and cattle (1822), against cruelty to dogs (1839 and 1854), and against baiting and cockfighting (1835

and 1849). Later welfare campaigns moved into the more private world of animal cruelty, including the keeping of caged birds and vivisection.

The object of the SPCA was 'the mitigation of animal suffering and the promotion and extension of the practice of humanity towards the inferior classes of animated beings'.[14] It relied on the legislation to change people's behaviour, whereas groups like the Animal Friends' Society and the Association for Promoting Rational Humanity towards the Animal Creation looked to influence people's behaviour towards animals by educating them – the latter through its *Voice of Humanity* periodical.[15]

Thankfully conditions improved for the resident, and transient, animals that lived in and passed through the capital. But alongside the vision of London as a hell for animals, there is no disputing that animals helped shape the city both physically and in everyday life, and provided Londoners with (among other things) food, entertainment and livelihoods: their role needs to be recorded as part of London's history.

It would not take much to have cattle rampaging through the Smithfield streets: Thomas Sidney Cooper, *The Old Smithfield Market*, 1887, oil on canvas.

Livestock: Londoners' Nuisance Neighbours

The existence of large numbers of livestock in London had been an accepted part of city life since Roman times. Before railways and refrigeration, cattle, sheep, pigs and poultry were permanent fixtures in the metropolis and its suburbs. They were bred and reared by Londoners, and there was also a transient population for sale at London's livestock markets that had been driven from all parts of Britain and Ireland. Livestock touched nearly every Londoner's life; but it was not generally a pleasant experience for human or animal. The reason for the collision (quite literally in many cases) between man and beast was the seemingly insatiable demand for meat that Londoners became well known for.

London's love of meat

Pigs were kept in abundance in Roman Londinium. The forested areas around the city, such as Highgate and Hampstead, provided pannage for large herds of pigs, and pork and bacon were the most common meats eaten by the more affluent, while the poor used scraps to flavour soups and stews. Pigs' lard was part of a soldier's daily ration, and blood and fat were also mixed into the sausages that made up the army's iron rations when it was away fighting.[1] Other meats arrived in Londinium on the hoof after being driven along the Roman road network from around the country: beef was the favoured meat of the army and the wealthy, although sheep and goats were also prized for their milk as well as their meat.[2]

By the Middle Ages the meat in Londoners' diets was strictly rationed due to the Catholic Church's observance of days when the meat of quadrupeds could not be eaten. Fish, chicken and goose were the main substitutes. Meatless days fell on Fridays, Wednesdays and Saturdays, plus other festival days, making it necessary to abstain from red meat for nearly half the year.[3] But despite these restrictions, the demand for beef and mutton was strong enough to restart the droving trade established by the Romans. In 1562 Alessandro Magno, an Italian merchant, visited London and was astonished at the amount of meat eaten:

> It is extraordinary to see the great quantity and quality of meat – beef and mutton – that comes every day from the slaughter-houses in this city . . . Truly, for those who cannot see it for themselves, it is almost impossible to believe that they could eat so much meat in one city alone. The beef is not expensive, and they roast it whole, in large pieces. They do not care as much for veal as we do. Apart from chickens and other birds which one finds everywhere, they have many swans, much game, and rabbits and deer in abundance.[4]

In Stuart times the Yeomen of the Guard, founded by Henry VII at the beginning of his reign in 1485 to act

M. Dubourg after James Pollard, Christmas at a London 'Meat Stall', from *The London Markets* (1822).

as his private bodyguard, became known as Beefeaters because of the size of the meat rations they were given: as late as 1813, the 30 yeomen at St James's Palace received 24 pounds of beef, 18 pounds of mutton and 16 pounds of veal per day to share.[5]

By the mid-1850s, Londoners' appetite for red meat had not faltered: there were thousands of eating houses and coffee shops selling 'juicy, well-trimmed [mutton] chops, crowned with a sprig of parsley',[6] whereas pork and bacon were still the main meats eaten by London's working classes.

The demand for meat increased as London's economic power and human population exploded: the population doubled between 1801 and 1841 to reach 2.3 million by 1850, and annual meat consumption doubled from 1750 to 1850, reaching 122–53 pounds

per head; the large range presumably depending on social class.[7] To supply this market about 140,000 cattle and 1 million sheep were needed in 1810; by 1828 this had risen to 150,000 cattle and 1.5 million sheep and by 1853, cattle numbers had risen to 277,000 head and sheep to 1.6 million head.[8]

All of these animals came into London to be sold and slaughtered, giving the metropolis the dubious honour of being the only city in Europe, and probably the world, with a livestock market – Smithfield – and thousands of slaughterhouses at its centre. This market coped with the greatest volume of domestic livestock destined for slaughter of any city in history.[9]

Animals destined for Smithfield Market

Smithfield was originally established as a market site in about AD 950 in a field immediately outside one of the gates in the London Wall. This field was chosen because animals could be conveniently watered at the old Horse Pool, which lay between the Moorfields (now EC2Y) and Smithfield.[10]

In about 1174 the site was described by William Fitzstephen (*d. c.* 1191), clerk to Thomas à Becket, as a 'smooth' field where a celebrated horse market was held every Friday. 'In a separate part [of Smithfield] are located the goods that country folk are selling: agricultural implements, pigs with long flanks, cows with swollen udders, woolly flocks and bodies huge of kine [cattle].'[11] Smithfield was also used as a common place of execution in the thirteenth century. In addition it was the home of the three-day Bartholomew Fair, which began as a cloth fair in the reign of Henry II (r. 1154–89), and was the site of jousting tournaments for the nobility in the fourteenth century and, in the sixteenth century, an arena for burnings at the stake.[12] But Edward III (r. 1327–77) granted Smithfield formal market rights in 1327 and the market expanded. It was held on Mondays and Fridays, with cattle, calves, sheep, lambs and pigs sold on both days.

The market was further extended, and paved and drained for the first time, in 1614, and was described as 'a most capacious market for [about 4,000] black cattle, sheep, horses, hay and straw, with pens or folds, so called of sheep there parted and penned up to be sold on market days'.[13] Before the agrarian revolution in the eighteenth century, the market was not held after the autumn as livestock was killed before winter due to lack of forage after the autumn stubbles had been eaten. With the introduction of new winter crops, such as turnips, animals could be fattened over winter, and therefore Smithfield was supplied with livestock all year round. This meant that Londoners could eat fresh beef and mutton during the winter,

instead of salted meat.[14] With improvements not only in feedstuffs, but also in breeding stock, agricultural advances also directly increased the carcass weights of livestock: by 1795 the average carcass was twice as heavy as that produced in 1710.[15]

Before the advent of refrigeration, steamboats and railways, London's supply of animals came from across Britain and Ireland on the hoof. Cattle from Scotland, Ireland and Wales would arrive at grazing pastures outside London wearing iron shoes or cues, secured with broad-headed nails.[16] They had been driven by country drovers along drovers' tracks which criss-crossed the country, travelling at about 2 mph for 12 hours a day – the trip from Wales would take 20–25 days – and staying overnight on pasture, often in fields called Halfpenny Field, because the charge was a halfpenny per head.[17] After such a tremendous journey, the cattle arrived emaciated and were fattened up outside London on grazing grounds for two to three weeks. Daniel Defoe estimated in 1727 that Norfolk graziers bought up 40,000 Scottish cattle a year to fatten for sale at Smithfield;[18] Welsh cattle were fattened on the salt marshes of Essex and Kent.[19]

Shorter distances were travelled by sheep, which came from Lincoln, Norfolk, Somerset and Devon. Pigs were very difficult to drive because of their obstinacy and greed – they were often muzzled during travel, and would only cover 6 to 10 miles a day. The 14,500 pigs driven to London from Ireland, via Wiltshire, in the 1830s undertook a journey which would have taken hundreds of days.[20] However, they mainly came from East Anglia, Surrey and Buckinghamshire, sometimes wearing knitted woollen boots with leather soles to protect their feet.[21]

As for poultry, thousands of geese, the chosen bird of the poor at Christmas, were also driven from East Anglia from August onwards, so they could feed on the harvest stubbles as they travelled to London in time for Michaelmas in September.[22] To protect their feet prior to the long journey, they were driven first through tar, then sawdust and grit.[23] By the 1550s exotic New World (American) turkeys had been introduced from Spain and were reared in huge numbers in East Anglia.[24] They were available in the London markets having been driven west during the run-up to Christmas – they were allowed to roost in the trees at night during the journey.[25] The closer the poultry came to London, the more the roads deteriorated into muddy ruts, and the birds were usually transferred into wheeled vehicles and taken to the poulterers' area of the City – particularly Leadenhall Market.

To visualize the number of animals coming into London – and hence the meat supply demanded – the report of the 1850 Royal Commission, which was set up to decide the future of Smithfield,[26] used the analogy of climbing to the top of a mile-high tower

made of beer barrels to see the beasts approaching the city from all directions:

Herefrom we might discover the Great Northern road stretching far away into the length and breadth of the land. Lo! as we look, a mighty herd of oxen, with loud bellowing, are beheld approaching from the north. For miles and miles the mass of horns is conspicuous winding along the road, ten abreast, and even thus the last animal of the herd would be 72 miles away, and the drover goading this shrinking flank considerably beyond Peterborough . . . as the clouds of dust clear away, we see the great Western road, as far as the eye can reach, thronged with a bleating mass of wool, and the shepherd

Drovers resting their charges on the way to Smithfield at Highgate Archway tollgate and tavern, 1825.

at the end of the flock (ten abreast) and the dog that is worrying the last sheep are just leaving the environs of Bristol, 121 miles from our beer-built pillar. Along Piccadilly, Regent-street, the Strand, Fleet-street, Cheapside, and the eastward Mile-end-road line, for 7.5 miles, street and causeway are thronged with calves, still ten abreast; and in the great parallel thoroughfares of Bayswater-road, Oxford-street, and Holborn, we see nothing for nine long miles but a slowly-pacing, deeply-grunting herd of swine. As we watch this moving mass approaching from all points of the horizon, the air suddenly becomes dark – a black pall seems drawn over the sky – it is the great flock of birds – game, poultry, and wild-fowl, that . . . are come up to be killed: as they fly wing to wing and tail to beak they form a square whose superficies is not less than the whole enclosed portion of St. James's Park, or 51 acres. No sooner does this huge flight clear away than we behold the park at our feet inundated with hares and rabbits. Feeding 2,000 abreast, they extend from the marble arch to the round pond in Kensington Gardens – at least a mile.[27]

Foreign animals were also imported into London to meet demand. The unfortunate cattle mostly came from Prague, Prussia and Bavaria, which meant that they had to travel for between seven and twelve days by land and sea to reach Smithfield.[28] These animals deteriorated in appearance, and hence in value, during their arduous journeys and their meat usually ended up in the cheap East End markets, while British- and Irish-born animals went to the West End markets. That is not to say that the latter were in any better condition when they reached London on the hoof (unless they had been fattened outside London): it was estimated that when animals came by railway in the mid-nineteenth century, rather than being driven,

each cow saved 40 pounds in body weight, sheep 8 pounds and pigs 20 pounds.[29] This prevented a lot of meat being wasted and also negated the need for fattening before sale, so made economic sense for the animals' owners.

Other animals that were sent to Smithfield did not have far to travel at all, such as the worn-out dairy cows from the City's cowsheds, and the 'town-made' pigs that were bred and reared in the London suburbs.[30]

Smithfield Market procedures

The driven animals destined for Smithfield would be gathered at several points outside the City the day before market: in Mile End, Islington (where overnight housing could be secured for 150,000 cattle and 460,000 sheep), Knightsbridge, Newington, Paddington, Bayswater and Holloway. The animals were then transferred to the London drovers, who would move them by torchlight during the night into the streets around Smithfield.

If any visitors tried to visit the market (if they had even wanted to), it would have been nearly impossible to pass through the streets in the vicinity, and they would have been most disappointed if they were expecting to see an imposing market doing justice to the reputation of the Roast Beef of Old England. The Royal Commission reporters of 1850 described the visitor's reality:

What they do see in reality, if they have courage to wend their way along any of the narrow tumble-down streets approaching to Smithfield, which the Great Fire [of 1666] unfortunately spared, is an irregular space bounded by dirty houses and the ragged party-walls of demolished habitations, which give it the appearance of the site of a recent conflagration – the whole space comprising just six acres, fifteen perches,

'Fiend-like practices in night-time Smithfield', from an issue of the *Animals' Friend*, 1838.

roads and public thoroughfares included . . .
This narrow area [is] surrounded with slaughterhouses, triperies, bone-boiling houses, gut-
scraperies, &c.[31]

The most auspicious time to see the market in full
swing was at 1 am or 2 am on the Great Day – the
Monday market before Christmas – when the market
was full to its capacity of 4,100 oxen and 30,000 sheep,
besides calves and pigs. To get this many animals into
the market was a logistical nightmare, with animals
backing up for hundreds of feet in the approach roads:
Giltspur Street, Duke Street, Long Lane, St John's
Street, King Street and Hosier Lane.[32]

The moving of the animals fell to the 2,000-odd
London drovers who, by 1851, were licensed by the
city authorities. They paid a certain sum for the
privilege and wore a numbered brass badge on the
left arm. These drovers were employed and paid by
salesmen (who had the stock consigned to them by the
owners) to meet the livestock expected by road, or
rail, and bring it to Smithfield; no stranger could ever
have managed to bring in and arrange the cattle as
they did. Their only tools were their sheepdogs and a
goad, which was a stick the thickness of a stout man's
thumb, just over 4 feet in length, with a ¼-inch iron
point at one end. While waiting outside the market,
the drovers would hold their charges in groups, known
as 'off-droves', using brute force and their tools until
the animals could enter the site.

The *Chambers's Edinburgh Journal* described the
market's procedures to its readers,[33] and was greatly
impressed by the speed and efficiency with which
the drovers filled the site with animals. At 10.30
pm, the sheep arrived at the permanent pens, which
were capable of holding twelve sheep comfortably,

but would fit between sixteen and eighteen at a squeeze. The drovers were able to fill around one-third of the sheep pens by midnight, when the herds of cattle started to arrive and were fixed, using ropes, to the strong market railings. For the next seven to eight hours, the oxen, sheep, calves and pigs took their places, the latter arriving at around 5.30 to 6 am, along with a multitude of carts and small wagons (two-storied with a crate on the vehicle and another swinging between the wheels) containing calves and lambs.

To give an idea of the commotion created by this sequence of events, the market at bursting point was described in all its hellish detail by Charles Dickens in *Oliver Twist* (1838):

It was market morning. The ground was covered nearly ankle deep with filth and mire; and a thick steam perpetually rising from the reeking bodies of the cattle, and mingling with the fog, which seemed to rest upon the chimney tops, hung heavily above . . . Countrymen, butchers, drovers, hawkers, boys, thieves, idlers, and vaga-bonds of every low grade, were mingled together in a dense mass: the whistling of drovers, the barking of dogs, the bellowing and plunging of beasts, the bleating of sheep, and the grunting and squealing of pigs; the cries of hawkers, the shouts, oaths, and quarrelling on all sides, the ringing of bells, and the roar of voices that issued from every public house; the crowding,

The Smithfield drover, complete with arm badge, from William Henry Pyne, *Costume of Great Britain* (1808).

pushing, driving, beating, whooping and yelling; the hideous and discordant din that resounded from every corner of the market; and the un-washed, unshaven, squalid, and dirty figures constantly running to and fro, and bursting in and out of the throng, rendered it a stunning and bewildering scene which quite confused the senses.[34]

As the pigs and carts were entering the market, the 600-odd salesmen, with their ink-bottles hanging down in front of their waistcoats, took up their posts. The buyers, mainly carcass butchers (as opposed to retail and cutting butchers), crowded around the salesmen and each carried a pair of scissors in the breast or waistcoat pocket of his blue apron. After inspecting the animals and bargaining with the sales-man, a deal was struck by shaking hands, a transaction that was deemed irrevocable. The salesman then recorded the name and price agreed with the buyer in his account book and the buyer took out his scissors and cut a mark, or his initials, into the hair on the hind-quarters of the calves. When cows and bullocks were purchased, the hair of each animal's tail was cut off; any other cattle had a few hairs pulled out and tied round the tail. Sheep were ruddled (painted) with the buyer's mark. These symbols were to show that the animal had been bought, to stop others wasting their time. The buyers did not give their money directly to the salesman, but to one of the seven or eight market banks, which was done to prevent unpaid market tolls. The Corporation of London, which controlled the market, had collected these tolls since 1400, which in 1851 amounted to 2*d*. on every twenty sheep sold, and 1*s*. 8*d*. on every twenty cattle.

Once the agreed amount had been deposited at the bank, the animals were delivered to the butch-ers' premises by another set of drovers employed by the butchers and, dictated by demand, were killed in their private slaughterhouses. The leading butchers

slaughtered animals every day, so it was usual for them to purchase three days' worth of animals – this could be 20 cattle and 100–120 sheep – at each market.[35] The market closed on the Monday at noon, and carts, wagons and other vehicles could pass through the site, although if it was particularly busy, business would not end until about 3 pm. Unsold stock was taken to the cramped neighbouring lairs, where it remained until the next sale day.

The 'Smithfield nuisance': attempts at closure

The animals and the 'noxious' trades around Smith-field began to have an impact on Londoners' lives in the mid-eighteenth century, when Smithfield was no longer suburban but had become embedded in the heart of London. It had St Paul's Cathedral looming over it, St Bartholomew's Hospital was its neighbour, and houses, slaughterhouses and all manner of busi-nesses processing dead animals surrounded it.

Londoners called for the 'nuisance of Smithfield' to be relocated outside the city boundaries.[36] The list of complaints was always the same (the following is from 1835):

> the shameful desecration of the Sabbath [ani-mals were moved into Smithfield on the Sunday night], the personal accidents, and dangers to passengers resulting from the cattle and sheep being driven through the streets to and from this market, and in their progress to the innumer-able slaughter-houses of individual butchers.[37]

Hence it was not just the market site that became unacceptable, but also the arriving animals being driven across London. In 1755 influential residents in the still separate villages of St Marylebone, Pad-dington and Islington petitioned Parliament, in part, for the right to provide a turnpike road for the cattle and sheep on their way from the north and west to

Smithfield. The 'New Road' was London's first bypass and followed the route of what is now the Marylebone, Euston and Pentonville Roads; then through open fields and on to the outskirts of London. Work began in 1756 to avoid livestock congesting the east–west route via Oxford Street and High Holborn – previously there had been 'frequent accidents' and 'great inconveniencies' caused by driving cattle through the main roads.

However, this did not stop the drovers from using the old route, to avoid the tolls. So in 1766 the complaints continued: the architect and civil engineer John Gwynn stated that the sale of cattle at the centre of the metropolis was 'intolerable' – Smithfield had become 'a nuisance at once extremely dangerous as well as inelegant and inconvenient'.[38] There was even legislation introduced from 1774 to prevent the 'great Mischief' caused in the streets because of 'improper and cruel' driving of cattle, by unauthorized persons, using dogs, or stones, bricks or other missiles. If convicted of this foolhardy behaviour, the penalty was a payment of up to 20*s.* or one month's hard labour.

Attempts to remove the market formally began in 1808–9 when a memorial was presented to the Lord Mayor from 177 farmers and graziers, 99 salesmen and butchers, and 30 Smithfield residents who demanded that the market be moved to the open fields at Clerkenwell-fields, Islington.[39] They argued that the Smithfield site was too small to contain the number of cattle, and therefore the amount of meat, which was demanded by the population of the growing metropolis. Due to the resulting squeeze cattle were bruised and lamed.

The damage to animals was further increased by the horrific cruelty inflicted by the drovers, so the butchers were concerned with the resulting economic loss of bruised meat. One of the largest wholesale butchers estimated in 1828 that he lost between £300 and £400 a year 'on account of the carcass so readily putrefying from the *bruises* inflicted, and the rapid

wasting of the animal from feverish irritation, produced by cruelties and long driving'. A reserved total loss for the butchery community each year was estimated at £62,000.[40] The same type of complaint was heard at the Royal Commission, when Mr Slater, the Queen's butcher in Kensington and Jermyn Street, stated that he could not often sell mutton from the market to West End tables, because the meat was so disfigured by blows. This meat would often turn putrid within 24 hours after death.[41]

However, the Corporation of London either ignored the repeated pleas for Smithfield's removal, or extended the market as much as was possible when buildings surrounding Smithfield were pulled down. It had no thought of building another cattle market elsewhere.

Infuriated beasts on the rampage

It was quite astonishing to most Londoners that nothing was done to remove Smithfield, especially when there was a daily risk of meeting an overdriven bull on the London streets 'from Islington to Brixton, from Mile-end to Kensington',[42] in broad daylight. Even by 1849, when the railways were handling over half of the cattle arriving in London,[43] the animals still had to be driven to Smithfield from the London termini, including Euston, Shoreditch, Paddington and Nine Elms.

That no Corporation member had ever been fatally trampled or gored by cattle horns was obvious, otherwise the market may have been relocated more quickly. Incidents involving runaway cattle were reported in the newspapers with alarming regularity, stated *The Era* newspaper in 1849:

> Supposing it is only now and then that a respectable and somewhat paralysed pedestrian gets gored to death, a loitering boy has his brains dashed out, or a hapless servant-maid becomes

impaled on her way home with her beer; supposing it rarely occurs that the cry of 'Mad bull!' frights the street from its propriety, and a score of butchers rush violently after what the newspapers term 'An infuriated animal', slaughtering him in a gentleman's library, or a tradesman's china-shop, after he has done all manner of mischief.[44]

Not only were people's lives put at risk, but, as 'Opifex' wrote to the *Morning Chronicle*, business was also interrupted and property damaged – such as in Holborn, where broken windows were evidence of rampaging bullocks, as were damaged parlours and coffee rooms.[45] Several months later the same newspaper ran a report titled 'The Smithfield Nuisance', which told of a bullock that had escaped and rampaged through the streets, pursued by a huge crowd.[46] It smashed a shop window and took out the front of a public house, collided with two cabs (injuring or knocking down the horses), threw a woman into the air, causing serious internal injuries, scattered several market stalls, forced its head through a plate-glass window and broke the mahogany frame, and gored a man. Only days earlier, a bullock had dashed off the streets into a schoolroom full of children – luckily with no casualties.

Some cattle on the rampage had been deliberately terrified so that they would run people down, giving criminal gangs a prime opportunity to rob several victims. A gang of 500–600 thieves caused chaos in Spitalfields during September 1826 when they ambushed drovers on the way to Smithfield, stealing cattle, then driving the beasts through the streets during the night. Within a fortnight over 50 people had been robbed by the gang, and five people were lying in the London Infirmary 'without hopes of recovery'.[47]

Sheep also damaged private property and householders along the animals' routes would close their garden gates, because experience had taught them that 'if one poor sheep, beguiled by the apparition of a blade or two of fresh green grass, bolt in upon your flower-bed, the whole flock is sure to follow, and then you have the spectacle of half-an-hour's hunt, by means of an angry drover and a worrying sheep-dog, to get them out again.'[48] Pigs also created chaos, as seen in a news report from the 1830s: 'A hog went into a house in Turnmill Street and very much mangled a young child, and 'tis judg'd would have eaten it, the nurse being asleep, had not a neighbour who heard it cry, run in to its relief.'[49]

Cruelty to animals

The animals were so injured during the market process that one witness at the Royal Commission in 1850 stated that 'a grazier will not know his own beast four days after it has left him.'[50] Those coming into the market had usually been driven for hours, if not days, without adequate food or water. They were exhausted and thirst-mad, and some collapsed in the streets and were unable to continue on foot. In these cases a low-loading trailer, with a tailgate and a crane worked by a crank, was engaged to drag the harnessed animal on to the vehicle and then into lairage by the market.[51]

The cruelty was mainly due to Smithfield being too small to accommodate the animals. The Commissioners worked out that 70,000 cattle and 540,000 sheep were sold at the market in 1698, increasing to 236,975 cattle and 1,417,000 sheep in 1849. However, the only increase in the area of the market was in 1833, when just under 2 acres were added. Cattle were tied up to the rails that ran along the length of the open space, but this was not an easy operation, as the cattle were not cooperative and had to be dragged up to the rails with ropes. During the scuffle it was common for the drovers to break their fingers when the ropes slipped – there was barely a drover who did not have twisted fingers.[52] Because there were not enough of these rails, cattle were often forced to stand

Illustration of drovers
keeping control over cattle
in Smithfield Market, 1849.

in 'compasses' or 'ring droves' – in a tight circle facing inwards. It was particularly difficult for the drovers to get them to form the circle in the first place, and also to make them stand patiently. Sheep were squeezed into the hurdles so tightly that they had to lie down upon each another, but they made no sound, unlike the pigs that squealed while they were moved.

Charles Dickens wrote a fictional account of an amateur seller, Mr Bovington, who witnesses the treatment of his treasured cattle as they pass through Smithfield under the guidance of the drovers:

> A sticking of prongs into the tender part of their feet, and a twisting of their tails to make the whole spine teem with pain . . . Across their horns, across their hocks, across their haunches, Mr Bovington saw the heavy blows rain thick and fast . . . constantly dropping gouts of the blazing pitch [from the drovers' burning torches] upon the miserable creatures' back; and to smell the singeing and burning, and to see the poor things shrinking from this roasting, inspired a sickness, a disgust, a pity and an indignation, almost insupportable.[53]

'Hocking' was a favourite punishment meted out by drovers to reluctant cattle – blows were inflicted onto the hind legs to make the animal lame, then the other leg was also attacked. 'Pething' was hitting them over the horns.

As already noted, the earliest legislation against driving cattle within London and Westminster in an 'improper and cruel manner' to Smithfield market was enacted as part of the Metropolis Acts of 1774 and 1781, and the Metropolitan Police Acts of 1822 and 1833. However, this was not because of any welfare concerns, but because of the danger to the public from terrified stock stampeding through the streets. It was not until Richard Martin's Act to Prevent the Cruel and Improper Treatment of Cattle of 1822 that cruelty to the animals was criminalized per se.[54] The law stated that anyone who 'cruelly beat, abused or ill-treated' livestock (including horses and sheep) would be fined between 10s. and £5, and if they were not able to pay, they would be sent to the House of Correction for up to three months.

But it was initially difficult to prosecute anyone, as the SPCA was not established until 1824 and the Metropolitan Police until 1829. It was left to individuals to make complaints to a Justice of the Peace or magistrate, but the SPCA worked to ensure that Martin's Act was implemented to prevent the 'unmanly outrages daily perpetrated in our public streets on innocent and defenceless animals', which proved so shocking to 'foreigners coming amongst us for the first time'.[55]

In a typical case of 1849, four defendants were taken to court for brutality against three oxen, which they were driving from Smithfield to a slaughterer on the south side of the Thames at Chapel Yard, off Union Street, SE1. Once in the yard they deliberately started to goad the oxen, hocking them for no apparent reason but their 'own diversion'. Each was fined 40s., and in default they were sentenced to fourteen days committal.[56]

By 1851 police officers were working in the market and looking to prevent acts of brutality by their presence. They would chastise and/or arrest drovers if they saw cruel practices.

Why did Smithfield Market persist?

Despite the overt animal cruelty in the streets, and the danger to the public from marauding cattle, the market continued to exist in the metropolis even after centuries of complaints and the Royal Commission which recommended its removal. The obstacle to moving Smithfield was the powerful Corporation of London, made up of the Lord Mayor and his Alderman. This body had been granted monopoly of all cattle markets within 7 miles of London by Edward III under the Charter of the City of London in 1327.[57] This meant that it received all the tolls and dues associated with the market, which was hugely profitable. Even in 1851, when much 'country-killed' meat was bought to London, causing a slump in market receipts, about £300,000 changed hands every week at the market.[58] The Corporation made money on each sale and every entry – around £3,000 to £4,000 a year.[59] It was no wonder that 'the fierce

and protracted resistance opposed to the abolitionists by the civil authorities at once assumes a natural and intelligible aspect and character.'[60]

In a move to bypass the Corporation, private money was poured into an alternative to Smithfield in March 1836. However, Mr Perkins's Islington Cattle-market between Lower Road (now Essex Road, N1) and the Regent's Canal only survived for seven months. It was spacious – 15 acres within its walls – and had open and covered lairs for 8,000 cattle and 50,000 sheep. But the Corporation breathed a sigh of relief as butchers (and other buyers) continued to use Smithfield because it was more convenient to their premises. Sellers were forced to go where they could get the best prices. The Islington market remained in use as lairage for animals on their way to Smithfield. It was briefly reopened in 1847 with water troughs and room for 20,000 cattle, but still the business did not come.[61] It finally took the weight of parliamentary committees, the Royal Commission and the Secretary of State to bring about the Smithfield Market Removal Act of 1851; the effort had to be powerful to compel the Corporation to adopt reform.

The new market – the Metropolitan Cattle Market – was less than 5 miles from the City in Copenhagen Fields, Islington, and was opened on 13 June 1855 by Prince Albert. It lay up the Caledonian Road, 1¼ miles from King's Cross. The site embraced 74 acres (twelve times the area of Smithfield), with the market itself covering 15 acres. It could accommodate 7,000 cattle and 42,000 sheep,[62] and had a covered calf and pig market. On site there were also private and public abattoirs – the private abattoirs being rented by the regular slaughterman who killed livestock for butchers, while the public abattoir was for those who killed their own stock at the market. Comfortable lairage for sheep and 3,000 cattle was also on site for before and after the market, and there were railway links right into the market from the north, which would benefit the sellers as 'the value of the animals themselves will be greater, when thus spared the hazard and fatigue of struggling through busy thoroughfares'.[63]

However, enormous numbers of animals still had to be driven through the City from the south, east and west to arrive at the market, and be driven back, after their sale, to the Newgate Shambles for slaughter.[64] Foreign cattle, especially from Ireland, were landed at Blackwall and driven 6 to 7 miles to the market, then harried back half the distance to the slaughterhouses in Whitechapel.[65]

Although drovers were able to move stock through a larger number of routes in and out of the market (so there were not the roadblocks associated with Smithfield), the new cattle-driving routes ruined the tranquillity of the surrounding genteel districts, such as Camden Town. Many residents were forced to relocate, as they could not cope with the animal traffic that ruined their peace twice a week on market days.

This was not the only problem with Smithfield's replacement. Although the facilities were much more spacious, one journal reporter speculated, before the market opened, that the cruelty the animals suffered might increase because the 'supervision which a jealous, antagonistic public exercises upon Smithfield will be to a great extent withdrawn'.[66] He was right. Sheep were still forced into the pens, nearly to the point of suffocation, so the grazier did not have to hire another pen; the goad was still used by the drovers; and sheep still had no access to water. One periodical writer estimated that most sheep would not have had water or feed since they had left their pastures – usually between two and four days before. He also estimated that the sheep lost about 10 per cent of their value by the time they arrived at market. However, one dealer told the reporter that he had seen sheep being allowed to drink in a pond once they had reached town when they were really thirsty. They had drunk until they killed themselves – nothing would get them away from the water.[67]

Eventually, a charity was formed in 1859, principally to provide water fountains for humans. By 1867 it had already built fourteen large troughs for the street animals, many of which were on their way to the Metropolitan Cattle Market. The charity changed its name in that year to the Metropolitan Drinking Fountain and Cattle Trough Association to reflect its resolve to build more drinking troughs for cattle, sheep, horses and dogs: 'The intense suffering which is experienced by all kinds of animals from thirst in the streets of London has long been a source of anxiety and grief to all humane and benevolent persons.'[68] By 1868 there were 99 cattle troughs scattered throughout London, and twenty years later this number had increased to 679 troughs in London and its suburbs.[69] Many were sited along the drovers' routes into London: at Highgate Hill and Haverstock Hill in the north, Kilburn and Maida Hill in the west, Battersea Rise in the south, and Stratford, Plaistow and the Barking Road in the east.[70]

One wealthy campaigner who tried to make a difference to the management of the animals during transport was Angela Burdett Coutts (1814–1906). She employed cattle trucks to bring four cows down from Edinburgh to the Metropolitan Cattle Market early on Monday morning. They were watered and fed en route, so they arrived looking well. But *The Examiner* newspaper noted that unless the prices fetched were high, the outlay for travel would be too great.[71]

The London-centred trade in livestock eventually diminished in the early twentieth century, and the Metropolitan Cattle Market closed in 1939. The only remnant of the market today is the clock tower which stood at its centre – on the edge of Caledonian Park.

After its closure on Monday, 11 June 1855, Smithfield lay vacant for thirteen years. The opportunity to abandon the riotous Bartholomew Fair had also been taken the same year. In 1868 the London Central Markets, colloquially known as 'Smithfield', was built

Illustrations of Old and New Smithfield Market (1830, 1899). Note the pitcher and the bummarees moving the butchered meat around.

on the site and functioned as the largest wholesale meat market in the country, replacing the old Newgate Market that was demolished in 1869. The market took two years to build and incorporated lifts which brought up carcasses from the basement, where they had been delivered on the Metropolitan Railway, which linked Smithfield to all parts of the UK. The railways delivered meat until the early 1960s, when road haulage took over.

Smithfield is still in operation today, but instead of the area echoing to the night-time bellowing of livestock and shouts of drovers, its neighbours are harassed by the roaring of lorries' refrigeration systems as they wait to unload their cargoes of meat. The London drovers were replaced by three types of self-employed workers who, until the market was refurbished in the early 1990s, manually transported the carcasses before hygiene regulations disallowed the practice:[72] the 'pullers-back' pulled the meat to the tailboard of the vehicles, the 'pitchers' carried the meat on their shoulders into the market to the appropriate stall and the meat porters, known as 'bummarees', used old wooden hand barrows with steel-rimmed wheels to move the cuts of meat when they were sold. Trading opens at four in the morning and finishes at noon, with all traces of blood, flesh and sawdust washed from the streets each day.[73] It is an efficient and hygienic way of dealing with London's meat supply which befits the prestigious City of London – a world away from the centuries of market horrors experienced by animals ultimately destined for Londoners' stomachs.

London's piggeries

The animals driven into Smithfield did not account for all the livestock in London, which in the mid-nineteenth century included

> extensive back-yard agriculture, not merely half-a-dozen hens in a coop of soap boxes, but cow-stalls, sheep-folds, pig-sties above and below ground, in and out of dwellings, on and off the streets, wherever this rudimentary factory farming could be made to work.[74]

Pigs had an ancient history in the City. After the Romans left, they were found in Lundenwic (Anglo-Saxon London) around the Charing Cross area as pigs were useful for recycling household waste while providing bacon and fat for cooking.[75] By 1281 it seems that London was full of pigs: a City of London

regulation tried to stop pigs roaming freely in the streets, and in 1297 a further regulation required pigsties to be removed from the roads. Although the pigs were ridding the city of decomposing waste so it did not become too hazardous, they were becoming a health danger themselves. Swine known as St Anthony's pigs were regularly seen on the City's dunghills. These animals, according to John Stow in his *Survey of London* (1598), were starved pigs taken from Smithfield by the overseers of the market and given to St Anthony's Hospital, Threadneedle Street. These pigs were then released into the streets to scavenge, with a bell around their necks and a slit in one of their ears so they were easily identifiable. When a pig had fattened, it was taken back to St Anthony's to be killed and eaten.[76] But wandering pigs were a hazard; they sometimes started fires by brushing straw into dying embers, and they often bit or even killed small children – a sow attacked the MP Sir Hugh Cholmley (*b.* 1600) when he was eight years old.[77]

On a commercial scale, pigs were often kept in large numbers in the backyards of dairies, distilleries or starchmakers, where they lived on buttermilk, lees and the refuse of the wheat after the starch had

The 'Piggeries' of Notting Dale, 1855, from *Ragged Homes and How to Mend Them* by Mrs M. Bayly (1860).

been removed (and some pulses) respectively. In the eighteenth century 3,000 pigs were fattened each year at Messrs Johnson's Distillery at Vauxhall, 3,000–4,000 at Benwell's in Battersea and 2,000 at Bush's in Wandsworth. The starch manufacturer Stenard's fattened an average of 2,700 pigs and Randall & Suter's kept 600–700 per year.[78] Distillers also fattened hundreds of cattle during the brewing season from October to May.

However, pigs were mostly found in residential areas, and sometimes in houses: in 1862 on Latymer Road (between Kensington Potteries and Wormwood Scrubbs), two pigs lived in an upper room of a house in a corner; the room also served as a residence and workshop for two shoemakers and their wives and children.[79]

Shepherd's Bush was known as *the* pigsty of the metropolis in 1850 because every house had a pigsty: 'the air [was] sonorous with the grunting of porkers.'[80] Another area renowned for its piggeries since the 1820s was the Potteries in Notting Dale (now known as Notting Hill), Kensington, where many Irish people lived. They were renowned for their small-scale pig-fattening; their companion pig was the 'jintleman who pays the rint'.[81]

The area festered in filth and the stench of pigs until 1849, when cholera wiped out many lives in the Potteries and the health inspectors entered the area. They found 3,000 pigs being looked after by 1,000 people, living in 250 hovels over eight acres.[82] Dominating the area, in size and in terms of filth, was a lake of stagnant water called the Ocean (now covered by Avondale Park and Kenley Street), described as 'a receptacle for dead animals and filth of all descriptions, and into which the adjacent piggeries and privies have been drained for the last 20 years . . . [an] abominable nuisance'.[83]

Many attempts were made by health inspectors to remove the piggeries because of the danger to public health. However, in 1856 there were still 1,041 pigs

being fed on pig wash, the refuse and offal collected from houses, clubs and hotels in the West End, boiled up in huge copper cauldrons.[84] Officialdom was thwarted by the pig keeper Samuel Lake, who had originally bought the land at Notting Dale and rented it out to other pig keepers who were being evicted from Connaught Square, w2. They had been known as the Pigmasters to the West End establishment,[85] because their pigs traditionally lived off the scraps from Mayfair houses. When Lake leased the land to the other keepers, he stated that the land was to be used for the purposes of pig-keeping, and only a special Act of Parliament could overturn this clause and get the pigs removed.[86] The Potteries' pigs finally left in 1878, although an RSPCA report of 1939 showed that there were still 18,000 pigs in the metropolitan area – a fact attributed to the resurgence of backyard pig keeping during the Second World War.[87]

Poultry

Families also kept fowl, rabbits and pigeons in their backyards, and sometimes their homes, to provide protein and pocket money. During his enquiry into the sanitary conditions of the working classes, Edwin Chadwick (1800–1890) found that poultry was being reared in town bedrooms in 1842.

On a larger scale, Poultry (the street) was the special quarter of the London poulterers up to Elizabethan times. Thousands of live birds were reared and kept in cellars and attics in cramped conditions and usually in complete darkness. Poultry was forcibly fed and confined in cages. Geese and ducks had their webbed feet nailed to the floor to stop them wasting energy.[88] When the birds were fattened they were slaughtered, plucked and scorched in Scalding Alley, now St Mildred's Court. When the poulterers left the area, for unknown reasons, they moved to Gracechurch (or Gracious) Street near Leadenhall and Newgate Markets.[89]

Christmas Eve in
Leadenhall Market,
1845: *the* place to buy
your Christmas goose.

By 1850 Leadenhall was reputedly the largest and best poultry market in London, with many other animals sold there, including rabbits from Ostend. There was one famous Leadenhall goose called Old Tom whose story is told on a plaque on Lime Street Passage within the market.[90] According to *The Times*, Old Tom died in 1835, aged 37, and was buried in the centre of the poultry market after having lived there for twelve years. He had become 'the patriarch and guardian of all the geese and goslings that came into the market, and he was never known to let one go astray. He was a favourite with all, and the pet of many.'[91]

His extraordinary tale began in 1797 when he was hatched in Ostend and employed as a decoy to lead gaggles of geese for 10 miles to a boat leaving Calais, destined for London. By accident in 1823 he was sent to Leadenhall along with his companions, after supposedly becoming infatuated with one of the ganders in his charge, and when this was discovered his owner sent a series of letters begging for his safe return. The goose was easily picked out because he answered to the name of Tom, but he never returned to his native land as he always managed to evade capture. Instead he was sold to one of the poulterers and became, according to his original headstone, 'The chief of geese, the poulterer's pride'. During his time at the market, though, Old Tom did have some narrow escapes – in 1829 he was mistakenly sent to Mr Levy's shop in Houndsditch with eleven other geese, nine of which were already slaughtered when the order came to halt his execution.

By 1857 about 250,000 geese were sold in London during the run up to Michaelmas, but the majority came in by railway already dressed and ready for the spit. Those that were still driven live to the market came from farms 12 to 15 miles away. The geese came in

forlorn and draggle-tailed flocks, amounting to hundreds in number, through a devious route of back and bye-ways, to the yard, or, it may be, the underground cellar of the consignee ... they must be well fed in confinement, at a considerable cost in cramming, or they will lose in weight of flesh.[92]

These fattened geese would appear everywhere in the markets, including Farringdon Fish Market,[93] and butchers' shops.

Dairy cows and milch asses

Other livestock kept in London eventually ended up in butchers' shops, but it served another purpose before it entered the meat supply. Demand for milk in London, before railways began to carry regular supplies in from the country in the 1850s, was entirely met by cows owned by suburban, and later urban, cow keepers who could deliver milk to the customer before it went sour. Milk Street, EC2, was London's medieval milk market, and John Stow wrote in 1598 of an abbey near Aldgate which had a farm attached with 30–40 dairy cows. The young Stow would fetch milk 'always hot from the kine, as the same was milked and strained'.[94]

In 1794, dairy herds were mainly found in Edgware Road, Hackney, Mile End and Islington, with the Board of Agriculture estimating that 8,500 cows were milking in London.[95] Islington had been an area celebrated since the sixteenth century for its dairy farms and rich pastures for cattle grazing. One of the largest keepers was Richard Laycock (who gave his name to Laycock Street), who in 1810 kept 500–600 short-horned cattle on 225 hectares of pasture.[96] He milked at 4 am and 1.30 pm, and fed his cows a healthy diet of brewers' grains,[97] turnips, cabbages, potatoes and hay; they were let out onto grass for the night. The cows were young, not more than three or four years old, and when their milk yields fell away they were fattened for the butcher.[98] There was also lairage at

Laycock's for thousands of cattle and sheep on their way to Smithfield, containing strawed pens, with feed and water available. There was additionally a cattle pound – one of many in London – in Upper Street, Islington, which would detain stray animals until their owners came to retrieve them on payment of a small fee.

As London spread, the green fields around it were swallowed up, and cows were forced to become urban dwellers without access to pasture, although in 1837 Green Park was still 'a large field cropped down like velvet ... cows grazed before the eye', and as late as 1905 Londoners could still get fresh milk from the eight cows which stood tied to posts in the summer in St James's Park (there were four cows in the winter).[99] The park milk sellers were licensed by the Home Secretary and mainly sold warm milk, straight from the cow, in little mugs to those of a delicate nature or to young children who were brought to the park by their nurses. In smarter residential areas cows were brought to the door to be milked – if the milk was cold, then there had been water already in the can before the cow was milked, which was a common method of adulterating milk to increase its volume.[100]

However, most London cows were not lucky enough to enjoy fresh air. In 1829 there were at least 71 cowsheds in London, and by 1850 there were 20,000 dairy cows; some buildings housed 500.[101] Even when railways started bringing country milk into London in 1852, there were 13,000 cows.[102] The larger dairies, such as those in Islington, were luxurious compared with the smaller urban dairies that were concentrated in a belt stretching from Clerkenwell to Hyde Park Corner to take advantage of the West End market for milk. Sometimes these cows lived on the first storey and were milked on the second. In 1850 the public were made aware of the dangers and cruelties associated with their innocent-looking cans of milk through the pamphlet *Observations on London Milk &c.* by a surgeon called Hodson

Rugg. He described one cowshed under the Adelphi Arches where the cattle were usually fed entirely on a diet of brewers' grains and distillers' wash from London businesses,[103] which, although it stimulated milk production, caused great suffering in the cows. Rugg wrote:

> The result is, their milk-producing organs are stimulated to a wonderful degree; they yield enormously, but soon become diseased; their gums ulcerate, their teeth drop out, and their breath becomes fetid. Though thus diseased, they do not fall away in flesh, but, on the contrary, puff up and bloat to an appearance of great fatness, their joints become stiff, so that they cannot with ease lie down, and rarely or never come out alive.[104]

The milk produced by the cows was thin and bluish because of the by-product waste they were fed, and this meant that to be sold it had to be adulterated to make it appear wholesome. Rugg wrote of molasses, water and whiting being added to the milk, but also sheep brains, which gave the milk a richer appearance in texture and colour.

Unhygienic cowsheds and the diet of the cows were further risks to public health. A newspaper review of Rugg's pamphlet commented on the 'effluvium which is constantly steaming forth from those repositories of corruption', and *Punch* grimly joked in 1852 that Londoners would 'have to wait until there was another February with 5 Sundays to be able to get a clean glass of milk'.[105] Others argued that diseased cows' flesh was only fit for 'cats' meat, or for converting into animal manure', but instead it was used in sausages for the poor.[106]

Frontage of an old dairy in Stroud Green, built in 1836, depicting the stages of dairy production.

Many of the dairy cows in London also suffered from the lung infection of pleuro-pneumonia, which had been brought into England from Holland in 1842 (when import restrictions were lifted in the interests of free trade). These Dutch cattle were destined for the City dairies and the disease spread rapidly in the cramped and unhygienic cowsheds, with affected cattle showing the signs of near death: 'carbuncle, phlegmon and boils'.[107] The cattle were sent to Smithfield, where unscrupulous butchers bought them and sold the diseased meat on to the poor. But the disease was passed to other cattle at the market. Foot-and-mouth also became a chronic problem in London cowsheds in the 1840s (another foreign import), and it was estimated that of the 12,000 cows kept in London in 1862, there was an annual loss of at least £80,000 through disease and accident.[108]

Another disease which nearly decimated London's dairy cows was the Cattle Plague of 1865 and 1866–7. The disease first appeared in London in Mrs Nicholls's sheds in Liverpool Road, Islington (formerly Laycock's Farm). It was brought in from Russia by thirteen cattle that were sold at the Metropolitan Market. It was and is highly infectious, proving fatal to cattle within a few days. Within three months the number of cattle in Islington had fallen from 1,317 in 71 licensed cowsheds to 314 in 45 sheds (although many animals had been sent away for safety).[109]

The effects of the plague reverberated across the livestock industry, as there were 82 centres of infection in the country.[110] Cattle were slaughtered if they became diseased and, in some cases, so were those cattle that were 'contacts' – those seemingly healthy animals that had been in contact with the disease. Restrictions were placed on cattle movements and in 1869 the Contagious Diseases (Animals) Act placed restrictions on the import of foreign cattle. This led to the creation of the Foreign Cattle Market at the redundant Deptford Dockyard on the Thames in 1871, where cattle, sheep and pigs from European scheduled countries (known to have endemic disease or a recent outbreak) had to be landed and slaughtered within ten days of disembarkation. This 23-acre site provided pens with food and water for 4,000 cattle and 12,000 sheep, as well as open pens which could hold thousands more animals. The workshops and boathouses of the dock were converted into slaughterhouses – described by the campaign group Council of Justice to Animals in 1911 as 'one of the dark places of the world' because of the horrendous conditions.[111] In 1871, 45 per cent of foreign cattle and 39 per cent of foreign sheep went inland alive to the Metropolitan Market, but by 1880 only 22 per cent of imported cattle and 9 per cent of sheep went there;[112] the majority were slaughtered at Deptford. This market finally petered out in 1912 when shipments of live cattle from North America and Canada stopped.[113]

By 1906 there were still 15,000 cows in London,[114] but the housing conditions and standards of cleanliness had greatly improved due to the dairymen having to operate within the guidelines of health inspectors; the Dairies, Cow-Sheds and Milk Shops Order of 1879 stipulated that licensed dairies had to have satisfactory lighting, ventilation, cleansing, drainage and water supplies. These sanitary measures reduced the numbers of dairies in London because of the cost of converting existing sheds. But in any case, the numbers of dairy cattle had been falling since the 1880s, when the market for urban cow beef collapsed, as did the profits from selling manure to farmers and market gardeners. The wholesale cowshed milk price had also declined.[115] The cowsheds had also moved into the East End from the West End because of laxer sanitary regulations; rents were lower and feed was easily transported from the breweries and hay merchants.[116] However, cowsheds clung on: there were ten cows in a small byre in Clipstone Street, off Euston Road, as late as 1926, and the longest survivor was S. P. Snewin in Oldhill Street, Hackney, whose herd survived into the 1960s.[117]

Asses' milk on sale in
Kentish Town, *c.* 1760.

Cows were not the only livestock that provided milk to Londoners. Since 1780, Dawkins of Bolsover Street, W1, had been selling asses' milk.[118] It was a luxury costing twice as much as cows' milk, because the yields were low, and it was a favourite cure used by physicians to nourish weak individuals and invalids suffering especially from consumption – the milk was more sugary and less 'cheesy' than cows' milk.

However, its reputation as a medical cure suffered occasionally as fashions changed: in the late 1790s the celebrated Italian opera singer Mrs Theresa Cornelys (1723–1797), who had fallen on hard times, opened up her house in Kensington as a place for respectable company to breakfast on asses' milk. Donkeys were kept on the premises, as foreign fashions dictated, but Londoners had moved on from the miraculous asses' milk diet and Mrs Cornelys ended her days as a prisoner for debt in the Fleet Prison.

London's association with asses continued past 1895. A journal visited a dairy near the Marble Arch, at Hyde Park, which housed twelve to fourteen donkeys that were enjoying a holiday from their usual drudgery, because they had each produced a foal (which was with them) and were in milk.[119] They each produced about a quart a day, after four milkings, so London's 50 milch asses (in 1890s) would produce a single churn. The milk was sent out to West End mansions, and also sent by rail; donkeys were even sent by rail with a set of instructions for their management and milking to wealthy believers in the milk cure. Other than for medical use, customers used asses' milk as a face wash, on their breakfast tables, or mixed with blacking to impart a greater shine to their shoes.[120]

Slaughterhouses

When asses finished producing milk they were usually sold or sent back to their normal jobs as draught animals or seaside rides. If they were too old to work, or diseased, they were sent to the knacker's yard. Other livestock that was either past its best, such as broken-down dairy cows, or destined for meat, was sent locally for slaughter; the metropolis was full of private slaughterhouses owned by butchers, as had been the case for centuries.

It is not difficult to guess what King Edward Street, near Newgate Street, and the east end of Newgate Street were once associated with, when looking at their respective former names of Stinking Lane and Bladder Street. The whole area was full of slaughterhouses, surrounding London's main meat markets, known in medieval times as Eastcheap (now known as Cheapside) and St Nicholas Shambles, which ran along the present line of Newgate Street from the Newgate to St Martin's-le-Grand. Other,

later markets that also sold flesh, besides other wares, were Clare Market and Stocks' Market. Slaughterhouses flourished.

There were huge objections to having the slaughterhouses in the centre of the City, mainly because of disease concerns and the smell, but it proved difficult to dissuade the butchers from killing animals on their premises because they were conveniently close to the dead-meat markets, and animals could be killed when they were required. This was particularly helpful in the summer, helping to ensure that the meat did not deteriorate: in 1849 the summer evenings of Friday's Smithfield Market could see up to 1,200 cattle and 12,000 to 15,000 sheep slaughtered, ready for Saturday's dead-meat markets.[121]

The first to try and ban the metropolitan slaughterhouses was Henry III (r. 1216–72), who issued an ordinance preventing the slaughtering of cattle any nearer the City of London than the town of Knightsbridge, but this seems to have been largely ignored.[122] Nearly a century later, on 25 February 1362, Edward III tried again by commanding that no bulls, oxen or pigs should be killed in St Nicholas Shambles, because

> the air of the city is very much corrupted and infected [from the] putrified [animal] blood running down the streets, and the bowels cast into the Thames [at Butchers' bridge, or quay] whence abominable and most filthy stinks proceed . . . sicknesses and many other evils have happened to such as have abode in the said city, or have resorted to it.[123]

Butchers would have to take their animals either to the town of Stratford (Stratford le Bow) or Knightsbragg (Knightsbridge) to be slaughtered and gutted. Any butcher who slaughtered in the City would lose the flesh of the animal and be imprisoned for a year.

But, again, this evidently did not dissuade butchering in the City, because John Strype mentions in

A Survey of London (1720) that in Elizabethan times (possibly 1563) an Italian physician had said that one of the causes of the Plague was the killing of cattle within the City.[124] The Italian had said that the Queen should build some slaughterhouses in the suburbs.

By the 1830s there were private slaughterhouses operated by the London carcass-butchers principally in Warwick Lane, around the dead-meat markets of Leadenhall and Newgate, and in High Street, Aldgate (known as the 'Whitechapel butchers').[125] With the miasma theory of disease still predominating – in Edwin Chadwick's words 'all smell is disease' – the 'deadly exhalations' still emanating from these slaughterhouses increased the calls for public abattoirs in the suburbs.[126]

However, the situation was no better in 1849 when the health supervisor responsible for enforcing sanitation complained of the 'filthy condition' of the slaughterhouses in the neighbourhood of Saffron Hill and Cow Cross, near to Smithfield.[127] An outbreak of fever in the nearby Infant School was credited to the disease-ridden abattoirs.[128] Although City slaughterhouses had to be registered and inspected by the City Commissioners of Sewers from 1848, and licensed from 1851, it was not until 1855 that the Nuisances Removal Act gave London's local authorities the power to remove piles of excrement, refuse and waste from slaughterhouses that were in residential or business areas.[129]

It is already evident that these slaughterhouses were not the modern hygienic abattoirs of today. The greatest challenge to the urban butcher was the slaughtering of cattle, because of their size, weight and strength. They were most commonly stunned into unconsciousness first using the spike on the poleaxe – an axe with a blunt protruding metal spike opposite the blade. But first the animal had to be held in position by having its head roped to a ring attached to the floor or wall, so its forehead was easily exposed to the slaughter man. One accurately aimed hit should have been enough to cause the cow to collapse, unconscious, but this was rarely achieved. A pithing cane was then inserted into the hole made by the poleaxe and agitated to destroy the brain tissue; supposedly this made the meat more tender. Then the animal was hoisted by one, or both, hind legs and its throat was opened. The carotid arteries and jugular veins were then severed (known as a sticking or being stuck). It bled rapidly to its final death.

Pig were easier to manage and were hoisted and stuck while still conscious, although preliminary stunning did prevent them from squealing, which otherwise would have annoyed the neighbours. Sheep, lambs and calves were usually laid on their backs in a cratch or wooden cradle, and slaughtered by transfixion – stabbing the throat with a knife to bleed the animal without stunning it – to preserve the brain tissue so it could be eaten.

Because the killings happened in public places, those passing could see the bloody spectacle. This was thought to 'brutalize young minds' that were already numbed by the harshness of the poorer London streets. In the nineteenth century complaints also focused on the cruelty suffered by the animals. It was 'objectionable and repulsive', wrote one commentator,

> to see bullocks or sheep driven, often with violence, through a narrow doorway (frequently alongside of the stall where meat is hanging up, thus alarming and offending the senses of the animals) into back premises, odorous with blood and offal, cannot but create a feeling of pain and regret in the mind of the casual passer-by.[130]

It was evident that sanitary legislation incorporating a clause against cruelty in slaughterhouses from 1847 onwards was not in the least effective at preventing animal abuse. The social explorer James Greenwood described in *Unsentimental Journeys* (1867)

Slaughtering sheep and cattle in a slaughterer's den near Newgate Market, from an issue of the *Animals' Friend* (1840).

the scene he saw in the premises of Messrs Venables and Dixon, 'the celebrated sheep-slaughterer' near Newgate Market:

I saw a barn no larger than a drawing-room, in which were eight men gory to the elbows and with their faces speckled red. But, limited as was the room, the eight men did not have it all to themselves; there were likewise in the room at least fifteen sheep – alive, half dead, dead, and half undressed, and hanging from beams completely muttonised. By the door there was a great sweltering pile of fleecy hides, and in an extreme corner was a hideous wooden tank, with bars across the top, and along the bars was a row of freshly-slain sheep. As fast as the dressers lugged one from the crimson bars to the stone floor, a hot and saturated giant, looking hideous

through the gloom that lurked in the place, plucked another from the frantic live ones, who were penned against the wall, and who, having the blood of their fellows before their eyes and on the floor, causing their feet to slip, stared about them and uttered sounds such as I never before heard sheep utter; except one, and that was in Old Smithfield Market, and I heard somebody say that [it] had been kept without water till driven mad. I trust I am not mawkishly sentimental; but when I saw emerging from that dismal den, foggy with the steam of blood and departing breath, and contrasted the sad, limp bodies of the poor animals with the rosy carcasses that came from the country in the wicker hampers – when I saw the former, borne along on the butcher's back, wag their heads mournfully, and as though aware of their ignoble appearance – I could scarcely forbear wagging my own sympathetically.[131]

One journal reporter even advocated the use of the newly discovered anaesthetic chloroform to take away the pain of the brutal deaths meted out at abattoirs. He further believed that public opinion would force this method on 'reluctant butcherism' and that the RSPCA 'could not act more efficiently in their humane vocation than in urging its early adoption'.[132]

Although private slaughterhouses were identified as a public nuisance in the 1700s, the butchers resisted all attempts to remove their City premises, and slaughterhouse-licensing records showed there were still 1,500 metropolitan premises in 1873, only reducing to 350 in 1905.[133] The eventual decline of the London slaughterhouses was due to the dwindling number of livestock to be slaughtered: most of the live cattle imported into London were foreign and, because of disease restrictions, went via the abattoirs at Deptford; imports of chilled and frozen beef from Australia, New Zealand and South America grew rapidly from 1875 to 1895, and an increasing proportion of domestic beef was country-killed and shipped directly to London Central Markets via rail or road.[134] Private slaughterhouses did persist though in London until 1927, when they were finally abolished.[135] And chloroform was never introduced.

Noxious trades

It was not just the slaughterhouses that appalled Londoners, but also the offensive industries that were supported once the livestock of London had been slaughtered – no part of the animal was spared. In the Middle Ages, the noxious trades had been banned from the City and moved to the suburbs,[136] but as London spread, the occupations of blood boiler, bone boiler, tripe boiler, trotter scraper, paunch cleaner and gut spinner were all undertaken in the midst of

hospitals, workhouses, schools and residential areas, which created horrendous living environments.

In 1846 John Simon, the Medical Officer of Health in the City of London, called for the urban noxious trades to be removed to the countryside. They were blamed for causing the cholera outbreak in London in 1849:

> If we arrest, and turn towards the suburbs, the *cart loads* of half putrid *bowels* that go teaming through the streets of the City of London to be twisted into *fiddle-strings* on the catgut maker's wheel – if along with the catgut spinners we also eject from our crowded streets to the open country the pestiferous factories where the fat of animals is converted into *tallow*, their bones into *glue*, their hides into *leather*, their stomachs into *tripe*, and their blood into *Prussian blue* – if we make the starch manufacturer remove his *pigs*, and the *London milk* manufacturer his cows (so far as cows be needful for his ingenious trade), from those City dungeons, darksome and foul, where now they stand degenerating till *their very feet rot off* . . . then may we expect in London exemption from *preventable disease.*[137]

London's trade in fur and skins deserves attention because its centre moved to the suburbs and totally colonized a whole area. Budge Row was known as Bogerow in 1342; it was so called because of the boge or budge fur (lambs' skins) that was prepared and sold there. This area was the centre of the London fur and skin trade and an ordinance dated 1345 required all furriers to dwell in Walbrook, Cornhill and Budge Row.[138] However, by the nineteenth century the only skins and leather market in London was at Leadenhall, but this trade moved to the New Leather Market, Weston Street, in Bermondsey in 1833.[139]

The noxious trades associated with cattle hides and sheepskins also moved to Bermondsey, and by 1851, when Charles Knight wrote of Bermondsey,[140] all of them (except for one or two businesses) were located over on the Surrey side of the river. Charles Dickens Jr (1837–1896) visited the area and noted that

> the air reeks with evil smells . . . it is a sight to see the men pouring out from all the works. Their clothes are marked with many stains; their trousers are discoloured by tan; some have aprons and gaiters of raw hide; and about them all seems to hang a scent of blood.[141]

There had been mention of tanneries in Bermondsey since 1392, mainly because of Bermondsey's location: a series of tide streams supplied a large quantity of fresh water twice a day, and there was a supply of oak trees nearby which provided the bark used in the tan pits to cure the hides into leather. The hides were first exposed to lime to loosen the hair, then the hides were scraped in preparation for the tan pit. After spending time in the tan pits, the tanned leather was hung up to dry. Once dried, the currier continued to stain and soften the leather.

The sheepskins supported another industry in Bermondsey. Outside the leather market were the fell-mongers who removed the wool from the skins and cleansed the pelt (which is what is left after the wool is removed) of its fat and impurities. The wool staplers then took the wool to sell to hatters and the woollen and worsted manufacturers, while the pelts were taken to the leather dresser, who prepared the skins and any other thin leather, such as goat, deer and dog skins. More delicate skins were tanned using chrome alum and oil instead of oak-bark.

The New Leather Market provided all parts of the animal for other industries. Horns were used by comb makers, knife-handle makers and other horn manufacturers; refuse was taken by glue manufacturers to extract the gelatine, and certain boys had 'the privilege of going over the ox-hides . . . and

trimming off the ears and the pieces of flesh left on the skull. These are piled in heaps, and sold [for eating] at 3*d.*or 4*d.* a lot.'[142] What the boys left behind was snapped up by a gigantic, sleek raven which hopped around the roof and floors of the market, as recorded by Greenwood. When Greenwood enquired as to whom the raven belonged to, a man told him that the bird belonged to no one, but was found on top of a shed as a fledgling and had made his home there. Asked why the raven had a broken wing, the man replied: 'When he was quite a little chap, a boy out here wanted to belong to him. They had a fight for it. That's how he got his wing broke.'[143]

Livestock on show

With the livestock of London now reduced to its skins and bones, it is worth noting that there was one class of livestock that was greatly admired in London while it was alive – unlike the countless number of nameless animals that innocuously arrived in London to meet their deaths.

At first these 'star' animals were exhibited at the London fairs as freaks of nature because of their extraordinary size. Gigantic pigs were often on show at Bartholomew Fair; presumably because after they had been exhibited, they could be spit-roasted to earn their owners even more money. Early in the eighteenth century, a Buckinghamshire pig was shown that was 10 feet long, 4 feet 4 inches high, and had a 7½-foot girth. By 1779, the prize pig at the fair had grown to 14 feet in length, but his bulk made it difficult for him to stand: 'When he rises from the ground for the spectators to see him, he roars in such a manner that his voice seems to mix, as it were, with the earth.'[144]

One of the most famous animals was the Lincolnshire ox painted by George Stubbs in 1790 when it was brought in a covered wagon, drawn by eight horses, to be exhibited daily in Hyde Park. The ox stood at

6 feet 4 inches high and weighed 3,000 pounds. Its owner, John Gibbon, had won him in a cockfight. Gibbon sold him at Tattersall's auction house, near Hyde Park Corner, and he was then put on show at the Lyceum in the Strand. He stayed there for almost a year, alongside a rhinoceros and three ostriches, until his death, which was caused by a lack of exercise and generous feeding. This had caused his legs to swell and his muscles to waste. He collapsed and was slaughtered the next day. Two weeks later, part of his huge carcass was displayed – and the public paid a shilling to view it.[145]

Deformed animals were also exhibited as freaks of nature. In 1654 Evelyn recorded seeing a six-legged sheep, which 'made use of 5 of them to walke', and also a goose 'that had 4 leggs, two Cropps, & as many Vents, voyding excrement by both, which was strange'.[146]

However, the real stars of the livestock world were to be seen at the annual four-day Smithfield Club Cattle Show. The Smithfield Cattle and Sheep Society, as the organizers were first known, was formed in December 1798 to encourage the economical rearing and fattening of cattle, pigs, and sheep to feed the growing population: well-known agriculturalists took the role seriously because 'the improvement of the rural arts was looked upon as a patriotic duty'.[147] However, at the show the entrants were mainly sensational because of their size and fatness.

Initially the show was held at a livery stables in Dolphin Yard, Smithfield, but in 1806 the 61 animals were judged by butchers and renowned breeders at Mr Sadler's Yard, Goswell Street (now Road). The owners had to certify the beasts' age, duration of fattening, work (whether they had been used as draft animals) and the food consumed. After exhibition, the animals were slaughtered and the judges took into account the dead-weights of the offal and quarters of the animals before they awarded the prizes. But it became increasingly difficult to judge the animals based on their dead-weight results, mainly because the butchers' figures were not accurate. So in 1895 several new classes were created to award prizes to the best carcasses in show. The animals in these classes were seen alive one day, slaughtered in the Metropolitan Cattle Market overnight and their carcasses judged, exhibited and sold to butchers the following day. The show soon began to attract the attentions of the rural and town public; not just for the huge animals on show, but for the sight of their carcasses hanging up in the most famous butchers' windows afterwards.

The butchers who bought the prize-winning cattle did not do so for financial gain, but rather for the kudos of selling the meat, which increased their reputation, fame and renown. Larger butchers were able to exhibit the animals in private rooms before they were slaughtered, whereas smaller ones would often rig up exhibitions on the kerbs outside their shops.

After the show outgrew the premises at Goswell Street, the event moved to the more spacious Horse Bazaar in Baker Street in 1839. Between 20,000 and 25,000 people visited this four-day show.[148] Its popularity soared when royalty began to visit and in 1862 the Cattle Show moved to the New Agricultural Hall in Islington, where 132,000 people viewed the exhibited animals.[149]

The appearance of the animals changed over time. The glory at Baker Street had gone to the 'immensely corpulent' and 'shapeless' stock on show that had been purely bred for fatness.[150] But this proved to be a 'very unscientific business, with a tendency to deteriorate the stock rather than improve it'.[151] Even London Zoo was cross-breeding Berkshire pigs with Indian wild hogs to try to improve on the 'somewhat overbloated candidates for porcine honours' at the Club Show.[152] After the show was installed at Islington, the judges started to award prizes not merely on weight, but also on 'symmetry and other qualities more desirable in cattle than mere bulk'.[153] However, the pigs were not so lucky and were poetically described as 'elongated balls of animated lard of mountainous dimensions'.[154] They were so fat that they were uncomfortable:

> Their very existence is evidently a burden under which they pant . . .They cannot get on their feet, but must lie prone to the hour of their death; and even as they lie, they would be smothered were not their snouts propped upwards by a friendly log, to enable them to inspire the air. They have looked their last upon the world, for fat has long since blinded their eyes and their little black muzzles peep forth from the round globes of cheeks, like the stem of a ripe pippin from the swelling fruit. Altogether, one does not compassionate them on their approaching fate, but rather feels inclined to congratulate them that their deliverer, the butcher, is not far off.[155]

The pigs, and other livestock, slimmed down over the years and the Royal Smithfield Show moved to Earls Court in 1949. It continued until 2004, when the prime livestock classes were seen for the final time in London. There was other exhibited livestock at the Royal Agricultural Hall, as the Islington Hall became known (it is now the Business Design Centre), notably prize cattle and goats at the Dairy Show (with its 'concomitants of poultry, pigeons and bees'[156]). The Crystal Palace hosted the Poultry and Pigeon Show, which also included classes for rabbits. But the end of the Smithfield Show saw London's troubled history with livestock come to a close.

Unloading cattle, pigs and sheep at the Baker Street Bazaar for the Smithfield Club Show, 1856, illustration. Note the rugs on the star exhibits to keep them clean before entering the ring.

Recreating the past: a sheep drive from Borough Market to Smithfield Market across the London Millennium Footbridge in June 2006, part of 'London Architecture Week'.

Today there are still places to see livestock in London, but these are in quiet city farms where the animals are kept from marauding through the busy streets. The first of these was established in Kentish Town in 1972, with others following in Hackney, Vauxhall and Spitalfields. The only time Londoners will see livestock walking over London Bridge these days is during a re-enactment of the right of Freemen of the City to herd sheep (usually) over the Bridge toll-free. This tradition began in 1237 and was extended to include Tower Bridge, Blackfriars Bridge and Southwark Bridge as they were built. However, according to the Corporation of London, the right no longer applies as there are no remaining livestock markets in the City, although sheep were driven over London Bridge on its 800th anniversary in 2009.

The void left by the demise of livestock around the streets of London was filled by an increase in the numbers of working animals that were needed to keep the burgeoning economy and population of London in a seemingly endless whirl of activity. To these, mainly horses and dogs, we now turn.

two

Working Animals: Straining Every Muscle

Throughout London's history up until 1947, when the Ministry of Transport banned all horse-drawn vehicles from using major London routes in peak traffic hours,[1] horses, ponies and donkeys were the hardest-working animals to grace the city's streets. The horse population grew alongside the human population, providing transport and a means of distributing the goods which poured into London via the railways, canals and ships. Although there is scant evidence of the actual numbers of horses employed by Londoners, their numbers peaked at the turn of the twentieth century, although estimates range widely from 200,000 to 700,000 working horses at this time.[2] Many of them were hired from 'jobmasters'.

Contemporary reports noted London's extraordinary draft-horse population, such as this observation of 1841:

In passing through Fleet Street, Cheapside, and some of the other principal thoroughfares ... the vehicles are so densely wedged together, that if one could walk on horses' backs, and on the tops of waggons, omnibuses, coaches, cabs, and so forth, without the risk of slipping his foot, he might proceed two or three hundred yards without once touching the causeway.[3]

While draft horses were worked for a profit and plied their trade mainly in the City and the East End, the other class of working horses in London could mainly be found in the West End. These were loss-making pleasure horses – the carriage horses and riding horses mainly used by the well-heeled of London during the season (which lasted from Easter until the 'Glorious Twelfth' of August).[4] But whether used for draft or pleasure, the life of the London-based horse was filled with dangers and hardship caused by both man and the environment, and was relatively short. However, horses helped to shape the economic and social history of London for centuries and provided a whole fleet of occupations with a livelihood. According to one horse lover, their presence on the streets in the nineteenth century also had a 'very beneficial effect on the national character; it had a humanizing effect on the population'.[5]

Medieval and early London

Although it is hard to estimate the number of horses in medieval London, evidence suggests that their presence in London was widely noticed. The draft-horse traffic caused hold-ups on the major routes around London, with complaints made in 1479 about the carts that blocked the route from London Bridge to the Tower while they stood waiting to pick up loads of fish at Billingsgate.[6] The Coroner's Rolls highlighted human deaths from being run over by horse-drawn carts and a groom drowned after he was thrown from the horse he had taken to water at the Thames.[7] Even dead horses caused problems for London citizens.

Edward William Cooke, *A Hay Barge off Greenwich*, 1835, oil on panel. Hay came in from the Essex countryside to feed the thousands of working horses.

There was an ordinance prohibiting the skinning and burial of horse carcasses within the City walls; in 1304 a tanner called Richard de Houndeslowe was brought before the Mayor for doing just that, and also for casting carcasses into the ditch (presumably the City Ditch at Ludgate).[8]

Horses were essential to the daily business of the City, both commercially and privately, but most Londoners wouldn't have owned the animals as the cost of buying and keeping a horse was out of reach – even horse bread, the staple diet of the horse made from beans and peas, cost a halfpenny a loaf.[9] Londoners could hire a horse and cart from the *traventers* to move the occasional heavy load, and could also hire a *hakenei* (road horse or everyday horse) from a hackneyman, at considerable cost, for rides out of the City – at this time London could be crossed on foot in about twenty minutes.[10]

Apart from trade and pleasure horses, London was also home to heavy horses employed for civic duties:

After Jan Griffier the Elder, *The Thames at Horseferry, with Lambeth Palace and a Distant View of the City, c.* 1710, oil on canvas.
This private coach-and-horses with attendant footmen is on the Horseferry, where Lambeth Bridge stands today.

the *carectarius* (carthorse) used by rakers to pull rubbish wagons, those used by London Bridgewardens to transport mainly timber and stone to maintain London Bridge, and the teams of four horses used to pump water by the Shadwell Waterworks Company from 1669 to serve nearly 8,000 homes from the Tower of London to Limehouse Bridge and from Whitechapel to the Thames.[11] These carthorses were nothing like today's heavy horses, and were probably more like hefty ponies by today's standards, so often large teams of them were used for heavier work.[12]

Meanwhile, the character of London's medieval streets was influenced by the size of riding horses, as stipulated by Henry Fitzailwyn, London's first mayor from *c.* 1190 to 1212. He decreed that the overhanging projections or jetties on the upper floors of houses had to be at least high enough for a man on horseback to pass under.[13] The landscape outside the City's walls was also largely dictated by the need to produce pastureland and hay to feed the growing urban horse (and livestock) population. During the Commonwealth, the trees of St John's Wood were felled and grassland was planted, which produced two or three cuts of hay a year.[14] Hay and straw were brought into the City

and sold at the Haymarket three times a week, from 1657, and in Whitechapel, Smithfield, the Borough and, from 1800, in Paddington.[15] In February 1774 over 1,300 hay and straw carts arrived at the Haymarket, and between 1827 and 1828 over 26,000 loads of hay and straw were registered with the toll collectors. The area became so clogged up with traffic that an act of 1830 finally moved the hay market to the new Cumberland Market, east of Regent's Park.[16]

Horses used for pleasure became increasingly important during the Restoration, when Charles II reopened Hyde Park to the public and railed off an inner circle in the northern half of the park, which became known as the Tour, and later the Ring. This became the rendezvous of fashionable society, and beauty, during the late afternoons of the London season, when they would promenade in expensive, ornate four-wheeled coaches pulled by two or more handsome, large coach horses. The coaches were lumbering, heavy looking vehicles which could carry six passengers inside, and two footmen and a coachman.[17]

To ensure that the nobility and gentry came into London with the most perfect team of horses to show off, the family's coachmen often walked their

The height of the coaching era: the courtyard of The Swan with Two Necks, off Cheapside, 1831, aquatint with etching.

specially purchased coach horses into the City at the beginning of the season.[18] The horses and carriages would then be kept either in mews stabling adjoining their grand houses in Westminster, Kensington and Chelsea, or in livery stables nearby which could accommodate between 80 and 100 animals.[19]

Alongside the private coaches, the seventeenth century also saw the emergence of horse-drawn public transport in London. The hackney coach, which was often a cast-off private carriage, stood waiting for fares from 1634 at the maypole in the Strand (where St Mary-le-Strand Church now stands). Although coaches had been let out for personal hire

at London inns from 1625, the idea of introducing them onto the streets grew popular. By 1637 their numbers had become a nuisance and Charles I limited London and Westminster to 50 hackney coachmen, each with a stud of twelve horses. However, their success was assured and by 1771 there were 1,000 coaches plying the streets.[20]

The eighteenth century: London's coaching era

While coaches worked within London, the City's coaching inns had already created flourishing stagecoach businesses which provided regular transport services connecting London with the rest of the country. But it was not until the 1780s, when coaches were used to carry mail as well as passengers, that coaching boomed. Previously a network of mounted post boys had delivered the 'General Post' throughout England, but by the end of the eighteenth century 80 mail coaches left London's General Post Office in Lombard Street each evening, having first collected up to ten passengers and their luggage from coaching inns.[21] The mail coach horses of London were insignificant in number compared with the thousands of London-based horses, but they were a glorious sight to see as they galloped in and out of London on their 10-mile 'stage' of the journey. The departure of the mail coach from the George and Blue Boar, Holborn, was described in *Coaching Days and Coaching Ways* (1893):

Tom Hennesy languidly mounts on to his box, assumes the whip as a marshal does his baton. 'Let 'em go' he says 'and look out for yourselves'. The ostlers [stablemen] fly from the chestnuts' heads – the four horses spring up to their collars – the guard performs 'Oh, ea, what can the matter be?' on his bugle and we are out of the coachyard before we know it, stealing down Holborn Hill with the 'fine, fluent motion' which as De Quincey described could be experienced on any crack coach which was finely driven.[22]

They looked equally impressive en masse during the annual parade of mail coaches at Millbank on May Day, which took place during the 1830s – coaching's heyday – to celebrate Queen Victoria's birthday. The horses from all the large London coach proprietors made a procession from Westminster through the Strand, Fleet Street and Ludgate Hill by the Old Bailey, and ended up at the new General Post Office building in St Martin's le Grand.[23]

The horses were generally stabled in the inn courtyards by the hundred, although the Bolt in Tun, Fleet Street, and the Bull and Mouth, St Martin's le Grand, built underground stables to accommodate the large number of coaching horses required.[24] They were well fed and looked after, worked only one hour in 24 and rested on the fourth day, but they were only useful for about four years, according to W. J. Gordon, whose *The Horse-world of London* (1893) chronicled the daily lives of all the major types of London-based horse.[25] Their working lives were short because of the speed at which they had to travel, and the state of the roads (pre-macadam) on which they had to fly, harried by a driver who cared not for their welfare, but for the timetable he had to meet. One journal writer in 1847 rejoiced on behalf of the 'Poster' (post) horse that the mail-coach era had come to an end the previous year, thanks to the railways.[26]

The nineteenth century: Rotten Row and riding horses

The introduction of better carriage springs and macadamized road surfaces made it possible for the heavy, capacious coaches of the previous centuries to be exchanged for smaller, lighter, two-wheeled carriages. These could be pulled by finer horses, and often by only one, which made the Cabriolet carriage a transport option for more Londoners. The horse was usually a thoroughbred type and a quick trotter – being 'showy' was the primary requirement, according to one journal in 1847:

Showy action is now so indispensible in the metropolitan horse for every purpose . . . He must [also] stand motionless while his aristocratic owner enjoys his colloquy at the coronetted carriage-window; must not want the application of the toy-whip, or pull so as to stretch or

W. G. Simmons, *Rotten Row*, 1867, hand-coloured engraving. The cream of society in Hyde Park; women rode side-saddle and both sexes wore top hats.

twist the fingers of the white, lemon, or pink kids [gloves] . . . [27]

The fashion for horses with showy movement also extended to what was known as the park hack or ridden horse that was seen mainly in Rotten Row in Hyde Park. Rotten Row was a sand-and-gravel, 80-foot track 1.5 miles in length that was full of riders during the season. In the later eighteenth century, and the early part of the nineteenth century, The Drive, between Rotten Row and the statue of Achilles, again became fashionable for carriages, and Rotten Row was fashionable for riding – even ladies were commonly seen riding side-saddle in public. [28]

Men had been riding in Hyde Park for centuries – even Samuel Pepys had tried to impress Charles II by kitting himself out in the newest riding garb and hiring a horse to ride – but the horse was too high-spirited for him and he failed to come to the King's attention. [29] Riding lessons for the nobility and gentry had been offered at Monsieur Foubert's Academy since 1679 in Sherwood Street in Piccadilly. [30] The Foubert family was said to instruct young ladies and gentlemen in how to 'witch the world with noble horsemanship'. [31] However, the frequenters of Rotten Row certainly were not all competent riders: an editorial in *The Examiner* in 1863 stated:

In Rotten Row there are many fresh, high-spirited horses, ready to follow any example of misbehaviour, and the rush of one at speed will set off others, and perhaps end in a run away and some frightful accident. A good half of the horse-people in Rotten Row are bad riders, some old and nervous, others young and inexperienced. Many have no seats, more have no hands, and no skill to manage their horses if anything should make them skittish or disposed to take themselves off. [32]

Several weeks earlier, the Member of Parliament W. E. Gladstone had been thrown from a horse in Rotten Row when it took fright. He suffered cuts and bruises and took to his bed in Carlton House Terrace for several days. [33]

The nineteenth century: carriage horses

By the later nineteenth century, the glamour of 'rank and fashion' attending Hyde Park had degenerated, complained the Guards Officer and social commentator Captain Gronow in 1860:

Democracy invaded the Park and introduced what may be termed a 'brummagem society,' with shabbygenteel carriages and servants . . . [in earlier times] 'pretty horsebreakers' would not have dared to show themselves in Hyde Park. [34]

It seems that London's pleasure horses were by then firmly in the sights of City workers, tradesmen and the like. Most of these carriage and riding horses were hired from the jobmaster or from local horse-livery stables. One jobmaster in the 1860s estimated that over a thousand horses were stabled at livery every morning within the City while their suburban-living owners or hirers went to work for the day. [35] In fact, the 150 jobmasters in London that Henry Mayhew mentions in his *London Labour and the London Poor* (1861) had been increasingly supplying rich people with the 'best horses in the world' since the railways had arrived in London. [36] This was probably because people coming for the season found it cheaper to hire horses in town than to bring their own, and private mews stabling did not have the 'best of reputations' by this time. [37] In 1893 Gordon estimated that 80 per cent of the 'magnificent horses that draw the family coaches' were on hire from jobmasters. [38]

High-class carriage horses generally arrived in London at about four years old and were trained for eight months among the hubbub of London to behave like gentlemen: to stand well, back and turn gracefully, draw up stylishly to a door, look nice while 'under window criticism', carry their head and lift their feet well, and work with a companion in a pair.[39]

His life was relatively easy while in the care of the jobmaster, where he was stabled on straw beds, and as well cared for 'as the plate at a silversmith's'. But he often was not treated so well when out on hire, and in 1900 Canon Samuel Wilberforce labelled 'the bad-tempered coachmen of the aristocracy' as the worst class of driver for ill-treating horses.[40]

The carriage horse was also subjected by many coachmen to an overly tight bearing-rein for excessive periods of time. This piece of leather was part of the bridle and, buckled to the bit, it passed over the head and attached to the harness on the horse's back. It was misused on fashionable carriage horses to keep their heads fixed artificially high, to make them look proud. But this caused their windpipes to be continually outstretched so they could not get rid of foam in their mouths, sometimes caused fractured jaws, and led to huge pressure on their spines. Their tails were also sometimes 'nicked', with the tendons/muscles severed, to create an artificially high tail carriage.

It was often the case that worn-out carriage horses, or those unequal to the job, were sold on as cab or omnibus horses. This was a real come-down in life for them and the start of a slippery descent into drudgery and ill-health, as chronicled in Anna Sewell's *Black Beauty* (1877).

Other high-class carriage horses had a better life in London; they were the Queen's horses, the black brigade and the wedding greys. In 1893 there were 700 black horses belonging to London's 'black masters', which were hired by 'funeral furnishers' to pull hearses.[41] They were all Flemish stallions, imported when they were nearly three years old. It took them a year to acclimatize to London, get over their travel illnesses and be trained to their stately task. The largest 'black master' was Samuel Dottridge of East Road, Shoreditch, who had 80 horses, all named after contemporary or deceased politicians, artists, musicians, actors, poets and churchmen. They were usually taken out as teams of four and Gordon was amazed at their docility, seeing as they were stallions.[42]

Wedding greys were also kept for hire: Tilling the jobmaster needed at least 40 greys to cover an average of six weddings a day all year round. They were never hired out for any other purpose.

The nineteenth century: public transport horses

The lives of the horses used in public transport were not so rosy. The hackney coach was gradually taken over by the Parisian *cabriolet de place* or cab, after it was introduced to London in 1823. This small, two-wheeled vehicle was drawn by one horse and was originally licensed to carry only two passengers. Cabs were cheaper than coaches and could be driven at far greater speeds, but there was a great danger of them overturning. Many passengers feared getting into them, but an improved version known as the hansom cab made them more popular. By 1841 there were about 1,500 cabs in London – twice as many as hackney coaches – and by 1888 there were about 11,500 hansom cabs and four-wheeled 'growlers', either waiting at the 600-plus cab stands or plying the streets for fares (which caused a great nuisance to other road users).[43] One reason for the increasing reliance on cabs by Londoners was, according to Henry Curling's pamphlet *A Lashing for the Lashers* (1851), that those who used to walk around the town were becoming more slothful, and also that the fashion for being driven around town had descended the social ladder.[44]

London cab horses were widely regarded as 'unfortunate animals', whether they worked during the day or night, stated Gordon. They worked six days a week, sometimes travelling up to 40 miles in a normal day, pulling half a ton of carriage and driver, excluding passengers.[45] They rested on the Sunday, during which they spent all day in their mews stabling being fed to prevent them from getting bored.[46] Their replacements, the Sunday cab horses, were part-timers that worked on other vehicles during the week. The regular cab horses were generally Irish, with many shipped over from Waterford, and they would travel unshod to prevent them damaging each other during the sea voyage, with their lips tied down to keep them quiet.[47]

These horses would be stabled in London and given names – never Christian names but often 'after some trivial circumstance connected with its purchase [like the weather conditions] or from some event chronicled in the morning newspapers'.[48] As is apparent by the slapdash choosing of names, cab owners mainly regarded the horses as machines, and as long as the horses came back at the end of their seven- to twelve-hour shifts in a reasonably sound state, cab owners were not worried about the treatment their drivers had meted out to them.[49]

Cab drivers were widely regarded as some of the greatest 'miscreants as inhabit the earth', known for their brutality, drunkenness, avarice and ill-temper.[50] The problem was that drivers had to make a certain amount of money for the cab owner before anything went into their own pockets, so they went after every likely fare and delivered passengers to their destinations as fast as they could without a thought for the horses. In *Sketches by Boz* (1836–7) Dickens noted, drily, that this hectic pace frequently caused cab horses to fall: 'We are not aware of any instance on record in which a cab-horse has performed three consecutive miles without going down once.'[51]

Cabs eventually declined in popularity as the numbers of omnibuses and trams rose, mainly because of the vagaries of the 'voluntary addition' charged by the cabmen on top of the distance driven.[52]

When the cab horses were not being harried through the streets, they waited peacefully at the cab stands eating the 'vitals' that their drivers provided for them. Many observers commented on the personalities of the horses that shone through, if only passers-by would take time to look at them properly.

The naturalist Frank Buckland (1826–1880) entertained his readers with an amusing account of a cab horse's quiet revenge on his driver:

A cab-horse in a four-wheeler at the stand by Palace Yard; the cab-horse fast asleep with his head hanging down; the cab-man also fast asleep, leaning against the horse. The cab-horse (I suppose in his sleep) kicks the man; the cabman instantly wakes, and kicks the cab-horse in return. 'You brute,' he said, 'I can kick as well as you can,' and then they went on at it again – the cab-horse and the cabman kick for kick for a minute or so, till at last I settled the dispute by saying, 'Hi! Cabby, four-wheeler, so to so-and-so!' 'Right you are,' said the man, and we all three trundled off, as though nothing particular had happened.[53]

It only took three years for cab horses to become exhausted and, if they hadn't already dropped dead in the streets, they were gradually retired from service, ending up pulling the Sunday morning cab.[54] The cab owner would then dispose of them in one of the metropolitian auction houses, to be sold on as a tradesman's horse.

The life of the London omnibus horse was little better. These cumbersome horse buses, originally pulled by three horses but later by a pair, were brought to London in 1829–30 by George Shillibeer. They were licensed to carry twelve passengers inside. A few carried another two passengers, and the total weight for the team to pull topped a ton-and-a-quarter per horse.[55] Every horse travelled 12 miles a day, at speeds of about 5 miles an hour over a route of 4 to 5 miles. By law, the drivers were only allowed to stop for three minutes in one or two places along this route to rest the horses, but often drivers took more breaks if they were low on passengers. If they had a full bus, they made no rest stops along the way. In 1841 the *London Saturday Journal* insisted that strangers to London would be amazed at the speed at which the ponderous-looking omnibuses travelled through uncrowded streets, with the horses often at a gallop.[56] But what really damaged the horses were the frequent stops and starts they had to make, which 'knock[ed] their legs to pieces' and often made 'their necks quite raw under the collars'.[57]

The largest horse owner in London in 1875 was the London General Omnibus Company (LGOC) with 8,000 horses.[58] This number rose to 10,000 horses by the early 1890s (nearly half of all omnibus horses),

Hansom cab horses patiently waiting for fares, 1860.

and reached nearly 16,700 horses in 1901 – although ten years later the LGOC ran its last horse bus, in preference for motorized vehicles.[59] These horses were brought to London from provincial fairs and sent to a depot in either Paddington or Spitalfields, where they were sorted based on their preference for different road surfaces – granite, asphalt, macadam or wood.

Once moved to their new yards, they were trained up for fitness, paired up with their future companions and found collars that fitted. Aside from their feed, shoeing was a major cost in their upkeep; they went through one set of shoes a month, and often needed frost nails in cold weather to prevent them from slipping. However, it was fairly common for horses to fall, either through slippage or overwork, and two out of every three horses died in the service.[60] Only those horses likely to recover were taken care of; the others were 'remorselessly weeded out'.[61] Back at

Two horses drew the weighty omnibuses over the rough cobbled streets, photograph from mid-1860s.

Horse-drawn tram running between Greenwich and Westminster, 1885.

their stables the foreman would try to overcome the minor ailments that affected many omnibus horses: paralysis of the back, sore throat, nails in the foot, fever in the foot and congestion of the lungs.[62] Gordon witnessed one foreman sympathetically ordering, 'a pint and a half of ale for one horse, mustard for another, a blister for another, poultices for two or three, and "a drop of whisky for the roan at the far end"'.[63]

The Road Car Company, with about 3,000 horses, was the second-largest omnibus horse owner. Its Fulham yard, in Farm Lane, was the 'finest omnibus yard in Britain', according to Gordon.[64] It housed 700 horses (mainly Scottish-bred) on two storeys and the stables were the horses' refuge from the noise, the weather and the road surfaces of London.[65]

Horse-drawn trams were the last of London's horse transport to be established. Trams were supposed to make horses' lives easier by reducing the resistance of the vehicle, but the horses were actually made to pull a load that was 20 per cent heavier because of the tram's weight and its increased passenger capacity. It was also difficult to pull on a sunken tram rail, especially when it was full of dirt, and horses had to deal with hills and routes which required about 500 stops a day.[66] There were just under 10,000 tram horses in London, mostly working two-horse cars, with each pair averaging 13 miles a day.[67] The North Metropolitan (Tramways) Company owned the most horses out of the thirteen London tram companies – 3,500 in 1893 – but when it was founded in 1871 it hired omnibus horses from the LGOC.[68]

Railway horses and cartage agents

The coming of the railways did not decrease the need for horse-drawn transport; quite the reverse. Passenger numbers on public transport increased and railway companies started to deliver the goods they brought into London and collect those they shipped out of the city. They owned more heavy horses (for moving heavy goods) and trotting horses (for the lighter goods) than locomotives.[69] Horses were also used in goods yards and sidings, moving goods and shunting railway wagons. Gordon estimated that the railway companies owned a total stud of 6,000 horses in 1893.[70]

The Great Western Company prided itself on its magnificent stud of over 1,000 horses, stabling half of them in a four-floor stabling block complete with infirmary in South Wharf Road, Paddington. Heavy van horses were the most numerous type at the stud, and their work began at 2 am on Monday when the vans went off to Covent Garden. This made for a bustling week: 'What the trains bring the vans must take, what the vans bring the trains must take, be it much or little.'[71] A four-team of horses drawing the heaviest van would be a moving mass of 13 tons, making it one of the heaviest things going through the London streets, while the single-horse railway parcel cart was one of the fastest.[72] Van horses, like all other heavy horses in London, were originally farm horses and were gradually acclimatized to London life over two months before starting railway work. They would last on the streets for five years before the jarring stops and starts took their toll. But at that point they were not sent to the auctioneers but moved to the veteran stables near the goods yard, where they helped drag the vans up the steep slopes of Paddington station.[73]

The other railway company of note for its stud was the London and North Western Railway, which had a curiously small 650-horse stud because it contracted out half of its cartage work to Messrs Pickford and Co. The railway horses were stabled on Chalk Farm Road (now Stables Market), and a labyrinth of tunnels built from 1854 allowed them to travel underground from their stables to their work in Camden Town Goods Yard, so they did not have to cross the tracks; cast-iron grilles set into the road surface at regular intervals provided the tunnels with their only source of light. The same network of tunnels, known as the Camden catacombs, was used by other heavy

horses, such as the shire horses of Gilbey's – the wine, spirit and liquor company that owned warehouses, bottling plants and goods sheds with access to the railway – and those that worked on the Regent's Canal towpath.[74]

Pickford's (new) stables were also attached to the tunnels. Its previous stabling, for over 100 Clydesdale horses, had been in the basement under its warehouse in the goods depot,[75] but this had burned down in June 1857. Luckily nearly all the horses were turned loose from their stables in time. Images in the *Illustrated London News* and written accounts of the fire captured the terror of the horses involved:

> The animals, the instant they got into the open road, ran in wild confusion about, to the danger of trampling down the many thousand persons, including men, women, and children, who flocked towards the spot . . . The whole of the horses were got out with the exception of one a remarkably fine though savage animal, known as the 'Man-hater', and which could only be managed by the man who drove him. As this man was not present the poor brute was left to perish, and on Wednesday, after the fire was subdued, his remains were found burned to a cinder.[76]

While Pickford's worked for the railways and needed heavy horses, most other general carmen and cartage agents around London used lighter horses. The largest of the household carriers – which moved the public's parcels – was Carter Paterson, which had a stud of 2,000 horses stabled in twenty depots across London, with its headquarters at Goswell Road, Clerkenwell. It dealt with any parcels that the Post Office's parcel post would not carry, from overly large or bulky items such as servants' boxes as they moved jobs, to baths and garden tools. Its horses, therefore, were required to draw all types of vehicle from box furniture vans to the parcels cart.[77]

Private businesses also found it economical to own a stud of horses to collect goods and make deliveries. By the mid-1700s, Fortnum & Mason Ltd in Piccadilly had set up stables in nearby Mason's Yard, mainly to collect goods such as 'Harts Horn, Gable Worm Seed, Saffron and Dirty White Candy', imported into the docks by the East India Company.[78] Furniture stores such as John Maple & Co. Ltd in Tottenham Place had their own horse-drawn delivery carts, and in 1828 the newsagents and stationers W. H. Smith (which added 'and Sons' to its name in 1846) provided the fastest and most efficient newspaper-delivery service in London with a fleet of small carts and horses.[79]

These carrier horses, about 19,000 of them, varied in quality from the excellent to the indifferent. The latter were often ex-cab or omnibus horses on their final job before being sent to the knacker's yard.[80]

London's dray horses and carthorses

The heavy teams working in London learnt their trade on the farm before coming to the Big Smoke. They usually became ill on first arriving in London and it took at least a week for them to acclimatize. They were generally a very docile lot, for reasons which the *New Sporting Magazine* explained:

> They are never really distressed, or ... punished to make exertions ... They [the drivers], unlike the coachman or groom, have no pride in seeing a horse fast at his work: they are slow themselves; and provided the horse obeys the motion of the whip, and 'come 'ither who's' or 'gee who's', or backs the dray, they do not care if he is half an hour doing it.[81]

Several classes of heavy horse were described in *The Horse-world of London*: the coal horse, the vestry horse (which carted rubbish) and the brewery horse. Coal horses were worked by the railways and shipping companies that imported 5 million tons of domestic coal into London each year, and also by the coal merchants who distributed the coal to households.[82] The first-class horses were the heavy dray types, which were mainly black or dark bay.[83] Their working day began with breakfast at 4 am; they were out to work at 6 am and did not return until between 7 and 11 pm. A full load weighed no less than 3 tons, which was often taken long distances.[84]

However, the coal horse's day involved plenty of standing around while being loaded and unloaded: 'the horses [stand] gently bobbing their nosebags and utterly indifferent to the dust and din.'[85] Drivers tried to avoid hills, but where they were unavoidable two vans would climb the hill together, with two horses each pulling the vans in succession. The hardest route was from Smithfield to the Angel along St John Street, which was uphill on a slippery granite track – 'if [the horse] can stand that slippery track he can stand anything', noted Gordon.[86]

The life of the vestry horse was similar to the coal horse's in that it had to move extremely heavy loads, but had plenty of time to rest while its cart was being loaded. The 1,500 vestry horses moved 1.3 million cart-loads of refuse from London streets during the year; two or three loads of rubbish each day, taking eleven hours, with each load averaging 2.5 tons.[87] Both of these types of horse were English-bred, which meant their forelegs did not easily give way compared with those of foreign animals, which 'strained the back tendons with the constant jar of his feet as he has plodded along the granite, asphalt, or wood'.[88]

The vestry horses, although they were municipal horses, were still of good quality, especially those that worked on the streets of Marylebone, Battersea, St George's Hanover Square and Kensington, and often won prizes at the annual London Cart Horse Parade. This parade, established in 1886, was held on Whit Monday and aimed to improve the general

Jacob the dray horse stands in The Circle, Queen Elizabeth Street, SE1, in memory of the Courage dray horses that were stabled there.

condition and treatment of London's working carthorses by encouraging drivers to take an interest in their welfare.[89] But the vestry horses made a happy pairing with their drivers anyway since drivers were matched to their horses by their gait, so that they walked at similar speeds.[90] Drivers also got a bonus of a sovereign or two a year for keeping them in good condition.[91] Vestry horses were more adept than their heavy brethren at avoiding nails on the road left over from demolished buildings, as they had to pick their way through the rubbish heaps to keep clear of all sorts of dangers.[92]

The most powerful of the heavy brigade were the 3,000 horses owned by the larger London brewers, and Messrs Courage's shire horses were the finest of them all.[93] Courage's horses were kept at Horselydown Lane, SE1, near Tower Bridge. From the sixteenth century, Horselydown was the place where working horses could rest before crossing London Bridge into the City, and today the site of the Courage stables from the early nineteenth century is marked by a statue, *Jacob: The Circle Dray Horse*.

These brewery horses, in teams of three, pulled loads of 8 tons during the week, and their working lives were cut short when they failed to pull hard enough as this disrupted the team and demoralized the other horses.[94] But still their working lives were between six and seven years, so they were some of the longest survivors in the London streets. After they had been retired they were usually exported to

Horses and carts collecting sand and gravel from a spritsail barge beached at Lambeth in 1934.

Hamburg on the 'sausage boat' rather than going to the knacker's yard, and returned to the shores of the UK as sausagemeat.[95] However, during their lives the brewery horses seldom had bad tempers because they were in good health, worked regularly and shod very well – at Courage's each shoe was made specially to fit and was never allowed to wear out.[96] The last shires to leave London were those of Young's at the Ram Brewery in Wandsworth in 2006. They delivered beer to pubs within a 3-mile radius of the brewery and were all black with four white socks and a blaze down the middle of the face.

Jobmaster horses: the doctor's horse, the Post Office and the emergency services

Gordon estimated that by the end of the nineteenth century, nine-tenths of quality London horses were hired from jobmasters.[97] One of the largest was Tilling of Peckham, with a stud of 2,500 horses, all of which were good-looking and obedient as it would not have been good for business if he had loaned out poor-quality animals. He 'jobbed' for 'the duke, the doctor, and the drayman; for all sorts and conditions, from the Lord Mayor and Sheriffs to the washerwoman limited'.[98] He also owned the horses which had pulled the Tilling omnibuses and cabs since 1864, the horses of the Regent's Park Canal Company, the horses that pulled the Board of Works carts, Peek Frean's biscuit vans, brewery bottled-beer vans, several London tram lines, the Fire Brigade (jobbed since 1880), the Salvage Corps and the Metropolitan Police.[99] As can be imagined, the yards were open day and night and they bustled with life. Often the arrangement with the jobmaster meant that the horses were fed and shod at the jobmaster's expense, although the horses were often stabled at the hirers.

Doctors needed strong and fast horses that could travel long distances, but could also draw up to the patient's door with style – this was no horse belonging to a humble general practitioner.[100] Those doctors who practised in Harley Street and Cavendish Square often had six horses on hire so they were always fresh. GPs' horses, on the other hand, had hard lives without

Illustration of Messrs Meux's brewery horses, 1830, at the Horse Shoe brewery, Tottenham Court Road.

much rest or comfort in the stable, or on the street. They were worked particularly hard in the winter, when cases of influenza were rife, and often had to stand for hours in the cold and rain. If a GP had only one horse, he would often walk on a Sunday to give his weary horse a rest.[101]

Since 1837 all the Post Office's trotting horses were jobbed by one Mr McNamara, who had 600 horses spread over London: in his Finsbury headquarters and many local branches. Like most working horses, they came to London aged five – any earlier and they were not suitable for London cartage work as, according to one authority, they were 'like children and catch every ailment that comes along'.[102] The Post Office horses were always at work from 4 pm Sunday to 10.30 am the next Sunday, so they only had a few hours of undisturbed rest, but, surprisingly, they worked longer than most horses – for six years – mainly because they were well looked after and had few ailments.[103] If they were ill, the horses were entitled to sick leave, as shown in a note from 1898 stating that 'Mr T. C. Poppleton's horse of The Post Office is suffering from sore shoulders and unable to perform his official duties.'[104]

It was more common for the 130 jobbed Fire Brigade horses to require medical treatment than the Post Office horses. Although they ignored the sparks which sprinkled their backs from the unguarded funnels of the steam fire engines, they did suffer from accidents and jobmasters had to have a ready supply of horses in emergencies.[105] Tilling's fire horses were grey, a purposely conspicuous colour, so that the public were quick to clear the roads ahead of them. They were a spectacular sight:

Hear the clatter of hoofs mingling with the clang of the alarm bell . . . the flying manes, the wide, distended eyes and nostrils of the gallant beasts; watch them . . . with admiring wonder, straining every muscle, needing no lash in their headlong career, while the busy traffic of the street parts to give them right of way.[106]

Horses had been used to draw fire appliances since the formation of the privately run London Fire Engine Establishment (LFEE) in 1833. Horses were also used to pull escape vans, which carried long ladders, and hose carts. The London County Council-run London Fire Brigade was formed in 1904, but horses were still employed after the first mechanized engines came into service in 1907,[107] and they were not phased out until 1921. The last pair of fire horses – Lucy and Nora – left Kensington Fire Brigade Station in November of that year.

Many of the older fire stations around London today date from 1900 to 1916 and were designed to cater for horses. When the alarm was raised, a system of pulleys and hooks lowered the harness, which was pre-attached to the vehicle shafts, from the ceiling onto the horses' backs at the sound of an electric bell. The harness would self-fasten underneath the horse by the release of a spring (no buckles were used). The waiting horses would already be wearing bridles. During call-outs to large fires, such as the Regent's Park Explosion in 1874 when 5 tons of gunpowder and several barrels of patroleum being towed on the Regent's Canal exploded, the Fire Brigade was supported by the police and the Royal Horse Guards from Albany Barracks, who were brought in to keep order, salvage as much as possible and help the firemen to work the fire engines.

One might also expect ambulances to arrive at the scenes of disasters, but there was still no formal ambulance service (for street accidents) in 1903.[108] London had horse-drawn ambulances after the 1880s, but they were attached to the London hospitals and were mainly used for transporting patients with infectious diseases. When the last horse-drawn hospital ambulance was used in September 1912, one journal noted that it was 'a day that marked the end of the once familiar

R. G. Reeve, *London Fire Engines*, *c.* 1830, hand-coloured aquatint with etching. Note the three different insurance companies racing to get to the fire first.

sight of urchins pursuing the slow-moving vehicles shouting "Fever!"[109]

If an accident happened in the streets, it was up to the police to decide what to do. This usually involved hailing a cab and having the injured parties taken to hospital, or taking the cab horse and harnessing it to a hospital ambulance. This situation was not ideal and there were calls for horse ambulances to be kept at fire and police stations, where horses were already waiting to respond to emergencies.[110] But before the formal reorganization of the Ambulance Service in 1930, the horse-drawn ambulance was already a vehicle of the past.

Buying horses

Having introduced the main types of working horse in London, it is necessary to look at where these horses were bought and sold within the city. First-class riding and carriage horses were either traded at Tattersall's auction house or bought through private dealers, who were commissioned to find the perfect horse for the client. Many of the quality dealers in the nineteenth century had been finding horses for the London market for centuries, such as the 300-year-old Cox's of Stamford Street, Waterloo Road. George Cox, the last of the family to run the business in the nineteenth century, bought at least 300 horses from Paris each year, where the best horses came from (at least according to his guarantee).[111] Dealers also purchased heavy horses for many of the London breweries.

Trade horses of high to medium quality were usually sold at auction houses: Aldridge's Horse Repository in St Martin's Lane and Rymill's in the Barbican – the two main houses – and Stapleton's out in the east, Ward's in the west, and the Elephant and Castle in the south.[112] Aldridge's or the 'Horse Bazaar' was established in 1753 and held auction sales on Wednesdays and Saturdays until 1926. *All the Year Round* described the buyers who attended as a motley assortment; the majority of them were London dealers, coachmen, grooms, cab men, job-masters and omnibus owners.[113] Stables surrounded the sale yard, and the horses were brought out on to 'the course' to be trotted and cantered up, and have their legs felt and their mouths checked by the punters. All types of horse were offered, from first-timers to 'many-other-handers', and to suit all pockets: redundant government-owned horses, the surplus stock

of London jobmasters after the season was over, Irish horses, horses from Belgium, hunters and ladies' hacks.

Aldridge's and the other auction houses were also trusted sources of horses: 'if the auctioneer says of a horse "warranted sound", you may take his word.'[114] Unfortunately this was not the case of horses sold at Smithfield Market, where the underclass of the horse world could be found. Along with the horse fair held at the nave of St Paul's Cathedral during the Reformation,[115] Smithfield had been the place to buy horses since William Fitzstephen had described it in the eleventh century. In medieval times it was known for the quality of its horse sales on a Friday:

It is a delight to see the palfreys [quiet horses, usually ridden by women] trotting gently around, the blood pumping in their veins, their coats glistening with sweat, as they alternately raise

Smithfield horse market in an engraving of *c.* 1820 after *A View of Smithfield* by Jacques Laurent Agasse.

then lower both feet on one side together. Then to see the horses more suitable for squires, rougher yet quicker in their movements, simultaneously lifting one set of feet and setting down the opposite set. After that the high-bred young colts, not yet trained or broken, high-stepping with elastic tread. Next packhorses, with robust and powerful legs. Then expensive war horses, tall and graceful, with quivering ears, high necks and plump buttocks. Prospective buyers watch as all are put through their paces: first, their trot, followed by their gallop.[116]

However, certainly by the sixteenth century, the Smithfield horse fair, the dealers (coursers or corsours) and the horses (known as scrub-horses[117]) had a very bad reputation. According to one researcher, 'The size and anonymity of the market there certainly attracted shady characters from all over the country, intent on selling stolen animals or palming off worn-out jades at inflated prices.'[118] In 1828 it was stated that the horse fair was a means of bringing together 'all the rogues and thieves within ten miles of London', and that it was 'the most abominable scene that can be imagined'.[119]

Even when the Metropolitan Market was opened at Islington in 1852, the horse fair did not really improve, despite the presence of the police. James Greenwood visited the London Horse Market in 1867 and warned that it was no place for amateur horse buyers to attend, as they would never be able to spot the subtle tricks of the 'copers' and would likely be sold one of the many 'spavined, weak-knee'd, wall-eyed monstrosities' that were palmed off as quality horses. About 200 horses – many of which, said Greenwood, 'making such a pitiful collection as made one quite melancholy to contemplate' – had been subjected to 'vamping and tinkering' to make them appear better than they were.[120] One practice was to cover up the pulmonary disease of glanders, which was feared as

much as the cholera in humans, by 'calking' the nose with hog's lard to 'mend his wind for a few hours'.[121] Another trick was to inflate the deep pit above the eye found in old horses so that it temporarily filled with air to make them appear younger.[122] Gordon remarked that the horse fair was full of 'screws': kickers, jibbers, roarers, the broken-winded, bolters and those with bad tempers.[123]

To show off the horses, ponies and donkeys, an avenue was cleared in the crowd and the animals were made to trot down the aisle to show 'their mettle'. The avenue was dotted with men with whips who yelled and lashed out at the frightened animals to 'encourage' them in their movement.[124] Many of the animals, rather than being auctioned, were strawed, which meant that a bunch of straw was tied or plaited into their manes and tails as a sign that the seller was open to reasonable offers.[125]

Despite the market's appalling reputation, most of the horses and ponies were bought by costermongers (the street sellers of fruit, vegetables and fish) for pulling their carts, and by other small tradesmen. Also among the horses were some 'fine specimens' of racks – fleshless horses, simply skin and bone – which were bought by knackermen.[126]

It was a sad end for many London horses at the market, said Greenwood, because often they had started off life as magnificent hunters and the like, but had for some reason become injured or unusable, so had been sold on to an easy carriage life. From there they had descended into a dreary life pulling omnibuses, and were then plunged into the misery of the London night cab. By the end of their working lives, perhaps blinded, with aching bodies, Greenwood believed they were hoping for some knackerman to snap them up and put them out of their misery, but because of the tinkering of the copers they were sold on again to work until they dropped.[127]

Goats were for sale in another part of the market. These were sold as chaise-goats for pulling carts (as alternatives to dogs), but were also often sold as horses' stable companions. There was disagreement among commentators as to why. The *Leisure Hour* journal noted that goats had 'from time immemorial' been in horse yards as they were conducive to the health of the horses, whereas *Once a Week* journal believed that it was because goats would run from fire, and that horses would follow them out of the stables.[128]

Costermen and their donkeys

Greenwood believed that the Horse Market should have been renamed the Ass Market after its most numerous animal. It was the only place in London, and for 5 miles outside London, where the humble donkey or moke could be traded.[129] Most of the 3,000 donkeys that went through the market each year were destined for use in costermongers' carts,[130] but others would find themselves pulling laundresses' carts, being ridden or being milked in the capital's ass dairies. Each type of donkey could be readily identified, according to Greenwood:

The donkey that had passed its life in the society of [coster] men . . . carried its ears aslant, leant negligently on three legs, and was a blackyard donkey from its impudent tail to the tip of its ruffianly nose; when the butt-end of the whip-stock was brought down on its back with a noise like the banging of a barrel, it merely winked its eyes contemptuously and backed deliberately against the whelk man's stall, its close proximity to which had been the original cause of the chastisement. How different was the behaviour of the sleek [ridden] Clapham ass, with its dainty white saddle-cloth and decently blacked hoofs! So of the neat laundry donkey, meeker even than its neighbour the chaise-goat, and only less bashful and seemingly washed out than the two unfortunates from the milk purveyors.[131]

Most costers aspired to owning a donkey cart of their own, although many only hired their donkeys from the jobmaster, and they 'almost universally treat[ed] their donkeys with kindness', according to Henry Mayhew.[132]

Charles Dickens, writing for *All the Year Round*, went to Billingsgate Market to see whether he could find any ill-treated donkeys, but was pleasantly surprised to find them all well fed and not overloaded. He asked a policemen why the costers' donkeys were all treated well: "Cos it's their interest, sir; they would be fools to ill treat their best friend', was the reply.[133] A writer from *The Contemporary Review* was witness to one particular act of kindness between a coster and his donkey on the London streets:

I saw a constermonger lad with a donkey, which had made a dead stop in a street where there were no lookers-on save myself. When the donkey stopped the driver did the same, looking at it for a minute or so intently and kindly, as one would look at a friend in distress. Then he went nearer, and said, in a coaxing tone which, I regret, I have not power of committing in any way to paper, – 'What's the matter with you? – give's a kiss!' At this, the donkey rubbed its nose against its master's cheek, as if it quite understood both the tone and the words. The day was very hot – that was the 'matter' with the donkey; and the poor lad felt a good deal of sympathy for it. Perhaps each was the only friend the other had in the world.[134]

However, as already mentioned by Greenwood, the donkeys were continually thumped by the costers with sticks while in the market; this was not meant in a cruel way, but just as 'a matter of habit when talking', explained Dickens.[135]

Dickens added that donkeys were also ill-treated when their owners became drunk or when they were

An illustration of a coster and his 'moke', 1876.

given over to people 'who had no interest in them', such as the riding donkeys on Hampstead Heath. A dozen donkeys were originally introduced on to the heath in 1817, to the delight of the ladies in the neighbourhood, who rode them side-saddle,[136] but as their popularity grew they were shamefully used by their owners, he wrote. The donkey men would buy them from the Horse Market in the spring, when they were at their most expensive, but it was worth the cost. An officer of the Humane Society told Dickens: 'They can make more by them in a day than they are worth, and they don't mind killing them.'

Donkey-riding on Hampstead Heath, from Gustave Doré's *London* (1872).

Dickens agreed: 'Have you not seen a sixteen-stone materfamilias, with her whole family of daughters, ruthlessly riding as many donkeys to death on Hampstead Heath, utterly regardless of their sufferings?'[137]

By 1893 there were about 13,000 donkeys in London, but the number of donkeys being ridden was few because the London County Council had introduced a licence for donkey hirers which limited their studs to five animals.[138]

Cruelty and prosecutions

It was not always the case that costers looked after their donkeys and, before the mid-nineteenth century, most of London's horse population was badly treated. The reason for this poor treatment was not really wanton cruelty on the part of the owners/drivers (although there were many 'brutish' drivers about), but ignorance and a desire to get the most out of the animal.

Gordon highlighted the ignorance issue when he remarked that by 1893, the horses in London were in a much better state than they had ever been:

The average horse is treated much better than he used to be; he is better fed, better housed, and more intelligently looked after, and he lives longer, works more, and is better worth looking at than in the merry days of the past.[139]

Another writer in the *New Sporting Magazine* in 1847 explained the economic issue of pushing horses, but also alluded to the innate cruelty of some men:

It is singular, but fact, that in a general way all animals are used more cruelly by the very persons who get their bread by them than by any others …There seems a kind of devilish feeling in men, as if they wished to punish or, at all events, to be careless of the feelings of the animal because they are in a certain way under obligations to him.[140]

So how did it come about that costers, and other drivers, changed their behaviour towards their animals? Dickens went in 1864 to see the Mule and Donkey Show run by the RSPCA at the Agricultural Hall and admired the costers' affection for their smartly turned-out donkeys and carts. But he also touched on the reason behind the show:

Donkey-drivers, who had for years been receiving lessons in humanity from the officers of the society, came up to show what progress they had made in the art of persuading donkeys to do their work without the argument of the stick.[141]

The (R)SPCA also worked on the public and on passengers to report instances of cruelty which could be prosecuted under the newly emerging animal cruelty legislation, kick-started in July 1822 by Martin's Act to prevent the cruel treatment of livestock and horses.

According to one alderman in 1835, there had been 'a marked reduction in the beating of donkeys with large clubs seen on the streets since the enforcement of Mr Martin's Act'.[142] In the early 1830s the *Voice of Humanity* journal contained lists of prosecutions the SPCA inspectors had brought before the courts – usually for cruelly whipping horses drawing hackney coaches, carts and private carriages.[143] At this time, the police were not required by law to intervene if they saw cruelty, so the inspectors were vital to the SPCA's work. However, as part of the Police Act of 1831, police had to stop any 'wanton and furious driving', or drunken driving which could endanger or cause injury to the public.[144]

Newspapers, particularly the *Morning Post*, covered the cruelty cases. The following examples are not the worst cases, but some reports are truly horrific to read:

1832: Fined 10*s*. for whipping horses on a sore place called 'a raw', which had probably been artificially created to make them more sensitive to the whip so they increased their efforts to pull their omnibuses which were crammed with people.[145]

1849: Wounds on an omnibus horse painted over with flour of brimstone, and the holes in the raw flesh plugged up with fullers'-earth – the horse had been sent out to work by its master and dropped down dead near Hyde Park.[146]

1863: Torturing a cab-horse: wounds on back, shoulders, and withers created by a rubbing harness; fore knee badly broken, lame on all four legs, and in such a poor condition that its bones were nearly protruding through the skin – the master said that he'd have never let the horse out for work if he'd seen how bad it was.[147]

1866: Over-loading of coal horses – 3-ton load, including the waggon, put behind the 'broken-winded' and lame horse; wounds on shoulder from the collar. Seen being flogged up the steep

Camden Road. Owner of coal company fined 40s. plus costs, and driver sent to prison with hard labour for 3 weeks.[148]

One magistrate in 1861 was so sick of dealing with 'disgraceful acts of cruelty' that after he had sentenced a man for violently beating donkeys with a wooden staff merely for amusement, he handed out a sentence of fourteen days in the House of Correction with hard labour and swore that he would send the next successfully prosecuted person to prison for a month.[149]

But, even with the enforced legislation, there was still one class of horse which seemed to be exempt from ill-treatment in the minds of the drivers and the public: those known as 'gibbes'. These were horses that were believed to be unwilling to move forwards, and deliberately pushing backwards, when asked to pull a load, because of sheer laziness or bloody-mindedness. In reality, a letter writer to the *Morning Post* explained, these horses were probably overloaded, weakened through lack of feeding and/or disease or suffering from a 'psychological disturbance'.[150] The pandemonium of London was enough to unsettle many horses when they were hemmed in by traffic. One chestnut horse drawing a hansom cab in Oxford Steet was described in 1907 by the writer Stephen Reynolds:

The horse, a gawky young chestnut, thin and badly clipped, was sweating and trembling and mouthing its bit, but it could not move. For some reason or other it had utterly lost its nerve. It was powerless to do more than stay where it was. Its joints twitched in and out. The traffic roared and clattered around. Two men caught hold of the spokes of each wheel and tried to turn them. Two men pushed behind the cab. The driver lashed with his whip. At last the frightened chestnut tottered up the street, and the fools on the pavement laughed

aloud as if it had been a joke. We soon overtook that cab. Once more the horse stood helpless and trembling.[151]

Reynolds concluded, like many before him, that London was no place for animals:

If men build cities for themselves, they have no right to take horses into them. The nature of that chestnut will be maimed for life . . . Why could they not have given it a little time to regain its nerve . . . I see they could not. The almighty, unnecessary push of London was behind it. It had to move on, and move quickly.[152]

Despite the good work of the RSPCA, it was constantly harangued in letters to the press, usually to the *Morning Post*, for overlooking cruelty on the streets. It was likely that it was aware of the cruelty but did not have the resources to bring cases to court, or that the legislation to bring about successful prosecutions was not yet in place.

A gentleman signing himself as a 'Lover of Horses' also highlighted the cruelty of the law which prevented horses that had fallen injured in the streets from being shot almost immediately; rather the owner of the animal had to be found – which could take hours – and his consent given before it could be killed and taken away by the knackerman.

[Meanwhile] the poor animal, tortured by pain and thirst, lies groaning in agony, a distressingly piteous sight to any feeling person, a hardening, degrading spectacle to the numbers who crowd to gaze on it.[153]

Improving conditions for working horses

Aside from the RSPCA and the AFS, there were many organizations that sprang up in the nineteenth century which aimed to improve the lot of London's working animals. By 1867 the Metropolitan Drinking Fountain and Cattle Trough Association was providing drinking troughs for dogs, livestock and horses throughout the city.

Since medieval times horses had been watered in the Thames, but due to pollution this was impractical, and troughs were built outside public houses instead. However, carmen and others wanting to water their horses had to buy a drink in return, so frequently the horses did not get to quench their thirst. Sometimes there was a verse written on the trough: 'All that water their horses here / Must pay a penny or have some beer.'[154]

By 1870 there were 153 Association troughs set up to avoid this problem and give free water for horses and by 1885 over 50,000 London horses were drinking from them each day. During the hot summer of 1912, the trough at the base of Gladstone's statue at Aldwych, Holborn, was used continuously.[155] The drinking troughs were still greatly in demand in 1931, even though the motor vehicle was replacing the horse. A census of the horses that used 64 of the Society's troughs from 9 am to 5 pm on one particular day showed that the least-visited trough had 35 horse-drinkers, while the most visited catered for 1,025 horses; a total of 20,000 horses drank from the troughs during that particular day.[156]

Another major problem for London's horses was the variety of paved streets that they had to work on. In 1871 the Assistant Surveyor of Marylebone and the Foreman of Works were summoned by the RSPCA to answer for repairing the road surface along Regent Street with granite chips to a depth of 6 inches without crushing them down first, so they cut horses' feet.[157]

Providing respite: an Association trough at Tooley Street, Southwark, *c.* 1930.

69

Letter writers to the *Morning Post* were also at the forefront in highlighting the plight of horses as they slipped their way across wet and frosty London, with calls of: 'Put down more gravel, change the pavement [paving] or shoe the horses differently.'[158] Fallen horses would often sprain, dislocate or fracture their shoulders and had to either be destroyed where they fell, or limp into the accident boxes at the Animals' Institute, Kinnerton Street, Wilton Place. This organization opened in June 1888 and took on the cause of 'London Horses v. The London Streets', headed by one Mr Atkinson, who saw the streets as 'veritable death traps' for horses.[159] He made several recommendations: for the roads to be resurfaced to make them less slippery, for the curvature of the road surface to be reduced, for the use of asphalt as a road surface to be stopped, and for the police to be allowed to have an animal put down

immediately without having to find its owner, as well as to prevent and punish drivers guilty of overloading their horses.[160] The Institute even held an 'Exhibition of Appliances for the Prevention of Injury to Horses from Slipping on the Roads' in its museum, with prizes given for ideas to improve horseshoes, street surfaces and so on.[161]

Another organization dedicated to encouraging kindness to animals introduced many ideas to improve the lot of working horses in London. Our Dumb Friends' League (ODFL) was established in 1897 and in 1900 proposed an ambulance service for horses that had fallen in the streets, whether injured or exhausted in hot weather or through sickness.[162] In its first year, one horse-drawn ambulance removed 65 injured horses.[163] By 1907 enough voluntary contributions had been raised to provide all twelve metropolitan

'The Streets and the Weather', *Illustrated London News*, 1855. Horses slipping on icy roads was a common occurrence.

Postcard of Jack the trace horse, sponsored by Our Dumb Friends League, who helped horses pull loads up Wimbledon Hill in the 1920s.

boroughs with a horse ambulance to deal with horses, which by then were increasingly being injured because of the congested traffic in the main thoroughfares of London.[164] And by 1910 fourteen ambulances were removing over 3,000 patients a year. An annual parade of the horse ambulances on May Day through London's main streets helped to raise awareness of their existence.[165] In 1924 the ODFL, then known as the Blue Cross, introduced the first motorized horse ambulance and in 1936 it was used to return a mare, belonging to a dairy company, back to the company's stables after she gave birth to a foal in Bloemfontein Road, Shepherd's Bush, while drawing a van. Six police-men helped to get the mare and foal into the ambulance and they were later reported in *The Times* to be doing well after their ordeal.[166]

In 1912 the ODFL proposed a trace-horse for use on Kingston Hill (on the Kingston side) in the autumn to help pull loaded horses up the hill, which was 'steep, long, narrow, and has a very slippery surface, so that horses are often seen much distressed'.[167] In 1921 Jack the trace horse was installed on Wimbledon Hill.[168] By 1931 another Jack, who won his fourth successive

title of London Van Horse (of the Year), had pulled about 17,000 tired horses up Wimbledon Hill for over four and a half years.[169] The trace-horse was still working there in 1937, but the following year there were insufficient funds to keep him at work.[170]

But perhaps the ODFL's greatest achievement was the building of an animal hospital in Hugh Street, Belgrave Road, Victoria, in 1906 on the site of the Duke of Westminster's stables. This hospital gave free medical advice to owners and treatment to animals, including horses and donkeys. This was not the first animal hospital in London. Many of the larger job-masters and the railways, for example, had their own infirmaries for sick or injured horses, and when it opened in 1871, horses made up 70 per cent of the cases seen at the Brown Animal Sanatory Institution (also known as the Brown Institution, 1871–1944) in Wandsworth Road, sw8.[171]

The most established veterinary hospital was that of the Royal Veterinary College in Camden Town, which opened in 1791. Before then, horses had been treated since at least medieval times by marshals, or farriers, who would advise on the purchase of horses, make horseshoes and nails, shoe the horses, and try to cure them by handing out medicines and performing simple surgery.[172] When the college opened, the initial focus of work was the treatment of horses,[173] as they were vitally important for civil and military purposes and the rudimentary knowledge of the farrier was not effective, with lameness often caused by poor shoeing. Infectious diseases, such as glanders, were also rife.

However, the working horses of London did not really benefit from the work of the college because of the high cost of treatment. But in 1879 the college opened the doors of its outpatients' department, or the 'Poor Man's Corner',[174] for all working horses that were most likely to need vetinary assistance because of overwork, gross negligence or ignorance. Most of the horses and donkeys brought in by costermen, laundrymen and carters were treated by the students for persistent lameness.[175]

There was one other organization which, instead of offering veterinary treatment, gave horses, mules and donkeys a chance to rest if they were ill or overworked. The Home of Rest for Horses (now known as the Horse Trust) was established in 1886 by Miss Anna Lindo after she was inspired by *Black Beauty*. The farm at Sudbury, near Harrow, became a holiday home for many London equines. It was really aimed at those small tradespeople and cab drivers who had only one horse which they worked into the ground because if the horse rested, their business stalled and they could not afford to hire another. These people were dependent on the health and endurance of their horses for their sustenance and when the horse became ill, it had to be sold off to the knackers as there was no money to send it to the surgeon or to pasturage to get some rest. All the horses needed was a few weeks' rest, then they could continue to work: 'this is not a project based on sentimentalism, but on proper business lines.'[176] Owners could hire replacement animals at minor cost. In time, the farm at Sudbury became a retirement home for favourite horses, so they did not have to be sold to the abusive cabmen or destroyed.[177] The home moved to Acton in 1889, then to Cricklewood from 1909 to 1933. When the intake of cab horses declined, their places were taken by the thousands of tradesmen's horses that still worked in London.

Slaughter

For many London horses, the final trip to the knackerman was a release from working life. However, despite the efforts of humane societies, it remained one of the most frightful experiences that they had to endure. There was no legal provision for welfare or cruelty matters until 1849; the slaughteryards wantonly abused the horses in their 'care'. The only regulation that knackers had to abide by was the 1786 Knackers Act, which required the knackerman to hold a licence and an inspector to record a description of the animals in a book in order to try to prevent the disposal of stolen horses.[178]

A letter to the *Morning Chronicle* in 1818 demanded to know why inspectors stood by and watched the ill-treatment of some 'wretched' horses the writer had seen at a yard in Clerkenwell. They'd been bought by the 'Trackers or Knackers' in batches from Smithfield and were starved for days before being slaughtered: 'many of them were gnawing each other's manes . . . others were absolutely screaming from the pain of starvation, and . . . others, more fortunate, dropped down dead.'[179]

The situation was no different in 1831, when the *Voice of Humanity* reported on a visit a correspondent had made to a yard in Osborne Street, Brick Lane, Whitechapel, which slaughtered 40–50 horses a week. He found many horses that had been sent to be slaughtered actually being hired to work during the night,[180] when it was less likely that the drivers would be caught by those concerned with animal welfare. The situation was, no doubt, similar in other 'licensed' yards, such as those in Edgware Road, Marylebone; Ball's Pond, Hackney; Maiden Lane, near King's Cross (slaughtering 500 horses a year); and Market Street, Paddington (slaughtering 200–300 horses a year).

Unfortunately the AFS continued to document horrendous conditions at the yards, and in 1843 officers of the Metropolitan Police corroborated its observations.[181] The stomach-churning reports described barely alive horses surrounded by dead and decomposing animals – one worker stated that they need not do any slaughtering when they had so many horses dropping down dead naturally.[182] It was not until 1849, with the extension of the Cruelty to Animals Act, that many of the abuses were stopped: manes had to be cut off when the horses arrived at the yard so they were disfigured and could not be hired to work, and they had to be slaughtered within three days and in the meantime provided with adequate food and water.[183] By 1893 Gordon wrote of 'the practical zootomists', as the knackers were beginning to call themselves, as carrying out their slaughtering operations 'to the letter of the law'.[184]

He focused on Harrison Barber Ltd,[185] which had seven depots around London, the largest being in Garratt Lane, Wandsworth, which was established in the late eighteenth century. The company killed 26,000 London horses a year; day and night the slaughterhouses never rested.[186] While many of the horses were old or injured, there were also some good horses that were killed when their owners died so they would not fall into cruel hands; horses that had bolted and caused injuries to their riders; horses that had begun to kick and bite; and sometimes 'the mildest mares who … [had] upset their mistresses by taking a wrong turn'.[187] According to the *Morning Post*, there were still also cases of stolen horses being artificially lamed, aged or given wounds so they could be sold on for the knacker's price.[188]

Gordon described the aftermath of the slaughtering process. A cart was dispatched to collect an injured horse on the streets, and within half an hour the animal was killed with a poleaxe, and being cut up – every part of the horse, like livestock, was used by other industries. All 70 tons of the horsemeat processed each week by Harrison Barber was sold to the cat's meat man, and Gordon mentions the long queue of carts waiting to collect the meat from the slaughteryard between 5 and 6 am.[189] London donkeys usually ended up with a Mr Gill who supplied them wholesale to the Veterinary College for dissection, as their anatomy is almost identical to that of a horse. Donkeys were not wanted by the knackerman as there was not enough meat or other goodness in them to cover the cost of transporting and slaughtering them.[190]

The decline of horses on the streets

Slaughter was the literal end for London horses, but their fairly sudden withdrawal from the London streets from the late 1930s marked the beginning of the end for Londoners' close relationship with the horse. The demise of horses in the city could easily have been caused (by our modern health and safety standards) by the number of accidents and human deaths which they caused. The unpredictability of horses, and the noises and sights that they were subjected to in the streets, made them a danger to pedestrians. Figures from the Registrar General of 1867 showed 164 deaths caused by people being run over by horses or carriages in the streets, and another 1,467 less serious accidents. Newspapers commonly contained reports of people who had been run over by horses and vehicles, such as in 1806 when a spooked carthorse galloped off in James Street, Haymarket, and ran over a man who tried to stop him. The cart's wheels went over the man's head and part of his body, leaving him unconscious, while the horse rushed

The last horse-drawn mail van leaving the King Edward Building in 1949, drawn by Peter.

across the Haymarket and dashed its head through a shop window, 'by which means it was stopped'.[191]

However, horses were far too useful to be banished from the streets just because they caused accidents. It was the compulsory purchase of tradespeople's horses during the First World War, which saw horses seized for the army and shipped across the Channel, that caused an initial loss of good London horses. Thousands of horses were 'under subsidy with a view to immediate use' in times of foreign invasion, and it was always a fear of the jobmaster that he could lose his entire livelihood and be left out of pocket because the Government would never pay prices equal to the quality of his studs.[192] After the mass exodus of horses to the Continent, all the horses left in London were of poor quality, and MPs submitted a report to the Home

Secretary about the 'deplorable state' of so many of those remaining. They suggested the following remedies: 1) Police should be given definite orders to stop horses that are unfit, overloaded or being over-driven in the streets; 2) The Royal Veterinary College should help horse owners in the care of their horses; 3) Better-quality hay should be available in the City; and 4) The Ministry of Food should check whether horses received too little in rations, as well as too much.[193]

It was not until the 1930s that a serious decline in the numbers of working horses occurred, mainly due to the introduction of motorcycles, motor coaches, vans and cars. Londoners, in their fancy new vehicles, complained to the newspapers from at least 1932 about the remaining horse traffic in the streets. *The Times* carried a typical letter exclaiming that horses were a 'source of obstruction and delay' in the streets and also that the animals were not suited to the urban traffic-laden environment (a view that had already been expressed by Stephen Reynolds):

> The exhaust fumes from motor vehicles, and the constant stopping and starting which modern control of traffic involved, made the lot of the horse to-day anything but a happy one. Traffic signals, pedestrian crossings, and other road safety measures could not fail to distress horses drawing laden vehicles, and in hot weather or when the roads were frost-bound their plight was still more pitiful. The only alternative to partial restriction in the general interest was the wholesale reconstruction of most of the existing thoroughfares, and this would be financially prohibitive.[194]

From 1937 to 1938 the volume of horse traffic in London decreased by nearly 66 per cent, according to a census by the Metropolitan and City of London Police, mainly owing to a trial ban on horse-drawn traffic in the major London thoroughfares by the Ministry of Transport in January 1937.[195] Campaigners such as Major-General Sir John Moore of the National Horse Association of Great Britain had argued against the 'evil' of this ban, pointing out that the small trader could not afford a motor vehicle if he were not allowed to use a small pony and cart.[196] But it seems that some trades, such as dairies and greengrocers, continued to use horses since they found it more economical to deliver to numerous customers in a moderately small area using horse-drawn vehicles, even when petrol consumption was only 'two miles to the gallon!'[197] Peter, who pulled a mail van, was still on the streets until 1949.

Petrol rationing and shortages during the Second World War also meant that horses clung on in London, mainly due to the reversal of the ban on horse-drawn vehicles in October 1939.[198] At this time the 40,000-odd horses working in London were deemed part of the war effort.[199] In the event of gas attacks or bombing, the Royal Mews at Buckingham Palace, along with many other London sites, was offered as an emergency horse standing for twenty horses, with a first-aid post and a horse ambulance on stand-by.[200]

However, after the war ended horses almost disappeared completely from the streets. In 1966 *The Times* made a list of horses still in the City, according to Anstee's the forage merchants: six City of London police horses and 197 Metropolitan Police horses; 21 working horses at Young's Brewery; twelve shires at Mann Crossman's Brewery in Whitechapel; 28 shires at Whitbread's; one horse, Captain, at the coach merchants Charles Franklin in the summer, and four in the winter. Rothman's the tobacconists had an old coach drawn by two Windsor greys, and Taylor's the perfumers were starting horse-drawn deliveries again.[201]

London's remaining horses: state and public duties

Today it is quite rare to meet with horses in London. After the recent demise of the London brewery horses, there are only a few privately owned horses working on the busy streets. In 1987 Mohamed Al Fayed re-established the Harrods green-liveried, eight-strong team of black Friesian horses that made deliveries to local hotels and palaces within a 4-mile radius of the famous store. In rotation, the horses spent six days at a time in Knightsbridge before having a well-earned rest at Fayed's Surrey estate. The horses are still associated with Harrods today, despite Fayed's departure.[202] Cribb & Sons undertakers have twelve Friesian horses stabled in Essex, which have been making regular trips into London since 1985, complete with black-plumed headdresses.[203] But, aside from the riding-school horses which are seen in Hyde Park, the Queen's state horses,

The Irish state coach drawn by six Windsor Greys outside the Royal Mews.

cavalry and artillery horses, and police horses are the main equine presence in the capital.

The Queen's horses are stabled in the most exclusive address of the London horse world – the Royal Mews at Buckingham Palace. In 1893 Gordon noted that it contained 'extremely roomy stables' where 'not a straw is out of place'.[204] The Mews was also 'probably the most accessible stables in London to the public as cards of admission are freely granted by the Master of the Horse'.[205] One can visit the stables today, although the horses are not always on show.

The Royal Mews was originally at Charing Cross on the site of the current National Gallery. It had been known as the King's Mews since Edward I's reign (1272–1307) and was used to house hunting hawks until 1534, when, according to Stow, the stabling of

the royal horses at Bloomsbury (then Lomesbery) burnt down. Horses ousted the birds of prey when the King's Mews was converted to accommodate them. However, Edward Hall's *Chronicle* (1548) states that on August 1534 the Charing Cross Mews was destroyed by a fire which 'brent many great Horses and great store of haye',[206] so it is more likely that the horses were there before the fire, and not as a consequence of it. It was rebuilt several times but the horses were gradually transferred to Buckingham House (afterwards Palace) after George III acquired it in 1761. The move was completed in 1824 when George IV moved into Buckingham Palace as a full-time resident and the Charing Cross site was finally demolished in 1830.

Under Queen Victoria the Mews became extremely busy. She described it as 'a small village which belongs to Buckingham Palace'.[207] She and Prince Albert kept up to 200 horses there and her children learnt to ride and drive miniature carriages in its riding school, which was built in 1765. In 1841 there were ladies' saddle-horses, gentlemen's saddle-horses and hacks, servants' hacks, eight grey phaeton ponies (the Ascot racecourse team), road-teams and state horses – eleven duns and nine black Hanoverians.[208] However, by 1893 the Queen's stables had diminished and she no longer rode, although she did have six favourite carriage horses that she used regularly out of the 90–100 horses that were still at the Mews.[209]

State horses only appear on ceremonial duties, and are as much a part of royal pageantry as the crown and sceptre. Today there are ten Windsor Greys, of the same stock that was kept at Windsor during Victoria's reign and used to pull the family's private carriages. They still draw royal carriages and when on duty their manes are plaited with purple ribbon. In the event of a coronation, eight of the greys draw the Gold State Coach. There are also twenty bays in the Mews, which are plaited in crimson ribbons when on duty.[210] They fulfil a variety of escort and transport duties, including driving visiting heads of state to and from official ceremonies.[211] These horses may be spotted being exercised in Hyde Park and around the London streets, with their grooms riding in long brown coats. They have also pulled the daily mail carriage that has taken post from Buckingham Palace to St James's Palace since 1843. In August and September the state horses are given a holiday at Hampton Court.

Just as royal horses have traditionally been greys or dark coloured, the horses of the London-based Household Cavalry Mounted Regiment have, since its origins in 1660, been a certain type of black horse, all with similar conformation.[212] These carry out ceremonial and escort duties on state and royal occasions.[213] Most Londoners and visitors know of the existence of the household troops because of the

Queen's Life Guard that stands on daily duty from 10 am to 4 pm in Whitehall outside the entrance to Horse Guards – this being the official main entrance to both St James's Palace and Buckingham Palace. But during the nineteenth century, when the Royal Horse Guards were kept at Albany Street Barracks near Regent's Park, the horses were also used as back-up for the mounted police to control crowds, such as those at the Bloody Sunday demonstrations in Trafalgar Square in November 1887. In 1893 Gordon noted that with support from 275 cavalry horses and 375 mounted police, the five million Londoners 'are content to behave themselves'.[214]

Postcard of the Life Guards, 1953, part of London's pageantry.

Like royal horses, cavalry horses were and are treated well. A Mr King recalls that in his youth, in the 1920s, he and his friends would go to the Albany Barracks, where the sentries would let them in (this would never happen today). They would then help the soldiers clean the horses and give them their nose-bags after returning from guard duty: 'Oh we did work hard. They were very well treated, those horses. It was always VIP treatment for them.'[215]

The cavalry horses moved into their current home at the Knightsbridge Barracks, near Hyde Park, in 1932. The barracks were built in 1793 and since the last rebuild in 1967–70, they provide accommodation for 514 soldiers and 273 horses, including the 17-hand-high, piebald Drum horses. The horses are kept on two levels, with two ramps – one up, and one down – leading to the parade ground. The ramps, according to an unofficial Household Cavalry website,[216] are kept free of ice in the winter by heated coils which are embedded in the concrete to prevent the horses slipping and falling. Plans were announced by the Ministry of Defence in June 2012 to sell off the Knightsbridge Barracks and relocate the cavalry to a new site in central London – nothing has happened yet.[217]

The other mounted regiment seen in the London streets and parks is the King's Troop (Royal Horse Artillery) – known as the Troop – which was established in 1947 when George VI expressed a wish that a troop of Royal Horse Artillery should take part in ceremonies of state. There were 111 black horses stationed and trained in St John's Wood Barracks on Ordnance Hill. Best known as the Queen's ceremonial Saluting Battery – six horses pulling First World War 'thirteen pounder' state saluting guns – they still perform as part of royal anniversaries and state occasions, including funeral processions. They also relieve the Queen's Life Guard for one month in the year when the Household Cavalry leaves London to holiday the horses. The Troop moved out of London in February 2012 to relocate to the former

barracks of the Royal Artillery in Woolwich, which has been converted to accommodate the horses.

London-based police horses also play a part in ceremonial occasions, alongside their usual public-order details: they top and tail state processions, such as the one at the Queen Mother's funeral, and marshal tourists wanting to see the changing of the guard at Buckingham Palace.[218] They also escort the troops to their guard duties. In 1982 Echo the police horse was one of those injured, while on escort duty, in the IRA Hyde Park nail-bombing incident – seven horses were killed, along with four men. After being treated, Echo was too nervous to go back on the beat and he retired to the countryside, unlike Sefton the Household Cavalry horse, who returned to work after recovering from 28 separate wounds. Members of the Royal Family have also ridden police horses on ceremonial occasions, such as Winston, who was ridden consecutively by George VI and the Queen at Trooping the Colour from 1947 to 1956. His obituary in *The Times* in 1957 stated that he was 'chosen as the royal mount because of his good manners and indifference to noise and traffic'.[219]

News reports of the student protest in 2010 showed London's police horses in their most commonly known role – that of crowd control. However, police horses were not originally introduced to keep the peace, but rather to act as another crime-fighting arm of Sir John Fielding's Bow Street force with the aim of catching the plague of highwaymen who infested London's turnpikes. In 1758 Fielding initiated 'two Persuit horses and proper Persuers',[220] and another six horses and men were added to the mounted patrol during 1763. The experimental horse patrol was disbanded in less than two years, even though it was an 'acknowledged success', and horses were not employed for another 40 years until 1805 when the regular Bow Street Horse Patrol was established. This consisted of 52 men and horses to protect all main roads within a 20-mile radius of Charing Cross, especially Hounslow

London's mounted 'Peelers' on duty at Derby Day, 1860.

Heath, Finchley Common and Epping Forest.[221] The men wore blue uniforms with scarlet waistcoats – so they were known as Robin Redbreasts – carried handcuffs and were each armed with a pistol, heavy sabre and truncheon. In 1839 the Horse Patrols were absorbed into the newly created Metropolitan Police.

When railways arrived and the highwaymen threat diminished, the patrol's work switched to guarding against livestock theft as rural unrest and poverty became rife. According to one report in 1872, the mounted branch was very successful:

They regard themselves as constituting the aristocracy of the body, and look down on the foot police . . . The horse police are the sole protection against these marauders [rural burglars and livestock thieves], for so rapid are the movements of the trotting horse, in the light trap with the thin spoked wheels, that no ordinary policeman could hope to come up with or intercept it. The police patrols, however, come up with him by hard riding, and do not always keep to Her Majesty's highway.[222]

Aside from their crime prevention role, the patrols were used as a messenger service between the Metropolitan Police stations before the arrival of the telegraph, and they also began their role of public order. Their presence at the Chartist meetings in 1848 saw them working alongside the cavalry, but gradually the mounted police took over when order was threatened,[223] which must have been a shock for the all-conquering horses (and men) used to open country pursuits. During the Bloody Sunday demonstrations in 1887 one police horse was deliberately hit around the head by a rioter, who claimed in his defence that the horse was 'almost on the top of him'. The man was eventually charged with cruelty to the horse.[224] Other similar cases showed how much affection Londoners felt for police horses: in 1931 an unemployed protester at Victoria Embankment deliberately struck a police horse over the eye with a banner pole. 'The mare jumped in pain, and it was found that its right eyeball had been punctured and was hanging out', reported *The Times*.[225] A veterinary surgeon at Harley Place confirmed that her eyesight was lost, but the eye would not need to be removed; either way, the horse was no longer fit for use. There followed great public interest in the horse, which was never named, evidenced by the hundreds of letters to the judge in the case, the police and the Veterinary College asking about her condition and offering a good home, rather than seeing her sold on or ill-used.[226] The man was given six weeks' imprisonment with hard labour for attacking the horse.[227]

Other police horses became famous for other reasons. The first FA Cup Final to be held at Wembley Stadium in 1923 saw up to 250,000 people storm the

Nuisance training of police horses; they have to be able to cope in the London streets.

127,000-seater stadium and spill onto the pitch. Kick-off was delayed by 45 minutes while police horses were used to disperse the crowds from the turf. The press later christened the event the White Horse Final because of images of Billie the grey police horse, who was the most eye-catching of the horses there, seemingly sailing through the crowds as they parted in front of him. The White Horse Bridge at the new Wembley Stadium commemorates the event.[228]

Three other police horses found glory during the Second World War when they received the PDSA Dickin Medal,[229] which honoured, and continues today to honour, the work of gallant animals. Olga, Upstart and Regal had all been on duty in London during the Blitz, and Olga had been confronted by a flying bomb which demolished four houses in Tooting and shattered a plate-glass window right in front of her. After bolting for 100 yards, Olga returned to the scene and remained on duty with her rider, controlling traffic and assisting the rescue organizations.[230]

At the turn of the twentieth century, the Metropolitan Mounted Branch comprised 126 horses, with a reserve of twelve kept and trained at the Remount Depot at Adam and Eve Mews, Paddington, until 1919, when the new Training Establishment was built at Imber Court in Thames Ditton, Surrey. The young remount horses brought into Imber Court were less heavy, less common-looking and altogether classier animals than those previous employed. Training involved, and still involves, 'nuisance training', in which the animals get used to noises such as gunfire, bands and football rattles, and sights such as waving flags and fire; walking quietly over people lying on the ground; traffic training and walking up steps. This last skill was useful in the 1920s when rioters in Trafalgar Square threatened to enter the Grand Hotel until their way was blocked by a police horse that nimbly walked up the steps.[231]

Once trained, after six or seven months, horses are assigned to one of eight stables within the Service.[232] The headquarters of No. 1 District, Mounted Branch (responsible for the West End), is at Great Scotland Yard, where the horses climb up a gently winding slope carpeted with coconut matting to their stables. The newest stables reopened in Hyde Park in April 2010, after being closed for six years, and house at least five horses that patrol the three main London parks alongside their usual duties.[233] Today 120 horses do shift patrols of three to four hours in parkland or troubled estates,[234] are a large presence at riots, demonstrations and disturbances, and undertake crowd control at football matches and other sporting events. However, calls to cut spending by the Metropolitan Police in 2010–11 could see the mounted police, and all its horses, removed from duty.[235]

The other police force in London – the City of London Police – also has a mounted branch of ten horses, which could be under threat. The City's horses are grey, although there is one piebald on active service, and they wear red-and-white striped headbands on their bridles to distinguish them from the Metropolitan Police's horses. They have patrolled the Square Mile of the City since 1873, although the horses used initially were hired from local livery stables on an ad hoc basis and a specialist horse unit was not established until 1931. The horses were stabled at City Greenyard, once the City pound where stray animals were kept, until 1940 when the stabling was bombed during the Blitz. The horses returned to London in 1946 to live alongside the Whitbread Brewery's white shire horses in Garrett Street, until they moved to their current home at Wood Street (Cheapside) Police Station in 1966. The same building also houses the City of London Police's dog unit, which was established in the 1950s and is currently made up of ten general-purpose police dogs (Alsatians), eight explosives-search dogs, five cash-, drugs- and weapons-recovery dogs, and three passive-drugs dogs (spaniels and labradors).[236]

Working dogs

The Metropolitan Police also has a longer-established Dog Support Unit of about 250 dogs. Bloodhounds were the first dogs tentatively used by the force after the Mitre Square and Berner Street (now Henriques Street) tragedies – the fourth and fifth Whitechapel Murders by Jack the Ripper in 1888. The idea was to use the scent-tracking hounds to catch the killer, and two hounds, Burgho and Barnaby, were brought down from Scarborough to be tested in Regent's Park and Hyde Park at tracking people, including Sir Charles Warren, the Commissioner of the Metropolitan Police. The trials were deemed successful, although the press thoroughly ridiculed the 'bloodhound theory'; their

The first Metropolitan Police dogs: Labradors patrolling in Peckham, 1938.

mocking may have led to Sir Warren not wanting to purchase the dogs without further trials. Their owner, Mr Brough, left Barnaby in London with his friend Mr Taunton and he was called in by the police to track a burglar from Commercial Street, E1, but the scent trail was not fresh enough for the dog to follow. After being told of this incident, Mr Brough demanded that Barnaby be returned to him immediately because of the danger of him being poisoned if it was widely known that he was being used to track burglars.[237]

Brough had left London by the time the body of the Ripper's last victim, Mary Jane Kelly, was found, but Taunton told *The Times* it was unlikely that Barnaby would have been any use, as her body was not found until daylight and the streets were crowded with people.[238]

Despite police dogs being successfully used and respected in France, Germany and Belgium, it was not until 1914 that 172 police constables were authorized to take their dogs with them on patrols – a motley mix of sheepdogs, collies, mongrels and even a Pomeranian – and proper dog trials did not begin until 1935. The Home Office trialled bloodhounds, dobermans, Alsatians, boxers, rottweilers and giant schnauzers, but the best all-rounder for temperament, defence (not by grabbing by the arm, but by hindering progress) and tracking ability was the Labrador.[239]

The work of dogs during the Second World War further cemented the use of dogs in the force. In 1945 several PDSA Dickin Medals were awarded to dogs for locating air-raid victims during the Blitz; Rex the Alsatian, a Civil Defence Rescue Dog, was honoured for

outstanding good work in the location of casualties in burning buildings. Undaunted by smouldering debris, thick smoke, intense heat and jets of water from fire hoses, this dog displayed uncanny intelligence and outstanding determination in his efforts to follow up any scent which led him to a trapped casualty.[240]

Labradors were not officially introduced into the Metropolitan Police until 1946, but by July 1947 they had 'arrested' thirteen people, mainly thieves. One woman had her handbag snatched in Hyde Park and Jessie (in another report she's called Lassie), described as a golden and black Labrador, was released by her handler when the woman was heard to scream.[241] Jessie 'pounced on [the] man who was being chased, pinned him to the ground, and waited until Police-constable Shelton arrived'.[242] The dogs were initially trained along with the police horses at Imber Court, but were moved to their current training ground at Keston, Kent, in 1953. By then, Alsatians had joined Labradors as the police dogs of choice, and together

they enjoyed particular success in reducing handbag snatchings in Hyde Park and generally protecting the area around Buckingham Palace.

The force authorized dog numbers to rise from 158 in 1954 to 272 in 1958,[243] although due to limited training facilities operational numbers were about 100 dogs short. By this time the dogs were being used to clear Teddy Boys and other hooligans (later to be football hooligans) off the streets, because, as *The Times* stated, 'being controlled by a dog involves loss of face for a lot of these youngsters who are little dictators in their own set'.[244]

Figures in 1962 showed that 150 police handlers and their dogs in the metropolitan area had achieved more than 2,500 arrests in the year, over 1,000 of which had been brought about solely by the skill of the dogs. The dogs had also had considerable success in finding lost or missing people and had been instrumental in the recovery of a good deal of stolen property. The force also introduced a Flying Dog Squad in this year, which involved two dogs and handlers being sent out each night in mini-vans linked by radio with the 999 service, so they were already mobile and could get to a crime scene early.[245]

The dog's worth to the London police, and the London public, seems to have been proved since its stuttering introduction to the streets. The evidence is in crime statistics and also the awarding of three PDSA Dickin Gold Medals to police dogs for their life-saving work following the London terrorist bombings in July 2005: Vinnie (British Transport Police dog), Billy (Metropolitan Police dog) and Jake (City of London Police dog) searched for secondary explosive devices to clear a path for the emergency services to reach the many casualties.

Highly trained, specialist police dogs are a breed apart from London's past working dog population. Like horses, dogs were used from medieval times for all purposes. In 1486 Dame Juliana Berners spoke of three types of draught dog in her *Boke of St Albans*: the turnspit, the butcher's dog and the midden dog. The turnspit was a small dog, usually with a long body and short crooked legs, which was put into a wooden wheel that rotated the kitchen spit via a pulley so that meats were roasted evenly over the fire. Once the wheel was set in motion, the dog was forced to run to keep up with the motion and this constant pressure on its forepaws caused the legs to turn out – much like the dachshund's.[246] The butcher used large dogs to make meat deliveries and keep control of cattle, and midden dogs were used to haul rubbish to the midden or rubbish dump. The earliest attempt at a complete classification of dogs was Dr Johannes Caius's *Of Englishe Dogges* (1576, translated from Latin) and he included the water drawer, which was used to draw up water by turning a wheel that it was attached to; the messenger/carrier that carried letters and so on, attached to its collar, for its master; the tinker's cur that carried the tools of the travelling tinker in a dog pack-saddle; and the butcher's dog.

The other profession of London dogs involved pulling carts and trucks. The latter vehicle was a large box with a double opening lid on the top, on large but light wheels, which was used mainly by shopkeepers to transport goods to their customers. It was usually drawn by a young man using a T-bar pole, and a large dog helped to draw the trunk from its position underneath the box. One journal in 1841 (after dog carts/trucks were banned) described the dogs that had been used:

These dogs were admirably trained for the purpose; and drew weights which would appear incredible to those who had not witnessed their achievements in this way. They were for the most part very spirited animals; seldom needing the application of the lash. Indeed, so great was the exertion they made, that they often worked themselves to death . . . I mean the very small carts which were drawn entirely by dogs. These

Lilliputian carts were used for a variety of purposes, and were sometimes drawn by one dog, although occasionally by as many as three. The dogs were duly harnessed as if they were horses, and were trained to their duties as drawers of these vehicles in a wonderful way. In many cases the persons, mostly boys or young men, charged with them, or to whom they belonged, sat in the carts themselves, and drove the tractable creatures whip in hand, just as if they were horses. They proceeded at an amazing celerity through the streets; frequently exceeding hackney coaches and cabs in the rapidity of their movements. The only thing to be regretted was, that they were not only often overburdened, but very cruelly used by those who had the charge of them.[247]

The final comment about the lack of consideration for the dogs' welfare had been used as an argument against dog carts since the 1830s, when during the hydrophobia (rabies) panic of 1830 working dogs were muzzled on the streets. Not only did this increase their 'misery' because they were unable to pant properly or drink, but it was thought that if they were driven mad by thirst they would be more likely to bite someone when they were released from their work.[248]

The other argument against dogs pulling carts was that they were, according to a jury's decision reported in the *Morning Post*: 'a dangerous nuisance in the streets of the metropolis, and ought to be done away with by the magistracy'.[249] This call followed a court case concerning the death of a wealthy elderly gentleman in York Street, Borough, after he was run over by a dog truck travelling at between 12 and 14 miles an hour. It was pulled by a 'powerful, fierce animal' whose energy the driver could not hold back, and one of the truck's wheels ran over the man's head.

The Metropolitan Police Act of 1839 eventually prohibited the use of dog carts within a 15-mile radius of Charing Cross from 1 January 1840. While the

A rather healthy looking St Bernard-type dog pulling a cart in Covent Garden at middle
right, sketch by George Scharf, *c.* 1820–50.

humanitarians and the hydrophobia-panicked campaigners were thrilled, the decision to remove dogs from the streets of London was deeply regretted by those who used the animals to earn their livings – dogs were cheaper to keep than horses and donkeys and were more manoeuvrable, and a dog would also guard the goods being transported. Many Londoners, especially those around the Notting Dale Potteries area, were then without a livelihood and had to turn out their dogs as strays as they could not afford to keep them for nothing. If they could be afforded, goats became substitutes for working dogs and, as seen earlier, they could be bought at Smithfield Market, complete with carts.

Working dogs have long since left the streets of London (except for a few guard dogs), and now Londoners with room to accommodate their needs regard dogs solely as pets. But English mastiffs, the best guard dogs in their time, were also regarded by the Romans as matches for bears and lions in the amphitheatre. This introduces the other purpose of London dogs through the ages; as sporting animals.

three

Sporting Animals:
Natural Instincts Exploited

The history of London's sporting pursuits has relied heavily on the presence of animals, which created a tale of high drama, cruelty and pageantry. Today sporting animals are rare in London and it is hard to imagine that some of the most popular entertainments in the city since the Roman invasion involved animals (dogs, bears, bulls, badgers, cocks, rats and so on) fighting each other – these contests were known generally as animal baiting. These blood sports, along with hunting, were enjoyed by all classes in society, and even children were encouraged to watch them to instil a 'heroic' fighting attitude in them. Thankfully London was also the centre of enlightenment against animal cruelty and slowly legislation was passed to ban these cruel sports, though illegal dog fights and rat killing took place in the nooks and crannies of London's streets, and still do today. However, many Londoners looked to non-violent sports as a way to indulge their other passion of gambling: the city's race courses and dog tracks provided the sporting vehicle. Other less violent sports also enjoyed their time *en vogue*, such as jousting, pigeon shooting, polo and horse leaping – now known as showjumping.

Blood sports: Roman amphitheatre contests

In 1988 the site of London's Roman amphitheatre was discovered in excavations of the Guildhall Yard. The arena was probably built at the end of the second century in what was then the outskirts of Londinium near the military barracks at Cripplegate. The dig revealed two small rooms, or antechambers, built on either side of the entranceway to the amphitheatre, with doors leading in from the outside passage and out into the arena. These were probably used as waiting rooms for people and animals before they went into the arena – slots cut into the arena threshold of one of the rooms may indicate that it had a wooden sliding trapdoor which could be raised to release the animals.[1] It is likely that the first blood sports Londoners saw were these Roman entertainments. There is little evidence of which animals were used in the London amphitheatre, but the Romans were very impressed with the English mastiffs they came across and an officer was appointed to train them for the contests of the amphitheatre: three of these huge dogs were thought to be a match for a bear, and four of them for a lion.[2] They would possibly have fought alongside wild dogs, lynx, bears, wolves, bulls, horses and some exotics imported from North Africa and Asia Minor. In the Coliseum in Rome, these exotics would have been crocodiles, lions, tigers, elephants, rhinos, hippos, ostriches, hyenas, gazelles, camels and giraffes; they were kept in cages beneath the arena, winched to the surface in lifts by a system of ramps and pulleys, and released suddenly into the arena through a series of concealed trapdoors.[3]

There were three types of Roman animal blood sport: armed men fighting animals, animals fighting each other (such as elephants versus bulls) and unarmed criminals facing the wild animals as their punishment. The *venationes* or wild beast hunts were part of the morning games at the amphitheatre – an appetiser to the gladiatorial contests – with exotic and domestic animals facing gladiators known as *venatores* and *bestiarii*. Among these, there were specialized professions like the *taurarii*, or bullfighters. Most *venatores* would fight with a *venabulum*, which was similar to a long pike. With this they could stab at the beasts while keeping themselves at a distance.[4]

Enormous numbers of animals could be killed during these spectacles: 9,000 were dispatched during the opening celebrations at the Coliseum in AD 80. But they were not merely slaughtered, as this would not have been appreciated by the Romans. The animals stood a chance of being left alive if they fought well and earned the audience's mercy. They were primed to fight by being kept starved before the hunts, and were also whipped into a rage if required.

The entertainment of animals killing criminals – called *ad bestias* or 'to the beasts' – was scheduled for noon and took on several guises: a criminal could have had the unenviable task of separating, using a hook, a bear and bull which were chained together; the likelihood was that they would either turn on him while he attempted this, or attack when they were freed from each other. Alternatively the criminal would be whipped and forced to face a lion or other wild animal, tied to a stake, or wheeled into the arena in a little cart and left there as prey.[5]

So London was no stranger to the sight of blood sports, if we assume that the Romans staged such 'delights' to entertain the masses. But there is little evidence of blood sports in London again until Fitzstephen's account of twelfth-century London entertainment, in which hunting, cockfighting and animal baiting were favourite pastimes.

Hunting

Hunting was initially valued as a simulation of warfare, but it was also both a necessary way of providing food and a sport to be enjoyed by all Londoners. According to Fitzstephen, the 'immense forest' that lay close to North London was

> densely wooded thickets, the coverts of game, red and fallow deer, boars and wild bulls ... Most of the citizens [of the City of London] amuse themselves in sporting with merlins, hawks and other birds of a like kind, and also with dogs that hunt in the woods. The citizens have the right of hunting in Middlesex, Hertfordshire, all the Chilterns, and Kent, as far as the river Cray.[6]

This hunting of the Home Countries was granted by Henry I (r. 1100–1135). However, there were strictly designated areas in which the different classes of society could hunt. The ordinary Londoner could hunt in unenclosed land outside the royal forests and free warrens – the latter were given by kings to lords.

Following the Norman Conquest, William I 'made' large forests, which were not solely woodland, as we understand the word today, but also pastures. These 'forests', such as the great forest of Waltham (now in outer northeast London), of which Epping Forest is one of the last remaining fragments, were solely for the King's use. William also forbade the killing of red roe and fallow deer, boars and hares. This was not popular, according to an Anglo-Saxon chronicler in 1087: 'The rich complained and the poor murmured but he [William] was so sturdy that he recked nought of them.'[7] Financial penalties were also introduced under the Forest Charter for owners of dogs that bit wild animals, and for men who chased animals so hard that they panted.

The prize animal in the royal forest was the red deer stag, which was reserved for royalty and noblemen

A lymerer and his scenting
hound sniffing out a stag
for the day's hunting,
c. 16th century, woodcut.

to stalk and kill; under different kings the penalty for unauthorized hunting of these stags was blinding, the loss of limbs or even death. The stag hunt in medieval times (as seen in contemporary tapestries) was a romantic set-piece:[8] a huntsman called a lymerer would go out early in the morning with his lymers (scenting hounds) and find a stag, noting its size, strength and health. On his return, he would describe the quarry to the king/lord and his company while they ate a hearty breakfast. The lymerer and his dogs were later used during the hunt if the stag confused the hounds with evasion tactics (doubling back, taking to water or swapping with another stag), the scent dogs working out where the stag had gone so the hunt could continue.

Before the hunt began several relay hounds were dropped off in small packs along the route the stag was likely to take, to give the pursuing hounds fresh impetus. The main pack consisted of snub-nose hounds, which hunted by smell and were not fast, and greyhounds, which hunted by sight and were very fast. Once the relay hounds were set, the lymerer and his dogs would rouse the stag. When it broke cover, the shout of 'Tally-Ho' would announce that the hunt was underway. Once the stag was cornered, the hounds were kept back while the master of the hunt dispatched the stag using a sword. But this was a difficult job as the desperate animal would be slashing and kicking in self-defence. The hounds were given the choice titbits from the stag and were treated extremely well, including having their feet bathed and greased on their return to the kennels. Sometimes the stag would be hunted in a more leisurely way, with the king and queen and other nobility shooting at the animal with bow and arrows as it was driven by hounds past their stand.[9] Or, as Henry VIII (r. 1509–47) requested, the deer would be rounded up (200–300 deer in Henry's case) and greyhounds would be let loose to chase them.[10]

Other beasts of the forest were the hind (female red deer), fallow deer, wild boar and wolves – although the latter were extinct around London by the mid-fifteenth century. Only bishops, abbots and barons could hunt these other beasts of the forest.

The other area with privileged hunting rights was the warren, which was often owned by private individuals and religious houses that had been granted free warren by early kings on land outside the forests. Staines, for instance, was retained as a royal warren until the right was rescinded in the reign of Henry III.[11] The beasts of the warren were the hare, rabbit, fox and also the roe deer from 1338, when it became labelled as a nuisance for driving away the highly regarded red deer and fallow deer – this led to its extinction in Epping Forest by the sixteenth century.[12] There were birds of the warren, including pheasants, partridges, woodcocks and herons. Anyone found hunting without the owner's licence could be fined £10 and have his snares, traps and dogs impounded. And any dog living near to the royal warrens had to be 'lawed' – three claws of its forefeet were cut close to the ball of the foot to prevent it from chasing the beasts.[13]

The general public had the right to hunt within the Home Counties outside the forests and warrens: in medieval times in Southwark woods, for example. But rather than hunting for the love of blood sports, as the nobility did, most London citizens hunted with their dogs and hawks to fill their cooking pots, or to remove wild animals that threatened their domestic animals, such as foxes, polecats, martens, wild cats, hawks, buzzards and perhaps eagles.[14]

Londoners' right to hunt was eventually flouted by the hunting enthusiast Henry VIII in July 1536, when he issued a proclamation stating that henceforth 'the games of hare, partridge, pheasant, and heron' would be 'preserved and kept for his owne

disport, pleasure and recreation' within a loop from his palace at Westminster, to St Giles, to Islington, to Highgate, to Hornsey Park and to Hampstead Heath and back to Westminster via Marylebone. Anyone caught hunting or hawking within this area would be imprisoned, or worse, depending on Henry's 'will and pleasure'.[15]

Henry kept this area (a large part of the modern West End) mainly for hawking, which involved following the flight of a bird of prey either on horseback or on foot as it hunted the area for prey. The most celebrated birds, and the choice of royalty, were the gyrfalcons (or gerfalcons) of Norway. They were magnificent hunters and were used to catch large birds; their favourite quarry, aside from wild duck and cranes, was the heron, but it was a fearful enemy because of its speed, high-altitude flight and pointed, powerful bill.[16] Lower down the bird hierarchy, the lord flew a peregrine falcon, the knight a saker, an esquire a lanner, a yeoman a goshawk and the clergy were associated with sparrowhawks.[17]

The royal falcons and other birds of prey were housed in the King's Mews on the north side of Charing Cross. The building's name is derived from 'mew', the time when falcons moult and cast their feathers; during this flightless period they were housed in mews.[18] It was probably Edward I who first keep birds there in the thirteenth century, and they remained there for about 300 years until the mews was converted to horse stabling. This explains why the term 'mews' is associated more today with horses than with birds of prey. But the royal birds didn't disappear: the treasury lists of 1702 show that they were still used for hunting. These lists include payments to the 'Serjeant of our Hawks' and to ten falconers.[19]

Apart from hawking, Henry VIII loved the stag hunt. Within his great London hunting grounds he kept private deer parks – now the West End royal parks. St James's Park was a meadow before Henry had it drained and enclosed by four brick walls in

GERFALCON

PEREGRINE

MERLIN

HOBBY

GOSHAWK

SPARROWHAWK

Birds of the mews; different hawks for different social classes.

1532 to create a 'nursery for deer': to keep the deer in, and the poachers out. During the Commonwealth the deer disappeared, but St James's Park did revert to being a deer park again when Charles II ring fenced the central area.[20] Henry also fenced off Hyde Park after the Reformation and had it stocked with deer in 1536. Subsequent royalty used this park for hunting and for hawking around the ponds, and James I (r. 1567–1625) entertained foreign dignitaries with a deer hunt. Jacob Larwood writes of one of these hunts in *The Story of London Parks* (1874):

Then the clear echoes, nestling in the quiet nooks and corners of the ancient forest, were awakened by the merry blasts of the horn, the hallooing of the huntsmen cheering the dogs, and the 'yearning' of the pack, as they followed the hart to one of the pools where it 'took soil,' [ran into the water] and was bravely dispatched by his Majesty. After that followed the noisy 'quarry,' in which, of course, 'Jowler' and 'Jewel,' the king's favourite hounds, obtained the lion's share.[21]

James I was extremely fond of his greyhounds, which he regarded as the lords of the canine race, with spaniels as gentlemen and scent hounds the yeomen of dogs.[22] On every stag hunt he attended, he would personally cut the animal's throat and daub his courtiers' faces with the blood, which they were not allowed to wash off. It was 'customary for ladies and women of quality … [to] wash their hands in the blood, supposing it will make them white'.[23]

Eventually Charles I granted Hyde Park to the public in 1637, and the deer were kept as ornamentals until 1831, when they were finally removed because of the number of pet dogs that gamekeepers were forced to shoot when they chased and worried the deer.[24]

Henry also acquired Marylebone Park (now Regent's Park) in the late 1530s, and Marylebone manor house

and the farm were used to house the Keeper of the Park. The park was used for hunting by subsequent royalty up to Charles I, who leased it to two supporters in return for military supplies. On Charles's death, Marylebone Park was sold; the sale included 124 deer worth £130.[25] But the park was still used for hunting with dogs and guns in the mid-1680s, according to the nineteenth-century historian Thomas Macaulay.[26]

It was the gamekeepers of the royal parks who, among their other jobs, had to arrest poachers who were then brought before the Middlesex judiciary. In 1612 three men were arrested for 'stealing of deere forth of His Majestie's Park at Marribon'. Fines of £50 and £100 were taken from the men and they were bound over to appear at the next sessions, though the case was never concluded.[27] More dramatic were the poachers, and the unfortunate labourer who was paid to hold their dogs, who were executed at Hyde Park Gate for shooting deer at night in 1619.[28] In 1723 George I passed the Black Act, which made it a felony (a hangable offence) to poach red or fallow deer, hares or rabbits in a royal park or warren.

Hawking eventually declined as land was enclosed and built on, and guns became widely used. But hunting with hounds continued to be practised by all classes of society. There are several eyewitness accounts of stags being chased from the countryside into the suburbs of London: in 1796 a stag swam across the Thames from Battersea and into Lord Cremorne's gardens in Chelsea. It then ran along the river bank 'as far as the church, and turning up Church Lane, at last took refuge in Mrs Hutchins's barn, where he was taken alive'.[29] When the supply of wild deer around London dwindled, a home-reared stag would be put in a cart, driven into the countryside and released for the hounds to chase. Carted deer hunting was introduced to the Royal Buckhounds in the 1780s, and during the following decade most hunts, royal and otherwise, were chases after carted deer. A young boy recorded one such hunt in his diary

On the road to Epping

Uncarting the Deer.

The first obstacle reduces the field.

Illustration of the dangerous Epping Forest hunt, 1888. Note the use of a carted stag because indigenous deer had been mercilessly hunted.

in 1829 when the hunt passed outside his school-room window:

> The stag set off in the direction of Paddington and, coming to the Grand Junction Canal, swam across towards the Church. It so happened the door was open and he bounded in and was caught inside the Church! The poor creature who was a victim to this inhuman 'sport' must have given chase at least 35 miles, as he was started at Hounslow and had made a long circuitous route.[30]

From the fifteenth century more affluent citizens would hunt out for entertainment with the Lord Mayor's staghounds, which were kept in the 'Dogge Hous' in 'More Fyeld', according to Ralph Agas' Tudor map of London. The hounds were used for the Citizens' Common Hunt, which was described by Stow in 1562. The Lord Mayor and his alderman and assorted dignitaries hunted the hare and the fox, with a dinner in between, at Tyburn Conduits: 'There was a great cry for a mile, then the hounds killed him [the fox] at St. Giles; great hallooing at his death and blowing of horns; and the Lord Mayor and all his company rode through London to his place in Lombard Street.'[31]

By the end of the eighteenth century the Lord Mayor's staghounds had been reduced to being used only once a year at the Epping Forest hunt, following a carted stag, which would often stand stock still with bewilderment when it was released from its confinement in front of the hunt.[32] The Epping hunt was instigated in 1226 by Henry III and was traditionally held on Easter Monday. It was originally a 'solemn' affair played out by the Citizens' Common Hunt, although it was a dangerous one: in 1774, two horses fell down dead after colliding with each other, and in 1793, 100 horses came back riderless, with many riders ending up in St Bartholomew's Hospital.[33] But the Epping hunt deteriorated into a 'farcical show' when the City of London abolished the Common Hunt in 1807 and the annual hunt was taken over by 'the dissolute populous of town coming out on any quadruped they could lay their hands on'.[34] One commentator in 1810 wrote of the majority of Cockney horses as being 'not capable of keeping up with a lame goat'; 'The equestrian display was highly ludicrous and laughable.'[35]

The *Morning Herald* report of the hunt of 1826 revealed its chaotic organization: it did not actually start until 2.30 pm because the stag was being exhibited, for threepence a view, at a variety of public houses where around 3,000 hunt followers were enjoying a meal of beef, beer, bacon and brandy.[36] At the allocated time, hundreds of huntsmen gathered in two long lines leading away from the stag cart to make an avenue for the stag to stride down after being released. The animal was decked out in flowers and ribbons and had streamers tied to its antlers. When the stag saw the hounds waiting at the end of the horse-lined avenue, it bolted through the line of huntsmen and was off – the chase began. But only around twelve staghounds and their keepers actually pursued the stag; the rest of the crowd were too drunk, fell off their horses or were not brave enough to follow the hunt. They did not know where the stag was killed, but apparently enjoyed the outing immensely.

This circus continued, but with fewer and poorer quality hounds. Without the Lord Mayor's hounds, the hunts in the surrounding area were loath to send their best dogs for the 'Cockneys' to trample.[37] The last Epping hunt was held in 1847 and *The Era* newspaper was enraged by the 'disgraceful exhibition . . . a cruel, wanton, unEnglish and unsportsmanlike affair' which saw the doe chased by seven dogs – she was 'a fat creature; resembling a donkey in some respects; and, as we are told, *blooded* [bled], so as to be unable to leave the neighbourhood of the Roebuck [public house], where a brisk business was going forward'. The dogs basically harassed her until she could go no further and she was caught and returned to her cart, 'bruised, bleeding, and gasping'.[38]

Private hunts continued around London, though. The Old Berkeley hunt was started by the Berkeley family, which originally kept 30 huntsmen and a pack of hounds in the village of Charing (now Charing Cross) and hunted in the vicinity. It expanded its hunting ground to cover 'Kensington Gardens to Berkeley Castle and Bristol'. But it eventually stopped hunting around London because of 'the advancing waste of bricks and mortar, and the increase in the value of land arising from the spread of London westward'.[39] Another factor was

the pressure of a swarm of nondescripts who, starting from every suburb of London, were glad to make a meet of foxhounds their excuse for a holiday on hackney or wagonette, overwhelming the whole procedure by their presence and irritating farmers and landowners, to the great injury of the hunt.[40]

However, the Enfield Chace hunt was the last hunting pack to meet on the boundary of Greater London as it stands today; it even hunted on areas now flush with the Underground's Central Line.[41] The hunt began in 1935 and since 2001 has been combined with the Cambridgeshire hunt.

Shooting and duck hunting

The medieval sport of hawking was gradually replaced by shooting with guns: this was perhaps when hunting became 'unsporting', as the animals did not have a fair chance of escape, which only escalated with bagged foxes, carted stags and the shooting of mutilated domestic birds.

Shooting became a formal blood sport in the eighteenth century when large bags of partridges and pheasants were exterminated, leading to red-legged or French partridges being introduced into many land estates, such as in Wimbledon before 1751.[42] Rough shooting was also a popular sport, mainly for snipe and woodcock, and occasionally grey plovers. For wealthy men this was superseded by pigeon shooting, where pigeons were let out of traps and shot by a line of guns. It came into vogue in about 1790 with the sport headquarters at the Red House (Tavern) Club in Battersea. This closed in 1850, but was the leading venue for pigeon shooting as 'the crack shots about London assemble there to determine matches of importance, and it not unfrequently [sp.] occurs that not a single bird escapes the shooter.'[43] According to Mayhew, any birds that did escape were picked off by onlookers, often Lambeth costermongers, and wounded birds were retrieved by boys and their specially trained dogs.[44]

The Gun Club was founded in 1860 at the Hornsey Wood House (Tavern) in Harringay; development moved it on in 1867 to the Hurlingham Estate at Fulham, which led to the formation of the Hurlingham Club. This popular sport later declined: out of the club's 1,500 members prior to 1891, only 200 were shooting members, so the sport gradually ceased – finally being replaced in popularity by polo.

The fate of pigeon shooting was sealed when George Anderson MP exposed cruelty in the sport during parliamentary debates for the Cruelty to Animals Amendment Bill in 1883.[45] In the early days of the sport, wild blue-rocks were the birds used and they were unmutilated, so testing the skill of the shooter and giving the birds a fair chance of escaping. They cost about £8–£10 per 100. But Anderson claimed that although the birds were called blue-rocks, they were, by then, only tame household pigeons; so tame that some would refuse to fly when the trap was open. The trappers therefore resorted to certain methods to make the birds move: yanking out the bird's tail feathers and applying pepper or turpentine to the raw skin or sticking a pin into their rumps. Anderson also claimed that trappers would accept bribes to make the pigeons fly in a certain direction as they left the trap, by gouging out either eye with a pin or a fingernail (the bird would fly in the direction it could see). Pigeons also had the upper mandible of the bill bent over and stuck through the soft part of the lower, possibly to confuse the birds in flight, making them easier shots.

Lord Westbury immediately wrote to the papers to deny that Hurlingham and the new Gun Club at Notting Hill used these cruel methods, but a Revd Doctor from a London parish wrote to Mr Anderson with first-hand accounts of the practices at both establishments. The slight on Hurlingham was confirmed, and the papers reported that the 'Princess of Wales and other Royal and aristocratic ladies have boycotted Hurlingham, at Her Majesty's own suggestion, until pigeon shooting stopped and urged other Ladies to do the same'.[46] The pigeon is still the Hurlingham Club's crest and until 1905 'clouds of live pigeons' were released each summer to mark the association with the pigeon.[47]

As opposed to the organized pigeon-shooting contests of the wealthy, the lower classes loved hunting ducks with spaniels and other dogs – the weavers of Bethnal Green bred a special small spaniel called a splasher for the purpose.[48] The most notorious areas for duck hunting around 1750 were the stagnant pools of St George's Fields in Southwark, Tothill Fields in

Partridge shooting in long stubble after the harvest – the hounds raised the birds.

Westminster and Hertford Street in Mayfair. The former area was well known for the Dog and Duck Tavern, which had a sign on its stone wall depicting a dog sitting on its haunches, with a duck hanging from its mouth. The pond near the Dog and Duck in Mayfair was surrounded by a knee-high board to stop excited spectators from falling in.[49] The 'sport' consisted of the ducks diving to escape the hunting spaniels, so they must have had their wings clipped. Sometimes an owl was tied to a duck's back, as described in Joseph Strutt's *The Sports and Pastimes of the People of England* (1801), so by diving she tried to escape her burden, and

> the miserable owl, half drowned, shakes itself, and hooting, frightens the duck; she of course dives again, and replunges the owl into the water; the frequent repetition of this action soon deprives the poor bird of its sensation, and generally ends in its death, if not in that of the duck also.[50]

A variation on this sport was practised in the latter part of the eighteenth century at the ponds of Tottenham Court Road and in the Long Fields, when a cat was thrown into the water and dogs were let loose on her.[51]

Thankfully duck hunting was out of fashion by 1800, probably because there were few large ponds left in London to sport in. However, some seeking the entertainment were forced to hunt on the Regent's Canal, for which they were fined sixpence and charged with disorderly conduct,[52] and also on the canal at Camberwell.

Baiting of animals: bull-baiting

As well as hunting, in his account of entertainments enjoyed by Londoners in the twelfth century, Fitzstephen introduces the 'sport' of baiting animals to their death:

> On most festival days during winter, before lunch, boars foaming at the mouth and hogs

Woodcut showing bull- and bear-baiting on Bankside: a real crowd pleaser, *c.* 16th century.

armed with 'tusks lightning-swift' fight for their lives; they'll soon be bacon. And fat bulls with horns or monstrous bears, under restraints, are set to fight against hounds.[53]

Bull-baiting from the medieval period was actually regarded more as a necessity than an entertainment, as it was believed that a bull needed to be stressed in order to tenderize its flesh before slaughter; local by-laws stipulated that bulls had to be baited before death, otherwise butchers could face considerable fines. This was believed until the eighteenth century, when regulations fell into disuse, but bull-baiting continued for its entertainment value.[54]

Initially bulls were baited in the streets of London and its suburbs; the earliest recorded arena was the bullring in Southwark High Street in 1542.[55] The bull was restricted by a 15-foot rope or chain on its neck collar, or the base of its horns, attached to a stake in the ground or an iron ring in a stone. The awaiting dogs were normally set on him one at a time, although this was not always the case, and they aimed to seize the bull by the nose and tenaciously hold on until the bull stood still – called pinning the bull – even if the bull got free of the stake. Bouts could last for over an hour and a half and the dogs, or their owners, would sometimes compete for a silver collar and a gold-laced hat.[56]

Originally mastiff dogs, large, strong dogs renowned for their fearlessness and ferocity, were used for baiting. But by late Stuart times, bulldogs had been bred to bait rather than just being used by butchers to move cattle. They were more ferocious and smaller than mastiffs, and much more active when fighting. Bulldogs would hang onto a bull's face with 'invincible obstinacy', according to the wood engraver Thomas Bewick in his *History of Quadrupeds* (1790).[57]

Despite the dogs' tenacity – dogs often had to be pulled back by their tails and needed to have their jaws forced open to release their hold – it was not an easy task to pin a bull. The Duke of Würtemberg, on a visit to London in 1592, noted the breeding and mettle of the dogs that tried to fasten onto the bull, but the bull fought back.[58] A practised bull would try to get his horns underneath the dog and toss it in the air, as seen by Pepys in 1666 and John Evelyn in 1670, when dogs were tossed into the spectator boxes and, in Evelyn's case, 'full into a lady's lap, as she sate in one of the boxes at a considerable height from the arena. Two poor dogs were killed.'[59]

The London diarists had all seen bull-baiting at the Bear Garden in Southwark as part of a programme of blood sports and animal baitings, but later much bull-baiting was held on an informal basis. In 1760 the *London Evening Post* described a baiting on a Monday evening in a field by the roadside near Edgware:

the Mob of the Country were inhumanly diverting themselves with a Bull-baiting, to the great Scandal of the human Species, and to the Reproach of those who have it in their Power to put a Stop to such Diversons. It was a prodigious Milk-white Beast, with about twenty Dogs at him, which he toss'd almost as fast as they came near him, but not without being greatly torn by them, his Head and Face being one continued Gore of Blood.[60]

It is apparent from this report that the contemporary view of bull-baiting was one of abhorrence. No longer was it a formal sport patronised by the wealthy, but it was supposedly perpetrated by the lowest in society, many of which were members of the working-class 'fancy' societies who bred bulldogs especially for baiting and fighting.

Some of these bulldogs became celebrities and large amounts of money were gambled on baiting contests. The *St James' Chronicle* reported a 'truly brutish Meeting' in 1762 at St George's Fields, but noted the fine collection of bulldogs that were gathered. One particular bitch was 'as good Blood as Putney Peg, or Teddington Diamond'.[61]

Bear-baiting

The same mastiffs and bulldogs were used to bait bears, which was London's first organized sport with paying spectators.[62] There was no practical use to bear-baiting, as there supposedly was with bull-baiting; it was purely for entertainment.

Bear-baiting was so popular among all classes in society that by the sixteenth century bears were long extinct in England and they had to be imported;[63] it was an expensive sport. The Crown, from the reign of Richard III (r. 1483–5), even had its own bearwarde or Master of the Bears who would provide bears and dogs for baiting contests wherever royalty required; this often meant that they 'took over' suitable dogs and bears from their owners.[64]

Although there were several sites around London, there was really only one place for royalty and ordinary citizens to watch bear-baiting, and that was on the south side of the Thames, at the Bear Gardens in Bankside, in the manor of Paris Gardens. The Spanish ambassador was taken to the bear-baitings in 1544, probably as a guest of Henry VIII, and he described it thus:

> It is not bad sport to witness the conflict. The large bears contend with three or four dogs, and sometimes one is victorious and sometimes the other. The bears are ferocious and of great strength, and not only defend themselves with their teeth, but hug the dogs so closely with their forelegs that, if they were not rescued by their master, they would be suffocated.[65]

It is not clear whether these baitings took place in the open air, or in arenas, but certainly by 1572, Braun and Hogenberg's map of London shows two amphitheatres on the Bankside labelled as 'The Bowll Baytyng' (pulled down in 1613[66]) and 'The Beare Bayting'. They stood in adjoining fields, separated by a piece of land containing several ponds. The bears could have used these water pools, as recorded in Dresden in *Brown's Travels* (1685): they had

> *fountains* and *ponds*, to wash themselves in, wherein they much delight: and near to the pond are high *ragged posts* or *trees*, set up for the bears to climb up, and *scaffolds* made at the top, to sun and dry themselves; where they will also sleep, and come and go as the keeper calls them.[67]

Unlike bulls, which were also baited in the arenas, bears were not killed because they were too valuable. There were usually eight of them, and were esteemed based on how well they fought – the most popular bears were given names such as Harry Hunks or Sackerton. Pictured on the 1572 map, the mastiff dogs – 120 of them, according to the Duke of Würtemberg in 1592[68] – were separately kennelled on either side of the plots, and were depicted as jumping up and straining on their leashes. These dogs, and the bears, were fed on offal and refuse from Newgate shambles.[69] But excavations at Benbow House, Southwark, also showed that aged horses were butchered to feed the baiting animals.[70]

Every Sunday afternoon the baiting attracted huge crowds of around 1,000 people per arena.[71] Spectators (mainly men) would pay a halfpenny, one penny or tuppence depending on their seating requirements. Raphael Holinshed's *Chronicles* (second edition) noted that in 1583 the old and underpropped scaffolds round the bear garden collapsed under the weight of spectators, killing eight men and women and injuring many others. That this disaster happened on a Sunday was 'a friendly warning to such as more delight themselves in the crueltie of beasts, than in the workes of mercy'.[72]

The bear fights back: Henry Alken, 'Bear Baiting', print from the series *National Sports of Great Britain* (1821).

Latterly, when the 'Beere Bayting' arena (as it was labelled on Hollar's 1647 map of London) was also a part-time theatre (the Hope), baits were held on Tuesdays and Thursdays. It was finally pulled down in 1655 and Thomas Pride, the Sheriff of Surrey, shot the surviving seven bears under the orders of Oliver Cromwell (1599–1658), who suppressed baiting and the theatres.[73] Charles II revived one final bear garden from 1658 to 1683 on Bankside – the one visited by Pepys and Evelyn.[74]

As already noted, baiting contests took place in other venues apart from Bankside. The tiltyard at Whitehall Palace was used to bait bears until the Horse Guards building was built on this site – the last performance was recorded as June 1663.[75] Bull- and bear-baiting (and fox hunting) was even played out on an iced-over River Thames during the Frost Fairs,[76] the most documented of which was in 1683–4, when

prints depicted circles of spectators opposite the Temple Stairs watching a bear- and bull-bait. In the time of Queen Anne, bear- and bull-baits were held at the Bear Garden in Tothill Fields, Westminster and, most auspiciously, at the Bear Garden in Hockley-in-the-Hole, Clerkenwell, which replaced Bankside as the Crown's official baiting arena in 1686–7.[77]

Baits at Clerkenwell were held on Mondays and Thursdays, and the animals were paraded solemnly through the streets on the day as advertising. The sports on offer were similar to those staged 200 years before at Bankside, with the exception of a few added entertainments: in 1710, 'a bull to be turned loose, with fireworks all over him; also a mad ass to be baited'.[78] Other informal venues for baiting in the late 1700s included Kennington Common; Devil's Lane, near Muswell Hill; Temple Mills, on Hackney Marsh; Putney Common; and Wormholt Scrubs, Kensington.[79]

Baiting of other animals

Meanwhile, back at Bankside, the crowds didn't just come to see baiting. A full range of cruel and sickening (by today's standards) blood sports was offered. The Spanish ambassador previously mentioned wrote in 1544 that after the bear-baiting,

> a pony is baited, with a monkey on its back, defending itself against the dogs by kicking them; and the shrieks of the monkey, when he sees the dogs hanging from the ears and neck of the pony, render the scene very laughable.[80]

Nearly half a century later, in 1598, a German traveller saw the whipping of a blind bear by six men,[81] and James I was most partial to afternoon baiting at the Tower of London. He used all sorts of animals for sport. On 3 June 1605 the keeper of the lions was ordered to put into the yard a lion and lioness – they were not keen to enter, so burning torches were used to persuade them. Two racks of mutton were thrown down to them, which they devoured; then a live cockerel was thrown down, which they killed and ate; then a live lamb was lowered by rope into the yard. The lions, probably full from their previous meals, just sniffed the lamb and so the lamb was taken back up again. The King was bored by this, so ordered a fresh lion into the yard, on which he set three 'lusty' mastiffs – the dogs were all killed by the lion.[82]

More exotic animals were baited in other, smaller venues in London. It was a 'very large African Tyger' that was baited with six dogs in 1717 at the Boarded House, in 'Marrow-Bone-Fields, the backside of Soho Square'.[83] The previous year, a leopard had been baited on the stage, which was 4 feet off the ground. The Boarded House was also a prizefighting venue, and the animal baits were held as entertainments between bouts – the same programme could be seen at Broughton's Amphitheatre in Oxford Road, off Oxford Street.[84] In 1747 the 'celebrated white sea-bear [polar bear]' was baited at the Amphitheatre.[85]

In 1821 Londoners looking for novel baiting were delighted by a Spanish monkey called Mukako or Jacco Maccacco (or many other variants). This gibbon-type monkey weighed about 10 pounds and would fight any dog up to 20 pounds. The spectators would bet on how long the dogs would last during the fight, which saw Jacco staked on the end of a 6-foot chain. It was rumoured that this monkey could kill any dog within five minutes; it went for the dog's windpipe, then jumped on the dog's back and wrestled it to the ground before dispatching it with a bite to the jugular with its canine-like teeth. Jacco was said to have killed fourteen dogs in a row in the Westminster Dog Pit, Duck Lane, but came to a sad end when he was pitted against a dog double his weight called Puss, belonging to the famous boxer Tom Cribb. It was reported in 1822, in the House of Commons during a speech in favour of animal cruelty legislation, that 'Jacco fought the dog for half an hour, and the battle terminated by the dog tearing away the whole of the monkey's lower jaw, and the monkey's ripping up the dog's stomach. Both animals died in a few minutes.'[86]

But reports of Jacco, and the fight with Puss, were not as they seemed. The *Morning Chronicle* ran the supposedly 'true story' of Jacco and the fight in 1825. The monkey originally came from the 'Isle of Macacco', where he was bought by a sailor and taken to London. This sailor kept him for three years, but then Jacco bit off three of his fingers and a man from Hoxton at Ratcliffe Highway bought Jacco and put him up as a raffle prize. His new owner was a silversmith who could not cope with Jacco's aggression, so took him into the fields to be killed by dogs, but none of the dogs succeeded. A spectator said he had a dog for the job and a fight between Jacco and the dog was held in Bethnal Green, but the monkey was indestructible. So Cribb's Puss was the next to try. However, the battle had actually lasted only two and a half minutes (not the half-hour reported in Parliament), when Puss was taken off the stage. She lived for another two years and had two litters of puppies, whereas Jacco jumped onto his house (which was next to the stake) in triumph after the fight, and eventually died fifteen months later of a chill and a lacerated sore throat.[87]

The gentleman sportsman Grantley F. Berkeley (1800–1881) revealed in his autobiography that he had visited Duck Lane to see the acclaimed monkey fight Cribb's Puss, but was disappointed at the sight of the monkey:

> In the centre of the pit was chained to a ring a large, ill-looking monkey. There was nothing about him suggestive of an animal that had ever conquered, or that was boldly expecting a battle; he cowered to the floor, and seemed to wish that some hole would open into which he might creep for protection.[88]

Berkeley then noticed that as Cribb was holding his dog before the fight, he nicked the dog's jugular vein with a lancet before setting it down. During the fight, a pool of blood appeared around the dog (seemingly from Jacco's bites) and eventually the fight was declared a draw. The dog was removed from the stage and Jacco jumped on top of his house as the winner. Cribb held the 'injured' dog in his arms – and stopped the bleed – while the crowds dispersed. Berkeley told Cribb: 'I'm down on it all; the monkey never bit your dog. You bled her . . . I knew it when I saw the care you took of her jaws and head.' Cribb replied: 'Mum, sir's, the word – you knows it, but it makes a pit.'[89] It seems that the dogs, and the punters, were bled!

The fight against animal baiting

Between the fifteenth and nineteenth century, the fight against animal cruelty (of which the baiting of animals was a large concern) centred around one belief, which initially was not widely held: that the tormenting of animals for entertainment sake was unacceptable.[90]

In the Tudor and early Stuart periods, the baiting arenas enjoyed royal patronage and protection, so even though there were Protestant and Puritan attacks against bear-baiting as 'a filthy, stinking and loathsome game',[91] they did nothing to affect the popularity of the matches. Bull-baiting was, of course, still a required part of butchery at this time.

However, rather than for its cruelty, bear-baiting was suppressed by royal decree and by the London Corporation for other reasons: in 1546 Henry VIII banned baiting in Bankside after Easter as part of his 'Suppression of the Stews' anti-prostitution programme (baiting brought in the punters),[92] and the Lord Mayor wanted bear-baiting to stop in 1583 because the people assembled were likely to spread the plague. In the latter case, Bankside was out of the City's jurisdiction so the order was ignored.[93] During subsequent plague outbreaks, though, the baits were suppressed.

Other early legislation against bear-baiting was concerned with the fact that baits were held on Sundays, which was supposed to be a sacred day reserved for religious contemplation. Even the clergy were guilty of this sacrilege, as recorded by the Puritan churchman Thomas Cartwright in 1572: 'If there be an animal to be baited in the afternoon, or a jackanapes to ride on horse-back, the minister hurries the service over in a shameful manner, in order to be present at the show.'[94] There was a motion put before Parliament in 1601 for A Bill for More Diligent Resort to Churches on Sundayes, which cited bear-baiting as a 'Brutish Exercise' which should not be 'used' on the Sabbath.[95] By 1617–18 it was an offence under James I (the most bloodthirsty king to date) to bait animals on a Sunday as it was classed as an 'unlawfull' game.[96] This law was reissued in 1633 under Charles I.

During the Civil War (1642–51), baiting at the Bear Garden in Southwark was outlawed totally, as public meetings in all their forms were deemed favourite resorts of plotters and rebels. During Cromwell's Protectorate (1653–8), the baiting of animals in London was banned. Perhaps Cromwell was swayed by Puritan arguments against baiting, but Cromwell hoped to limit 'the excesses of (sinful) humanity' because this entertainment brutalized the spectators, leading to betting, drinking, swearing and sexual perversions.[97] Cromwell had the Bankside bears killed in 1655, but private contests still continued around London, although they were less frequent and less popular.

After the Restoration, baits were once more held in public, but, alongside Puritan ideals, others (mainly the educated middle class) began to view baiting of animals as inhumane and evidence of an uncultured and savage society. Evelyn and Pepys both showed their disgust at the sports shown at Bankside in 1666 and 1667: Pepys calling it 'a very rude and nasty pleasure', and Evelyn calling the baiting of a 'gallant' horse (which had supposedly killed a man) by dogs, a 'wicked and barbarous sport . . . I would not be persuaded to be a spectator'.[98]

Although law did not ban baits, local magistrates began to prohibit contests, such as in Clapham in 1693 after the campaigning of the 'Clapham Sect' – a group of Christian leaders, many of whom were MPs (the most visible being William Wilberforce), who mainly lived close to Clapham Common.[99] High and Petty Constables enforced the magistrates' orders with the help of the public: a bait at Kensington Gardens in 1787 was temporarily stopped by the constable after it was reported by the Minister of Paddington.[100]

However, there were still informal bear- and bull-baits in London, and often the public were in danger from the gatherings. Bulldogs attacked spectators and infuriated bulls were reported to have gored people to death, such as in 1761 when 'the Slaughter Man belonging to Brook's Market attending a Bull-baiting in Tothill Fields . . . venturing too near the irritated Animal, was gored in such a manner that it is expected he will not live.'[101] An inquiry into the state of policing in London in 1817 contained a report from Mr Fielding, a police magistrate, which noted that the prohibitions were ignored at 'one end of the metropolis' – the police were powerless to stop it.[102]

What was needed was proper legislation. The first attempts to make bull-baiting illegal were brought before Parliament in 1800 by Sir William Pulteney. He cited the cruelty to the animal, the danger to the public of being gored and also of being hurt by the bulldogs, and that it was 'productive of great mischief, idleness, and riot'. But the main opponent, William Windham, Secretary of War, dismissed the argument with distain, saying, 'it is beneath the dignity of the Legislature to interfere with matters of such a frivolous nature . . . [and try to] curtail the amusements of the lower order.' Windham argued that if bull-baiting was banned, then bans on hunting and shooting would have to follow (which were sports of the aristocracy!).[103]

There were several more attempts by others who proposed legislation to stop bull-baiting nationally, all to no avail. However, The Metropolis Act in 1822 made it illegal to keep or use a baiting arena within 5 miles of Temple Bar, because these places were magnets for 'idle and disorderly Persons . . . to the Interruption of good Order and the Danger of the public Peace'. This measure was used by the SPCA to bring indictments against certain London pits for causing a nuisance: in July 1830 it brought to court John King of the Westminster Pit, Duck Lane, for bear-baiting.[104]

There was also evidence at this site of a badger being baited after the bear. It was kept in a narrow box, which was opened so that a dog could try and drag the badger out. The dog that pulled out the animal the most times in succession was the winner. Mr King was found guilty of causing a public nuisance and told to remove the badger and bear. But the *Voice of Humanity* reported that there were, sadly, other pits to be found in West Street, Smithfield; New Inn Yard, Tottenham Court Road; Edgware Road, Paddington; Mint Square, Borough; Old Saint Pancras Church, near Camden Town; and others.[105]

It was up to Richard Martin MP to campaign against bear- and bull-baiting and 'other cruel practices' from 1825 onwards. Finally, after the Great Reform Act became law in 1832, the 'protests of decent folk could no longer be set at naught',[106] and all baiting of animals was made illegal under the Cruelty to Animals Act in 1835. However, there were some notorious areas where bull-baiting was still permitted (or police officers turned a blind eye), such as Hackney and Bethnal Green.[107]

Cockfighting and cock throwing

Cockfighting was one other blood sport that was as resilient as baiting. It too was mentioned by Fitzstephen as a twelfth-century London entertainment, and was enjoyed especially by children:

> Every year on the morning of Shrove-Tuesday, the school-boys of the city of London bring game cocks to their master, and in the fore part of the day, till dinner time, they are permitted to amuse themselves with seeing them fight.[108]

Cocks were/are innately disposed to fight when they confront each other, so it was deemed to be a 'noble and heroic recreation' to watch their strength and determination when fighting to the death – hence schoolmasters trying to instil bravery in their pupils by encouraging cockfighting.[109] The following description gives an idea of the sights and sounds of a full-blown cockfight:

For fully three minutes one confused mass of wings and feathers was seen; blow succeeded blow with startling rapidity, and the feints and parries that could be occasionally seen were surprising . . . As they were put down again [one untouched, the other with a deadly injury] . . . No thought of yielding was in the gallant bird's breast, as again and again he rose and struck with all his force at his antagonist, hoping yet by a lucky blow to win the victory; but it was not to be; his blows became weaker and weaker, while his lusty foe struck hard and sharp, and, ere long, drove his keen weapon [spurs] through the brain of the gray cock, and crowed a shrill note of triumph.[110]

During the reign of Edward III in the fourteenth century, cockfighting became a fashionable adult amusement, but it was not encouraged because it was 'productive of pernicious consequences'.[111] It was prohibited by public proclamation in 1363, along with other 'idle and unlawful pastimes', such as football. Instead, subjects were encouraged to practise archery.[112] Henry VIII was the first monarch directly to encourage cockfighting in his subjects after he built a cockpit at the Palace of Whitehall. It was a grand 'castellated building with a pointed roof and a weathervane in the shape of a lion'.[113] Henry's influence was perhaps to turn the sport into a professional gambling pursuit, performed by specially bred and trained birds.

Fighting cocks were looked after by 'feeders' and reared on a special diet – brandy, raw steak, maggots and urine were some ingredients[114] – and specifically trained for fighting. Their wings were clipped, their wattles and combs cut off, and their feet fitted with artificial spurs made of sharp steel or silver. Cockfights were usually 'Mains', where two rival teams were paired off for individual contests, until there was only one cock left alive; a rougher version was

Cockfighting in St James's Park. 'John Bluck', *Royal Cock Pit*, 1808, engraving.

the 'Welsh Main'. Most spectacular was the 'Battle Royal' when a large number of cocks were put in the pit together.[115]

The bloody gore of cockfighting was bound to be enjoyed by James I, and he continued to use the cockpit at Whitehall. James was, according to a French ambassador, so keen on the sport that he watched a fight twice a week.[116] And no fair or racehorse meeting was complete without a cockfight in Stuart times. One particular fan was the poet and writer Gervase Markham, who wrote a pamphlet in 1614 called *The Choice, Ordering, Breeding, and Dyeting of the Fighting Cocke* in which he stated: 'there is no pleasure more noble, delightsome, or voyd of cozenage and deceipt than this pleasure of cocking'.[117]

Several cockpits opened in London in the seventeenth century – cocking's heyday. The pit in Drury Lane was built in 1609, but converted into the Phoenix Theatre in 1616–17; there were other pits in Jewin Street, Gray's Inn Lane and Shoe Lane. Henry's Whitehall pit was turned into the Cockpit-in-Court Theatre by Inigo Jones in 1629–32 and was sited on what is now the parade ground of Horse Guards.[118]

It is no surprise that in May 1653 the Protectorate (which deplored all Stuart entertainments) banned cockfights. It was not so easy to condemn cockfights on the grounds of animal cruelty (compared with other animal-baiting contests), because the cocks naturally fought to the death. But it was the gambling that accompanied the sport which the Puritans disliked –

and every bout of a Main involved heavy betting on the winning fowl.

At the Restoration, cockfights once again became extremely popular and Charles II fought his own light-coloured, red-and-white birds. The Royal Cockpit was built in about 1671 for Charles at the top of Cockpit Steps (leading up from Birdcage Walk) in what is now Queen Anne's Gate.[119] However, Pepys's writings indicate the new sensibilities which began to regard the blood sports of old as inhumane. He visited the newly opened Shoe Lane pit (off Fleet Street) in December 1663 to see a cockfight and was amazed to see a wide variety of spectators from 'Parliament men to the poorest 'prentices, bakers, brewers, butchers, draymen, and what not; and all these fellows one with another cursing and betting. I soon had enough of it.'[120] But he tried the cocking again in April 1668, this time at the new cockpit in Great James Street, off Theobalds Road, Holborn. Again he noted the 'mixed rabble of people' who spectated and was almost disgusted by the cocks themselves for their cruelty towards each other.[121]

Nearly a century later, in 1762, James Boswell (a Scot) visited London. He resolved to be a 'true-born Englishman' and visit the Royal Cockpit near St James's Park for a five-hour festival of cockfighting. He felt 'sorry for the poor cocks', but when he looked around to see if any other spectators were moved by the plight of the fowl, he 'could not observe the smallest relenting sign in any countenance'.[122] This cockpit was pulled down in 1810.

Despite the seemingly changing tide against cockfighting, another Royal Cockpit was built in Tufton Street, Westminster, and in the mid-1700s hosted the major fighting cock-training yards – the Cockpit Yards, where one might experience 'the effluvia of the Great Unwashed. Yet hither came the cream of the *beau monde*, including Royalty itself.'[123] The fact that cockfighting was enjoyed by London society helped it to remain free of the statute books, but cockpits eventually became illegal in London in 1833, under the Metropolis Act, and throughout the rest of the country in 1835, alongside animal baiting pits. Cockfighting as such was finally banned in 1849, though it continued as an underground 'sport' outside the range of the Metropolitan Police.

Another 'sport' involving cocks had long since been abolished in London, but it was a traditional part of Shrove Tuesday for many Londoners, especially children: that of cock throwing. Rather than actually throwing the cock, as the name suggests, the cock was tied to a stake and stones, cudgels and other missiles were thrown at it. One campaigner described the unsporting pastime in a letter to the *Public Advertiser* in 1757:

> [The cock] is fastened to a Stake, while some lubberly Fool of Six Foot high, armed with a Stick sufficient to level a Goliath, at a small Distance, is to divert himself by breaking every Bone in this poor Creature's Skin. First the successful Hero breaks a Leg; then the courageous Cock stands on one; the next Trophy is a broken Wing, the second Leg then falls a Sacrifice to the Hero's Rage. Still the Cock clears his Ground, and when he can no longer stand to face his Enemy, he is put into a Hat, and becomes the Hero's Prize if his Stick but touch him. At length he wins him; the Owner is pleased with the Money he has made, and the Victor glories in the Conquest of so stubborn a Foe.[124]

However, by the 1750s there were loud calls to ban the practice, because it was believed to breed barbarity and cruelty in children. By 1762 London magistrates were ordering constables to do their utmost to suppress the 'shameful' custom.[125] Happily, in 1783, the *Whitehall Evening Post* concluded that cock throwing had been 'laudably abolished: for it was a species of cruelty towards an innocent and useful animal; and such a cruelty, as would have kindled compassion in the heart of the rankest barbarian'.[126]

Despite legislation to abolish all animal fighting in 1835, there were two 'sports' that tended to be ignored. They carried on in private arenas, such as London's sporting taverns, with little police interference: dog-fighting and rat killing.

Dogfighting

Contests between dogs had been a regular part of London entertainments probably since the Roman occupation, after Caesar was impressed with the huge and fierce *Pugnaces Britanniae* (War Dog of Britannia) – probably the mastiffs that he found in the City. But regular dog matches peaked during the Stuart period, with Charles II banning matches in 1664 because of the excessive gambling that they attracted.

In the early 1700s dogs were set against each other between bouts of prizefighting and the animal baits. The fights, which were advertised in the newspapers, took place at venues such as Figg's Great-Room in Oxford Street; Mr Stokes's Amphitheatre in Islington Road and also in Tothill Fields (along with ass races and other 'heroic games').[127] These dogs were either pure-bred old English bulldogs, or bulldogs crossed with terriers to make them more nimble and speedier. The most renowned fancier of classic bulldogs in nineteenth-century London was Ben White. He had a 'trial ground' in Harper's Field, and later in Conduit Field, Bayswater, where clients could try out dogs, either on some unfortunate badger or in combat with each other.

In its heyday, dogfighting was a classless sport – even the nobility owned fighting dogs. It was reported in the newspapers that the 42-pound fighting dog known as Belcher (who had fought 104 battles and never lost) was exchanged for a gun and a case of pistols by his new owner, Lord Camelford, in 1803.[128] But by the 1820s, the enlightened attitude of the

middle classes, which culminated in Mr Martin's proposed bills against bull-baiting and dogfights in 1823, saw dogfighting fall in regard to a lower-class pursuit and being described as 'barbarous and disgraceful'.[129] Police made patrols of Spitalfields, Bethnal Green, Hackney Road and the surrounding neighbourhoods on Sundays to prevent dogfighting in 1822, which was by then classed in London as a public nuisance.[130] By 1835 dogfighting pits were outlawed, but the sport carried on illicitly, according to James Greenwood, in about 50 different 'slums, and corners, and crooked ways of the great City [in] establishments devoted to the "showing" of dogs'.[131]

Greenwood investigated one of these Sunday evening 'dog shows', which had been advertised in *Bell's Life* (a weekly sporting newspaper). It led him to the Duck, Duck Street, in Bethnal Green where the landlord, Mr Lerinke, had a terrier weighing 3½ pounds, who would 'kill with any dog in the world at his weight'.[132] The punters came in large numbers with

shrill-voiced ratting dogs, and fighting terriers, fighting bulldogs, struggling and straining their leashes to get at each other, with their red eyes starting from their heads, and their black lips curled back from their fangs, howling, yelping, barking shrilly and spitefully, or growling with a deeper rage from the bottom of their wide, red throats; while their masters, savages as themselves, roared out horrid blasphemy . . . [some owners sat apart] stirring up their dogs to show their mettle, or clenching their muzzles and holding still their writhing limbs when for business reasons it was desirable that their tremendous courage should not be made too public.

Other dog fights were held in home-made pits behind houses. In 1875 constables caught four men in Webber-Row, Waterloo Road, Southwark, in the act of encouraging two bulldogs to fight in a backyard pit on a Sunday morning. The dogs were separated with difficulty and washed; the constables also found a badger in a cask in the backyard shed.[133]

The situation has changed little in today's London, where certain areas of London, especially Islington and Finsbury Park, are known for illegal dogfighting. In a crackdown operation, the Metropolitan Police launched a Status Dogs Unit to tackle the problem of dangerous dogs being bred and sold to fight – in the first year after its launch in 2009 more than 1,070 dogs, including 900 pit bulls, were seized.[134]

Rat killing

The sport of rat killing also seemed to escape the police enforcement of other anti-cruelty legislation – perhaps because the rat was seen as vermin, and it was natural for terriers to want to kill this prey. And what better way was there for the well-employed rat catchers in London to dispose of these animals?

Most matches were advertised in the newspapers and played out weekly in the public houses known for their sporting contests, such as The George in Gravel Lane, Southwark, and The King's Arms, Coal Yard, in Drury Lane.[135] The dogs and their owners would be shown into an upstairs, or back, room of the tavern, which contained a makeshift pit, 15 feet square, surrounded by wooden sides that tilted inwards at the top to prevent rat escapees. There was nothing formal about these meetings.

James Greenwood described a night's ratting at the Turnspit, Quaker's Alley, Somers Town, in 1874, where 'The Fancy' (enthusiasts) brought their mastiffs, yard dogs, terriers and bulldogs to test their prowess at killing rats.[136] The rats were bought for four pence each, and once they were thrown into the pit, a dog was let loose on them. Some dogs were terrified of the rats and were kicked out of the pit by their owners for being cowards, while others ran through the rats quite easily. It was common for younger dogs to be pitted

against rats that had their 'teeth drawed' – the teeth were pushed out using a thumbnail – so the dogs would 'enjoy' the experience and not get hurt. It was such a popular evening's entertainment, according to Greenwood, that even less well-off men would rather see their dog after a rat than have some bread to fill their hungry stomachs.

In between the amateur rat killings, matches between two rival dogs were played out to see who could kill a certain number of rats in the fastest time. Bets were taken on the winner. The most documented, and celebrated, ratting dog was Billy, who lived at the Westminster Pit in Duck Lane. This terrier only had two teeth and one eye – the other lost to a rat bite – but in 1825 he had already killed over 4,000 rats in his career.[137] By 1832 Billy held the record for killing 100 rats in 5½ minutes, or 3.3 seconds per rat. This record stood until 1862, when Jacko, owned by Jemmey Shaw, was two seconds faster at killing the 100 rats.

It was not just dogs that took part in the rat sports. Samuel Province, aged fifteen, also killed 100 rats in less than five minutes at the Westminster Pit, just like a dog would: on all fours and seizing the rat in his mouth, and biting to separate the head from the body.[138] Henry Mayhew also met a rat killer who used dogs and ferrets to rid London houses of rat infestations, but he also, for a sovereign a time, would bet that he could beat a dog at killing rats. He was very much ashamed of doing this and had a scar on his neck where a rat had bitten him.[139]

It was a dangerous sport for dogs too. Mayhew visited a tavern famous for its ratting matches in the 1840s, which was decorated with prints of famous dogs and also the stuffed heads of dogs in glazed boxes. One bull terrier was represented with a rat in her mouth; she could kill a dozen rats as big as herself, but she was killed by the sewer rats in the end – the proprietor's son explained to Mayhew:

for sewer-rats are dreadful for giving dogs canker in the mouth, and she wore herself out with continually killing them, though we always rinsed her mouth out well with peppermint and water while she were at work.[140]

Mayhew also interviewed Jemmy Shaw (also known as Jimmy), the owner of one of the largest sporting taverns in London – the Blue Anchor in Bunhill Row (now the Artillery Arms) – and the first to establish 'rat sports' in London, about his supply of rats. They came, said Shaw, from professional rat catchers who hunted the field ditches and hedges around London after the harvest, the barns and straw stacks of farms, warehouses around the city, the Docks (including on ships) and the sewers. These six or seven different types of rat could not be mixed as they fought each other, and if Shaw did not sort the stock, his cages would be full of dead rats by the morning.[141] He reckoned to buy in 300–700 rats a week – about 26,000 a year[142] – from the rat catchers and he had to feed them on good-quality barley meal, otherwise they would turn cannibal.

Rats were also pitted against each other on the streets, in back alleys and out-of-the way locations to avoid attracting police attention. In an article

Ratting at the Blue Anchor tavern, Bunhill Row, Finsbury, in the 1850s, which was enjoyed by all walks of life.

titled 'Amusements of the Moneyless', *Chambers'*
Journal described the 'gladiator rat, champion of all
England', who lived in his 'master's bosom',[143] was
brought out whenever a challenge was accepted from
another rat. Invariably this champion rat killed off
any competition.

Non-violent sport: betting on horses

Aside from their love of violence, blood and gore,
gambling equally enthralled Londoners. They bet
on the outcome of all blood sports, and also on other
non-violent animal sports. Although there is no concrete evidence, the Romans probably introduced
their sport of chariot racing to the Londinium amphitheatre. And, like its successor horse racing, a meeting
was an opportunity for heavy betting on a series of
races.[144] There were usually four teams of horses and
their drivers to support – the *factiones* (teams) of
white, green, red or blue. The chariots were built
purely for speed, being as light as possible, and they
were usually drawn by a pair of horses (a *biga*), three
horses (a *triga*) or a team of four (a *quadriga*). The
driver of a *quadriga* had to be expert in order to control his charges, but crashes in chariot racing were
frequent and usually spectacular.

A full-length race was about 4,000 metres around
a track with tight turns at either end, and because the
race was on sand there were no lanes. There seem to
have been no rules either, as such; the first to finish the
course was the winner.

The first horse races recorded in London were
those run at the weekly horse sale at Smithfield Market,
according to Fitzstephen.[145] Sometime during the
sale, the 'common horses were ordered to withdraw
out of the way', and the 'strong and fleet' horses were
called forward. From Fitzstephen's description, there
seem to have been no rules, and the 'grand point' of
the race was 'to prevent a competitor from getting
before them'.[146]

It is clear that 'running horses' were part of the
inventory of early kings; King John (r. 1199–1216)
was the earliest.[147] But it is not clear whether races
were held in London, until Charles I established
horse races in Hyde Park. These races were held in
'the Ring' and were combined with coach races and
foot races – as witnessed by Pepys in 1660 and 1658
respectively.[148]

Race winners were originally presented with a
bell, but this changed to a silver cup and prize money
under Charles II.[149] Horse races were still being held
in Hyde Park until the late 1790s, when descriptions
of the races appeared in the *Sporting Magazine*.[150]
Other advertised London race meetings in the
1700s were held on Hackney Downs and Hackney
Marshes, on Finchley Common, at Highgate and
Tothill Fields.[151]

There was also a course near Jack Straw's Castle,
a pub on the west side of Hampstead Heath,[152] but
according to newspaper reports, it was not well patronised. The September meeting in 1732 only featured
one race, with the winner collecting a modest 10
guineas. Horse races at this time involved two or
three horses running three heats over 4 miles each.
So they could be galloping a total of 12 miles in one
afternoon.[153] During the only race of the day on
the Heath, three horses started and raced two heats
before Merry Gentleman was declared the winner.
According to Park's *History of Hampstead*, the races
'drew together so much low company, that they were
put down [by the magistrates in the 1740s] on account
of the mischief that resulted from them'.[154] It is not
easy to image a racecourse on the Heath today because
of the scars left from the gravel pits, but the road
above provided an elevated platform for the spectators.

In the nineteenth century London once again
enjoyed (albeit, again, briefly) the joys of the turf,
when a 2½-mile racecourse called the Hippodrome
opened on the Bayswater slopes of Notting Hill in June
1837. One member of the sporting press described it

as the 'most perfect racecourse that I had ever seen'[155] and eulogised its facilities: a training ground for 75 horses and a site for horse exercise that was particularly safe for females to ride over.

The opening day saw two races; the first with three horses, and the second started with four horses. However, despite initially being ranked among the most favoured of London's societal rendezvous, there was a fault with the 'perfect' racecourse: it was built on deep clay soils which made it a quagmire in wet weather. This made the course unpopular and after stumbling through several seasons, it became apparent that it was not financially viable. The last race meeting was held in June 1841. The land was parcelled off to developers and St John's Church now stands on the racecourse site. Only a side street in Notting Hill called Hippodrome Place, and Hippodrome Mews, serve as a reminder of this piece of London's racing history.

Twenty-seven years later, London's faltering racing scene once again saw another racecourse try to pull in the punters. The result was a course at the Alexandra Palace ('Ally Pally'), Muswell Hill, at Hornsey; first opened in 1868. It was nicknamed the 'Frying Pan' on account of its shape, and had treacherous twists and turns that made it dangerous – the jockey Willie Carson said that the place 'wanted bombing'.[156] But the evening race meetings, instigated in 1955, were very atmospheric, although the whole 5-furlong course could not be viewed from the grandstand, as the start was hidden by trees. The Jockey Club eventually withdrew the course's licence in 1970, because of its financial losses and the need to invest huge amounts to improve safety for horses and riders. The calls for the Ally Pally racecourse to be reopened occasionally surface, with the racing pundit John McCririck being one of its greatest supporters – he even wants his ashes scattered at its furlong post.[157] But it is unlikely that the course (you can still make out the frying-pan shape) will see horses running again.

View of the short-lived Hippodrome racecourse in Notting Hill, *c.* 1840.

Despite its rather poor efforts to maintain a racecourse, London became a great centre for horse racing, because Tattersall's was *the* place in Europe to buy racehorses: their mission was 'to procure for the nobles and gentry of the Continent fresh supplies for their studs of the finest English horses'.[158] Mr Tattersall came to London in the early 1770s and originally sold horses at auction in the yard of the Barley Mow tavern in Piccadilly, but when the growing number of horses could not be accommodated, he moved to new stables at the Hyde Park turnpike in May 1772.[159] The auction-mart entrance was at the southeastern corner of St George's Hospital, now Grosvenor Crescent, where horses were paraded in the courtyard within the premises (which extended into the grounds of Lanesborough House, now the hotel). Horses were trotted up and down a gravelled avenue so spectators could see their movement before being halted in front of a wall. This was so their 'points' were 'well displayed' and potential buyers could get a closer look at them, and even check their heartbeat and lungs.[160]

Originally sale day was Thursday, but this changed to Monday (and also Thursday during the height of the season) with the sale horses arriving on the Friday, and being stabled next to the courtyard. It was not only racehorses that graced the 120 stables,[161] but hacks, hunters and carriage horses. However, it was a

The inner courtyard of old Tattersall's, where horses were put through their paces.

place of class, where 'men of taste might enjoy the glimpses afforded of the most beautiful specimens of an exquisitely beautiful race, without being perpetually disgusted with the worst of all things – that of the jockey or horse dealer'.[162] It was not just a place to purchase racehorses, but also the site of the subscription 'Rooms', which were frequented by members of the high-society Jockey Club. The site also became the centre of betting, which regulated bookmakers throughout the country.[163] Tattersall's then moved in 1865 (not far away) to the junction of Brompton Road with the main road through Knightsbridge, near to Albert Gate, where it remained until 1939 when it moved to Newmarket, Suffolk.

Betting on the dogs

London's track record with greyhound racing has been similarly chequered. The relationship started off well, as the first greyhound race ever held in England was played out in September 1876 in a field near the

Welsh Harp tavern in Hendon.[164] The greyhounds chased an 'artificial hare'. However, the sport did not take off and it became popular in America before returning to British shores. The headquarters of the Greyhound Racing Association was at Tothill Street in Westminster, and the first track was opened in Manchester in 1926, followed by tracks in London: White City Stadium at Shepherd's Bush (on the site of the stadium which had been built for the 1908 Olympics), which opened in June 1927, followed in September by one at Harringay and another in December at Wembley Stadium.

The racing was instantly successful, with 15,000 spectators at the opening of the White City – which later saw regular crowds of over 50,000 people, sometimes 80,000, and even 100,000.[165] Before the opening meet, commentators believed that the London dogs would be handicapped by a 'lack of schooling and training' at running around the oval track after the mechanical hare, compared with the more experienced Manchester dogs.[166] But the London dogs provided good sport on the night and excelled themselves:

> The finishes, perhaps, were not quite so close as usual, but cleverness and experience told nearly every time, and the keenness and gameness of the dogs were indicated, first, by their howling and pawing at the doors of the starting box and, then, by their refusal to give in so long as a breath of wind remained to them. Trainers already tell stories of the older dogs' hatred of being beaten by another dog – a hatred that far transcends the desire for the mechanical hare's blood.[167]

Meetings were held three evenings a week at White City, on alternate nights at Harringay Park and four times a week at Wembley. There were enough dogs kept in London to supply all of these stadiums with racing greyhounds – many of which were kept in the owners' backyards. One incident reported in *The Times* tells of a neighbour complaining of between twelve and sixteen greyhounds that were barking in a Shoreditch backyard. He had threatened to poison them if the owner did not get rid of them. However, trial evidence showed that the dogs were being provoked by children dangling a cat over the fence – and the case was dismissed.[168]

Greyhounds were sold at Aldridge's Repository in St Martin's Lane, with newspapers reporting good business at the first sale of the year in 1929 – 77 dogs were sold for a total of £1,457.[169] Although privately owned, the dogs were trained during the winter months at White City (Harringay may have had a similar set-up) by six well-known trainers who each took on 40 dogs to care for, and train, ready for the new racing season at Easter.[170] The young, untrained Wembley greyhounds were taken to the Hampshire countryside to chase wild hares to 'give them the hunting zest', and older dogs that had become 'track-tired' were also given the country air to reinvigorate them.[171]

Some believed that as long as the dogs retained their interest in chasing the mechanical hare, then the new sport of greyhound racing would become very popular with the public; especially once the dogs became 'as familiarly known as racehorses . . . [then] there will be a great intensification of enthusiasm'.[172]

The best known of the early greyhounds was Mick the Miller, who only raced at White City between 1929 and 1931, but won 51 races out of 68 (including two Derby races), winning £10,000 in prize money.[173] His speed records did not last long, but he is still considered one of the sport's greats because of his spirit and because the excitement which he generated helped to popularize the sport. On his death his body was gifted to the Natural History Museum; it is currently on display at the museum's sister site at Tring in Hertfordshire.

However, the sport was attacked by others as soon as it started for being 'a city casino for the poorer

Greyhound racing. An advertisement for 'Ladies Night' at White City Stadium, 1933.

classes'.[174] It not only encouraged thousands of women to participate in gambling, as they regarded dog racing as 'essentially feminine' because of the 'absence of cruelty' in the sport, but was also a 'school of juvenile gambling'.[175] 'Going to the dogs' encouraged dissolute practices and was also regarded as a poorer form of sport than horse racing. So much opposition was mounted against plans to hold greyhound racing at Crystal Palace, Alexandra Palace and Kennington Oval that they were abandoned.

However, defying the critics, by 1929 there were three other London greyhound tracks at Clapton, Wimbledon and West Ham. Even as late as 1958 there were fifteen London tracks, including Catford, Slough, Romford, Wandsworth, Dagenham and Walthamstow.

But attendance figures slowly dwindled and 1984 saw the closure of the White City track, followed in December 1998 by Wembley. Today Wimbledon Stadium is the only greyhound track left in London, with races held on Friday and Saturday evenings.

Other horse sports: jousting

Gambling and the love of blood sports did not wholly dictate the sports that Londoners enjoyed: there were also contests involving horses that provided the necessary thrills and spills to entertain the crowds.

Apart from betting on the 'running horses' at Smithfield, the medieval Londoner's passion for sporting horses extended to watching warhorses carry their riders during jousts. The earliest bouts were recorded in the reign of King Stephen (r. 1135–1141). Fitzstephen noted that every Sunday in Lent after lunch, 'a fresh swarm of young gentles' on chargers and 'steeds skilled in the contest . . . apt and schooled to wheel in circles round', go outside the City gates, possibly at Smithfield, to compete with 'the sons of ordinary citizens' armed with lances and shields.[176] The steel points of the lances were capped for the younger boys during these mimic battles, which trained them for warfare.[177] The horses were excited by events: 'their limbs tremble; they champ the bit; impatient of delay they cannot stand still'.[178] The jousts ended with men unseated, and others fleeing in terror at the sight of the charging horses.

However, another twelfth-century writer, Geoffrey of Monmouth, described the jousting contests in a rather more derogatory way in his *History of the Kings of Britain*: 'a game on horseback, making a show of fighting a battle, whilst dames and damsels looking from the top of the walls . . . do cheer them on'.[179] This was the spectacle that graced many pageants, and formalized jousting took on many romantic ideals – far removed from its initial role as warfare preparation. Only the richest, most powerful and most privileged people in society took part in jousting, because by paying to enter the contests they could, according to historian Ian Mortimer, 'prove themselves worthy of their status through public demonstrations of their courage, strength and skill'.[180]

Knights would ride into the tiltyard on richly ornamented horses, which were highly trained and known as destriers or Great Horses.[181] These were the strongest and finest warhorses, and equipment in the Royal Armouries at the Tower of London shows the horses to have been between 15 and 16 hands high – relatively small by today's standards.[182] Although the jousts were more controlled than those fought out in the fields by the young men, the sport was still extremely dangerous. Opposing knights rode towards each other at a fast canter, approaching left hand to left hand across a timber barrier called 'the tilt', trying to unseat each other with a direct blow from their levelled lances.

Mortimer estimates that a blow to the head from an opponent's capped lance would feel like being hit by a half-ton hammer. The force of impact would comprise a suit of armour weighing 80–100 pounds, a knight weighing 200 pounds who was seated on a high saddle on a destrier weighing more than 1,000 pounds, travelling at speeds of 40 miles an hour, and all this force hitting an area of a few square inches. If a knight was unable to fall off his horse, the impact would be fatal; if he fell awkwardly in heavy armour, further injury would also follow.[183] To win the favour of a lady, the knight had to unseat three challengers, then the lady would offer him her glove as a sign of betrothal.

There were several temporary tiltyards throughout medieval London. In 1331 the Cheapside tournament was held in the presence of Edward III – Stow noted that 'the stone pavement . . . [was] covered with sand, that the horses might not slide when they strongly set their feet to the ground'.[184] There was another yard on what is now Parliament Square, which was reserved for state tournaments. By Tudor times, the tournament was still in vogue and Henry VIII built a tiltyard at Whitehall Palace. It measured about 145 × 25 metres and saw many bouts. The traveller and writer Lupold Von Wedel in his *Journey through England and Scotland* described one tilt in 1584, which was an Accession Day tilt, held annually in Elizabeth I's court to celebrate her accession to the throne on November 17. The tournament lasted from noon to 5 pm, with spectators paying 12*d.* to get into the stands surrounding the Whitehall yard. The competitors entered the arena in pairs (each having paid several thousand pounds for the privilege), then rode against each other, 'breaking lances across the beam'.[185] Accession Day tilts continued in the reign of James I, and the last tilt was recorded in 1624, after which the Whitehall tiltyard was mainly used for animal baiting until 1660.

Polo

Another horse-related sport performed solely by the wealthy was polo. Brought to England from India, where the British Army played 'hockey on horseback', the first polo matches played in London were at the Lillie Bridge Grounds, West Brompton (near the present Stamford Bridge), from 1873 to 1875.[186] Polo was an exclusive amusement, mainly because of the costliness of the polo ponies – each of the eight

riders in a team used, and still use, at least four horses during a match as they tire quickly. According to *The Graphic* newspaper, which covered the first games, the ponies 'should be so full of vigour and vivacity as to sympathise thoroughly in the excitement of their riders, and yet ready to obey the least touch of the rein. Such animals, of course, command high prices.'[187] Polo's popularity as a spectator sport was limited as it cost half a crown to enter Lillie Bridge.

By 1874 polo was also being played at Hurlingham Park, near Putney Bridge, alongside the pigeon shooting. But the public was not allowed to see the sport as tickets were reserved for members. The Hurlingham (Polo) Club became renowned as 'the finest ground for polo in England', and games were typically played between the 1st Life Guards and the Royal Horse Guards, and the Lords and the Commons.[188] The rules of polo were formalized there in 1875, including the optimum height of the ponies at 14 hands high.[189] The public was eventually welcomed in 1927,[190] but the polo ground was turned into allotments as part of the Dig for Victory campaign of 1939. Polo only recently returned to Hurlingham Park in 2009 with the inaugural Polo in the Park event – three days of polo matches, with updated rules, open to the public, involving between five and eight international teams.

All the pageantry and splendour of a royal joust: Henry VIII jousting in the tiltyard he built at Greenwich, *c.* 1511.

Playing polo by electric light at the Ranelagh Club, 1880.

Hurlingham was not the only pre-war London polo venue: there was also the Ranelagh Club, which played at Barn Elms on the Putney side of the Thames (not far from Hurlingham), and the Roehampton Club. The Ranelagh Club was also famous for its pony racing, which was superseded by gymkhana events: there were obstacle races with a paper screen through which the competitors had to jump, egg and cup races, and bending through poles. One commentator stated that the gymkhana events were better than the pony racing and 'moreover is free from the racecourse influences that cannot well be kept apart from the other'.[191] However, pony racing did reappear, alongside the gymkhana.

Showjumping

After the day's polo matches had been completed at the Lillie Bridge Grounds in 1874, pony racing and 'leaping' contests were held.[192] The latter was not new to London audiences as this sport – in its loosest term – was the highlight of the Islington Horse Show (also known as the Metropolitan Horse Show) at the Agricultural Hall from 1864. Horses and ponies from around the country converged on London for this show.

The most popular show days for spectators were those dedicated to hurdle jumping, which played out after the 'monotonous parading of hunters, hacks, and ponies before the appointed judges'.[193] These classes involved the hunters jumping artificial gorse fences, five-barred gates and a water jump. They were judged on whether they cleared all the fences, and also on the horse and rider's jumping style – they were looking for fences cleared 'freely and in a picturesque style'.[194] But many of the horses were fazed by the intimidating atmosphere of their indoor surroundings. The crowds loved it when things went wrong, and it seemed this was what they waited for:

The refusals or mishaps of the various horses were received by the public with unbounded expressions of amusement and delight, while hearty applause was bestowed upon the skill of riders who took their horses cleverly over the fences, and upon the pluck and resolution of others, who, after hard and prolonged struggling, overcame their repugnance to face the hurdles.[195]

It was not only hunters that were made to jump these fences. Before the daily judging had begun, and also when it had finished, there was a

mad mêlée of rough-riders and 'pretty horse-breakers', who . . . have leave and licence, for the better entertainment of the public, to rush and scramble their unhappy horses over and through the revolving [turning when struck]

furze bushes which do duty at the Agricultural Hall for sporting fences.[196]

From 1890 electric lighting allowed jumping competitions to continue at the show into the evening,[197] and leaping contests were introduced for different sizes of pony and horse. The fences also became more garishly coloured and less natural looking, and the horses were increasingly bred to jump, rather than being hunters who had been hunting across the fields over real obstacles.[198] The timber and wall jumping contest was particularly popular, with entries having to jump a gate and wall, both of which were heightened until there was one winning clear. The last Islington Horse Show was held in 1895.

Audiences loved the thrills and spills of the showjumping event (back middle) at the Horse Show in the Agricultural Hall, 1866.

Leaping contests were also part of the Alexandra Palace Horse Show from 1873 to 1883, and the one-off horse show held at Olympia in 1887. Olympia was to become the host of the International Horse Show from 1907 when a leaping class was held. However, the formal sport of showjumping was not established until the British Show Jumping Association set out a formal structure and rules in 1925.

Professional showjumping at the Horse of the Year Show (HOYS) was staged every October from 1949 at Harringay Arena and then, after a decade, it moved to Wembley Arena before moving out of London and then into the NEC, Birmingham, after 40 years. This was the 'Champion of Champions' show, which included international showjumping and the Pony Club Mounted Games, which were (and still are) similar to the gymkhanas that once were held at Ranelagh (Polo) Club.

The first Olympia International Show Jumping Championships were held in 1972 just before Christmas; 400 horses and 800 riders took part and over 60,000 people came to watch. However, when the show first started, it was not just horses on show, but also racing camels. These unwieldy animals were paraded along Kensington High Street to promote the show. Today Olympia hosts the London International Horse Show.

London's connection with sporting horses continued with Greenwich Park welcoming the 2012 Olympians for dressage, cross-country and show-jumping events. Despite considerable local opposition to the site being used, horses eventually went ahead to tackle the portable cross-country jumps, which were made off-site and then installed[199] – one of the many restrictions on the horse events to prevent disruption to Greenwich Park users and the environment. Watching the riders tackle the cross-country course, Londoners could appreciate how their ancestors once watched aristocratic hunting parties jump ditches and hedges in the suburbs.

The Olympics brought much life back to the streets of London, especially in the East End, where once animals played a large role in entertaining the masses, not just in sporting contests but also by performing. These animals are next under the spotlight.

four

Animals as Entertainers: Performance, Peculiarity and Pressure

Performing animals, both domestic and exotic, were once a regular sight in London, with 'every street teem[ing] with incredibilities'.[1] From the Roman amphitheatre to the itinerant animal trainers of the early and late medieval periods, right up to the grand circuses that performed to packed theatres and halls, live animals have been used to entertain and delight Londoners, and even to provide generations with a frisson of danger as they watched powerful animals trained to perform on command. The variety of acts showed not only the trainers' ingenuity and imagination when devising performances for their animals, but also the large number of domestic and wild animals that were kept and trained in the city, although many were just passing through London with their foreign owners.

Performing street animals

The Roman amphitheatre would have been London's earliest place of entertainment. The oval arena was estimated to have been 70 metres long and 50 metres wide – large enough for Roman blood sports and chariot racing – but it is not clear whether animals actually performed there, or in the streets.

Perhaps the first animal trainers seen in London from pre-Norman times were the musical street entertainers – minstrels and jongleurs – who wandered the streets with their bears, monkeys, horses and cockerels. Contemporary illustrations from the thirteenth and fourteenth centuries reveal that these animals had been trained to perform human-like movements: bears would dance, tumble and pretend to be asleep, monkeys wearing conical hats would ride the bears like jockeys, horses would dance on their hind legs to the minstrel's pipe and tabor (a little drum about the size of a cap which was tapped with a small stick) and cockerels were trained to walk on stilts.[2] The entertainer would also fight mock battles with his horse, or hold up his tabor while his horse beat out a rhythm on it with its hind hooves.[3]

These early animal performers were mainly owned by foreigners who moved with their animals through London, performing on street corners, or wherever a crowd could be captivated. It was easy for animal trainers to cause a stir because there was a lack of entertainment which the poor could afford to see; an animal act may not always have been a novelty, but it was sure to entertain them for several minutes. Londoners conducted their lives, and businesses, on the streets – unlike today – and consequently London 'bustled', which meant that animals performed frequently during the day, but for seemingly little reward. These animals were also shown at London fairs to entertain the 'mob', but wealthier persons would also hire some of them to perform at their houses as after-dinner entertainment.

Thomas Frost's *The Old Showmen, and the Old London Fairs* (1875) noted that there were performing monkeys, horses and bears at Bartlemy Fair – or

Strolling entertainers moved about the capital in the 14th century – these horses have been taught several different tricks.

Bartholomew Fair – into the sixteenth century.[4] It was a three-day cloth fair until the early seventeenth century, when it became a more riotous two-week entertainment fest held every August. Ben Jonson in his play *Bartholomew Fayre* (1614) tells of 'dogs that dance the morris, and the hare o' the tabor'.[5] The animals were mainly trained to imitate the actions of men, which made their tricks all the more impressive – mere animals were magically elevated to acting like superior humans.

At the May Fair in 1707, showing in Pinkeman's Booth, were eight dancing dogs from Holland.[6] Hogarth's *Southwark Fair* (1733) portrays a dog dancing dressed in a cape, sword and hat, and holding a stick while his owner plays the bagpipes, and John Evelyn records seeing performing monkeys in 1660 at St Margaret's Fair in Southwark:

We saw also Monkeys and Apes dance and do other feats of activity on the high-rope, to admiration; They were gallantly clad *à la mode*, went upright, saluted the Company, bowling and pulling off their hats; They saluted one another

with as good grace as if instructed by a Dancing Master; They turned heels over head, with a basket having eggs in it, without breaking any: also with lighted Candles in their hands and on their head, without extinguishing them, and with vessels of water, without spilling a drop.[7]

Monkeys tumbling over chains or ropes must have been a fairly common source of entertainment even in medieval times: the monkeys were subject to an import duty, a source of income for the Exchequer, presumably because of the numbers imported into London.[8] Capuchin monkeys from South America were easily tamed, gentle and trainable. Although they were relatively scarce in the seventeenth century, they became common in the nineteenth century under the guise of the 'organ grinder's monkey', which would collect coins from the audience and generally amuse with its antics.[9]

Animal entertainers escaped the restrictions placed on regular theatres during the Commonwealth, but were banned from performing in the streets during the Plague of 1665. After resuming their acts, the animals seemed to begin to give more elaborate performances. Frost noted that there were more exotic sights in 1778: a 'foreigner' exhibited serpents dancing on silken ropes to the sound of music at Bartholomew Fair, and 'Arab and Hindoo' performers exhibited snakes dancing on the ground.[10] One home-grown snake performer was the snake swallower interviewed by Henry Mayhew around 70 years later.[11] The man revealed several tricks of his trade: he paid a halfpenny to youngsters to catch the 18-inch-long snakes in the woods outside London, then gave a man a shilling to cut out their stingers (which were under the tongue). He then scraped the slime off the snakes with his fingernails and finally used a cloth to clean them up – apparently slimy snakes tasted awful, but clean snakes only 'draw's the roof of the mouth a bit. It's a roughish taste. The scales rough you a bit when you draw them up.'[12] To swallow a snake he would hold it by the tail with his fingernails, then pinch it slightly to make it bolt into his mouth. It would travel about 2 inches down

Capuchin monkeys were the monkey of choice for the touring organ grinder. Edouard Klieber, *The Travelling Organ-grinder*, 1842, oil on canvas.

Dancing bears were a common sight in the suburbs of Victorian London, as in this photograph of 1900.

his throat, then curl the rest of its body into a ball in his mouth.

Dancing bears were the 'cheaper diversion . . . of the vulgar' and could be seen about London 'jauntily trip[ping] to the light tune of the Caledonian jig'.[13] They retained their place on the streets, with the 1810s being a particularly good decade for performers, and were even invited to gentlemen's houses to entertain the guests, according to a drum and pipe player Mayhew interviewed.[14] He played the fife and tabor with Michael, the Italy Bear. Michael was actually the name of the man who brought the bear, called Jenny, from abroad. Jenny was chained and muzzled and performed with a monkey called Billy, which was dressed as a soldier and sat on her while they walked the streets, although she was not keen on Billy sitting on her head, which was part of their performance. Michael would beat her with a

'large mopstick' if she was 'obstropolous'. Jenny's special trick was to turn somersaults in a tight circle around a stick, then to dance around it. She was never baited by butcher's bulldogs, although offers were made.

For all this work, Jenny was fed on bread and boiled potatoes or carrots, all in half a bucket of water. She was never fed meat, as Michael thought, or knew from past experience, that this would make her savage. Billy fared a little better: he was fed nuts, apples, gingerbread and anything else Michael could find. Besides Jenny and Billy, the troupe consisted of two dancing dogs, which Jenny particularly disliked. They jumped through hoops and danced on their hind legs. Unlike many street performers, Michael's animals made him plenty of money in London, especially in the West End. He took over £12 a week for himself.

Bears were still performing on London streets into the late nineteenth century, by which time they were becoming a public nuisance. A court case of 1898 recorded that a child was killed after a horse, which was pulling the brougham he was in, took fright at seeing a bear being led down Marylebone Road and bolted, overturning the carriage and throwing the boy out of it. It was reported that horses became fearful even upon smelling a bear. One juror thought that there should be an alteration of the law to prevent bears being taken about the crowded streets of London.[15]

Prosecution of bear owners for creating chaos in the streets was not new: in 1869 a newspaper report entitled 'The Performing Bear Nuisance' told how crowds watching a bear were repeatedly causing obstructions in traffic.[16] The police had to take the French performer and his 'frolicsome' bear into custody. Eventuallly, after much mishap, the bear was lodged in London Zoo while the owners spent a month in Coldbath Fields Prison.

One particular bear was 'a familiar acquaintance of most of the London police magistrates' in 1891–2.[17] He was a small Pyrenean bear about three years old and wore a steel muzzle on his nose, which was 'of apparently needless severity'. While the owner, 'a genial Provencal' who shared his bed with the bear, was in the dock receiving his dismissal with a caution, the bear would be in the police station reception area wooing the constables with his 'endearing ways'. These hardened policemen were so moved by his performance that they made a collection for him before he and his owner were released. However, street children took advantage of the bear's gentle nature and would goad him.

There were other mishaps: two Frenchmen nearly drowned after they took their performing bear to the Thames near Hammersmith Bridge to have a drink. The bear decided to wade into the water and play games – standing on its hind legs and bobbing its nose and eyes in and out of the water. Thoroughly enjoying its freedom, the bear had no intention of being caught and it took a waterman to eventually collect the men and tow the bear to the bank, where a great crowd had assembled. The bear 'now showed itself perfectly amenable to discipline, and marched off quietly with its masters'.[18]

Cruelty on the streets

Like all performing animals, the street animals were trained away from the public gaze and many different ploys and devices were used to curb their natural instincts and make them perform unnatural acts. Because of their assumed inferior status to humans, it was quite normal for many trainers to treat their animals as though they were without emotions or intelligence, and this resulted in some brutal treatment being meted out to the animals.

One performer who owned a 'Happy Family' outfit told Mayhew how his animals had been trained – in a kind manner – but hinted at the methods employed by some of his less scrupulous contemporaries.[19] This 'Happy Family', one of two in London at the time, consisted of having animals that were supposed to be sworn enemies living peacefully together in one cage: it was more of a marvel than a performance. It did not pay well, although crowds would gather to see the exhibit. This man owned two monkeys, three cats, two dogs, sixteen rats, six starlings, two hawks, a jackdaw, three owls, a magpie, two guinea pigs and one rabbit, which all lived in the same cage during the day. At night they all slept in their owner's room out of the cage – they used to sleep together in the cage in the backyard, but someone stole a monkey so he brought them indoors. Although the man did not give away his trade secrets to Mayhew, he did deny using certain methods:

People have a notion that we use drugs to train a happy family; they have said to me, 'It's done with opium,' but, sir, believe me, there is no drugs used at all: it's only patience, and kindness, and petting them that is used, and nothing else of any sort . . . It's a secret what I used [on a ferret], so I can't mention it, but it's the simplest thing in the world. It's not drawing their teeth out, or operating on them . . . I'm fond of my little stock, and always was from a child of dumb animals. I'd a deal sooner that anybody hurt me than any of my favourites.[20]

Some animals were not so lucky, and no mercy was shown to them even during their performances; the early viewing public did not seem to be upset by the brutality.

In the nineteenth century, when sensibility to animal suffering was surfacing, cruelty was hidden from the public, yet was quite commonplace. At Bartholomew Fair in 1828, 'The Pig-Faced Lady' was exhibited. But the 'Lady' was, in fact,

nothing but a bear, its face and neck carefully shaved, while the back and top of its head were covered by a wig, ringlets, cap, and artificial flowers all in the latest fashion. The animal was then securely tied in an upright position into a large armchair, the cords being concealed by the shawl, gown, and other parts of a lady's fashionable dress.[21]

Unlikely cage companions: 'The Happy Family' from the *Illustrated London News*, 1852, after a painting by T. Earl.

The RSPCA had been bringing cruelty charges against owners of performing bears since the early 1880s. One case in 1892 was against a Frenchman who had been mistreating a bear. He had made it perform by jagging it with a chain attached to a ring in its upper lip, making it cry out in pain. He was doing it for the real owner who was currently in prison for ill-treating the same bear. The employee was sent to jail for a fortnight of hard labour. After the court case, the bear was taken to the veterinary yard of Mr Thrale in George Street, W1, where stray dogs were normally taken. The bear was evidently dangerous and unapproachable – he had already broken a window – and there was a fear for public safety, so he was killed using a bullet into the brain after several unsuccessful attempts were made to inject a syringe of prussic acid into his open mouth.[22]

What with RSPCA inspections, convictions for illegal obstructions and the death of the child previously mentioned, it was not long before bears left London for good. One incident with an animal known as the Royal Bear also paved the way for a ban on the general public performing or 'engaging' with wild animals on the stage. This bear had been touring London in 1891 and wrestled with any man who bet 10s. that he could overthrow it. While it was at Sebright Music Hall on Coate Street, E2, one wrestling bout led to the death of a man later in the London Hospital. The coroner suggested that this sort of interaction with a wild animal was bound to end in disaster.[23]

Generally it was difficult to make a living from showing animals in the streets; it had never been particularly lucrative. In 1801 Joseph Strutt remarked that 'the miserable appearance of their [performing bears'] masters plainly indicates the scantiness of the contributions they receive on these occasions'.[24] And in the mid-nineteenth century Mayhew interviewed an 'old, ill and poor Italian' who owned three dancing dogs.[25] Originally he had arrived from Palma with ten dogs, but over the years some had died. He was kind to his animals, which he dressed in jackets and hats, and played music while they danced and jumped over sticks and through hoops. These dogs performed from 9 am to 7 or 8 pm, dancing between twenty and 40 times a day; and for all this effort, the performances were rewarded with only two or three shillings, and sometimes nothing at all.

Animal oddities

It was not only performing animals that slogged through the streets and exhibited at the fairs, but also the *lusus naturae*: unusual or deformed animal exhibits. These unfortunate curiosities of nature were marketed and gawped at from Elizabethan times.[26] Their popularity was astounding across all classes.

Many of the animals were shown at the London fairs. Ben Jonson, in his *Bartholomew Fayre*, writes of 'the bull with the five legs and two pizzles (he was a calf at Uxbridge Fair, two years agone)'.[27] In 1790 two rams were shown at Bartholomew; one had a single horn in its forehead, like a unicorn, and the other had six legs.[28] And in 1803 a two-headed calf, a double-bodied calf and a 'surprising large fish, the Nondescript' were exhibited.[29] In 1825 a four-year-old thoroughbred chestnut mare called Mabe was on show. She had seven legs, six of which were shod.[30]

Other curiosities were exhibited throughout the city, such as the little Turkey Horse which was only 2 feet high and 'kept in a box'. Shown in the early 1700s, it was accompanied by two black dwarves, and could be seen at the Mews Gate, Charing Cross, by her Majesty's permission.[31] Also in Charing Cross was another animal that caused a stir: the astonishing 'double cow'. For one shilling, the public could see one normal cow, but from the middle of her back there grew out the rear end of another cow. She could be milked from both her udders. It was reported that she was gentle and healthy enough, and it was said that she travelled 20 miles a day.[32]

Other 'oddities' were essentially frauds, but they still made their owners rather wealthy. There was the 'Talking Fish', which turned out to be a female sea lion who uttered two deep sounds like 'Mama' and 'Papa', and the Morocco Black Cat belonging to one Colonel Katterfelto, which he showed at 24 Piccadilly in 1783.[33] He was supposed to be able to 'extract gold from the body' of this cat, and it would also appear with a long tail which would miraculously disappear, then reappear. It was a sleight of hand, but Katterfelto was said to have won £3,000 in bets when he was in Piccadilly. Some reckoned that his cat was the Devil itself and he felt he had to mention in his advertising that this was not true.[34] The cat was later snatched from him in Manchester in 1790.

'Learned animals'

Learned animals were in a different class from the itinerant performing bears and dogs already mentioned. These were animals which appeared to use the human quality of intelligence to perform several feats of skill, such as arithmetic. In reality, many of these acts were fraudulent, but they were lapped up by audiences anyway.

The earliest recorded and probably most exalted learned animal was a small bay horse called Marocco or Morocco,[35] who wowed the London public on his arrival in 1592 or 1593. He was exhibited by William Banks, a man revered for his ability to train Marocco to perform incredible feats. Walter Raleigh says of Banks in his *History of the World* (1614): 'If Banks had lived in older times, he would have shamed all the enchanters in the world; for whosoever was most famous among them could never master or instruct any beast as he did.'[36]

Banks's training method was far from black magic. He had bought Marocco as a foal and had spent every minute of the day with the horse training him and developing a close bond. He used only kindness and

patience as rewards, and as punishment he did not feed Marocco his favourite loaves of bread. Banks revealed that all Marocco's 'powers' were directed by him through hidden signs made through his body or tone of voice, claiming that 'it is a rule in the nature of horsses, that they have an especiall regard to the eye, face and countenaunce of their keepers.'[37] Maracco's 'intelligence' was therefore learned behaviour cemented by positive reinforcement.

While in London they lodged at the La Belle Sauvage Inn on Ludgate Hill and their performances were given in an arena near Gracious Street (later Gracechurch Street); it was an exhibition reserved for the wealthier Londoners to view.

Marocco was particularly well known for one trick in which Banks ordered him to bow to the queen of England, which he did with great reverence, scraping his hoof on the ground. Banks then told him to do the same to the king of Spain, who was at that time Britain's greatest enemy. Marocco refused and when Banks insisted, the horse neighed furiously, bared his teeth and kicked out behind. For the finale, he chased Banks out of the arena. An early trick that was later pulled, due to it upsetting the ladies in the audience, involved the horse drinking a huge bucket of water and then relieving himself when Banks ordered. Another scene intended to embarrass the ladies was to pull out of the audience a pure, virginal woman and then a harlot of the streets; whether this was Banks's or Marocco's decision is unknown, but it caused much hilarity among the male members of the audience. The bawdy animal performance was perfect for the times and wealthier Londoners flocked to see the entertainment – it was so different from the blood sports they were used to.

Banks and Marocco left to tour the provinces from 1595 to 1597 and when they retuned to London they found it awash with other competing animal acts, such as Mr Holden's dancing camel, which was installed on London Bridge. But Banks was determined to regain

Marocco and William Banks performing in London, early 1590s.

his former pre-eminence. St Paul's Cathedral was at that time London's centre point, albeit somewhat neglected after a lightning strike in 1561 had damaged the tower. In February 1601 Banks led his horse up more than 1,000 steps of the spiral staircase out onto the cathedral's rotting roof. More than 520 feet above the ground, Marocco went through his dancing routine. Crowds swarmed on the ground, looking up to see the performance. Afterwards Marocco nimbly descended the steps and was greeted with rapturous applause.

Banks was a pioneer of his 'art' and many other animal performers followed in his wake when he and Morocco set off for France in 1608. But the noble and respected horse did not corner the learned animal market. The really impressive animals were those that were believed to be either too stupid to train, or too timid to appear on stage – unlike the horse, which had been a human companion trained for use in war, agriculture and travel since at least 4000 BC. Hence the sensational reports in April 1785 of 'The Wonderful Hare … the greatest curiosity ever shown in public'.[38]

It was exhibited around London and even appeared at the Sadler's Wells theatre, where it stood on its hind legs and beat a tambourine. Also on the same bill were the Singing Duck, the Dancing Dogs and the Learned Pig. A Mr Nicholson owned this pig,[39] a black boar, which originally was only shown at No. 55, Charing Cross. The interest in the animal was immense. The pig had been taught to pick up letters and numbers written upon pieces of card and to arrange them into words, the answers to mathematical questions or the time on a watch. Although the pig was able to perform with great aplomb, the reality of training him was a difficult task for Nicholson and the pig could still be exasperating – he caused embarrassment to Nicholson when he attended a private exhibition and the pig refused to answer when asked how many honest gentlemen were in the audience, or how many were free from mortgages. Nicholson had to apologize and 'in a confounded passion whipped his pig down the stairs'.[40] The pig was also the cause of some disruption when it was engaged at Sadler's Wells. The human performers on the same bill were so disgruntled to be on stage with a pig that they 'neglected their business',[41] and when the manager remonstrated with them they demanded that the pig be removed. The manager let them go and kept the pig – presumably he was less trouble and drew the desired audience.

Nicholson walked away a wealthy man after his time in Charing Cross, as he allegedly made over £2,000,[42] but the pig was worked hard during this time. He performed four shows a day, every day of the week. The caricature *The Wonderful Pig* (1785) by Thomas Rowlandson shows the rotund Mr Nicholson and the black, rather thin pig. When the anonymous author of *London Unmask'd; or the New Town Spy* (1785) asked Nicholson why the pig was so slim, he replied that 'a plenitude in the belly would diminish his pupil's adherence to discipline'.[43] The pig left London in September 1785, then returned in March 1786 to

Toby the Sapient Pig with Nicholas Hoare, 1817.

the Lyceum Theatre in the Strand. Again, he was a great success and the poet Robert Southey (1774–1843), who was Poet Laureate for 30 years, commented that the Learned Pig was 'a far greater object of admiration to the English nation than ever was Sir Isaac Newton'.[44] The Learned Pig may have died in 1788.

There was not another learned pig as famous as Nicholson's until Toby, the Sapient Pig, arrived in London in 1817. He was owned by one Nicholas Hoare, who marketed Toby well, showing him at Bartholomew Fair, Spring Gardens (off The Mall) and in Fleet Street, and even writing Toby's autobiography, which sold for a shilling. There was a succession of pigs of this name shown at Bartholomew Fair – it is doubtful that they were all the same pig – but the poet Thomas Hood immortalised the plight of all performing pigs in *The Lament of Toby, The Learned Pig* (1820):

Oh, why are pigs made scholars of?
It baffles my discerning,

What griskins, fry, and chitterlings
Can have to do with learning.

Alas! my learning once drew cash,
But public fame's unstable,
So I must turn a pig again
And fatten for the table.[45]

There was competition for Toby and Mr Hoare in the form of 'The Celebrated Dog, Munito', owned by Signor Castelli. Having received plaudits in Paris, Munito was shown at Savile House on the north side of Leicester Square.[46] There had been previous learned dogs in London since the mid-1700s, such as 'The New Chien Savant, or Learned English Dog', which was exhibited in Half-moon Court, near Ludgate. This dog was a border collie that could spell 'Pythagoras' with its cardboard letters, knew the Greek alphabet, answered questions in Latin, English and sacred history, and performed various acrobatic tricks.

Then came Munito, a large white dog resembling a poodle with a brown spot over his left eye. He was very popular on both the public and private entertainment circuit, and in 1817 Castelli had to rent larger rooms at 23 New Bond Street in Mayfair. His many tricks included picking out a card chosen by a member of the audience from a pack spread out on the ground in a circle, palmistry (where he would answer questions after looking at a person's palm) and dominoes. Munito was a regular sight on the streets of London and also in Green Park, where Castelli, dressed in his usual shabby clothes, would chat in Italian to Munito as they walked. In 1818, while walking through Green Park, Munito helped to save the life of a lady who was drowning in the lake, for which heroic efforts he and Castelli were awarded bravery medals from the Royal Humane Society (founded in 1774). Munito returned to London three times and his final shows were held at 1 Leicester Square, where he remained until June 1819.

Charles Dickens, writing in *All the Year Round*, revealed the secret of Munito's apparent intelligence after he had watched him perform twice.[47] Castelli would mark the card he wished Munito to choose with aniseed oil, which he kept in his waistcoat pocket – Munito's tricks principally relied on his sense of smell. Dickens also applied this principle to the performing Java sparrow that would peck at a deck of cards to pull out a card chosen by the audience: the cards each had a corner covered in sweet wafer paste and this was exposed by the showman to get the sparrow to pick out the required card. The same deceit was probably also practised by a troupe of 'Oiseaux Merveilleux' (Wonderful Birds) which appeared at Almack's Assembly Rooms, King Street, St James's, in 1852; they told the time, solved arithmetic problems in their heads, read minds and told fortunes, along with 'Exercises in Orthography' (spelling) and 'Tours d'Escamotage' (sleight of hand).[48]

But in the same article, Dickens also stated that he had seen cruelty used on stage to make animals perform correctly. Jacko was a large ape whose speciality was trick riding: '[after a mistake] we noticed that poor Jacko looked frightened, and received a sly cut of the whip; after a successful feat, he had a little sweetmeat from the pocket of the master of

An early drawing of Munito on his first visit to London in 1817.

the ring.' But this method of training had already been exposed to the public; in 1785 the *Morning Herald* said that

the increase of *learned animals* of the *brute* species, as horses, dogs, pigs, &c. must touch the feelings of every humane heart, when it is known that the tricks they perform are taught by the most excruciating torture.[49]

Theatrical acts

Aside from learned animals, another popular entertainment, especially in the music and variety halls, involved companies of animals acting out historic scenes of combat and warfare. In 1753 the Italian master Ballard installed his company of performing dogs and monkeys – known as The Animal Comedians – at the New Theatre, Haymarket, performing *Mrs Midnight's Oratory*. Their antics were meant as a supplementary attraction to the musical entertainments. The finale of their performance was a battle enacted between monkeys, which were defending the town walls with guns, and dogs bearing swords, which besieged the town. Amid smoke and noise from the fired guns, the dogs climbed up ladders, with several falling off into the ditch, to mount the ramparts and capture the town and raise their flag. As the smoke cleared, the monkeys and dogs 'sang' *God Save the King* together and bowed to the audience.[50]

The banner was passed on in 1775 to the dozen acting birds, probably canaries, which were shown at Breslaw's Exhibition Room, Cockspur Street, opposite the Haymarket. Joseph Strutt described their show in detail, in which they were dressed as soldiers and acted out the execution of a deserter by firing a cannon.[51]

Even the Theatre Royal, Drury Lane, succumbed to the obvious appeal of theatrical animals, and in December 1803 staged one of the first 'Dog Dramas',

The Caravan, which made a star out of a Newfoundland dog called Carlo that belonged to a neighbouring eating house. The climax of the show was Carlo jumping from a rock into a large tank of water to rescue a drowning child: 'The effect literally electrified the audience', said the manager, and the show made £360 during its near 100-night run.[52] In 1809 Carlo even published his own autobiography: *The Life of the Famous Dog Carlo*. Other 'Dog Dramas' followed at Sadler's Wells, Covent Garden Theatre (now the Royal Opera House), the Royal Pavilion in Marylebone, the Italian Opera House and the Alhambra Theatre, Leicester Square. These dramas starred trained dogs – such as Mr Cony's dogs Bruin and Hector – who performed either as heroes, or as assistants to the human hero, in attacking wrongdoers or rescuing victims, and received 'thunders of applause' for their efforts.[53] But there were 'mischievous wag[s] in the gallery who chose to throw a piece of meat on to the stage at some crisis in the action of the drama',[54] or imitate the call of a cat, just to cause trouble.

As unlikely as it seems, performing fleas were a known phenomenon. One of the most famous acts was that of Louis Bertolotto, 'The Industrious Fleas', exhibited in 1833 in Regent Street. He used human fleas, because animal fleas were not lively or strong enough,[55] to go through a performance of the siege of Antwerp with pin-sized cannons, a ballroom scene with four waltzing dancers and an orchestra of twelve, and a mail coach in harness. The act also included a single huge flea pulling a tiny [flea] elephant with a howdah on its back filled with flea passengers.[56] Mr Bertolotto had a workshop in Marylebone Street, which was visited by Charles Dickens for *Household Words* in 1856:

I entered and saw fleas, here, fleas there, fleas everywhere; no less than sixty fleas imprisoned and sentenced to hard labour for life. All of them were luckily chained, or fastened in some way or other, so that escape and subsequent feasting upon visitors was impossible ... [although] they have their supper, and in the morning also their breakfasts, upon the hand of their owner – sometimes he has nearly all his fleas on the backs of his hands at the same moment, all biting and sucking away.[57]

Much later, in 1885, Vidcoo's performing Russian fleas entered the Westminster Aquarium (the Aq, as it was colloquially known). These fleas of burden were all chained in brass collars, and wore flea harnesses. Vidcoo's exhibition also hinted at the first process in the training of fleas: they were chained by the leg to gradually remove their natural 'jumping propensities'.[58]

The Aq was another venue that used animal theatricals to entertain the visitors. In 1879 Senor Ortega and the bull Ligero was one of these sideshows. Bullbaiting had been outlawed in Britain since 1835, but Ligero was a huge bull trained to perform a mock bullfight so that no harm would come to his master. One newspaper stated that he was 'tame almost to stupidity' and would mildly retaliate when Ortega and his assistants tried to make him angry by throwing cloths over his eyes.[59]

Other acts at the Aq included Mlle Paula, with her snakes, crocodiles and alligators, and Mlle Orama, who wrestled with a huge bear.[60]

Musical acts

With street acts perennially popular, and some of them making quite significant sums of money, more ambitious animal trainers saw an opportunity to bring their acts to a more cultivated audience. Musical acts, in particular, had become more elaborate by the mid-eighteenth century and had moved into private rooms. In 1758 the 'Cat's Opera', announced by the famous animal trainer Samuel Bisset, arrived in the Haymarket alongside a trick horse, dog and monkeys:

'Bisset's pupils, furred and feathered, were regarded as one of the most wonderful exhibitions ever witnessed', stated Thomas Frost.[61] For this particular act, he had taught three cats to strike dulcimers with their paws to produce musical tunes while miaowing an accompaniment.[62] Cats, by nature (and indeed reputation) being solitary, sensitive and independent, were known to be unsuitable for this type of activity – so the entertainment was thought a marvel of training skill. Bisset cleared £1,000 after a few performances. [63]

Signor Capelli of Tuscany exhibited another troupe of cats in 1829. Alongside their labours of working a rice grinder, hammering on an anvil and drawing a bucket up and down in a well, they could also ring bells. They took up residency at 248 Regent Street, and their performance delighted a correspondent from the *Literary Gazette*:

> It is therefore a pleasure to us to see them [cats] raised in the scale of intellect, and again placed, by their cultivated abilities, in that station of respect which they seem not to have enjoyed since they were worshipped in ancient Egypt, or were, owing to their sagacity, the sworn companions of old witches in our own country.[64]

However, the reviewer continued in terms which today are regarded as pretty unpleasant, referring to one of the cats – a 'jet-black and maternal-looking negress' – who seemed to 'neither possess the intellect, sensibility, nor disposition to labour, of her red-and-white associates'.[65]

Other, more unlikely animals were also taught to sing, such as the singing mouse that appeared in 1843 at the Cosmorama Rooms, Regent Street. This mouse was reported to warble 'incessantly' for a quarter of an hour; 'its notes are low but clear, and not unlike that of the nightingale'.[66]

These unusual acts were still attracting audiences in the London music halls during the 1890s, when

The original 'Singing Mouse' and an advertisement for a rival mouse that was exhibited in a hairdresser's on the Strand in 1847, which customers could view for free.

'Mr Lavater's Dog Orchestra' took to the stage. This orchestra consisted of six mongrels, dressed in sumptuous costumes, playing popular musical tunes on the drums, violin, trombone and cymbals – the drumsticks and bows were attached to their paws with bracelets. Mr Lavater revealed in the *Strand Magazine* that he used 'curs' (mongrels) because they were cheap and easily replaced, and he told of their stage debut in Holland to demonstrate that training these dogs was not straightforward:

> They came out reluctantly . . . dazed by the glare of the footlights. When they *were* out, they sat there looking helplessly at each other as if to say: 'What on earth are we doing here?'

Then they did wrong things at wrong moments. Prince fell over his big drum. The others got up and tore aimlessly about the stage, scared by the trailing of their instruments behind them; and to crown all Jack, the trombone 'man', fell into the (human) orchestra. My Dutch audience were hysterical with merriment, and even my wife, who stood in the wings, couldn't help laughing, in spite of her vexation and dismay.[67]

Astley's: the beginnings of the circus

By the beginning of the nineteenth century there was one place in London that every visitor was encouraged to visit to see performing horses: Astley's

Amphitheatre. Back in the eighteenth century, this London landmark was the birthplace of the circus.[68]

Daring acts of horsemanship by skilled horsemen and women had been a London phenomenon before Astley's was established, including Thomas Johnson who, in 1758, was known as the Irish Tartar because the Tartars were then renowned horsemen. Johnson rode on one, two or three horses at full speed and 'even rode the single horse, standing on his head as the phrase is; but this posture giving pain to the spectators he discontinues it'[69] – it took him eleven years to learn this trick. Johnson performed in a field adjoining the Three Hats inn in Islington.

The financial rewards for these performers were substantial: Price, who was probably Johnson's instructor, amassed over £14,000 by performing at home and abroad. Another celebrated rider was Daniel Wildman, who performed an extraordinary show, as reviewed in 1772 by the *Daily Advertiser*:

[He] rides standing upright, one foot on the saddle and the other on the horse's neck, with a curious mask of bees on his face. He also rides standing up on the saddle with the bridle in his mouth, and, by firing a pistol, makes one part of the bees mount over a table and the other part swarm in the air and return to their proper places again.[70]

Debate raged about how Wildman managed not to get stung by the bees; in fact, he carefully held the queen bee in his hand so the swarm was contented.

A young ex-military man named Philip Astley (1742–1814) admired these performances of horsemanship and decided to set up in competition; but Astley tried something different and, in doing so, he invented the circus. In 1768 he set up what he termed a Riding School in a field called Halfpenny Hatch, near the present Waterloo station. It was a piece of ground enclosed by a flimsy fence and the ring was uncovered so that on wet evenings there were few in the audience. He performed a series of twenty daring military manoeuvres on horseback with the odd sword and pistol trick thrown in for good measure.[71]

Astley dressed in full military uniform, and performed on a dark bay stallion known as 'The Spanish Horse' or 'The Gibralter Charger', who had been gifted to him by General Elliott after he had been honourably discharged from the cavalry after fighting in the German War.[72] This horse was with Astley's for 42 years and retired after over 30 years of entertaining the public. He could perform all sorts of tricks, such as taking off his own saddle, washing his own feet in a bucket of water and grooming himself, but could also perform moves like the piaffe (trotting on the spot) in time to music, with fireworks exploding around him.[73] The stallion remained in the Astley stables on retirement, where he was given two loaves of bread a day, along with cakes, carrots, apples and anything else his adoring audience left him. When he finally died, in the care of Mr Davies (a subsequent owner of Astley's), his skin was tanned and converted into a drum skin.[74]

Astley purchased a second horse, called Billy, from Smithfield. He generally got his trick horses from this market, saying that he cared 'little for shape, make, or colour; temper was the only consideration',[75] and rarely paid more than £5. Billy was a great favourite with audiences, being as 'playful as a kitten with those he knew, and deeply versed in all the learning of the circus. Billy could fire off pistols, take a tea-kettle off a blazing fire, lay the cloth, arrange cups and saucers, and invite the clown to tea. All agreed that he could do everything but talk.'[76]

Billy was parted from Astley after the groom hired to care for Billy borrowed him for private exhibition in an attempt to get himself out of debt, but ended up being thrown into the Fleet Prison. Billy was sold at auction to pay the groom's debts. Two of Astley's riders found Billy by chance three years later; he was drawing a cart in Whitechapel. They bought him at a 'very moderate price' and he continued at the circus until he died of old age, 'universally respected and regretted'.[77]

It seems that Astley preached patient and kind training of horses. He was reputedly the 'best horse-tamer of his time, and as a judge of what may be called "trick horse-flesh", he has perhaps never been equalled'.[78] However, towards his two-legged employees Astley displayed a quick temper and was 'peremptory of speech and rude of manner'.[79] As he had great enthusiasm and energy for his business, he expected the same from his employees.

The business grew when he moved his horses to a timber yard at the foot of Westminster Bridge, in Stangate Street, Lambeth, in 1769 (now the Florence Nightingale Museum). Again, the venue comprised a ring open to the elements and canvas-covered seats. Astley's wife Patty now joined him during performances and he performed plenty more tricks, including

> riding two horses at one time, with one foot on the saddle, and taking a flingy leap over the bar, putting his toe in his mouth, and taking another leap, riding two horses with one foot on each saddle, without the bridle-rein and in this attitude, plays a tune on the fife.[80]

In 1772 a rival circus opened at Blackfriars Bridge, owned by Charles Hughes, who had the previous season been employed at Astley's. The Hughes's Riding School, as it was known, spurred Astley to broaden his performances: Daniel Wildman's 'Exhibition of Bees' was signed and Mr and Mrs Astley's five-year-old son John performed in public for the first time – he could ride on two horses.[81] At the start of the 1773 Season Astley renamed his establishment Astley's British Riding-School, but it was soon closed by the Surrey Magistrates as the venue was unlicensed.[82] Hughes's venue was also closed down

and never reopened, unlike Astley's, which reappeared in 1775 with additional entertainment, such as 'lofty tumbling' and 'Mrs Astley's surprising performances with the Bees'.[83] In early 1779 Astley changed the name again, this time to Astley's Amphitheatre Riding House, and Repository for Sound Horses, and roofed over his ring so that he could now perform by candle-light and during the winter.

The rivalry with Hughes erupted again in 1782 when Hughes built a permanent building called the Royal Circus and Equestrian Philharmonic Academy in St George's Fields, Southwark. Hughes's partner, the dramatist and composer Charles Dibdin (c. 1745–1814), introduced the 'equestrian drama' to London, or, as he wrote in his memoirs:

> I therefore proposed to have a stage, on which might be represented spectacles, each to terminate with a joust or a tilting match, or some grand object so managed as to form a novel and striking *coup de théâtre*, and that the business of the stage and the ring might be united.[84]

Aware of the competition, Astley had his own building remodelled by adding a stage, two tiers of boxes, a pit and a gallery. The domed roof was painted on the inside with branches and leaves, giving rise to the nickname The Royal Grove. This new building attracted a new audience, including the do-everything, go-everywhere Horace Walpole (1717–1797), and Astley's company received glowing reviews in the newspapers:

> Such Horsemanship [at Astley's] as we were yesterday evening witness to would, in the age of darkness and superstition, have been set down as nothing else but as feats of an infernal nature; instigated by the *Devil*, and performed by his *Imps*![85]

Besides the horse performers, Astley began to employ a wider selection of acts to keep his audiences amazed and entertained, such as the Dancing Dogs from France and Italy; the monkey General Jackoo from Paris (already mentioned by Dickens) who, among other things, danced on a tight rope; and the 'Gigantic Spanish Pig' ridden by a monkey.[86]

Astley's: horse spectaculars

When Astley's burned to the ground for the second time in 1803,[87] the Amphitheatre was again re-modelled. This time it was built to allow equestrian spectacles or 'hippodrama' to entertain the 2,500-seater venue. Now under the management of Philips's son John and Mr Davis, the theatre was endowed with a 130-foot-wide stage – the largest in England. The stage was built to withstand the weight and stress of the galloping horses and flying carriages that crossed it every night.

The chivalric hippodrama bought in huge profits for Astley's: *The Blood-red Knight* in 1810 was the best-selling horse spectacle, making a profit of £18,000.[88] Astley's also performed burlettas, short comical plays or pantomimes in which one or more horses performed. One of the favourites was the *Life and Death of the High-mettled Racer*, beautifully described in *Chambers's Edinburgh Journal* in 1835:

[The horse] appeared in the first scene as a racer, in all the life and vigour common to that high-bred animal, impatient of the rein, and champing on the bit till he started. In the next scene he appeared as a hunter, expressing his eagerness by pawing the ground, erecting his ears, and snorting, till he was off to the full cry of the hounds. Next, he appeared in harness as a post-horse, aged and fatigued, standing with knees bent and lowered head and when mounted, he went off with all the truth of such a reduced state.

He then appeared drawing a sand-cart, in a situation of positive decrepitude, with his head down, his lips dropped, enduring the seeming harsh treatment of an unfeeling master, till he finally dropped and died. You saw him stretched out with sharp angular projecting bones, parts of his hide galled, and his bare ribs boldly portrayed on his miserable sides. He lies thus, a most affecting spectacle to the pitying audience, and is about to be consigned to one of those men who purchase dying and dead horses for the sale of their skins. But, by a *coup de théâtre*, the once high-mettled racer is happily saved from this conclusion to his career. A magician enters, and, after some amusing jugglery, raises the animal to life and vigour. His skin instantaneously assumes its original gloss, his sores disappear, his bones cease to be visible, and he gallops off the stage amidst the plaudits of a thousand hands.[89]

This burletta included racehorses racing from the rear of the stage through the railed-off audience pit, and a fox hunt complete with fox and hounds played out at full speed. It was apparently so realistic that the audience joined in with the 'tally-ho' of the huntsmen.[90] Joining the rest of the eclectic company was Zephyr the 'flying stag', who gored a saddler who was called in to make an alternation to his collar. The man had been warned not to get too close because Zephyr was very savage.[91]

It was clear that Astley's assorted animals, but especially the horses, were the stars of the shows: there was no pretence of high culture.

In 1825 the new manager of Astley's, Andrew Ducrow, expanded the output of grand equestrian theatricals. Ducrow was a circus performer and he produced the wildly successful hippodramas of *The Battle of Waterloo* and *Mazeppa, or The Wild Horse*. Ducrow was known for his contempt for dialogue in his productions, shouting to his human cast: 'Cut the cackle, and come to the 'osses.'[92] Other animals joined the horses on the stage in some of the spectacles, such as Mr Carter with his lions, tigers and leopards which appeared in *Mungo Park* in 1844. Mr Carter as Karfa, the Lion-tamer of the Niger, fought with his animals, drove a pair of lions in harness and entered a cage with two adult lions and three leopards, 'over which he exercised such control that they seemed to be "spaniels" ... to remove all sensation of fear in the spectators'.[93]

Elephants, due to their rarity and grandeur, were always welcome additions to a performance, but did not always behave as well as their equine companions. In 1828, under the newspaper headline of 'An Unpolite Elephant', was a description of the debut of a small elephant from Exeter 'Change in *Blue Beard*.[94] The elephant's performance in the play seems to have gone without incident, but when it re-entered the ring to perform some tricks it decided to try and climb out of the ring into the audience, which caused terrified punters to scrabble for the exits. Three ladies were injured by the elephant's trunk.

Astley's soon became one of the most sought-after attractions for visitors to London, and it was immortalized in fiction, including mentions in Jane Austen's *Emma* (1815) and Dickens's *Bleak House* (1852–3) and *The Old Curiosity Shop* (1840–41). In the last, Kit takes his mother to Astley's:

> Dear, dear, what a place it looked, that Astley's! with all the paint, gilding, and looking-glass, the vague smell of horses suggestive of coming wonders, the curtain that hid such gorgeous mysteries, the clean white sawdust down in the circus ...[95]

Many theatre reviewers regarded Astley's as the original home of the hippodrama and circus, and even a whiff of the theatre suggested 'orange-peel, sawdust, train oil, and gas, mixed up with a goodly proportion of elephant and horse'.[96]

But disaster struck Astley's again in June 1841 when the theatre was destroyed for the third time. Accounts of the fire gave special attention to Ducrow's beloved stud of 50 horses and how many of them escaped. Those horses let out of their stables to escape the fire galloped through Stangate Street, Amphitheatre Row and the Westminster Road. But the grooms had difficulty rescuing several animals because when they were let loose, they automatically went towards the arena to perform. Unfortunately two horses and a donkey perished in the fire as their stalls were on the opposite side of the arena and valiant attempts to save them were thwarted by the heat of the fire.[97]

The fire broke Andrew Ducrow's spirit and he died in 1842. Astley's was eventually rebuilt and opened by William Batty in 1843, followed by Thomas Cooke in 1853 – both loyal to the traditions of Astley's. Batty was also keen on 'living' advertising, getting one of his riders (in response to a bet) to drive 24 horses, harnessed in pairs and pulling a van containing the theatre's orchestra, from Westminster Road right though the main streets of London.[98] Travelling at about 6 miles an hour, they caused plenty of havoc – but Londoners were aware that Astley's had reopened for business. Batty was also responsible for the sight which greeted hundreds of spectators in 1844 when a clown floated across the Thames from Vauxhall to Westminster Bridge in a tub pulled by geese.[99] Astley's once again became synonymous with horse-based entertainment.

Hippodrama in the theatres

It is possible that the hippodramas made famous at Astley's were first performed on a small scale at the King's Playhouse (now the Theatre Royal, Drury Lane) as early as the mid seventeenth century. Pepys commented on 11 July 1668 that he was at that theatre to see a play by James Shirley called *Hyde Park*, in which horses were brought on to the stage to

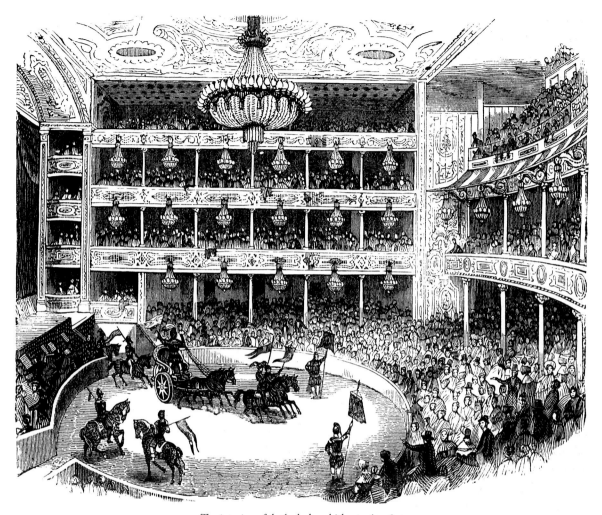

The interior of Astley's Amphitheatre in 1843.

depict a horse race. But as one later periodical stated, 'the horses probably were only required to cross the stage once or twice.'[100]

Astley's horses made appearances throughout the capital when their season had finished, beginning on 18 February 1811 at Covent Garden Theatre, where the group was introduced on to the stage during the mock battle which concluded *Blue Beard*. Stables were even built under the theatre for the horses. The audience was packed with people eager to see the horses, but some critics felt the horse show and theatre did not mix. It was a 'spectacle for the howling mob' rather than high culture, and according to one reviewer, the managers of the theatre, 'prostitute[d] the stage to buffoonery . . . to waste such enormous sums . . . is lamentable proof . . . of the degraded taste of the age'.[101] There were also concerns raised about the welfare of the horses being made to do unnatural tricks – another argument against letting horses on to the main London stages.

However, Astley's stud of horses regularly appeared at Covent Garden Theatre, even though there was some hissing heard at the start of one drama in 1814 and placards displayed which condemned the use of horses.[102] It was not only Covent Garden that saw the lucrative potential of using Astley's horses; they were a real pull for audiences used only to seeing human actors on the stage. Even Drury Lane, which ridiculed the use of the horses at Covent Garden by using artificial asses and donkeys in a pantomime in 1812, put on a drama (Moncrieff's *Cataract of the Ganges*) with 'real horses' and 'real water' in 1823.

Astley's: circus acts

All of Astley's owners realized that alongside the horse spectacles and the trick riding, the public clamoured for novel circus acts – and many of these were animal related. Elephants, as already mentioned, were popular and none more so than Mr Cook's Wise Elephants which were performing in 1854. These elephants were unusually acrobatic; one could even raise and balance his great body on his forelegs and 'slowly poise his reversed proportions in the air'.[103]

Lion-tamers were also regular visitors to Astley's, of which the most famous was the American Isaac

Van Amburgh in 1838. He was the first 'modern' wild animal trainer to capture the public's imagination and he made his tigers, lions and leopards share a cage – much against their natural instincts. His special trick was to put his head in a lion's mouth, which involved standing on the lion and grasping the bottom lip and the nostrils so hard that the pressure caused the animal to lose power in its jaws and allowed its mouth to be opened. However, as one lion-tamer reported,

> The only danger is, lest the animal should raise one of its fore-paws, and stick his talons in; and if he does, the tamer must stand fast for his life till he has shifted the paw.[104]

Van Amburgh would also introduce a child and a lamb into the cage during the routine, which the animals would leave alone. This feat was apparently achieved mainly because the animals were terrified of the fearsome punishment they received from Van Amburgh's iron bar or whip if they dared to go near

The American Isaac Van Amburgh with his lions at Vauxhall Gardens, 1848.

the vulnerable intruders. Van Amburgh was himself a frightening sight, wrote one reviewer, and his animals knew he was in control:

> There is something extraordinary in the visage of Mr Van Amburgh. His eye is extremely prominent, and has an expression which we have never witnessed in any other human being before, and we remarked that his very look seemed to awe his savage family . . . the fire in his eye and the severity of his punishment bringing them into perfect subjection.[105]

However, despite the iron control, during his residency at Astley's a tiger did get hold of him during a rehearsal and Van Amburgh had to fight for his life; eventually he beat the animal into submission with his fists and was able to appear in the ring that evening.[106]

Van Amburgh performed at venues throughout London during his visits, including Vauxhall Gardens, the Royal Lyceum Theatre and the English Opera House. Queen Victoria was so fascinated by his act that she commissioned Edwin Landseer (1802–1873) to paint a portrait of him in the cage with his cats. On one occasion, while he was performing at Drury Lane in January 1839, the Queen, who had already seen the show three times, paid a private visit to see the animals being fed.[107]

The only human death that occurred at Astley's (there were many serious falls from the horses reported, but no fatalities) was caused by a lion owned by Mr Crockett, 'The Lion Conqueror', in 1861. The unfortunate victim was a groom known as Jarvey, who was caught unawares by Havelock, one of Crockett's three lions, when they escaped from their cages. Jarvey was attacked as he tried to escape through a door and his death was presumed instantaneous. Crockett arrived too late, but managed to get Havelock to release the victim before Jarvey's corpse was dismembered. Crockett also managed to retrieve his three

prowling lions and that evening the performance went ahead as normal.[108]

There was one other incident at Astley's that ended in a fatality. In 1888 eight wild Siberian wolves were caged in one of the stables behind the amphitheatre, in the same area as seventeen valuable horses. One night all the wolves got loose (a vengeful former employee was suspected of sabotage) and attacked one of the performing mares, called Shrewsbury. They pulled her down and were at her neck and abdomen when the attack was noticed – she died within minutes.[109]

Even during circus performances, it was a fairly regular occurrence for the semi-wild animals to decide to revert to their pre-captivity nature, as seen when the 'Lion Happy Family' was performing at the Paragon Theatre of Varieties on Mile End Road. Herr Seeth's show consisted of five lions, two boarhounds and a couple of ponies that performed in the arena together, the ponies positioned on opposite sides while the lions and hounds circled and jumped over them. Three lions were then set to play on a see-saw. This was hardly an entertaining game for them as they had recently suffered a long sea voyage and had been moved around London ever since. As one newspaper stated, they 'felt hardly inclined to repeat their ocean experiences on *terra firma*. The whip cracked, and Herr Seeth perspired all to no purpose – the lions had made up their minds, and let him perspire.'[110]

Other London hippodromes

Between 1863 and 1871 London lost its horse-centred Astley's Amphitheatre when Dion Boucicault turned it into the Royal Theatre, Westminster, a theatre for 'bipeds, not quadrupeds'. It was not a successful venture and the reason for this was, according to one journal, that 'an Astley's without horses is as yet simply a misnomer, a shadow without a substance.'[111] This left Londoners without a permanent equestrian building until the New Royal Amphitheatre, Holborn, was opened on May 1867 'to revive the glories of the peaceful sawdust ring'.[112] One of the main attractions was 'The Fire King and The Salamander War Horse', which involved a horse going through a 'variety of evolutions whilst enveloped in a shower of fireworks, attached to the person of the rider'.[113] However, the Holborn Amphitheatre, too, was turned into a conventional theatre in 1873.

By this time the horses were back at Astley's under the management of brothers John and George Sanger, who were experienced producers of equine shows. They had previously leased the Royal Agricultural Hall in Islington to stage a 'Great National Hippodrome, Cirque and Tournament' in 1863, complete with jousting matches and chariot races.[114] The Agricultural Hall also became the home of what was to become known as the Royal Tournament.

In 1880 notices began to appear in the newspapers advertising 'A Military Tournament and Assault-at-Arms',[115] which consisted of 53 competitions, open to entrants from all the regiments in the country. The profits would be given to the Royal Cambridge Asylum for Soldiers' Widows. Eventually, over 770 entries were received, with cavalry, artillery and mounted infantry regiments competing in events such as

Tent-pegging, Cleaving the Turk's Head, Tilting at the Ring, Lemon Cutting, Sword against Sword mounted, Lance against Lance mounted, Lance against Bayonet mounted, Horizontal Bar and Vaulting Horse.[116]

Later productions included spectacular cavalry charges and heavy-artillery manoeuvres, and the show became known as 'A Grand Military Tournament' until 1906, when it moved to the larger Olympia, and then to Earl's Court in 1950, where it closed in 1999. In 2010 the British Military Tournament, featuring 145 horses, came to life again at Earl's Court in December.

With the Sangers at Astley's from 1871, the 'equestrian drama', 'grand horse dramatics' and 'scenes in the circle' were revived, much to the joy of Londoners, who had missed their performing horses. The Sangers also staged Christmas pantomimes featuring a wide range of animals: in 1879 Sanger's Amphitheatre (as it was then named) had a staff of 1,100 people, 180 horses, 60 ponies, eight camels and dromedaries, zebras, 'the horned horse', polar bears, four giraffes, and twelve 'ponderous performing elephants'.[117] And in 1885 the performers included 'a white poodle, a cat, a kangaroo which dances a polka, pelicans that "steal" food and an ostrich running around – doing "ballet" – in time to the music'.[118]

The Sangers' was not the only hippodrome in London at this time. Some equestrian companies were playing at suburban theatres: Covent Garden Theatre had the 'Grand International Cirque'; there was also 'Hengler's Palais Royal' in Argyll Street (now the site of the London Palladium); and the magnificent Olympia, also known as the National Agricultural Hall in Kensington, opened its first night with the 'Paris Hippodrome' in December 1886. This troupe decamped its entire staff of artists and its stud of more than 250 animals from Paris – demonstrating the status that performing animals had in London at this time.

Mr Wood, the Hall's general manager, told the newspapers that the 'great track', in which the tournament displays took place, was the largest in England – it would take a person five minutes to walk around it – and in that space the horses could 'go at their wildest speed, while a brigade of artillery may gallop at full stretch, giving a reality to mimic warfare impossible in any other hall'.[119] Outside the main arena were the stables and stalls of the performing animals – 86 staghounds and greyhounds, stags and does, six elephants, 150 horses and 45 ponies.

There was no account of the quantity of feed consumed by the animals from Paris, but figures relating to the 200 animals which visited the Crystal Palace in July 1876 – as Myers' Great Hippodrome – could provide a guide. The details were laid out in a hand-bill given to visitors:

> The area of stabling and harness-rooms at the Crystal Palace is not less than 27,456 ft square . . . the elephants, horses, and camels require about 10,000 lbs of corn, 8,000 lbs of hay, 8,000 lbs of straw, 2,000 lbs of bran and 3,000 lbs of potatoes per week, while the lions consume 400 lbs of beef per week.[120]

The great circuses come to London

Olympia, with its ample animal stabling, became the London home of the huge American circuses that toured the world. However, London had previously seen smaller American circuses, particularly Howes' and Cushing's Great United States Circus, which was at the Alhambra Theatre in 1858.[121] Among its biggest billings were the two 'educated mules' called Pete and Barney, who would throw people off their backs and, according to one reviewer, 'are entitled to have their names recorded as being in their mulish obstinacy the funiest [sic] of their race'.[122]

Another troupe visiting London was the Wild West Show. It set up in the 12-acre Kensington triangle (now the site of Earls Court 1) and was home to the American Exhibition where the first Buffalo Bill's *Wild West Show* was staged in 1887. The animal 'actors' included 170 bronco horse, Indian ponies and fear-some 'buckers', together with buffaloes, wild Texan steers, mules, elk and deer.[123] *The Era* newspaper noted that the bucking horses were the stars of the show because of their almost unnatural hatred of their riders: 'There was enmity, savage or sullen, in every attitude, and in every movement of these creatures.'[124]

Londoners were also treated to Frank Fillis's *Savage South Africa*, which followed at Earls Court in 1899.

This show brought over from South Africa a company consisting of 50 Zulus, 10 Boer families, 400 Basuto ponies, 80 buck, lions, tigers and elephants.[125]

However, the shows visiting Olympia were the pinnacle of circus entertainment. Between 1889 and 1890 Barnum & Bailey's *Greatest Show on Earth* came over from New York. The entourage consisted of 300 horses, 22 elephants, eighteen camels, 150 cages full of dangerous animals shown in the menagerie, and 100 head of led stock, including buffaloes, elk, moose deer and other large animals. The stagehands constructed five separate rings for circus acts, and these also accommodated the 'driving contests', including four-in-hands of moose and elk and great deer in tandems, pairs and fours. There were also performing lions, tigers, leopards and wolves.[126] *The Era* tried to cover the show in detail, but found it impossible – the writers had to make a second visit to give their account – which included:

> UNO – this graceful performer takes from a basket eight large pythons and some anacondas which she winds and hangs about her until she is almost covered with their scaly coils. Her performance is a surprising and thrilling one.
> MR WILLIAM CONRAD introduces his perform-ing camel and zebra donkey. In addition to the curiosity created by the latter strange-looking animal, the odd appearance of the camel as it gallops round the ring and leaps over the var-ious obstacles is most amusing . . .
> MR J. MAGOVERIN and his trained seals give a most quaint and comical entertainment. The manner in which these amphibious creatures 'flop' along to the little inclined planes placed for them to lie upon and drum upon tambourines is laughable and comic.
> MR CHARLES WHITE, besides exhibiting some well-trained and docile steers, introduces the clown bear Bruno. This amiable and inoffensive

animal submits to be clad in female attire, and nurses a baby and takes the arm of his master for a walk with equal equanimity.[127]

Barnum & Bailey revisited London in 1897; this time the company included 400 horses, 26 elephants, twelve seals, two polar bears, a performing chimpanzee called Johanna and two tigers. Unfortunately the circus' giraffe broke its neck during the sea voyage and died.[128] A reporter went backstage after the performance to see the impressive discipline of the animals (and humans):

They know very well when their task is finished, and need nobody then to lead them back to their stalls. Thus one sees relays of horses, troop after troop, with very few grooms in attendance on them, taking their turns behind the scenes, playing their little parts upon the stage, and then hurrying back to the manger in which they have perhaps been taught to look for the reward for good behaviour. It is the same with any of the animals in Barnum and Bailey's motley menagerie that happen to be cast for any scene in the arena. Dogs, monkeys, elephants, even camels acknowledge the potency of discipline, and the man who can teach a camel that may consider himself a master of his craft.[129]

Cruelty exposed: the end of an era

It was just as well that these international imports came to London because by 1893 there was no permanent hippodrome in London. Astley's – the last remaining – had to be demolished in March of that year because the building was declared unsafe.[130] However, animal acts were still in London and many were seen at the spectacular 'Noah's Ark' show at Covent Garden Theatre over Christmas 1893–4. There was every act conceivable, including pigeons on miniature trapezes, foxes playing leapfrog with ducks, a bear that went

to and fro on a globe balanced on a see-saw, baboons riding a donkey and elephants holding up a wire so their mistress could walk the tightrope.[131]

But the days of unregulated animal acts in London were numbered, as public pressure mounted for an end to the abuse of performing animals. In 1831 one lady wrote to the *Voice of Humanity* about the cruelty that must have been meted out on Astley's horses, under Ducrow, to make them perform 'contrary to their nature'. She believed they had been

tortured by red-hot irons, whipped till the tears have streamed from their eyes, deprived of rest and of food till their savage master has sufficiently tamed them to his will, lie down or get up at the word of command, fetch and carry, dance minuets.[132]

The Standard newspaper added to the debate by questioning the purpose of Charles Green's ascent by air balloon, while on horseback, in 1850. Green had first tried the act from the Eagle Tavern in City Road, EC1V, in 1828, when 'aerostation' was a science, but by 1850 he was in Vauxhall Gardens doing the same stunt as, according to the newspaper, 'a mere toy for the amusement of the multitude'.[133] The horse's hooves were firmly strapped into a light wicker platform which was suspended by cords from the hoop of the balloon. The pony, weighing only 200 pounds, was blindfolded and Mr Green mounted the animal before the balloon shot up amid cheers and laughter from the crowd. But the pony was evidently distressed.

By the late 1890s journals carried articles relating the cruel methods – starvation and water deprivation, spiked collars, hot irons, whips and so on – used to train the animals that were seen performing in the London variety halls, and which lived and trained unseen in the cellars.[134] Many of the troupes were from the Continent, and their owners had methods

Poster advertising Barnum & Bailey's three-ring circus, commonly known as the *Greatest Show on Earth*, 1897.

for training their animals which, when uncovered, were deplored by London's humanitarians. Much work was also done by humane groups, including the RSPCA, which campaigned to stop animals being used in 'improper and unnecessary performances'.[135] The real work, however, was in educating the audiences about the horrors that lay behind the faces of the apparently happy animal stage performers.

In 1899 the secretary of the Liverpool branch of the RSPCA, Walter J. Burnham, wrote to the *Liverpool Mercury* to make readers aware of three acts of cruelty towards performing animals that he had witnessed in London. The first involved a horse which was made to climb up a ladder on to a small stage and then to walk across a narrow platform, which from the audience's viewpoint looked like a thick rope.

On one of its crossings, the horse fell off the platform and landed in a safety net which was then lowered to the ground. The horse was made to perform again, even though it was obvious that the animal was shaken by the fall. The second incident related by Burnham concerned a pony that was parachuted down to earth from a platform high in the roof of the building it was made to perform in. The animal appeared to be quite calm, although Burnham questioned the cruelty which must have taken place in training this animal to perform such an unnatural and 'improper' stunt. Finally, Burnham told of a dog trainer he met in a West End hall who used a tiny whip during his performances, which Burnham said was so small that he thought there could be no charge of cruelty made against the trainer. But having inspected the whip, after noticing that the dogs all flinched when it touched them, Burnham found that it was made mainly of wire. He asks, 'Are there not thousands of ways by which the public can be entertained without putting animals to execute tricks for which nature never built nor intended them?'[136]

In the same year the RSPCA successfully prosecuted two men engaged at Olympia for cruelty to a pig during the Barnum & Bailey Show. They had a whip with an iron rod running through it, and a goad, which they used to hit the pig to force it onto its knees so it could be harnessed into a cart. The defendant said that the pig was vicious and no unreasonable force was used. The case was then discharged because the entertainer and his pigs promised to return to America.[137]

Also in 1899 a case involving an electrician and the French owner of a bear performing at the Aq came to court. The electrician had been asked to make an electric table which would give out shocks to the bear when it trod on the wires, which were hidden under a tablecloth. The bear's owner stated that the shock was not great enough to make his bear dance and when the electrician made the shocks stronger using more batteries, the owner refused to pay because the bear did not dance as he wanted it to. The bear's owner was made to pay the electrician,[138] but it became clear to the public that for their viewing pleasure, animals suffered unnecessary physical and psychological torture.

However, despite vigorous campaigning to ban animal-performance acts from groups such as the Performing Animals Defence League (PADL) – founded in 1914 – and celebrities like the author Jack London the issue was reduced to one of licensing.[139] Wild animals, such as lions and elephants, were only granted protection from those wanting to 'abuse, infuriate, tease, or terrify [them]' in 1900 under the Wild Animals in Captivity Protection Act, and most performing animals (excluding seals, dogs and monkeys) were not registered with the local authorities until 1925. The Performing Animals (Regulation) Act is still in use today and allows police and local officials, which may include a vet, to enter the premises on which animals are being trained and exhibited to check for signs of cruelty and neglect. Owners and/or trainers found to be offending have their registrations cancelled or suspended.

Apart from restrictive legislation, London audiences have increasingly shown their distaste for animal performers on the stage and in circuses. Animals now only rarely appear for entertainment. Ponies are still employed during the pantomime season, but whereas the London production of *War Horse* at the New London Theatre in Drury Lane in 2011 used life-sized puppets, in times past the play would have used real horses. There are no performing animals in the London streets either, only the occasional pet ferret or rat, or even young python on show for the pleasure of passers-by in Trafalgar Square or outside the Tate Modern.

Alongside the animal street performers and theatre spectaculars of London past, the city also teemed with exotic animals imported mainly from British colonies. Rather than performing, they were there to be marvelled and gawped at. Exotics, both dangerous and harmless, played their part too in the history of the city.

five

Exotic Animals:
The Allure of the Foreign and the Wild

By the 1870s London had become the centre of the European trade in exotic animals as a consequence of Britain's colonial trading network. Affluent Londoners could experience the thrill of seeing caged wild animals, even if not in appropriate habitats or being treated humanely, in several locations around the city. But exotic animals were not new to Londoners; despite high mortality rates during sea transport, they had been imported into the docks since the thirteenth century. Initially they were showy gifts given to the British monarchs as part of the ceremony of diplomacy between foreign rulers and heads of state – these royal exotics were housed in the Tower of London. Later, exotics were imported by traders and ships' captains, involved in trade or exploration, alongside their usual cargo – spices, gems, lacquer work, porcelain and silks – to sell to private menageries, or to showmen who wished to exhibit them to a keen public and, in doing so, make their fortune. Some of the exotics coming into London were companion animals belonging to the sailors, which they sold on.

By the early nineteenth century, the exploitation of London's exotics purely for profit, or the status they bestowed on their owners, was partly replaced by the early scientific community's wish to study and research these non-native animals, which led to the opening of a London-based national menagerie, solely for the purpose of zoological enquiry – eventually the site became known as London Zoo.[1]

However, it becomes evident when tracing the history of Londoners' relationship with exotic animals that the animals were in the care of, and at the mercy of, people who were ignorant of their charges, and this led to some astonishing acts of cruelty by today's standards. Most exotic animals had short and brutal lives in the metropolis.

The royal menagerie – Part 1

It is likely that from 1204, when King John brought three crate-loads of exotic animals back to England from Normandy, animals presented to (or otherwise acquired by) the monarch were kept at the Tower.

It is no surprise that African lions, and other large cats, were a favoured gift to present to English monarchs. Not only was the lion viewed as the King of Beasts and dangerous to capture, but lions had featured on the Royal Standard since Henry II's reign. The three lions *passant guardant* (lying down and looking out to the viewer) of royal heraldry were then known as leopards – which according to medieval texts were the offspring of a lion and a panther. So, rather aptly, three leopards arrived in 1235, sent to Henry III by his new brother-in-law Frederick II, Holy Roman Emperor. These animals were part of Frederick's private collection and made a significant wedding gift. However, their new keeper was bereft of skills to care for the animals: after 1240 there is no further record of their existence.

Matthew Paris, *The First Elephant to Arrive at the Tower of London*, 1255.

The only animal forlornly housed in the Tower at this time was a lion; its provenance is unknown, but its welfare fell to the Sheriffs of London, who paid for a keeper and 'chains and other things for the use of the Lion'.[2] This lion, and its medieval successors, lived a miserable existence chained in their dens. They were housed on the Tower's main entrance-exit causeway in small buildings at the Lion Tower (or Western barbican), in cages that measured a measly 2 × 3 metres, which would have been a tight squeeze for a beast 2.5 metres long.[3]

Conditions were slightly better for the African elephant which arrived in 1255, the first seen in England since classical times. This remarkable creature was a gift from Henry III's son-in-law, the French king Louis IX, who brought it back from Palestine on his return from the Crusades. It was landed at Whitsand, Kent,[4] and walked along the Canterbury–London road, making the final leg of its journey to the Tower by boat.

The chronicler Matthew Paris (*c.* 1200–1259) described it: 'The beast is about ten years old, possessing a rough hide rather than fur, has small eyes at the top of its head, and eats and drinks with a trunk.'[5] It was housed in a wooden house measuring 20 x 40 feet, about half the size of a tennis court (which was palatial compared with the lions' quarters). But, again, for want of specialist care, it died nearly two years later.

The 'pale' bear which arrived from Norway in 1240 arguably had the best medieval existence in the Tower. The creature was either a polar bear or a (white) brown bear. Whichever it was, it was the first royal animal that Londoners could have seen for themselves. The Sheriffs of London were ordered to buy it a muzzle, chain and rope so that the animal could be taken to the bank of the Thames, where it could wash and fish for salmon.

At least it was being fed its natural diet, unlike the second elephant to grace the royal collection. This animal arrived during the reign of James I as a gift from the Spanish king, and between September and April it was not offered anything to drink apart from wine: a gallon a day. Supposedly this would keep out the cold of the British winter. Rather unsurprisingly, like the first elephant in the menagerie, it did not live long.

Initially the royal collection was private, for the pleasure of royalty and their immediate circle, although a small number of privileged persons were allowed to view the animals. They must have been astounded by what was on display; animals which previously were only known through clumsy and inaccurate illustrations or through texts. For example, it was still believed in the thirteenth century that bear cubs were born as shapeless and eyeless lumps of flesh that the mother bear had to lick into their proper form.[6]

It was not until the 1420s that the gates opened to more visitors, but they had to have connections. And they had to pay the 3 sous admission fee, or offer their dog or cat as the carnivores' dinner. Unfortunately for the visitors, all the lions in the Tower died within the space of a few months in 1436. Although the animals were treated with awe when they were alive, they were worthless when dead and it appears that they were thrown unceremoniously into the moat and left to float until they putrefied and sank.[7] After these deaths (their cause is unknown, but is likely to have been a combination of very poor living conditions, food and misery), the menagerie lay empty until 1445 when Henry VI was presented with exotic animal gifts on his marriage to Margaret of Anjou.

By the reign of James I the Tower inhabitants were not just on show, but were being used to provide entertainment for the bloodthirsty king. As a taster, he would pit three mastiff dogs against one of his lions. He enjoyed the spectacle so much that he had the Lion Tower renovated to include a baiting yard, accessed from the lions' dens by trapdoors. There was also a water trough in the yard for them to wash in, as well as to drink from, and a separate feeding area. The dens, which were still there in 1799 (more than 175 years later), provided accommodation on two levels.

When James I and the Tower visitors were unable to see baiting, they often resorted to watching live animals being devoured by the lions. However, James also had a collection of more innocent and harmless animals, including an aviary of birds kept along what became known as Birdcage Walk, near St James's Park. His North American exotics included an opossum, flying squirrels, storks, a beaver (which was fed mainly on bread), herons and cranes. One of the cranes had a wooden leg which was created to replace an amputated limb; according to John Evelyn, it 'use[d] it as well as if it had ben natural'.[8] Pelicans were also part of the collection, which Evelyn examined closely and described as looking 'melancholy'.[9]

Following the Restoration of the monarchy in 1660, the popularity of the Tower soared, making it the most visited tourist attraction in the city. Besides the menagerie, the public could also see the Crown

A rather fanciful depiction of the lions in the Tower. Illustration by George Cruikshank from Ainsworth's *The Tower of London: A Historical Romance* (1840).

Jewels and Royal Armouries. However, the Tower faced competition from showmen travelling with exotic animals. Royalty had always known how to look after their proprietarial rights, so they issued a warning in 1697 prohibiting the exhibition of other exotic animals.[10]

Exotics on show – Part I

It is clear that the proprietary warning issued by the Tower in 1697 went unheeded, since by 1773 a catalogue of London sights stated that there were 'Lions, Tygers, Elephants, &c. in every Street in Town'.[11] Londoners of affluence had many opportunities to see exotic animals exhibited at fairs, in the courtyards of inns or in the newly popular coffee houses for a high admittance price.

Exotics such as the cassowary from the East Indies, a leopard from Lebanon, an eagle from Russia and an opossum from Hispaniola were not only popular with the crowds at Bartholomew Fair, but were also of interest to the serious student of natural history, and the famous naturalist Sir Hans Sloane (1660–1753) was among those who visited the fairs to study the captive animals.[12]

The first civet cat to be shown in London was kept at Moncrief's Coffee House in Threadneedle Street in 1698.[13] These animals, imported from Africa, were valued for the oil which is secreted from a pouch under the tail. This oil was used as a fixative base for perfumes and also as 'a cure-all for certain diseases of the head and brain, for fits and vapours, for bad hearing, barrenness, and depression of spirits'.[14] The owners of these exotic animals would have bought them either directly from ships' captains or from animal dealers who kept an eye on the cargo coming into the major port of London. The captain of a trading ship was frequently not just an employee, but a participant in the speculative venture of sailing abroad to buy and return with valuable traded cargo. If he was not the sole owner of the goods (including the animals) he was usually a part owner and would oversee the sale, and the collection of the monies from it.

Many animals brought from abroad would be kept as pets, such as parrots and monkeys. But many were too dangerous to be kept in private homes, although Samuel Pepys was given a lion cub by a Samuel Martin, then the British Consul in Algiers in 1674. It lived with Pepys at Derby House in Westminster and Pepys described his new friend: 'as tame as you sent him and as good company'.[15] What happened to the lion after it inevitably outgrew its welcome, we do not know.

The range of astonishing animals competing with those in the royal menagerie can be gleaned from contemporary diarists and also from newspaper advertising. Evelyn must have been feeling brave when, in 1654, he 'saw a tame Lion play familiarly with a Lamb: The Lion was a huge beast, I thrust my hand into his mouth, & felt his tongue rough like a Catts'.[16] The diary of scientist Robert Hooke refers to several animals he saw in the 1670s: 'India catt, Japan peacock, Porcupine, Upapa [African Hoopoe], Vultur, Great Owl, 3 Cassawaris' (1672); 'Saw Elephant 3sh' (1675); 'Saw tigre in Bartholomew Fair 2d' (1677); 'Saw Elephant have colours, shoot a gun, bend and kneel, carry a castle and a man, etc.' (1679).[17]

In 1684 Evelyn saw the first rhinoceros or 'unicorne' to be exhibited in London. She was four years old and was imported by several merchants of the East India Company. The amazing animal was sold for the astonishing sum of £2,000, and her subsequent owner(s) kept her at the Belle Savage Inn on Ludgate Hill. Visitors paid 12*d*. to view her, and two shillings if they rode on her back. She was led with a ring through her nose and was, according to Evelyn's diary:

Tame enough, & suffering her mouth to be open'd by her keeper, who caus'd her to lie downe, when she appeared like a [great] Coach overthrowne, for she was much of that bulke, yet would rise as nimbly as ever I saw an horse: T'was certainly a very wonderfull creature, of immense strength in the neck, & nose especialy, the snout resembling a boares but much longer; to what stature she may arive if she live long, I cannot tell; but if she grow proportionable to her present age, she will be a Mountaine: They fed her with Hay, & Oates, & gave her bread.[18]

Later the same day, Evelyn also went to see a young crocodile brought over from the West Indies:

It was not yet fully 2 yards from head to taile . . . & he went forward waddling, having a chaine about the neck: seemed to be very tame . . . They kept the beast or Serpent in a longish Tub of warme Water, & fed him with flesh &c: If he grow, it will be a dangerous Creature.[19]

Animals like the rhinoceros or crocodile that were unfamiliar to their owners were not well looked after

and, as Evelyn predicted, it was unlikely that they would live for long – the rhinoceros died after being in London for two years. One young female Indian elephant that died while on show in West Smithfield in 1720 was dissected, and the cause of death established by the anatomists:

It dy'd, as we [Sir Hans Sloane – President of the Royal Society – and William Stukeley] may reasonably suppose, for want of a suitable and proportionate method of food, and from the ignorance of the keepers, who expos'd it to cold and moisture, by stabling it in a damp booth and wet floor, not agreeable to its nature and the hot country it came from. Beside, it was upon cutting its great teeth of tusks, one being observ'd just broke forth. It's likely this pain, which was discernible from the creature's continual rubbing of the part, brought on a fever as is usual on such occasion. Its perspiration no doubt was stopt from the cold taken, and it had

George Stubbs, *Indian Rhinoceros*, 1770s, oil on canvas. This rhinoceros was exhibited in the Strand, and was painted by Stubbs at the request of John Hunter.

An artist's impression of a crocodile being shown in London as a live exhibit, 1739.

no stools for several days, which is a distemper these creatures are naturally subject to. All these disorders we may well suppose heightened by the great quantity of ale the spectators continually gave it. After it had languish'd for some time, by the advice of a farrier several strong purges and glisters were used; they not passing, it dy'd on the 4th of *October* 1720.[20]

Apart from being neglected through ignorance, some of these animals also posed a real danger to the public due to their inadequate housing. The second rhinoceros in London arrived 55 years after the one seen by Evelyn. It was from Bengal, in what was then called the East Indies.[21] The rhino was exhibited in Eagle Street, near Red Lion Square, Holborn, for half a crown, then later in the year was moved to the Golden Cross inn at Charing Cross.[22] According to the physician James Parsons, whose description and drawings of this rare animal appeared in the Royal Society's *Philosophical Transactions* in 1743, it was a two-year-old male whose temper made him particularly dangerous when he was struck or before he was given his morning rice and sugar (!). Parsons concluded: 'He is quite indomitable and intractable, and must certainly run too fast for a Man on foot to escape him.'[23]

Other less dangerous animals suffered further exploitation, not just from being exhibited, but from being anthropomorphized in a way which we would now regard as cruel. A female chimpanzee, the 'African Lady Mademoiselle Chimpanzee', was exhibited in October 1738 at Randal's Coffee-house in Lombard Street. Captain Henry Flower brought her from Angola on the Coast of Guinea in August, when she was about eighteen months old.[24] She was so popular that she was moved to Mr Leflour's White Peruke, in Charing Cross, where she was 'entirely dressed after the newest Fashion *A-la mode a Paris*, which is a great Advantage to the natural Parts she is endowed with'.[25] Again, she did not survive for long, dying on 21 February 1739. It was reported that she seemed to know that she was going to die and 'behaved in a great Measure like a Negroe in the like Circumstances'.[26] This casual racism is now difficult to read, but at the time Britain was engaged in the slave trade in which humans were a commodity available for sale and purchase. Sir Hans Sloane and John Ranby (surgeon to the king's household) dissected the chimpanzee's body and it was concluded that 'she was perfectly of a human Specie'. Her body was put on public view, and ladies were shown the sight by a 'Gentlewoman'.[27]

The royal menagerie – Part II

Nevertheless the Tower remained very popular throughout the eighteenth century and a visit to

London was not complete without 'going to see the lions'. The menagerie had moved from being a private collection to a public attraction.

However, despite their royal connections, the Tower lions were no better kept than the exotics seen on the streets. The menagerie was overcrowded, resulting in high mortality and a rapid turnover of animals. Ned Ward, a tavern keeper and later the writer of *The London Spy* (1703), commented in 1699 that 'the [lion] yard smelt as frowzily as a dove-house or a dog-kennel'.[28] Another visitor, the Swiss traveller César de Saussure, writing in 1725, described the enclosures as 'small and rather dirty', but he was enchanted by the four lion cubs and noted that visitors could 'fondle and caress them as if they had been little dogs'. That the public could get so close to the animals was surprising, especially as one young girl in 1686, who was a frequent visitor, had her arm so badly mauled that it had to be amputated. She had stroked one of the lion's paws

that it had stretched out to her through the grating of its den. She died soon after the incident.[29] By the mid-1700s conditions had improved for the lions, probably because the Tower authorities realized their value as a public attraction – money was finally the incentive. Their dens, although still cramped, were refurbished; the wooden floors were replaced with bricks and some heating was installed for the winter. They were also better looked after; the lions were fed on sheep heads and offal twice a day, while the other carnivore cats preferred raw dog flesh.[30] This better treatment resulted in lion cubs that survived into adulthood (in James I's time they had died in infancy). There was now a lineage of native-born lions at the Tower, all of which were named: among them Jenny, Helen, Pompey and Dido.

Although the lions were the chief attraction, other felines at the Tower were popular. Oliver Goldsmith described several of them when he visited to gain

Thomas Rowlandson's *The Monkey Room in the Tower*, 1799, hand-coloured etching and aquatint. The exhibit did not last too long!

information for his *A History of the Earth and Animated Nature*, published in 1774. He saw the ounce (a snow leopard), which was apparently quite tame. The tiger was a different matter:

[It] appears the most good-natured and harmless creature in the world; its physiognomy is far from fierce or angry; it has not the commanding, stern countenance of the lion, but a gentle, placid air; yet, for all this, it is fierce and savage beyond measure; neither correction can terrify it, nor indulgence can tame.[31]

Other inmates introduced during the 1760s were species from the Indian subcontinent as gifts by the East India Company: an elephant, a caracal (desert lynx), a rhino, an antelope, Bengal tigers and a 'Warwoven' bird joined the exhibition. And one inmate that delighted the visitors, because of his outlandish behaviour, was a baboon:

He has an admirable Art of throwing Stones, and will throw any Lead or Iron that happens to be within his Reach, with such Force as to split Stools, Bowls or any such wooden Utensils in a hundred Pieces.

If anything were flung at him, he would catch it and throw it back 'with great Dexterity'.[32]

However, it would have been too dangerous for the baboon to be in the new and sensational 'School for Monkeys' exhibition at the Tower in the 1780s. Surprisingly, despite their unknown dispositions, the monkeys were kept in a room in which the public could move freely among them. This was a domestic room with shelves and a fireplace, with no separating barriers. This meant that visitors would often be pinched and bitten by the animals, and many wigs were stealthily removed. Needless to say, the monkey room did not last long.

Other animals in the Tower did not survive for other reasons: 'scientific' experiments of the crudest sort could result in ghastly deaths. In 1791 an ostrich was fed nails to test the notion that the species could digest iron. When its corpse was dissected, 80 nails were found in its digestive tract.

One royal animal escaped the confines of the Tower of London, and was free to view – unless the visitor encountered one of the 'bent' keepers.[33] In 1762 a 'painted African ass' or zebra arrived in England from the Cape of Good Hope, imported by Sir Thomas Adams on HMS *Terpsichore* (a Royal Navy warship captured from the French). The zebra mare was presented to Queen Charlotte and turned out to graze in a paddock behind Buckingham Palace, alongside Buckingham Gate. The public was able to view her from the road and crowds, including a number of pickpockets,[34] flocked to see the exotic animal. George Stubbs was one such visitor, immortalizing her in his famous painting of 1763. A handbill advertising her exhibition spoke of 'a fine display of Elegance and Symmetry in its whole form and it is remarkable to swiftness'.[35] But the zebra was not enjoying captivity – as intimated in Stubbs's image – and the handbill added that she was 'so vicious as not to suffer any stranger to come near her'. The animal lived in the grounds of the palace for a decade, latterly in a stable-yard with its two elephant companions. In 1772 it was given to one of the Queen's 'domesticks' and was then toured around the country.[36]

A second zebra was acquired and, according to Goldsmith, this one was 'even more vicious than the former; and the keeper who shows it takes care to inform the spectators of its ungovernable nature'.[37] Lessons were also apparently learned when feeding the zebra: Goldsmith mentions that the original zebra 'would eat almost any thing, such as bread, meat and tobacco', while the second 'subsists entirely upon hay'.[38]

Queen Charlotte's grumpy looking zebra, painted by George Stubbs in 1763, oil on canvas.

Exotics on show – Part II

Apart from the royal animals, by the eighteenth century curiosity seekers could still see wonderous animals around the streets of London – from even further afield than India and Africa. Following the expedition of Captain James Cook in 1770, Antipodean animals began to arrive in England. However, it was not until November 1791 that the first live kangaroo was imported from Botany Bay. It was exhibited at No. 31, top of the Haymarket. One newspaper was overawed by its appearance:

It is not easy to describe the peculiarity of attitudes and uncommon proportions of parts which so strikingly distinguish the KANGAROO from all other Quadrupeds; it is now in its natural state of vigour and activity, and so remarkably tame, that Ladies may approach it without the least danger.[39]

If the advertising is to be believed, this male kangaroo, 'the only one in this kingdom', was then exhibited at the Lyceum in the Strand in November 1792.[40] By July 1793 it was at Exeter 'Change (see below), along

153

with a female kangaroo as part of a collection owned by Gilbert Pidock.[41] Having mated, their joey was born in 1801.[42]

However, while this may have been the first kangaroo to be shown in public, there was another male imported in August 1792. He was advertised as being ideal for those with female kangaroos wishing to breed.[43] And in May 1792 many people were reported as assisting in the capture of a kangaroo that escaped from the stables of T. Thirling, Esq., in Pentonville. 'It ran, or rather jumped several times round a field before it was secured.'[44]

Another rare animal was the 'Bous Potamous', 'Amphibious Beef' or 'River Cow' from sub-Saharan Africa, which could be seen alive at Sir Ashton Lever's Museum of Natural Curiosity (*Holophusikon*) at Leicester House – the largest private residence in London – in Leicester Square from November 1777.[45] This museum opened in 1774 after Lever moved his private collection of exotics from Alkrington Hall, near Manchester. Visitors could also see an elephant presented by his Majesty, the 'Oriental Tiger' and a 'Greenland Bear' (polar bear). Another hippopotamus was on show in 1800 at Brookes' Menagerie, 242 Piccadilly, at the top of Haymarket.[46] John Brookes was 'a big, ruffianly-looking man, generally known either from his appearance or his occupation as "Wild-beast Brookes"'.[47] He had originally sold, bought and exchanged exotic birds, but the promise of money to be made in the accumulation and display of a menagerie lured him into the big animal trade.

Exeter 'Change – Part 1

Another animal dealer who saw the potential in opening his collection to the public was Thomas Clark, who began exhibiting a permanent collection of animals in the Strand, on the first floor of the Exeter 'Change, in 1770. Below the menagerie, at street level, was a row of shops – an unusual set-up, but one that endured into the nineteenth century. Clark also leased the adjoining Lyceum. By 1788 the advertising for the Exeter 'Change claimed it to be the 'finest Collection exhibited to the Public these 20 years', featuring beasts shipped over from Asia, Africa and America. It was said that the large animals were secured in iron dens, that there was no offensive smell and that great care was taken to allow the public to view the animals in complete safety. The entrance fee was sixpence.[48] By September 1791 the Lyceum was exhibiting a rhinoceros, a zebra and two 'Imperial Sheep, a new variety, adorned with horns singularly grand and elegant'.[49] The Exeter 'Change collection included a lion, a pelican, vultures and an ostrich.[50]

The 'Change was sold off in 1792. It was leased in February 1793 by Gilbert Pidock, who took over the building and the majority of Clark's animals, bought at auction. Along with his own collection of animals (he had a travelling menagerie), he opened his 'Grand Menagerie of Foreign Beasts and Birds', which was aimed primarily at affluent visitors, who could afford the admission fee of one shilling (although servants were admitted for sixpence).[51] The collection included panthers, a tiger, a laughing hyena, a leopard and a 'Sagittaire [Secretary] Bird that kills the Snakes'.[52] By 1796 Pidock owned three Indian elephants which he showed in one room, and over 200 other birds and beasts in another.[53] It was a cramped existence for the animals, which were kept in cages lining the walls of the two rooms.

The collection was seldom mentioned in the newspapers until September 1797, when a tiger escaped within the 'Change and ate two or three monkeys. While it was busy devouring its prey, the keeper was able to approach the tiger unobserved and stab it.[54]

It would seem that Pidock was keen for his animals to be seen by the greater public as he regularly took a selection of animals to Bartholomew Fair. His menagerie became the chief attraction of the fair in 1796. In 1805 he took along a lion, tiger and elephant.[55]

However, in 1807 Pidock promised his public, via a report to the newspapers, that he would no longer expose his animals to 'that scene of riot and confusion', which was Bartholomew Fair. Instead, he hoped that the public would visit the 'Change, where the animals could be viewed 'without danger and disgust, but with infinite safety and satisfaction'. It is not clear what occurred at the fair, but it certainly deterred Pidock. As an interesting aside, Pidock intriguingly mentions in the same report that the young lion which 'jumped overboard' into the River Thames was now safely lodged in his establishment – London was certainly not a place for marauding exotics![56]

Early travelling menageries

Private collections of exotic animals had been shown at Bartholomew since 1708, when a 'Collection of Strange and Wonderful Creatures' was exhibited.[57] The travelling menagerie included a cassowary (billed as eating iron, steel or stones), leopard, eagle, opossum and monkey.[58] Other 'Beast Shows' were held in inn courtyards, such as 'Perry's Grand Collection of Living Wild Beasts' in 1748:

> This is to give notice to all Gentlemen, Ladies, and others, that Mr Perry's Grand Collection of Living Wild Beasts is come to the White Horse Inn, Fleet Street, consisting of a large he-lion, a he-tiger, a leopard, a panther, two hyenas, a civet cat, a jackal, or lion's provider, and several other rarities too tedious to mention. To be seen at any time of the day, without any loss of time. Note: This is the only tiger in England; that baited being only a common leopard.[59]

However, travelling menageries, by their nature, increased the risk of animal escapes. In 1810, as Ballard's menagerie passed along Piccadilly on its way to Bartholomew Fair, the horses pulling the wagon of leopards and monkeys were spooked and the wagon overturned. One monkey escaped into an oyster shop, and the leopard vanished into the basement of an unfinished house near St James's Church. Both animals were later recaptured, but a second monkey vanished.[60] Ballard was also the owner of the lioness that notoriously attacked the lead horse of the Exeter mail coach just outside Salisbury on 20 October 1816, causing terror to the passengers on board. The lioness was captured, but the injured lead horse had to be put down and a mastiff dog was also a casualty.[61]

Exeter 'Change – Part II

When Pidock died in 1810, Polito bought the Exeter 'Change animals at auction and continued to exhibit at the grandiosely renamed 'Royal Menagerie'. Lord Byron visited the menagerie in 1813 to see the lions being fed at 9 pm (this was changed to 8 pm in December 1823, allowing children to attend – Chunee Lah the elephant rang a large bell to announce feeding time).[62] Mesmerized by the sight of the wild animals, Londoners, both fearful and intrigued, watched the carnivores hunched aggressively over their horsemeat steaks. Byron was also taken with the evident fondness that the hyena and the elephant displayed towards their keepers, and described Chunee doing tricks such as taking Byron's money, then giving it back to him.[63]

Besides the performing elephant, the public was treated to animals behaving in 'cute' ways, which caused problems for the animals later in life. In 1818 an orang-utan, which had recently been imported from Borneo, was living on a diet of rich dishes, drinking ale and porter, not taking its usual exercise and being kept in comfort. Eventually it began to bleed from the nose and had an apoplectic fit, so was bled at the temporal artery until it recovered. The newspaper report concluded that by living in the 'true English style' and deviating from its natural life, its illness

The Royal Menagerie in Exeter 'Change, Strand, 1826.

showed its 'near affinity to man'.[64] After its death in 1819, the orang-utan's body was taken to the Surgeon's College in Lincoln's Inn Fields for further inspection by anatomists.[65]

The personable elephant Chunee (or, as some contemporary newspapers called him, Chuny) also came to a sad end in the 'Change. He had been imported from Bengal in 1810 and his first stage performance, a run of 40 nights in a pantomime at Covent Garden Theatre, was not a success. Chunee was reluctant to obeyed commands on stage and suffered from extreme flatulence. Worst of all, unaccustomed to humans in crowds, let alone a rowdy audience, his fear caused him to career off the stage, with resulting chaos.[66] To the relief of the theatre manager, the elephant's stage career ended when he was brought to the Exeter 'Change in 1812. We do not know how Chunee made his way up the wooden staircase of the 'Change to reach his den on the first floor, but he soon became the star attraction.

Unfortunately, as Chunee matured he came into musth (or must) and became ungovernable, which resulted in him nearly killing a keeper while he was in a rage (he had previously killed one keeper purely by accident, for which he was fined, by the courts, the nominal fee of one shilling).[67] By 1826 Edward Cross, a dealer in wild animals and a showman, was the owner of the 'Change and therefore responsible for the 5-ton Chunee, who was now battering the sides of his iron-bound oak-barred den and threatening to escape. Even though the floor of his den had been reinforced, the rest of the building had not. If he broke out he risked crashing through the floor into the shops below – and taking the rest of the animals with him. His trumpeting also stirred the other animals, including a lion, into a frenzy.

There had already been complaints from the public about passing horses being startled in the streets by the 'jungle' noises coming from inside the 'Change, so Cross could not risk a marauding elephant, and possibly other escapees, charging down the Strand. Cross ordered Chunee to be dosed up with a mixture of powerful purgatives to try and calm him down.

All attempts failed dismally and Chunee's rages increased until, on 29 February, he partially destroyed his den. A decision was taken to kill him.[68]

Poisons were collected, but Chunee refused everything laced with the arsenic. His keepers faced him with long pikes (spears) and harpoons to deter him from rushing at the bars, but desperate measures were needed. Armed troops from Somerset House military depot were engaged. In the end, it took policemen, keepers, soldiers and other individuals over an hour to shoot dead the frenzied and bloodied Chunee. Over 150 bullets were lodged in his body before he lay down in his normal resting position and died. Disaster for humans had been averted, but what a gruesome end: a terrible, painful death for Chunee, who was hardly responsible for the terror he caused to his captors.

Cross was distressed, but, ever the showman, he allowed the public to view the bloody corpse for several days. In a guilt-ridden and bewildered response, the newspapers were filled with dramatic images of Chunee's final resting pose, and poems and plays were written to celebrate the demise of London's favourite elephant. He had, after all, been the one who rang the bell at the menagerie to announce feeding time. But Charles Dickens, writing in 1836, projected human qualities onto Chunee and seemed appalled by his capacity for violence and his ungrateful behaviour. In *Sketches by Boz*, he wrote:

> The death of the elephant was a great shock to us; we knew him well; and having enjoyed the honour of his intimate acquaintance for some years, felt grieved – deeply grieved – that in a paroxysm of insanity he should have so far forgotten all his estimable and companionable qualities as to exhibit a sanguinary desire to scrunch his faithful valet, and pulverize even

Destruction of the Noble Elephant at Mr Cross's Exeter 'Change, 1826; the animal was variously said to be called Chunee or Chuny.

Mrs Cross herself, who for a long period had evinced towards him that pure and touching attachment which women alone can feel.[69]

Chunee's body was partially dissected in situ by anatomists and medical students after the neighbours complained about the putrid stench. It was also believed that neighbouring animals would contract diseases from the noxious bad air emanating from the decomposing corpse. A phrenologist took a plaster of paris cast of Chunee's head. Rumours started to circulate that Joshua Brookes, the celebrated anatomist and brother of animal dealer John, had eaten Chunee's flesh and Cross had fed him to the other animals, but they swiftly quashed the idea by writing letters to *The Times*.[70] A few days later Chunee's body was flayed by butchers, and carts doused in 'perfume' took his remains from the 'Change to various cat-meat sellers. But his skeleton returned in December 1828, complete with the bullet-ridden skull, to be exhibited in his battered den, and Londoners were able to properly mourn the elephant that had entertained them for seventeen years.

Another elephant caused a rumpus for Cross in 1827. Cross and several assistants were walking the animal through the Strand one evening to join a travelling exhibition. A passing drunk decided that it would be funny to pull and twist the elephant's tail. Even when Cross told him that he would enrage the elephant, he continued his annoying game and threatened to 'exterminate' Cross and his elephant. Mr Cross called the Watch and the man ran away. The elephant joined in the chase, which lasted from Newcastle Street to St Clement Danes Church, where the elephant caught up with the man and 'whipped' him with his trunk, sending him flying through the air and landing against some railings. He was unharmed and eventually the elephant was calmed, and the now-sober man was handed over to the Watch. Cross did not press charges as he

thought the man had been punished enough for his 'thoughtless conduct'.[71]

Aside from the elephant, Cross had one other publicized death in the 'Change. In 1820 a wolf escaped from the first floor of the building while it was in the hospital area. It found its way onto the roof, passed over two houses and entered the skylight of a house belonging to a trunk maker. The surprised and terrified workers evacuated the room, shutting the door behind them. The wolf then made its way out of the window onto the trunk maker's sign board, which was level with the window. Seeing an open window in the adjacent building it tried to jump, but the chain which was fastened to its collar became entangled, and it fell onto the street, dead.[72]

Cross had many breeding successes with his animals, such as the lions (the cubs known as the British Lions) and leopards, and he also exhibited new animals to the public: sea lions, boa constrictors, llamas, a gnu and a 'bonassus'. This latter animal was actually an American buffalo, but it was billed as 'extinct, till revived by the present specimen'. Wild animals were kept at the 'Royal Grand National Menagerie' (its final name) until 1828, when the Strand was being widened and the 'Change was demolished. It had been the home of exotic animals for over 40 years.

It was probably with relief that the neighbours of the 'Change took the news of its closure. Since 1816 there had been calls for the animals to be removed: several fires had broken out in the vicinity of the 'Change and there was alarm about what would happen if all the animals escaped, plus the menagerie was branded a 'nuisance' because of the 'incessant uproar and stench of [the] animals'.[73]

A taste of what might have happened occurred in December 1820 when a buffalo bull and two buffalo calves escaped into the London streets. They had been frightened by a curious crowd outside the menagerie which had stopped to see the animals before they entered the building. The chase through the streets,

The appalling living conditions in Polito's Royal Menagerie in Exeter 'Change, 1812.

including Bond Street, Grosvenor Square and Park Lane, did not result in any harm being done to pedestrians, although a horse was slightly gored. However, the bull did break a horn as he struggled to free himself after being captured, and he bled profusely.[74]

Another group glad to see the back of the 'Change was the emerging animal-welfare movement. Thomas Hood wrote of the plight of the caged animals using the 'voice' of his hero monkey called Pug in *The Monkey-martyr: A Fable* (1827). Pug stands in front of

> that intrusive pile [Exeter 'Change],
>   Where Cross keeps many a kind,
>   Of bird confin'd,
> And free-born animal, in durance vile . . .
> The desert's denizen in one small den,
> Swallowing slavery's most bitter pills –
> A bear in bars unbearable. And then

> The fretful porcupine, with all its quills
>   Imprison'd in a pen!
> A tiger limited to four foot ten;
>   And, still worse lot,
>   A leopard to one spot!
>   An elephant enlarg'd,
>   But not discharg'd;
>   (It was before the elephant was shot;)
> A doleful wanderoo [monkey], that wandered not;
> An ounce much disproporton'd to his pound.
>   Pug's wrath wax'd hot
> To gaze upon these captive creatures round;
> Whose claws – all scratching – gave him full assurance
> They found their durance vile of vile endurance.[75]

Cross's animals were moved to the King's Mews in Charing Cross in 1828. This is now the site of Trafalgar Square, but at the time Edwin Landseer's lions did not dominate the area, but a huge 150-foot-long wooden shed which held the skeleton of a whale. The move from the Strand to the 'Royal National Menagerie', as it was then known, precipitated a change of feeding time for the animals – from 8 pm to 4 pm – to accommodate the altered dining habits of upper-class Londoners.[76] But the King's Mews was a temporary home as the buildings were earmarked for demolition the following year to make way for the building of the National Gallery. Many of the animals moved to Cross's new venture, the Surrey Zoological Gardens, in 1831. Not a trace of the Exeter 'Change remains today, and in its place stands the Strand Palace Hotel.

The royal menagerie – Part III

After the closure of the 'Change there was only one place where Londoners could view a permanent collection of animals: at the Tower of London, which was enjoying its heyday. This was a turnabout in its fortunes, because in the early 1800s the Tower menagerie was suffering from the lack of gifts given to George III – as the older animals died, none were replacing them. There is mention of a lion in 1794, but it must have died soon afterwards. This animal managed to get its claws into a lady's gown as she passed too near to the grating when leaving the menagerie. The lady, a Mrs White, turned to see what she was snagged on and the lion made a swipe for her head, tearing out her eye and the whole of her cheek and badly lacerating her neck. The keepers managed to rescue her, but her injuries made a 'shocking and melancholy spectacle'.[77]

By the time the new keeper, Alfred Cops (Chunee's old keeper at the 'Change), arrived in 1822 there was only an elephant, a brown bear called Old Martin –

the first grizzly to be seen in England, who arrived in 1811 – and a couple of birds. The *Morning Chronicle* letter-writer known as C. T. expressed his or her disgust at the way 'a few wretched animals' were 'shut up in the gloomy confines of the ancient Tower of London'. This person also called for a national collection of living animals which the British Empire could be proud of, and which would further the science of natural history and provide entertainment and education for the poorer in society.[78]

Unlike his predecessors, Cops was a collector of exotics himself and he exhibited his animals alongside the royal collection. He was also keen to spend George IV's money and acquire animals, rather than wait for gifts. This was just as well, because the Nubian giraffe calf (or, as it was then known, the camelopard, because of its looks) sent to George by the pasha of Egypt was quickly dispatched to Windsor Park without stopping at the Tower. It was the first of its kind to be brought alive to England, landing at the wharf by Waterloo Bridge in August 1827. It was lifted from the barge using a crane, along with two Egyptian cows, which had provided it with milk during its journey. It was kept under Edward Cross's care at the Dutchy Wharf, Savoy, Strand.[79] Then, after a few days, it was moved to Windsor in a specially constructed van pulled by four horses.[80]

Due to Cops's knowledge and interest by 1830 the Tower collection contained about 300 animals: their housing was clean and well laid out. Tellingly, deaths due to disease and malnutrition diminished and the animals were breeding. Cops built an aviary and small-mammal and reptile house, and introduced novel sights, such as a zebra sufficiently tame to be ridden around the yard by a small boy (plainly not the zebra originally owned by Queen Charlotte), and lion cubs which could be freely petted by the visitors. The entrance fee of one shilling included the spectacle of feeding time at 3 pm and the *Morning Chronicle* stated in 1829 that it was: 'decidedly the most interesting Exhibition of the day'.[81] But this sublime state of affairs was superseded by the newly opened Zoological Gardens in Regent's Park and the animal welfare movement. The new Constable of the Tower, the Duke of Wellington (1769–1852), was also determined, it seems, to rid the Tower of both the animals and the nuisance visitors that they encouraged. His cause was assisted in January 1830 when a keeper was mauled, nearly to death, by an escaped leopard. Then George, a faithful supporter of Cops, died in June of that year; his brother William, shortly to be crowned William IV (r. 1830–37), had no interest in animals. By August 1830 it was announced in *The Times* that the royal menagerie containing 150 animals was to be transferred to the collection in Regent's Park (although they were not actually moved until 1831).

Cops's own collection of animals remained at the Tower and he continued to charge admittance to the public until, the penultimate straw for Wellington, one of the wolves escaped in April 1834. It terrorized a small terrier dog belonging to one of the families living in the Tower and came in range of children.[82] Then in August 1835, one of Wellington's soldiers at the Tower was bitten by one of Cops's monkeys and 'consigned for a considerable time to his chamber'.[83] Wellington sent a curt note to Cops: 'The King is determined that wild beasts shall not be kept there. Mr Cops had better dispose of his.'[84] The last animals – a bear, some monkeys and the birds – were sold to an American gentleman and the menagerie closed its doors on 29 October 1835. Over six centuries of the Tower of London being inhabited by animals had finally come to an end.

Nineteenth-century travelling menageries

With the closure of the Tower menagerie, the general public in London was only able to view temporary collections of animals in the travelling menageries as the Regent's Park Zoological Gardens only permitted limited public entry from 1847. These were a staple attraction at the London fairs, with the largest grouping at Bartholomew Fair. Thomas Frost described these menageries from childhood memory. Brass bands raucously played their music all day outside the exhibit to draw attention to the beasts on show. There were also immense painted images, suspended from poles, which showed the star animals of the exhibit. All were grossly exaggerated.[85] The animals inside the tents were not content. Frost pointed out that they travelled all over the country in cramped wagons, driven over rough terrain, with little ventilation. Once at the fairs, they were exhibited in cages set up in lines, open to the public's careless attentions, and continually subjected to the din of the bands outside their tents and the glare of gas lamps during the evenings.[86]

The menageries were good business, making their owners vast sums of money. In 1828 Wombwell's Menagerie made a profit of £1,700 and his main rival, Aitkins, made £1,000. Two smaller 'beast shows' made £150 (Morgan's) and £90 (Ballard's), respectively.[87] According to Frost, the largest expense was the animals' feed. He estimated that a lion or tiger ate 12 pounds of meat a day: the shins, hearts and heads of cattle. Bears were given meat in the winter, but otherwise had to be content with bread, sopped biscuits or boiled rice, sweetened with sugar. The quadrupeds' diet consisted of hay, cabbage, bread and boiled rice, with the elephants' diet supplemented with an 'unknown quantity' of buns and biscuits given to them by the public.[88] It was hardly surprising that a 'bonassus' (possibly the one seen earlier at the Exeter 'Change) exhibited by George Wombwell in 1829 died soon after it was sold to the Zoological Society, enfeebled by its past diet and confinement.[89]

Wombwell (1777–1850) was a cordwainer by trade, operating a boot- and shoemaker's shop in Old Compton Street, Soho. But he bought two boa constrictors from a South American sailor for 75 guineas and toured the local inns charging a penny per view.

Within three weeks, he had recouped his original investment. Pleased by this, he bought further animals from the London docks and established a 'Repository' in Commercial Road, in the East End, where he bought, sold and exchanged his animals and birds. By 1810 he had built up a menagerie that toured the country fairs, and later became the principal attraction at Bartholomew Fair.

Thomas Frost also recalled Wombwell's most famous animal, Nero the lion, who would allow his keeper, Manchester Jack, to sit upon him in his cage and would open his mouth, to the delight of the audience.[90] Such a compliant temperament was a boon for Wombwell's menagerie and to mark his importance in Wombwell's life, a statue of Nero, peacefully asleep, rests on top of Wombwell's grave in Highgate Cemetery. But this statue hides a painful truth: Wombwell submitted Nero to be baited by bulldogs in a fight he organized in Warwick in 1825. It was a horrific contest (which was deplored in the press) with an agonized Nero not fighting, merely swatting the dogs away with his paws. In the second fight, Nero was exhausted and suffered greatly from the attack of six fresh dogs. Eventually Wombwell stopped the spectacle, much to the crowd's disappointment and anger that Nero had not displayed any fighting spirit. Wombwell's next lion, Wallace, provided the necessary spectacle by tearing through the bulldogs.[91]

At Bartholomew Fair that year, the show cloths outside the exhibit were covered with images of the fight. Nero and Wallace were shown fearlessly tossing bulldogs into the air, with Wallace described as the 'Conquering Lion'. For sixpence, Manchester Jack would allow a member of the public into Nero's cage. This caused chaos within the tents as the paying customers were also able to view a further two lions, a lioness, two leopardesses with cubs, a hyena, a she-wolf and cubs, a polar bear, a pair of zebras, two wild asses and a large assortment of monkeys and birds.[92]

Wombwell's greatest competitor – Thomas Aitkin – was at the same show and his menagerie was deemed by William Hone, the editor of the *Every-day Book*

Wombwell's Royal Menagerie exhibition at Bartholomew Fair; sketch by George Scharf.

(1831), to be the better of the two exhibits: 'the number [of animals] was surprising, considering that they formed a better selected collection, and showed in higher condition from cleanliness and good feeding, than any assemblage I ever saw'.[93]

This menagerie was best known for its cross-bred lion-tigers or 'liger' cubs – the offspring of a tigress and a lion living in the same den. These cubs were tawny in colour, with dark stripes (rather like a tabby cat) that faded on maturity, and the males had very little mane. Because the tiger and lion were incompatible in the wild, these parents not only went against nature by breeding, but they were also tame enough to perform tricks. Their keeper put his head in the lion's jaws for nearly a minute, and had the animals jumping through hoops. He even performed the role of 'filling' in a sandwich of tigress and lion lying on their sides.[94]

The climax of the rivalry between Wombwell and Aitkin occurred in 1836. Wombwell had decided not to attend Bartholomew Fair as he was exhibiting in Newcastle upon Tyne. However, he learned that Aitkin was planning to be in London and rashly decided that he must make an appearance too. The journey down to London would normally have taken much longer than the fortnight he left himself, but by force-marching his animals he made it to Bartholomew for the opening, with the elephant walking at the head of the procession of animal wagons. Unfortunately Wombwell's elephant was exhausted by the journey and died the morning they arrived. Aitkin, in triumph, immediately put up a huge canvas sign excitedly proclaiming: 'The only living elephant in the fair'. Wombwell, undeterred and determined to make the best of his lot, published a large scroll stating: 'The only dead elephant in the fair'. The public, realising that an expired elephant was rarer than a living one, flocked to see, and poke, the dead one. For the duration of the fair, Aitkin's menagerie was largely deserted, much to his disgust.[95]

Nero reclining peacefully on the tomb of his keeper, George Wombwell, in Highgate Cemetery.

Travelling menageries were expensive to run: disease, mortality and accidents were common. Wombwell once had a 'fine ostrich', worth 200 guineas, which 'thrust its bill between the bars of his cage, gave it an unlucky twist, and in attempting to withdraw it, literally broke his neck'. He estimated that from the beginning of his career until 1834, he had lost, through death or mortal injury, about 10,000 guineas worth of animals and birds.[96]

Wombwell also seemed to be plagued with animals trying to escape from his Commercial Road winter headquarters. A polar bear imported in 1837 from the Davis Strait, in the Labrador Sea – the largest and oldest of three brought to London – broke loose and attacked one of the keepers.[97] And in 1839 a tiger escaped from the premises one evening and strolled up Commercial Road between the Regent's Canal and the bridges of Limehouse. The local inhabitants were horrified and greatly alarmed. It attacked a mastiff dog, played with it in the road, then made its way inside the iron railings of a house in Regent's Terrace. The police and keepers eventually retrieved the mauled body of the dog and caught the tiger using long poles with ropes attached. The magistrate, who was considering a charge of causing a public nuisance, questioned Wombwell. In his defence, Wombwell claimed that the tiger was perfectly docile as it was being trained to go on the stage at a London theatre – he said the dog had just upset the tiger. It was not long before the newspaper accounts of the tiger escape were being questioned. Was this a hoax or did a tiger really escape, causing local agitation? In any case, Wombwell did not miss out on the notoriety of his tiger and within a month it appeared on stage with attendant publicity.[98]

Wombwell continued to dominate the circuit: in 1840 Frost described his show as 'not only the largest and best travelling [show], but equal, and in some respects superior, to any in the world'.[99] He was by then showing various felines, bears, wolves, elephants, a rhinoceros, antelopes, giraffes, deer, assorted birds and monkeys. When Wombwell died in 1850 his obituary in *The Times* stated that he was 'the largest proprietor of wild animals in the world. No one probably has done so much to forward practically the study of natural history amongst the masses.'[100] His menagerie was shared out among three relatives, and the last collection was sold in Edinburgh by auction in 1872. Many of the animals were sold to the main animal dealers of London – Mr Charles W. Rice and Mr Charles Jamrach[101] – and taken to their respective premises at 130 Commercial Road and 180 St George Street, East (earlier known as the Ratcliffe Highway, now The Highway).

London's exotic animal dealers

Animal dealing in London, as stated earlier, was by this time well established. In addition to Rice and Jamrach, John D. Hamlyn of 221 St George Street, East, was best known for dealing in monkeys. He allegedly supplied all the monkeys for the Monkey Show at Alexandra Palace in 1889, but Mr Cross of Liverpool hotly contested this in the pages of *The Era* newspaper.[102] One of Hamlyn's advertisements read:

Proprietor of the Smallest Zoological Trading Establishment in the World . . . Note – There are several Dealers claiming to have the Largest Establishment, I am content to have the Smallest.[103]

James Morris had also traded in exotics since 1822 at the Trading Wild Animal and Natural History Stores at 81 and 97 Sclater Street, Shoreditch, and the Elephant and Camel Stalls in Cygnet Street, Shoreditch. His advertisement stated: 'A visit to the above Gigantic and Colossal Establishments will certainly repay anyone interested in Natural History Subjects. I Buy for Cash only, and Sell for Cash only.'[104]

Other animal dealers existed, but some exotics were also sold in the London markets, such as peacocks from India which were on display in Leadenhall Market, as described by *Leisure Hour* journal in 1861. The writer was dismayed at the conditions in which the 'proud and gorgeous peacock' was kept – he was cocooned in a swathe of bandages so he could not move; with his precious tail resting on a sheet of clean paper.[105]

However, Jamrach was the most celebrated animal trader in Victorian London. Charles's father, a dealer in birds and shells in Germany, established the business in London after visiting St Katharine Docks and seeing the large numbers of exotic animals being offered for sale.

Over time, Charles Jamrach (1815–1891) purchased his animals from several sources: collectors were sent out to capture animals with the 'natives' in Africa, America and India (but many animals did not survive the ordeal of capture), his agents and runners purchased animals from the ships in the London docks, or sea captains visited Jamrach to get 'shopping lists' of ordered animals to buy at foreign ports. Animals bought to order would arrive at the Wapping premises, in sometimes huge shipments.

Although the animals were not on show at Jamrach's, it was possible for the public to visit by appointment. Several newspapers investigated the depository, but their reports may well have scared off the faint-hearted. For the 'Wild Beast Mart', as it was termed in *The Graphic* in 1875, was in a rough neighbourhood and many of the wild animals within were the stuff of nightmares. It was situated in 'a narrow street blocked with heavy wagons, past low-crowned tenements, away in the murder-haunted East End'.[106]

The first part of the emporium was in St George Street – a retail shop selling shrieking parakeets, parrots and macaws, and also housing a museum full of curios from around the world. Down the road and around the corner in Betts Street were the 'stables' – a narrow yard lined on either side with cages and stalls, containing gentler animals or those which were sullenly subdued, such as lynxes, pelicans, baboons, emus, deer, antelopes and kangaroos (and latterly long-legged birds). At the end of the yard was a stable, often housing zebras and giraffes. Above this stable was a loft, reached by a steep staircase. Within the loft, closely packed together and enveloped in semi-darkness were, in the main, the recently embarked animals still in their sea-going containers. They were kept as close together as their health would allow. One correspondent from the *Daily News* described the moment he entered the loft:

A roar, a growl, a snort; a mad dash at iron bars; a frantic desire to flesh white and pointed fangs

in your carcase; rigorous writhing and tossing by some powerful body upon a wooden floor, and against wooden partitions, which shake and rattle under the shocks they have to bear, and a kaleidoscopic effect in which ferociously beautiful eyes, a savage mouth cavernously open, tawny bristly hair, and ponderous limbs and talons are intermixed confusedly, form your greeting as you pass from the topmost rungs of the ladder to the floor. It is only a young lioness . . . [but] you find yourself in a department in which a taste for human flesh, and a desire to make practical protest against confinement are very apparent.[107]

In those cramped conditions, probably without access to water, their 'protests' were hardly surprising. Alongside the carnivores were Jamrach's tame or domestic animals freely wandering about – wombats, rabbits and mandrills – and it was not unusual for dogs and cats to go missing when they accidentally went into the carnivores' cages.[108] One article noted that, 'it is odd to see the strange mixture of the domestic with the wild . . . the ducks quietly waddle under the very paws of a tiger'.[109]

The trade in exotics was a precarious business, both financially and in terms of handling dangerous animals. In 1879 'depressed' retail prices for several animals were published in *Reynolds's Newspaper* – the most expensive being a tiger at £300, and the least were 'other bears' at £8 to £16. Surprisingly, given its rarity, a polar bear was priced at £25 and ostriches were double the price of giraffes at £80 and £40, respectively.[110] Furthermore, sales were somewhat seasonal: fewer animals were for sale in the winter because the travelling menageries were resting and therefore not purchasing stock, and animals were easily killed off by the cold weather.

The fortunes of the animal dealers were also influenced by the general economic climate: during

An eclectic collection of exotics housed in Jamrach's Wild Beast Mart in 1873.

depressions, such as in the mid-1880s, sales of exotic animals crashed, but the 1890s were prosperous.[111] During this decade demand came more from America than the Continent, mainly due to the popularity of the menagerie at the World's Fair in Chicago in 1893. However, the European market was also buoyant due to low stocks of animals in European zoological gardens, which was partly due to problems in the African supply chain. Also at this time, circuses and private menageries were competing with zoological gardens and scientific societies for rare and interesting animals.[112]

It was common for dealers to lose animals before they were sold. Jamrach once lost four elephants and three tigers when a ship was wrecked in storms on its passage from India in 1873.[113] Animals also died in transit for other reasons: most often due to disease, usually caused by their close confinement between decks; exposure to the weather; accident (ostriches were known for breaking their legs in stormy weather);[114] or starvation, when the journey took longer than expected. Jamrach stated that animal losses between May and October 1885 cost him £647 – the price paid for the animals, rather than their market value.[115] Mortality on the land, which once included five elephants within a fortnight, was usually caused by the cold and damp of London – a chill finished them off. Monkeys were particularly vulnerable to the weather; Jamrach used to keep a chimpanzee as a pet in a cage in his office with which he would share his breakfast, but these were particularly susceptible to the cold and were carried off every fortnight, according to Charles's son Albert Edward, who took over the emporium.

There were several reported escapees from Jamrach's; most notoriously a tiger. Unlike Wombwell's dubious tiger escape, there is a statue to commemorate the event at the north entrance of Tobacco Dock. However, there were several versions of events reported in the newspapers and over time Jamrach emerged as the hero.

On 26 October 1857 a Bengal tiger escaped either on its way from the docks to the repository from a cattle van, or just outside the repository when it was being unloaded.[116] It broke out of its iron-bound cage and ran along the pavement in the direction of Ratcliff Highway, causing passers-by to run away in terror. Unfortunately, a young boy called John Wade, aged between five and eleven years old (depending on the report), was so stunned at the sight of the tiger that he froze. The tiger attacked him, or picked him up, and seriously lacerated his arm, face and head.

What happened next is again open to speculation. Early reports said that one of Jamrach's labourers used a crowbar to beat the tiger into submission, and one blow also landed on poor John's head. Later reports stated that Jamrach attacked the tiger with the crowbar, breaking its nose, then seized the tiger by the head, while the others secured the tiger with ropes.[117] Another report stated that the tiger, after being hit on the head by the labourer with the crowbar, was jumped upon by Jamrach, who seized the tiger's throat and managed to force it to release the child.[118] John did make a full recovery physically, but he suffered from terrible shock, which led his parents to press charges: Jamrach had already paid £10, but they wanted more. However, the court felt that Jamrach had been very courageous in his actions, and only increased the compensation to £60.[119] Mr Edmonds of Wombwell's Windsor Castle Menagerie later bought the tiger,

and an advertising picture was painted of the tiger with the boy in its mouth and labelled as, 'The tiger that swallowed the boy in Ratcliff Highway.'

Other escapees that were reported included a 4-foot-long lizard sighted in the Thames by a Bermondsey waterman. The man swore that it was an alligator.[120] The hardest animal to catch was a large baboon that freed itself from its cage, opened the window and crawled over the roof tiles to sit next to the warm chimneys. The neighbours panicked, and Jamrach was even threatened with legal proceedings if he did not recapture the 'odious creature'. It evaded capture for several days as it was 'more at home on narrow ledges and steep inclines than feet cased in boot-leather'.[121] Eventually it was enticed into an open window and had a blanket thrown over it.

Commemorating Jamrach's escaped tiger, this statue stands in the Tobacco Dock complex.

One unlucky bear never made it to Jamrachs. Muzzled and led by two sailors on a length of chain during the journey from the docks to Jamrachs, it broke its muzzle and attacked the sailors. It proceeded to kill a wolfhound and tried to attack passing horses and pedestrians. Finally, one of the sailors acquired a bludgeon and attacked the bear from behind, felling it. Instead of being sold to Jamrach, the bear's carcass was sold to a furrier for 10s.[122]

It would seem that Jamrachs was the place to sell and buy exotics. Among the buyers was naturalist Frank Buckland. He was a regular visitor and even named one monkey he purchased after the animal dealer – Jamrach is described in Buckland's *Notes and Jottings From Animal Life* (1886).[123] Van Amburgh, the celebrated lion-tamer, sourced several of his cats from Jamrach, and the artist Dante Gabriel Rossetti bought his adored wombat, called Top, from Jamrach in September 1869. Richard Bell (1833–1909), a Scottish landowner who kept his own menagerie, bought two emus and a suricate (meerkat). He wrote: 'the first time I was in London I was not long in finding my way to Jamrach's shop, which was, after the Zoo, one of the first places I visited'.[124] Jamrach was even mentioned in fiction, as the importer of the grey wolf Bersicker, which escaped from the Zoological Gardens and caused havoc in London in Bram Stoker's *Dracula* (1897).[125] Abraham D. Bartlett, the superintendent of the real Zoological Gardens in Regent's Park, was also a regular buyer from Jamrach.

London Zoo – Part I

Animals destined for Regent's Park fulfilled a very different role from those once kept in the Tower, the travelling menageries and Exeter 'Change. These animals were part of a specialist animal collection, which was intended for scientific research, rather than 'vulgar admiration'. When the Zoological Gardens opened in 1828, the general public had no access to view these animals, as they were the preserve of the Fellows of the Zoological Society of London and their guests.

The call for a 'scientific' collection of animals was set out in the 1824 prospectus for the Zoological Society. The text reflected the embarrassment felt by the co-founders that London, as the centre of the international animal trade and ruler of an empire on which famously the sun never set, did not have a national zoological garden.[126]

The prospectus went on to state the main object of the society: to introduce new animals, birds and fish to Britain 'for the purpose of domestication or for stocking our farm-yards, woods, pleasure-grounds, and wastes'.[127] It was up to the society to find further ways of exploiting animals for man's needs. To this end, it was vital to establish a collection of living animals to give 'a correct view of the Animal Kingdom at large, in as complete a series as may be practicable'.[128]

Frank Buckland took the hunt for alternative 'exotic' food sources literally. Using several species of deceased animal from the Zoological Gardens, he tried some experimental cookery. His biographer noted that Buckland ate elephant trunk soup (the trunk had to be boiled for weeks), roasted giraffe (which reportedly tasted of veal) and a pie made of the flesh of an aged rhinoceros.[129]

Scientific study of exotics

Although there had never been a repository in London for the scientific study of animals, exotics had been enthusiastically recorded since the seventeenth century, much like Buckland's taste experiments. The rarer imports, especially those from new British colonies, caused great excitement. In 1775 the first live electric eels were imported into London. Their presence led to group meetings, to test how many people standing in a line and holding hands could feel an eel's electrical charge pass through them. One meeting of Royal

Society members recorded that a chain of 27 persons could transmit the shock, and another party involved a chain of 70 people holding hands in a circle.[130]

A browse through *Philosophical Transactions*, the record of papers read to the Royal Society, reveals the variety of imported exotics in London, and their study and/or dissection by contemporary naturalists and surgeons: the rattlesnake from Virginia (1683), the 'cameleon' (1678), the opossum (1698), the ostrich (1724–5), the female sea lion or 'sea-calf', showing in Charing Cross (1742), the 'pinguin', or penguin, from the Falkland Islands (1768) and the 'nhylgau', or nilgai (1771). These animals, dead or alive, were either presented to the Society by merchants or brought back by naval captains from expeditions, or they were gifts to royalty or had been acquired for private collections.

The physician William Hunter (1718–1783) described the nilgai of the antelope family. The first breeding pair imported into London was brought over from Bombay as a retirement present for Robert, Lord Clive of India; the animals arrived in August 1767. Two more were brought over and presented to Queen Charlotte. Hunter asked to borrow these animals for study, and kept them in his stables at Great Windmill Street, Soho. Again, as in the case of the zebra, Stubbs painted them and when one died, William's brother John, an anatomist, was given royal permission to dissect it. William finally reported the findings to the Royal Society in 1771.[131]

Rather than William, John Hunter (1728–1793) was Britain's authority when it came to animal anatomy. The later anatomist Richard Owen (1804–1892) estimated that John's collection of animal bones, skulls, skins and organs contained about 500 different species, and according to Hunter's brother-in-law, Everard Home, 'no new animal was brought to this country which was not shewn to him; many were given to him; and of those that were for sale he commonly had the refusal'.[132]

Hunter became friendly with the keeper of the royal animals and was able to collect the carcasses when they died. He managed to dissect two elephants, an ocelot, an antelope, a caracal (desert lynx), a racoon and two hyenas.[133] He also acquired deceased specimens from Exeter 'Change, private dealers and travelling showmen, usually by paying generously to secure the corpse. Hunter even borrowed money from friends to pay for the carcasses: he once burst into the bookshop of a friend, begging to be loaned five guineas (a substantial sum) to buy 'a magnificent tiger which is now dying in Castle Street' (Leicester Square).[134]

John Hunter was not only interested in what was to be learned from the corpses, but also enjoyed live animals and owned a menagerie in the country at Earl's Court House in Earls Court. Passers-by would marvel at the zebra, Asiatic buffalos and mountain goats grazing in front of his house. The buffalos were also a regular sight in town as Hunter's farmhands used them to pull a cart loaded with vegetables and fruit to his town house at 13 Castle Street every Wednesday morning. Having delivered the produce, the cart would be filled with stable dung from the animals kept in town for use as manure, and also, in the winter, the putrid remains of his human and animal dissections, which were 'quietly disposed of' by the head gardener – whatever this may mean.[135]

John also kept lions and leopards at Earls Court, housed in dens beneath a hillock in the garden. Again, his brother-in-law recounted an incident involving the two leopards escaping their dens and finding their way into the yard, where they attacked Hunter's dogs. Hearing the commotion, Hunter rushed to the scene. He saw one leopard trying to climb the wall to escape and the other hemmed in by the dogs. Hunter apparently got hold of both leopards and carried them back to their den, then nearly fainted once he had time to reflect on his actions.[136]

Another anatomist, Joshua Brookes, kept birds and beasts in his garden. His brother John, dealer in animals, provided him with the beasts that Joshua kept on the corner of Blenheim Street, near Oxford Street. They were chained to artificial rocks. When the fire at the nearby Pantheon broke out on 14 January 1792, passers-by could see the eagle, hawks, racoons, foxes and other animals,

> terrified by the scene and incommoded by the heat, were panting and endeavouring to break their chains. The mob assembled, and fancying that the poor animals were roasting alive, kept up an alarming yell, and threatened to pull the house about his ears.[137]

Records do not reveal the fate of the animals, but several years later Joshua Brookes donated a white-headed eagle to the newly established Zoological Society of London. It was given the name Dr Brookes.

London Zoo – Part II

Before the animal housing at Regent's Park was built, many of the animals first donated or purchased were kept at the Zoological Society's headquarters in Mayfair's Bruton Street, inside a building and in its small garden. Others were kept in cages in nearby Camden Town and were wheeled every day to Regent's Park. In November 1827, before the Zoological Gardens opened, there were nearly 200, mainly donated, animals in the collection, including a bear, a leopard, two llamas, kangaroos and emus.

The grounds for the garden, initially only 5 acres, were leased to the Zoological Society by the Crown. It opened on 27 April 1828, but it was decided that the general public should be excluded 'to prevent the contamination of the Zoological Garden by the admission of the poorer classes of Society'.[138] It was not until 1847 that the public was admitted on Mondays and Tuesdays, and over Bank Holidays for one shilling. This princely sum was reduced the following year to sixpence on Mondays, and children were admitted on either day for this sum. This change came about due to public campaigns against the society attempting to monopolize knowledge of natural history – the most notable Fellow at this time was Charles Darwin – and also because the society needed public funds to expand. However, the public had to wait until 1857 to be admitted on Sunday mornings as well as the afternoons; previously Sunday mornings had been reserved for the Fellows.

By 1829 the permanent housing for the animals had mostly been completed. Some enclosures were plainly built with observation and study in mind, rather than the comfort of the inmates. The monkey poles consisted of a row of vertical poles to which certain species of monkey were attached, weather permitting. They were chained to the poles by a lightweight chain on a sliding ring, tethered to a leather belt around their bodies. This allowed the monkeys to move up and down their poles, on top of which there were small shelters. The bear pit was similar in that there was a pole in the centre of the sunken den, reaching up to visitor height. The bears stretched out to receive cakes, which the Fellows skewered onto the ends of their walking canes. Another poor practice, especially for the large cats, was the artificial heating of their small 'apartments' during cold weather, and also only providing a small awning to shelter them from the sun or rain; both of which caused untold damage to their health.[139] This was rectified in 1843 when new housing provided properly ventilated, draught-proof cages. But the situation did not improve for the snakes and monkeys, which were confined to badly lit, cramped and unventilated rooms: 'we counted fifty-eight [monkeys] in that one little room! If they were human beings, it is very certain that the Board of Health would have a right to interfere', stated *The Athenaeum*.[140]

In 1831, as described earlier, the collection of animals housed at the Tower menagerie was donated

George Scharf, *The Zoological Gardens, Regent's Park, showing the Bear Pit in Foreground*, 1835, lithograph.

to the Society, although they arrived periodically until 1834. The gift required more housing and more land was leased from the Crown.

The first elephant also arrived at the Zoological Gardens in 1831, having walked from London Docks – a journey of 8 miles – eating a hat and a bag snatched from two passing ladies en route. This Indian elephant was a crowd puller, named Jack, and a lady was allowed to set up a stall outside his enclosure selling rolls, cakes and fruit to feed to him, although fermented liquor was banned. It was reported in *The Times* that one day she sold cakes and buns totalling 36*s.*, 'all of which the elephant devoured'.[141] In 1836 four giraffes proceeded at their graceful loping pace (the journey took three hours) from the Brunswick Wharf, Blackwall, to the Gardens accompanied by a police escort. All transport was moved off the route because the newly arrived giraffes were unaccustomed to the hubbub of a modern city. Nevertheless they were still alarmed by a cow grazing in a field beside Commercial Road.[142]

The cult of celebrity shone on several animals throughout the gardens' history: the first 'star' was a chimpanzee called Tommy, who arrived in 1835 by night coach from Bristol. He was dressed in a cap and shirt, and lived in the keeper's apartments, but even these precautions did not prevent him from dying after six months. Richard Owen dissected Tommy. Another favourite with the public was Jenny the orang-utan, or the first Lady Jane as she was known. She lived at the Zoo for four years and delighted the crowds, including Queen Victoria and Prince Albert, by stirring tea in a cup and sipping it.

Despite some 'vulgar' displays of animal exploitation, 'scientific' study was still the focus of the Zoological Society's work. Curious, affluent gentlemen initially carried out this study of the Gardens' animals, but gradually the professional zoologist replaced the amateur by 1855. Scientific records were kept of the breeding success of the exotics and also their autopsy results, usually carried out by Owen, and later by Mr Salaman. Naturalists spent hours watching the creatures carefully, noting their habits, especially in the cases of animals of which they had no prior record. In 1851 the naturalist Charles Waterton met an orang-utan. After entering the cage, man and ape examined each other carefully (much to the amusement of the spectators) and Waterton was convinced that, 'the wild animal from the forest may be mollified and ultimately subdued by art'.[143] However, when Waterton left the orang-utan, it went to the front of the cage and promptly had a pee, which caused embarrassment to the ladies and great hilarity among the men.

Waterton concluded that, 'All monkeys are infinitely below us.'[144] It is evident that Waterton was not an observer of his fellow (male) Londoners, many of whom used the streets as a public urinal.

The young walrus that reached the Gardens in 1867 was also studied carefully – it was the first specimen to stay alive for any length of time. Its capture and travel to London were typical of the harsh reality experienced by many animals destined for the Gardens. It had been lured on board a whaling ship in the Labrador Sea by following its dead mother who was being towed behind a rowing boat to the ship. After being hauled aboard, it was tied to a ring-bolt on the deck and eventually induced to eat slivers of boiled pork. When the ship reached the Shetland Islands it was fed fresh mussels instead. After docking in Dundee, it was put in a large box with side

The Zoological Gardens' first giraffes landed in Blackwall in 1836 and walked through the London streets. George Scharf, *The Giraffes with the Arabs who Brought them Over to this Country*, 1836, lithograph.

openings and shipped by steamer to London. The journey took just under three months.[145]

Many of the behaviours observed in the Gardens' animals were reported at the Society's scientific meetings and also circulated in the newspapers for the education of the public, which was still not admitted. In 1845 an echidna or porcupine (spiny) anteater was added to the collection; this was the first time the species was exhibited alive in Europe, and observations on its housing, habits and feeding were presented in a paper to the Zoological Society by Richard Owen. However, as was to happen many times in the early history of the Gardens, it was trial and error when it came to managing the animals correctly. The echidna was fed on milk and bread – it did not eat the mealworms given to it – and was confined to a large, shallow box which had a bed of deep sand on half of the bottom, and crossbars covered the top to prevent its escape. It only lived for a few weeks; the fate of many of the newly imported species, until lessons had been learnt.[146] Many animals also suffered from the coal smoke-saturated, cold fogs that swept across Regent's Park.

Incidents were reported in the meetings, such as the case of the 11-foot-long boa constrictor that ate its 9-foot-long cage mate in October 1894: the press christened it the 'Cannibal Snake'.[147] Both snakes had been left to feed on two pigeons in the evening, but the next day the keeper found only one gorged boa. There was no sign of the smaller snake, or of the pigeons. It was expected that the boa would disgorge its companion, just as a boa constrictor had done in 1851 when it swallowed the woollen blanket that served as its bed. But this boa digested all it had eaten and was ready to receive another pigeon after 28 days.[148]

Once the public was admitted, animal celebrities became a useful marketing tool for increasing attendance. Perhaps the greatest star of the late nineteenth century was a hippopotamus called Obaysch (pronounced Obash). He was named after the island he was captured on in the White Nile when only a few days old. His sea journey from Cairo to Southampton, and then by train to the Gardens, was documented in detail by the press. Obaysch and his Arab keeper kept the public amused with his antics in the pool, *Punch* magazine christened him HRH (His Rolling Hulk), a dance called 'The Hippopotamus Polka' became popular and Cockney bus conductors would shout 'Don't let the 'orses see the 'ippo' when a fat man boarded.[149]

Obaysch's popularity was finally superseded in 1853 when a great anteater, the first to reach Europe alive, was purchased by the Society from a showman who exhibited the strange Brazilian creature in a shop in Broad Street, Bloomsbury. *Punch* magazine published a poem called 'A Howl from the Hippopotamus', in which Obaysch was portrayed as the deserted favourite. He whines, 'An American Ant-eater has put out my nose.'[150] However, the ant-eater lasted for nine days at the Gardens – probably because of its diet of milk and eggs, not ants – while Obaysch went on to father Guy Fawkes, and died of old age in 1879.

It was not long before admitting the public became a source of trouble for the Superintendent of the Gardens, as its presence inhibited the daily tasks of the keepers. Since the opening of the Reptile House in 1849 the snakes were fed live animals and birds, such as ducks, rabbits, mice and rats every Friday. This was done in public and the spectacle attracted enthusiastic crowds, which generally included a number of children. But by 1869 opinion seemed to change. A letter to *The Times* in May questioned the 'repugnant' and 'inhumane' spectacle of 'trembling rabbits [being] devoured by a serpent' and suggested that most of the public would be happy to view a stuffed boa if they knew no small animals would be eaten.[151]

Abraham D. Bartlett, the Superintendent at the time, did not give in to these demands, but did decide to substitute brown mice for the usual white mice, presumably on the grounds that white mice were, in the eyes of the public, more likely to resemble a small child's favourite pet. Eventually, the feeding regime

THE HIPPOPOTAMUS POLKA.

Obaysch the hippo inspired 'The Hippopotamus Polka',
a composition for piano from around 1850.

was changed so that the Reptile House doors were
closed at 5 pm on Fridays while feeding took place, and
only visitors who expressly wished to view the feeding would be admitted. By the early twentieth century
the regime had changed so that snakes were fed in
private on animals which had already been killed,
presumably humanely.

Westminster Aquarium

The public also made its feelings known, quite
rightly, about the way that marine mammals were
housed at the newly built Westminster Aquarium
(facing the Abbey and the Houses of Parliament),
which opened in January 1876. Its name was rather a
misnomer because essentially the Aq was an entertainment palace, as previously mentioned. But when

it was built, 31 show tanks of both fresh water and
seawater were installed. However, the water was not
clear enough to see the fish and aquatic life until
October of the same year, and even then not all the
tanks were occupied.[152] To stop mounting losses the
directors hired an ex-trapeze artist as entertainment
manager – The Great Farini. The tanks were then
used to display 'exotic' attractions of the sea.

A beluga whale arrived in 1877 after being brought
over from New York in a crate, bedded on seaweed
and soused every three minutes with seawater. On
arriving in London it waited until its tank, measuring
44 feet long, 20 feet wide and 6 feet deep, was filled
with fresh water, rather than saltwater. This took
two hours. Once installed in the tank, the whale was
offered live eels, which it did eat after being starved of
food while it had been travelling. This treatment was
alien to an animal caught off the coast of Labrador.
It died three days later after showing delirious behaviour, swimming up and down the tank rapidly and
hitting its head on the wall. The dissection showed that
it had died from congestion of the lungs, probably
caused by cold exposure on its journey from America.[153]
A letter to *The Times* from Bishop Claughton of St
Albans demanded that no 'repetition of so cruel an
experiment' should take place again.[154] However,
within the year, another beluga was confined at the
Aq. It died after a few weeks (despite the management's denials), only to be replaced by another brought
down from Blackpool.[155]

The disastrous keeping of marine mammals continued when the first manatee or 'West Indian
mermaid' arrived at the Aq in June 1878. Shipped
into Glasgow then down to London by train, once it
arrived in Westminster it went on hunger strike. It was
force-fed a mixture of milk and castor oil to cure its
supposed constipation, then started to accept French
lettuce. It ate about 100 pounds a day; mainly at night,
much to the annoyance of the public. Then it was
found in an empty tank on a cold December morning.

The facts were not clear, but it was suggested that either the keeper had not put the tank plug in properly, or the manatee had tried to commit suicide. It never fully recovered and died the following spring.[156]

Thankfully for the exotic animals on display, the Aq was sold in 1902 after its popularity plummeted.

London Zoo – Part III

The greatest public outcry concerning animals at the Zoological Gardens was over Jumbo. He was the first African elephant owned by the Gardens. Jumbo arrived in London in June 1865 and his keeper Matthew Scott soon became his trainer and favourite companion. Scott trained Jumbo to give elephant rides to children, which their parents rewarded by giving Scott a tip after their ride. However, as Jumbo approached maturity in 1881, he came into musth (just like Chunee earlier) and was banned from giving rides because of his unpredictable moods. He damaged his house, which had to be reinforced with timber buttresses, and no other keeper except Scott would enter Jumbo's den alone for fear of being attacked. He became such a problem that Superintendent Bartlett requested a rifle in December in case Scott was not present when Jumbo went berserk. With the elephant weighing 6 tonnes and standing at 11 feet 4 inches at his withers, contingency plans were needed – Bartlett did not want a repeat of Chunee's experience at the Exeter 'Change.

Jumbo was the largest elephant in Europe and, as such, he was potentially a prize exhibit for the American entertainer Phineas T. Barnum (1810–1891). Barnum approached London Zoo, as it was then colloquially called, in January 1882 asking if Jumbo was for sale and, if so, at what price. The Zoological Society jumped at the chance to offload their troublesome elephant and asked for £2,000, to which Barnum agreed.

There was an announcement in *The Times* on 25 January about Jumbo's purchase, which went relatively

The inspiration for *Winnie-the-Pooh*: Winnie with Christopher Milne.

unnoticed by the public and caused no fuss with the Fellows. However, when, on 18 February, Barnum's agents tried to load Jumbo into his travelling crate, he refused to enter it. He even refused to walk out of the gates of the Zoo to reach the docks. It was decided to try again in a fortnight but, during this time, the press got involved. The public, quiet when Jumbo's sale was announced, now waged a campaign to secure a reversal of the decision to sell him, as they believed Jumbo was showing distress at leaving his home. They also accused the Society of being unpatriotic. Jumbo's noisy neighbour Alice, who created a din when Jumbo was being moved, was referred to as 'Jumbo's little wife' and rumours started to circulate that Alice was in calf. A popular song of the time ran:

Jumbo giving rides to children: his size was remarkable. Matthew Scott stands to his left.

Jumbo said to Alice: 'I love you'.
Alice said to Jumbo: 'I don't believe you do,
For if you really loved me, as you say you do,
You wouldn't go to Ameriky and leave me in
    the Zoo.'[157]

Visitors, mainly children, flocked to the Gardens in a state of sentimental hysteria and left Jumbo gifts for his journey, such as dolls, books and even a sewing machine. There was a legal battle launched by some of the Fellows to try to implement an injunction against Jumbo's sale.[158] Throughout the mania, the Society reiterated its reasons for selling Jumbo; namely that he was a danger to the public and his sale to Barnum would remove the threat of him having to be killed.

'Jumbo's Journey to the Docks', from the *Illustrated London News*, 1882.

Eventually it was decided that Jumbo should leave. Bartlett asked if Scott could be sent away on holiday when Barnum's agents attempted to load Jumbo for a second time, because he had suspicions that Scott had given Jumbo a secret command to lie down. Scott, after all, was losing the elephant that provided him with a good living in tips. Bartlett then told Scott that Barnum had offered to let him travel to America with his elephant and Scott readily agreed to not go on holiday and to try again to induce Jumbo to enter his crate. The next morning, 23 March, Jumbo was loaded without a problem. It was not until past midnight that Jumbo's crate was moved by ten draught horses through the deserted London streets to St Katharine Docks. He was loaded on to a Thames barge and then onto a steamship headed for New York. Jumbo subsequently toured with Barnum's *Greatest Show on Earth*, but was accidentally killed in 1885 when he was hit by a goods train in Ontario.

It was a sad end for Jumbo, who had given rides to the children of London for seventeen years. This policy of training elephants and camels to be ridden was extended in 1904 to a zebra. The Zoological Society was against 'masterly inactivity' and it was urged to 'do something' with its equine stock,[159] so it was broken for the saddle. However, it died, possibly due to this practice, and after this death no other animals were domesticated.

Other zoo animals were trained for alternative uses. During the First World War the sea lions were commandeered to train as submarine detectors. They, and other sea lions around the country, were taken to swimming baths in London and trained to ignore fish which were released into the water (this was helped by them wearing leather muzzles), and to come to the surface and bark when they heard a buzzer sounding. This was the first stage in learning to detect submarines. However, by the time the sea lions had been fully trained in Wales, they were not required for active service as the hydrophone had been perfected. The sea lions were returned to the Zoo, where they continued to entertain the visitors.[160]

In 1925 chimpanzees were taught to sit around a table and 'take tea' – or rather fruit juice poured out by a keeper – and eat fruit off a plate. This 'Chimpanzee's Tea Party' was a staple of Londoners' childhood memories until 1972, along with petting tame animals in Pets' Corner, riding an elephant and feeding the animals. Eventually, an horrific incident resulted in a ban on feeding of the animals by the public. In 1967 an elephant called Diksie fell over her enclosure wall into a 5-foot-deep dry moat while trying to reach a bun held out by a visitor – or was she pushed by another elephant? She landed on her back, rupturing several internal organs and injuring her leg. She died as she was about to be hoisted up using a crane.[161] The ban was too late for one of the Zoo's best-known inmates, the hugely popular Guy the Gorilla, who lived in the Gardens from 1947 until 1978. He had been fed sweets while he was young and died under anaesthetic while his rotten teeth were being treated. His predecessor, Mumbo, the first gorilla in the Zoo, lived on a similar diet of fruit, but with sausages, beer and cheese sandwiches, boiled potatoes and mutton. Not surprisingly, he died within a few months of enclosure in 1887.[162]

There is a statue of Guy in the Zoo along with two statues of Winnipeg, or Winnie, as she was better known. She was an American black bear that had been rescued by Captain Colebourn, of a Canadian cavalry regiment, from a hunter in Ontario. She became the troop's mascot and travelled with it into Britain en route to the Western Front during the First World War. Colebourn donated her to the Zoo before the troop left for France and she lived there from 1914 until 1934. One of her biggest fans was a child called Christopher Robin, who named his own teddy bear Winnie after her.

The animals in London Zoo came close to being removed from their urban home in 1992 when it was announced that it was to close due to financial problems. But as a cost-cutting measure to allow its survival, animal numbers were reduced by 15 per cent. Attendance also increased after the threat of closure, and private donations allowed the newly agreed conservation, research and entertainment focus of the Zoological Society to develop. It seems that exotic animals will be in London for years to come, as long as people visit the Zoo, although elephants and other large animals, such as the rhinoceroses, left in 2001 to be rehoused at Whipsnade Wild Animal Park.

The other 'types' of exotic animal in London, to which we now turn, had a greater impact on people's lives than those behind bars. These were 1773 the (relatively) harmless exotics imported into London that were snapped up by the wealthy and tried out as pets for their novelty value – often with unforeseen consequences.

six

Pampered Pets and Sad Strays

Exotic and less exotic animals have provided companionship to all classes of London society for centuries as indoor pets, but it has not been the easiest of relationships for either animal or owner.

Exotic pets

At the eastern end of Cheyne Walk in Chelsea was Tudor House, the home of the artist Dante Gabriel Rossetti from 1862. Rossetti became obsessed by the wombats at the London Zoo, thinking they were the most beautiful of God's creatures, and he bought two. In a letter to his brother he described the arrival of one – called Top – 'a Joy, a Triumph, a Delight, a Madness'. Top had probably come from Tasmania to England aboard Prince Alfred's ship HMS *Galatea*, and then was bought by Charles Jamrach. Top only lived with Rossetti for two months, but made a huge impression on his owner and house guests. He would curl up and sleep in the middle of the table during dinner parties and he had the run of the house. On his death Rossetti was distraught and drew a pen-and-ink illustration of himself crying into a handkerchief as he looked upon the upturned dead body of this wombat. It is inscribed with a verse:

I never reared a young wombat
To glad me with his pin-hole eye,
But when he was most sweet and fat
And tail-less he was sure to die.[1]

Top was subsequently stuffed and placed in Tudor House's entrance hall. Rossetti's other pets included peacocks, armadillos, kangaroos, wallabies, a Canadian marmot or woodchuck, a Japanese salamander, deer, parakeets, a racoon, squirrels, mice and dormice, and two owls called Jessie and Bobbie. However, Rossetti did not have much luck with his animals: the young kangaroo killed its mother, which in turn was killed by the racoon; a white peacock released into the drawing room hid under a sofa and died, probably of shock; the dormice failed to wake up after they had hibernated; the armadillos dug under the neighbours' house and came up through the kitchen floor, sending the cook into hysterics; and the fallow deer chased a peacock and trampled on its tail until all the feathers came out. In disgust, the peacock flew up into a tree and started to make piercing shrieks which so annoyed the neighbours that there is still a clause in the leases of Cheyne Walk houses forbidding the keeping of peacocks.[2]

Frank Buckland's neighbours may also have been annoyed with the various exotic pets which lived at his home in Albany Street, Regent's Park. One of the most unusual was a kookaburra (then known as the 'laughing jackass') which would not laugh, until it one day escaped from its cage and flew free across Regent's Park, making its distinctive cry. Buckland was in despair until the Zoological Gardens brought the bird back, it having been handed in by a gentleman in nearby Stanhope Street, who had found the

Dante Gabriel Rossetti, *Rossetti Mourning the Death of his Wombat*, 1869, pen drawing.

pets, although they were often too delicate to cope with the climate. According to Jamrach, who sold many monkeys in the nineteenth century, ring-tailed or blue-faced monkeys made the best pets, as the former coped well with the climate and the latter were the most gentle.[8] Capuchin monkeys from South America also made popular pets. According to the naturalist C. J. Cornish (1859–1906), they were the only monkeys that could be thoroughly recommended as an indoor pet: they were beautiful, intelligent, could cope with the English climate, were good tempered and had 'pretty winning ways'.[9]

However, not all monkeys made ideal pets. They were, according to one female London vet in 1922, 'extraordinarily delicate little creatures, and suffer from all disorders, ranging from toothache to intestinal troubles'.[10] They were also liable to bite their owners. In 1683 John Evelyn wrote of several monkey attacks on sleeping children he had heard of – they had bitten out eyes, torn faces and eaten 'the head into the braine'[11] – but monkeys also attacked adults.

The portrait painter Richard Cosway (1742–1821) kept a monkey, and one friend who visited him at his London home found him

> laid on a Sofa in his night gown – and the calf of one of his legs bundled up; on my inquiring the cause he acquainted me that his monkey or baboon had tore a gt. Piece out of his leg; and that he was under Dr [John] Hunter's hand for a cure; the poor animal has been put out of its pain by the same hand and the Dr. had the pleasure of dissecting him & put him in spirits, in terror to all monkeys.[12]

It is not surprising that monkeys kept in London homes became violent, considering some accounts of how badly they could be treated through ignorance of their needs. One account written in 1890 stated that

kookaburra perched fast asleep at the foot of his bed. On its return home, Buckland cut the wing feathers off one wing to prevent further escapes.[3] It apparently sulked for months, but did eventually learn to laugh at regular half-hour intervals![4] Buckland's other animals included a Turkish wolfhound called Arslan, which had a penchant for killing small dogs (including the neighbour's lapdog), rats, a suricate or meercat called Jemmy, and a jaguar nursed back to health by Mrs Buckland after it was given to them by the Zoo.[5] Buckland also owned a succession of monkeys called Miss Susey, the Hag, Jenny, Tiny, Carroty Jane, Little Jack and Nigger. They were his constant companions in his study, which was renamed the Monkey Room, and he used to say: 'Love me, love my monkey.'[6]

Monkeys had been a particular favourite of Londoners since they were first imported in the thirteenth century.[7] They could make very entertaining monkeys were kept in tiny cages and fed on a range of inappropriate foods, such as cod-liver oil and salt herrings, or infants' food and tripe.[13]

The writer goes on to explain that at first the monkey's antics were endearing and it was given the run of the house, but when it became too mischievous it was often severely punished:

A very intelligent monkey was being taught, when its master (a working man) came home at night, to scramble on to his shoulder, take off his cap, spring on to the chest of drawers, and hang it on a peg. Unfortunately, the animal could not discern when its master was the worse for drink. One evening, when he was in that state, he wished to keep his hat on, as he was going out again. But the animal persisted in hanging it on the peg, and each time the man took it down Bruno replaced it ungently, tweaking his ears as it did so.

Lucas Horenbout, *Catherine of Aragon* with a pet monkey, *c.* 1525–6, miniature.

The man, in a rage, seized it, carried it to the sink, and held it under the tap – a fitter place for its drunken owner – while it howled pitifully. Then the poor drenched creature crept away, and never would touch his cap again.[14]

Another favourite exotic pet, and certainly less dangerous, was the opossum (now known as a possum) from Tasmania. These marsupials were described as 'sweet little things . . . when well treated'.[15] C. J. Cornish owned one, bought for £3, and he explained that it was the 'most fearless and affectionate pet' that he had ever known:

In the evening, when it was most lively, it would climb on to the shoulder of any of its visitors, and take any food given it. It had a mania for cleanliness, always 'washing' its hands after taking food, or even after running across the room, and was always anxious to do the same office by the hands of any one who fed it. It made friends with the dogs, and would 'wash' their faces for them, catching hold of an old setter's nose with its sharp little claws, to hold it steady while it licked its face. The staircase and banisters furnished a gymnasium for exercise in the winter, and in summer it could be trusted among the trees in the garden.[16]

Unfortunately, the opossum was becoming scarce because of demand for its fur, so Cornish also recommended the hardy American grey squirrel, the chinchilla, the South American coatimundi, the Indian mongoose and the meercat as alternative pets.[17]

According to another writer, meercats were not ideal because they developed respiratory problems during the winter months. 'Draughty floors are very trying to animals that live underground in the South African veldt.'[18] As a result, the same writer described the meercats being offered up to London Zoo for

Christian the lion living in the Kings' Road, Chelsea in 1970. No licence was required!

re-homing – they were so freely given as failed pets that the Zoo had to turn them away.[19] Other pets this writer had seen in 1909 were marmosets, the desert-living jerboa, the water tortoise, the chameleon and tree frogs.[20]

In wealthy London neighbourhoods in the early twentieth century, it was common for owners to return with unlikely pets from India and other parts of the Empire. Many of these animals were too big, or too difficult, to keep at home so they were housed nearby in a 'zoological boarding-house' run by a lady vet. She had in her charge kangaroos, small deer, foxes, tortoises, harmless snakes and

a cheetah, or a hunting leopard, which is really a capital pet – far less formidable than he looks, and quite a likely companion for promenades in the city streets, if only the lovely spotted thing would not attract so much attention.[21]

Another big cat was kept in London for about six months during 1970 – Christian the lion, probably the most famous animal to be sold through the Harrods department store's 'Zoo'. He was brought to Knightsbridge in 1969 from Ilfracombe Zoo in Devon with his sister, and they were kept in a small cage between Siamese kittens and old English sheepdogs. Christian's price tag was 250 guineas. Two Australians, John Rendall and Anthony 'Ace' Bourke, persuaded the Harrods buyer that they would be responsible foster parents for the then four-month-old Christian, and he lived with them on the King's Road, Chelsea, in an area known as World's End, in a furniture shop called Sophistocat that had a large basement. He lived in the shop, greeting the customers, and played outdoors in a local garden for five months, becoming a local celebrity through his TV and radio appearances. However, it soon became clear that Christian needed to be rehomed, and he was eventually released in Kenya under the care of *Born Free*'s George Adamson.[22]

In the 1970s Harrods stopped trading in exotic animals, although their archives do not show in what year exactly.[23] They now have a 'Pet Kingdom' rather than a 'Zoo', and the keeping of dangerous animals in London is limited by the Dangerous Wild Animals Act of 1976, which states that owners of exotic pets have to buy expensive licences for their animals and submit to welfare and safety inspections – although it is certain that London is still not only a centre of global animal smuggling, but also home to many illegally kept exotics and illegally dumped exotics that grow too big or are too difficult to look after.[24] There may even be young wolves hidden away, similar to the late Diable, which was kept as a pet in a Clapham back garden – unfortunately, it escaped and was killed in 1961. Its skin is in the Museum of London.[25]

Less exotic pets

In 1732 the *Gentleman's Magazine* wrote that most animals were cruelly abused in Britain, apart from a few privileged animals: 'Our Kindness to Brutes is chiefly owing to Whim and Caprice. Ladies are fond of a Lap-Dog, Squirrel, Parrot, Monkey, Cat'.[26] These pet animals were, as Keith Thomas states, 'company for the lonely, relaxation for the tired, a compensation for the childless'.[27] Initially pets were for the affluent, but as the nineteenth century dawned animals began to be welcomed into all Londoners' homes. Domestic pets are today the most numerous 'type' of animal left in London, apart from vermin.

Squirrels

The native red squirrel has been a 'privileged' pet since medieval times. It can be seen twice in the fourteenth-century Luttrell Psalter – one sits on a crowned lady's shoulder as she rides in a carriage, and a squirrel with a bell around its neck appears next to a kneeling woman.[28] When Hans Holbein was in London from 1526 to 1528, he painted an aristocratic-looking lady with a squirrel sitting on her arm, which was happily chewing a nut, and the cleric Edward Topsell (*c.* 1572–1625) said that apart from their love of eating woollen clothes, squirrels were 'sweet, sportful beasts and . . . very pleasant playfellows in a house'.[29]

Even in the mid-nineteenth century, the squirrel was still regarded by some as the 'king of pets':

First in the rank of innocent, playful, and confiding animals is our little friend the Squirrel. All life and vigour, he is continually inventing new tricks, and playing them off. Only let him see that *you* are pleased and attracted by his gymnastics, and his fun knows no bounds. He will throw himself on his back, bound upwards,

Hans Holbein the Younger, *A Lady with a Squirrel and a Starling*, c. 1526–8, oil on oak.

because he is very spiteful, and dangerous where there are children. Old squirrels bite severely, and leave their marks behind them for many a day.' It was also bad practice to buy a squirrel from a street seller rather than from a bird dealer – the writer warned that old squirrels had their teeth filed down to make them appear juvenile and to prevent them from biting.[31]

Most squirrels sold in London were taken from their nests in Windsor Forest when they were young and helpless, and placed with a cat that would act as a surrogate mother for up to a dozen squirrels at a time.[32]

Lapdogs

Lapdogs or small pet dogs also enjoyed pet status since the later Middle Ages as companions of 'wealthy females courtiers or those of privileged religious orders'.[33] These people had the 'Whim and Caprice',[34] and the money, to lavish attention on dogs that were not useful in any way – their only requirement was to be small and entertaining. Of all the dogs mentioned in Dr Caius's *Of Englishe Dogges*, only one pet dog was cited – 'the Spaniel-gentle or Comforter' – or toy spaniel. According to Abraham Fleming, who translated Caius's work:

> The smaller they be the more pleasure they provoke, as more meet playfellows for mincing mistresses to bear in their bosoms, to keep company withal in their chambers, to succour with sleep in bed, and nourish with meat at board, to lay in their laps and lick their lips as they ride in wagons.[35]

As far as we know, Charles II was the first king to publicly admit a love for lapdogs. He even named his own breed: his King Charles spaniels followed him everywhere. Evelyn wrote a tribute to Charles on 6 February 1685 in London:

downwards, backwards and forwards. He is here, there, every where, – all in a moment of time. And how pretty he looks, while poised on his two hinder legs (his forefeet suspended in air) to take a breath while you are watching his movements! . . . Their *forte* is play; their delight is unrestricted liberty.[30]

The writer owned a squirrel called Scaramouch that loved to tear up newspapers into tiny pieces, hunt the cat while riding around on the back of a spaniel dog and help himself to breakfast – he had his own chair, but would steal away, and hoard, the sugar. However, it was bad policy to buy an old squirrel, because he 'is not teachable, and very obstinate; next,

He took delight to have a number of little spaniels follow him, & lie in his bed-Chamber, where often times he suffered the bitches to puppy & give suck, which renderd it very offensive, & indeede made the whole Court nasty & stinking.[36]

James II (r. 1685–8) shared his brother's passion for toy spaniels and William and Mary (r. 1689–1702) popularized the Dutch pug. However, the ordinary London citizen would not have lavished love on dogs until the early nineteenth century, when the attachment to a pet became more commonplace and was more 'greeted with general sympathy than with disapprobation or derision'.[37] The craze for lap-dogs among London ladies was in full swing by the middle of the century. Whether the dogs were bought because they were loved, or because they were valuable fashion accessories, is another matter.

Ladies acquired their dogs from one of two sources: the working-class 'fancy' or pet emporiums such as Jamrach's. Wandering street sellers/breeders would frequent the fashionable quarters of London every day with lapdogs in their pockets, carrying one in their hand and walking another on a lead (some of them were stolen). They would sell to 'idle ladies, who do no work in the world, and imagine that they were born to do nothing', according to one journal writer.[38] Jamrach sold all types of Japanese dog, such as the long-coated pug and Japanese spaniels, and also Afghan hounds. In 1898 the Board of Agriculture made it difficult to import dogs, therefore increasing their prices. Jamrach was most disappointed when a Japanese dog worth £30 was devalued in one blow of a Persian cat's paw that destroyed its right eye.[39]

The indulgent treatment of ladies' lapdogs was much satirized in *Punch* magazine: the feeding of the dogs at the table, dressing them in costumes and allowing them free run in the house, and having servants bending to their every whim.[40] According to one journal writer, the rise of the lapdog in drawing rooms across London was a 'social nuisance'. He better described a lapdog as a 'man hound' because of its 'express purpose of frightening, worrying, snarling, and snapping' at visitors.[41]

It was no wonder that these dogs behaved as they did, according to one lady vet who took in lapdogs to board in 1922. She did her best to dissuade her rich and childless clients from lavishing their dogs with 'preposterous luxuries' – such as taking them to the Dog's Toilet Club in Bond Street,

'The West End Dog Fancier', from Gustave Doré, *London* (1872).

185

Thomas Blinks and Frederick Morgan, *Queen Alexandra with her Grandchildren and Her Favourite Pets*, 1902, oil on canvas.

where all sorts of products could be bought at prices which 'took one's breath away':[42] scented baths, perfumes, pocket handkerchiefs, fur coats, rubber boots and jewelled and golden collars. The dogs were also usually overfed on chops, steak, chicken and other rich food, and their every whim was indulged. One valuable but sick Siamese cat came into her surgery. It was particularly fond of playing with an expensive clockwork wooden motor car. She was warned that if the car stopped working 'the cat's spirits would suffer'.[43]

It was only after the First World War prompted social changes that pampered lapdogs began to be substituted for 'living dolls of the poor'[44] – adopted babies – which was encouraged by Queen Alexandra (1844–1925), even though she herself was devoted to her borzois and pekinese, and subsequently Queen Mary and her daughter Mary.

However, the craze for lapdogs has recently made a resurgence in 'fashionable London society', with Harrods pandering to the trend by holding an annual Dog Fashion Show called Pet a Porter. A Harrods Wedding Service for Dogs was even launched in 2006.

Beloved animals

Aside from (usually) overindulging their lapdogs and faithful hounds, wealthy owners also showed their devotion to their animals in different ways. In 1803 a duel was fought between two men after their Newfoundland dogs fought each other in Hyde Park. Colonel Montgomery dismounted and tried to part them, saying that he would knock the other dog down if it tried to attack him. The owner of the attacking dog, Captain Macnamara of the Royal Navy, replied that if the colonel knocked down his dog he must also knock him down. The resulting duel, after the dog fight, ended with the death of Montgomery.[45]

Other dogs were left money in their owners' wills. In 1805 Mr Berkely of Knightsbridge left £30 to four of his dogs – presumably for their eternal keep. These pets were the descendants of a faithful dog which had protected and saved Berkely from an attack by brigands during a journey through France and Italy. Sensing death was close, Mr Berkely called for two armchairs to be brought to his bedside for the dogs to sit on and, 'he received their last caresses, which he returned with the best of his failing strength, and died in their paws'. On his death stone busts were made of the dogs and placed at the corners of his tomb.[46]

London is also littered with memorials and small tombstones dedicated to beloved pets. Some are singular memorials, such as the burial site in the former front garden of 9 Carlton House Terrace, SW1 (the former German Embassy and now the home of the Royal Society), of Giro, the dog of Dr Leopold von Hoesch, the anti-Hitler German ambassador from 1932 to 1936. Giro was electrocuted by an exposed wire in 1934 and his headstone reads: 'Ein Treuer Begleiter!' (A True Companion!). There is a statue of William Hogarth and his pug dog Trump near to Hogarth's house on Chiswick High Road. Hogarth's image was originally unveiled in 1999, without his beloved Trump, who was added due to popular demand in 2001. Since 1997 a statue of Samuel Johnson's cat Hodge has stood outside 17 Gough Square, EC4, where Johnson lived for eleven years. The plaque reads 'a very fine cat indeed' (a Johnson quote), and Hodge sits on his owner's famous dictionary, alongside a pile of oysters which Johnson, according to James Boswell, used to buy for his companion, 'lest the servants having that trouble should take a dislike to the poor creature'.[47] A bust of Petra, the original dog of the children's television programme *Blue Peter*, also stood

The Dogs' Cemetery at Victoria Gate in Hyde Park.

in the *Blue Peter* Garden at BBC Television Centre, Wood Lane, until it was moved to the new BBC studios in Salford in 2012.[48]

However, the most impressive collection of animal tombstones is in Hyde Park at the Dogs' Cemetery, next to Victoria Gate and the Bayswater Road. There are about 300 stones in all, remembering beloved dogs, cats and a few monkeys buried there up to the First World War. The first to be interred was Cherry, a Maltese terrier, on the request of his master and family in 1881, because he was a member of their family:

> He was an accomplished dog of the world, and delighted in giving drawing-room entertainments. Dressed up as a soldier, in a little uniform coat, a helmet, and a musket, he was an inimitable sentinel. But as a sick baby carefully tucked up in a perambulator he always 'brought down the house' . . . So intelligent and so amiable a dog assuredly deserved a Christian burial.[49]

Once Cherry had been buried in the park, word spread and for twelve years an assortment of ladies' pets were given burials, as well as the fox terrier called Topper who was the mascot of the Hyde Park police station.[50] Most of the epitaphs are plain, but there is one that gushes with emotion.

> Sleep Little One Sleep
> Rest Gently Thy Head
> As Ever Thou Didst At My Feet
> And Dream That I Am Anear
> I Faithfully Loved And Cared
> For You Living – I Think
> We Shall Surely Meet Again.[51]

It seems that many of the dogs met their ends under the hooves of the horse traffic in the streets and one journal remarked, rather hard-heartedly: 'It would appear, however, that the very tenderness and care that are lavished upon them unfit them for the rude and heartless world, and make them unable to look out for themselves.'[52]

Dog stealing and dog skinning

This inability to defend themselves, and the fact that they were beloved dogs of the wealthy, made pet dogs a target for dog thieves, of which there were many in London – it was easy to distract a dog from its owner with the traffic, people, smells and sights of town all around. Charles II's dogs were regularly stolen, as intimated by a notice in the *Mercurius Publicus* for 28 June–5 July 1660, drawn up by the king himself:

> We must call upon you again for a Black Dog between a greyhound and a spaniel, no white about him, onely a streak on his brest, and his tayl a little bobbed. It is His Majesties own Dog, and doubtless was stoln, for the dog was not born nor bred in England, and would never forsake His master. Whosoever findes him may acquaint any at Whitehal for the Dog was better known at Court, than those who stole him. Will they never leave robbing his Majesty! Must he not keep a Dog? This dog's place (though better than some imagine) is the only place which nobody offers to beg.[53]

Between 1700 and 1800 there were almost 500 advertisements for lost dogs in the central London news-sheets, such as:

> 1786 – LOST, on Saturday last, May 5th, near Grosvenor-gate, a yellow and white Spaniel Dog, rather old, very fat, and has lost an eye. Whoever will bring him to Lady Robert

Manners, Grosvenor-square, shall have Two
Guineas reward.[54]

Gangs would stalk their targets to know their walking routes and when they were least watched by their
owners or dog walkers (servants).[55] Once the dogs
had been whisked away, often under the very noses of
their walkers, they would be hidden in the less salu-
brious parts of London, like Shoreditch, where the
known dog thief Taylor operated in the 1840s. This
man stole Elizabeth Barrett Browning's dog Flush, a
golden cocker spaniel, three times; twice in the streets,
and once on the doorstep of the house in Wimpole
Street, W1, where a decoy dog was used to attract his
attention. On the second occasion, Elizabeth herself
went with her maid to confront Taylor in the 'obscure
streets' of Shoreditch.[56] The thieves, after a prescribed
time (neither too soon nor too late), would visit the
owners saying that they had found the dog and would
need an amount of money to have it returned. When
asked how he settled on the amount of the reward, a
thief replied: 'Oh no, sir, we doos it by the feelinx of
the party.'[57]

Sometimes the thieves were caught when owners
went to the police. James Goude Sr, a livestock dealer and animal trainer, was imprisoned for four months
without hard labour for stealing a valuable black-
and-white Japanese spaniel on Christmas Eve in
1892. A reward of £10 was offered for the dog, and
subsequently Goude wrote to the owner offering to
restore the animal. They arranged to meet at a public house, Goude bringing the dog with him. He
handed over the dog, but the owner refused to pay
him the £5 he demanded, and went to the police with
his details.[58]

But dog thieves did not take pedigree dogs just to
return them to their owners. Some sold the dogs onto
professionals who ran a 'regular canine slave-trade to
the Continent',[59] so valuable stolen dogs were
whisked across the Channel to another life. Dogs,

'What have we done that we should be skinned alive?' Stray
cats were in danger on the streets from fur thieves, 1839.

both pedigrees and mongrels, were also sold on to
dog skinners, or even master curriers (leather dressers)
such as Mr Rout, of Coppice Row, Clerkenwell. Dog
skins were worth between 4s. and 4s. 6d. in 1831.[60]

The notorious dog skinner Doubleday spoke to
one journalist from inside Coldbath Fields Prison
about the process of catching the dogs: a piece of
bullock's liver was boiled hard to entice them, then a
rope with a noose was put over their heads and this
fastened round their necks, allowing them to be led
away to be skinned.[61] This was a particularly lucrative and easy job during the rabies alarm, when no
one thought anything of seeing a dog being noosed
and led away. Dogs were taken to the skinners' dens
in Whitechapel, Shoreditch, Tottenham Court Road
and Westminster; there were also outposts at
Greenwich, Ball's Pond in Islington, Lisson Grove
and Paddington, a noted place on the right of the
North Road, and a rendezvous in Long Acre.[62]

Another site was in Pettifield Court, leading into
Drury Court, the Strand, where in 1831, after a tip-
off, constables found the disgusting sight of up to 30
dogs chained to the walls and as thin 'as laths from
starvation', awaiting their deaths – which sometimes
were done via rigged-up gallows.[63]

Elizabeth Barrett Browning and her dog Flush in a watercolour by her brother Alfred.

Often constables only found dog carcasses when they visited suspected dog skinners, and therefore could not find the dogs' owners, so the culprits had to be released without charge. Two men came before the Bow Street magistrates in 1830 for possessing the skins of a black cat and a very large dog. A previous search of their rooms had revealed three dog carcasses and five skins all belonging to valuable dogs. But instead of being imprisoned and receiving a public whipping, they had to be discharged.[64]

Cats were also targets for the skinners, but they were usually skinned alive, according to the historian Alfred Rosling Bennett, as the 'furs taken in that fashion preserv[ed] their lustre longer and command[ed] a higher market value'. The skinner of the 1850s and '60s would place the cat between the knees and spike the back of the cat's neck to keep it still, then with 'dexterous and cunning incisions' would cut the skin and reverse the animal with a jerk to relieve it of its 'skin and fight, but otherwise uninjured'. Bennett added that stories were told of these 'pussies in this deplorable condition running home and mewing to be let in. One was said to have even reached the drawing room where its mistress was holding a reception and jumped on her lap.'[65]

Cats as pets

Cats were probably one of the most recent animals to enjoy fully fledged pet status in London; they did not

The most famous cat in London? This sculpture of Dick Whittington's cat stands near Highgate Tube station.

Sculpture of Samuel Johnson's cat Hodge outside his house at 17 Gough Square, just off Fleet Street.

become established domestic pets until the eighteenth century. Before then they were usually kept for killing vermin and were mainly the old English blue-and white cats – long since elbowed out by imported tabbies.[66] In the reign of Charles II, according to Daniel Defoe's *Journal of the Plague Year* (1665), the majority of London families owned cats for their hunting prowess, 'some having several, sometimes five or six in a house'.[67]

Even London's most famous cat, the companion of Dick Whittington (*c.* 1350–1423), was just a 'mouser' and not a pet. Though there is a bronze statue of the cat sitting on top of the Whittington Stone near the bottom of Highgate Hill (near Archway station), Dick only seemed to acquire his cat in the sixteenth century – prior to this, the legend omitted any men-

tion of it.[68] However, the cat legend remains intact today, not least in pantomime and children's books. The Whittington and Cat pub on Highgate Hill (now closed) used to display the mummified remains of a cat with a mummified mouse hanging from its mouth, supposedly the final remains of Whittington's famous companion.[69]

But despite their 'lowly' status, cat owners were often fond of their 'mousers' and many were well-kept and treated. Of all the cats in London, some of the most visible belonged to shopkeepers. These were often magnificent animals, such as the cat which lived in 1919 at the sausage and mash shop in Hammersmith Broadway. He was described by one journal as:

shining like a well-blacked boot, with eyes half shut, and the broadest of smiles upon his genial face, this cat sits within the doorway like some jovial innkeeper. Did the proprietor but know it – perhaps he does – this cat is a finer advertisement, a more convincing assurance as to the excellence of the fare within than all the notices upon its steamy windows.[70]

Equally remarkable were the enormous cats that could look over a tradesman's counter at customers while their hind legs were still on the ground. These cats were almost certainly descended from cats sold at Leadenhall, remarked one mid-nineteenth-century journal. Leadenhall cats were special 'thorough-bred grimalkin[s]', worth 10s. They were 'giants in size when full grown, and were moreover possessed of remarkable intelligence – we can pronounce them to be honestly worth the money'.[71]

Exotic and native caged birds

Caged birds have graced Londoners' homes for centuries. They were kept either for their song – nightingales and larks – or for their entertaining imitations of human voices – magpies and parrots. A number of small medieval pewter feeding bowls which clipped to the bars of bird cages can be found in the Museum of London – one of them was found by a metal detector on the Thames foreshore with birdseed still inside it.[72] Bird dealers selling natives and exotics first appeared in Tudor London. They supplied the wealthy, such as Henry VIII's one-time Chancellor Sir Thomas More (1478–1535), who was a collector of birds and allowed them freedom to fly about his Chelsea home. In Elizabethan times there are records of bejewelled silver birdcages, although none survive, and Charles II had many caged birds, including a pet starling.

Samuel Pepys recorded buying two cages for the canaries he had been given in January 1661. These wild green canaries would probably have been imported by Spanish dealers from their native lands, or from Germany, where they bred canaries out of the female birds from these Spanish shipments.[73] Pepys's last surviving canary lived until 11 January 1665, when Pepys wrote that he was 'much troubled' to hear that his 'poor canary bird' was dead. Another imported bird was the East India nightingale, or as it is now known, the mynah (mina) bird, which Pepys heard sing in 1664 in the Duke of York's rooms in St James's: 'There is a bird comes from the East Indies . . . talks many things and neighs like a horse and other things, the best almost I ever heard in my life.' Pepys was also plagued by a less than ideal caged blackbird that he had been given on 23 May 1663. This bird woke him up between four and five in the morning with beautiful whistling, 'only it is the beginning of many tunes . . . but there leaves them, and goes no further'.

In the early eighteenth century, birdman David Randall had a business in Channel Row (later Cannon Row), Westminster,[74] which sold delights such as singing nightingales, singing thrushes, fine cockatoos from the East Indies, canaries and bullfinches that sang tunes they had learnt from the flagelet (a small flute), parakeets and macaws that talked, and a parrot that whistled three tunes.[75] Teaching songbirds to learn tunes they had heard played on the flagelet was so popular that in 1717 William Hill wrote *The Bird Fancyer's Delight*,[76] which provided a range of sheet-music to play to the woodlark, blackbird, song thrush, house sparrow, canary, linnet, bullfinch or starling.

Poorer 'pets'

By the 1840s the reduced prices of native birds made many of them accessible to poorer Londoners, with Henry Mayhew stating that the bird catchers and bird sellers of London 'give to city-pent men of humble means one of the peculiar pleasures of the country – the song of the birds'.[77] Mayhew mentioned a pet shop in Pentonville that was supplied with linnets by the bird catchers. These were one of the most numerous, and hence the cheapest, London-caught birds, with many coming from Holloway, although they were not easily caged and half would die after a few days. The 'catch' of linnets for the London market alone was estimated at 70,000 a year, with one-tenth of them sold on the street. Young birds fetched 3*d.* to 4*d.* and the older birds accustomed to singing in cages reached 1*s.* to 2*s.* 6*d.*[78] The goldfinch was caught in similar numbers and was especially favoured by young women who appreciated the finch for its 'liviness, beauty, and sometimes sagacity'. It was also a long-lived bird of about fifteen or sixteen years, unlike other small birds, which rarely lasted for more than nine.[79] A favourite of the artisan class were song thrushes, which were either netted or taken from the nest when young and hand reared for the London market until they were old enough to feed themselves – a process known as 'rising' from the nest. These were favourites because they adapted best to caged life, since they had never know any different. The whole 'take' of thrushes was about 35,000 a year, with prices ranging from 2*s.* 6*d.* and 3*s.* for 'fresh-caught' birds and 10*s.*, £1 and as much as £2 for a seasoned thrush in high song.[80]

Beloved pets of the poor

It is more than likely that the dogs and other animals belonging to the poor were of far less quality in terms of breeding, but they were often more appreciated than the pets of the better-off because they were among the few possessions their owners had. In the 1850s it was common to see people in the streets dragging their possessions behind them in a cart on what was known as a London 'flitting-day', when rents were due. According to one report, a woman had a cat and a shrieking parrot secured onto her cart of meagre belongings:

to secure pussy the old woman had popped her into the parrot's cage, where she was lying very much at her ease, nearly asleep, and quite heedless of the clatter made by the rightful owner who, mounted on the swinging perch above her, kept scolding in a tone which could be heard far above the noise of carts and carriages.[81]

The animals would never have been left behind – unlike the wealthy's cats (see below). The same was true for an old sailor in Houndsditch who would not go to church, much to his neighbour's disgust, because he would not leave his squirrel Jack alone by himself. 'How is he to know I be comin' back?' the sailor would say. 'He giv' himself to my care, and I must be true to my charge.' But eventually the man went grudgingly to church, and then rushed back to find that Jack had broken out of his cage – his worst fears had been realized. However, after hunting for four hours, Jack was found in the oven, shivering and cowering with terror. Needless to say, the sailor never went to church again.[82]

Other owners neglected their children for the sake of their pets – and when it came to the poor, it was often men rather than women who thought more of their animals. One writer recounted his visit into 'Slumland', where he found frozen children outside a home while a warm fire burned indoors. The children explained that Benny was ill inside and he did not like noise. The patient was not an aged relative, but an old fox on its deathbed. Benny had originally been caught in a trap out of town, where the father, John, worked on an estate. He had nursed the fox back to health, although it remained badly maimed. The fox stayed with John after moving to London, but it was reluctantly kept full-time in a cage after the birth of the first child because it hated babies and would attack if it could. Benny was so precious to John that sometimes the children would go to bed hungry, as long as there was food for Benny. Life had not been good to Benny as he had outgrown his cage and could hardly turn around – 'its death must have been a merciful deliverance', remarked the writer. But Benny's death would greatly affect John, said his wife: 'I shouldn't be surprised if 'is death sent John ter the public [house]; they wus just like twins, they wus.'[83]

The same writer tells of a 'rather disreputable rat catcher' known to the police, who shared his life with an owl called Jim, which perched on his shoulder.

From time to time he would purposely blow the tobacco in its face, when it would put on a comical expression of insulted dignity, and move solemnly to the further edge of the chair. But always, after a pause, it returned to its first position.

Their relationship was cemented when Jim saved his owner's life by flapping his wings in the face of his sleeping master when burglars burst into the room. Later the rat catcher married and had a son, but he was finally caught by the police and sentenced to a long term in prison. He wrote a letter to his wife: 'Come to the court to say good-bye with babby and Jim. If you cannot carry both, bring the bird.'[84]

Some of the most vulnerable in society became so attached to their pets that they would kill for them. In the 1880s, at a London local prison, an order was issued for the extermination of all prisoners' pets, such as mice and sparrows, which were common companions, but a warden who attempted to carry out the order was stabbed.[85]

Veterinary hospitals

It was often the case that the Victorian poor could not afford for their sick animals to be seen by the newly emerging practitioners of veterinary science. But several sites across London opened their doors

for sickly, poor patients free of charge, and made their wealthier clients pay well for treatment.

The Royal Veterinary College in Camden Town provided in-house treatment for subscribers, with a special ward called 'The Nursery' for resident small dogs. One journal in 1891 sarcastically stated that many patients were King Charles spaniels and Skye terriers suffering from nothing more traumatic than ingrowing toenails.[86] However, the Vet College also hosted a Poor Out-Patients' Clinic; the area where the patients queued was known as the Cheap Practice Yard or Poor Man's Corner. Between the hours of two and four in the afternoon, the lecturers and their students would give free advice to owners and thoroughly examine the animals, giving out low-cost medicine. Students would perform any necessary operations. The professional vets would often see very ill pets that had already been seen by 'quacks' – there was as yet no legislation to prevent anyone setting up an animal dispensary.[87]

Pets could also be treated free of charge at the Brown Animal Sanatory Institution on the Vauxhall to Wandsworth Road.[88] By 1890 it had treated over 45,000 animals, of which 22,500 were horses, 11,700 dogs and 3,150 cats – and the remainder were smaller pets such as birds. The animals not only suffered from every form of disease, but were also injured or suffering from starvation – horses were also overworked. Over 34,600 animals were completely cured by 1890, while the remainder were put out of their misery as they were incurable or beyond help.[89] The hospital closed in 1939 (five years before the complete closure of the Institute) when it was only seeing about 1,000 cats and dogs a year. The fall in pet patients was partly due to the houses in the neighbourhood being turned into flats where pet-keeping was not allowed.[90] By 1906 animals could also be treated at the Animals' Hospital run by the Dumb Friends' League (later the Blue Cross) in Hugh Street at the corner of Belgrave Road, Victoria.

Owners waiting patiently
for the 'Poor Patient's Clinic'
at the Royal Veterinary
College, 1930.

Purchasing a pet

The pets of the poor and of the wealthy were on sale throughout London: in generalist pet shops and exotic animal emporiums, or from specialist street sellers who often gathered at the weekly animal markets. There were pet shops in Georgian London on the north side of Covent Garden which apparently sold everything from song thrushes caught on Hampstead Heath to marmosets in little outfits.[91] One description of a small Victorian pet shop in the Seven Dials district of St Giles deserves to be repeated in full, just to show the variety of animals on offer, and also the chaotic and somewhat dangerous way that pet shops were run:

> There used to be a small corner shop (now a sausage-and-mash house) which was very fascinating. Tiers of boxes crammed with living merchandise were displayed upon the pavement outside, the doorway was framed in crates and cages of parrots and the like 'taking the air'.

The window was generally filled with a job lot of rabbits, guinea pigs, pups and kittens. A bubbling, squealing, mumbling pandemonium, a kind of noisy 'utopian' commonwealth; where the brethren fought and slept, and took their meals – as the proprietor put it – 'jest any 'ow!'.

Pups and guinea pigs would fall asleep in mounds of twenty strong (very strong), and three and a half deep. Presently, as one watched the little heaving upturned chests, some brother at the bottom of the pile would suddenly be seized with a not unreasonable longing for a breath of air, and then the mound would boil and heave, till the nearly-suffocated pup burst triumphant into the light of day.

To the casual observer [the interior of the shop] was apt to give the impression of a dynamite explosion, or the last stages of an earthquake.

All the cages had apparently burst, at any rate they were mostly empty, whilst every variety of flimsy soap and candle box, temporarily covered with patches of wire netting, strewed the shelves, the floor, the cupboards, and the crazy table. Yes, there was a table in the middle of the shop, and to it were tethered a few bull-dogs, a mastiff or so, and an ancient nanny-goat. The constant wanderings of these animals in search of recreation and excitement gave to the table a perambulatory movement impressive in the extreme.

To reach the owner of this shop of shops one had to pick one's way gingerly amongst a litter of rabbits, placidly munching carrot tops, and apparently quite indifferent to the ferrets devouring chicken heads in an old tin bonnet box hard by; trays of silkworms eating mulberry leaves; bowls of goldfish; crusts of bread, honeycombed with meal worms; 'poms', chow-chows, parrots by the score, fancy mice by the drawer full, and puppies rivalling even the sprightly cockroaches in their numbers – which is saying a good deal.

Turn where he would, the nervous would-be purchaser saw nothing but teeming life in every crack and corner. All kinds of incongruous animals 'chummed in' together, and the very beams and rafters groaned beneath the weight of hanging parrot cages and rows of roosting poultry.[92]

This pet shop would not have been unusual, as the whole of St Giles was stuffed full of animal sellers up until the twentieth century, when their numbers declined. The weekly street market was full of wild and domestic British animals for sale: owls, hedgehogs, larks, thrushes, blackbirds, rabbits, jackdaws, snails, snakes, hawks, pigeons, turtle doves, starlings, squirrels, guinea pigs, hedgehogs and freshwater and marine fish.[93] There was a similar animal market at Leadenhall, which often caused problems for the neighbours when animals slipped out of their enclosures and invaded houses.[94]

The other main area of London associated with the animal trade was Club Row, off Bethnal Green Road, and the nearby Sclater Street. This latter area was a sprawling mass of men and lads carrying animals to sell, from white and yellow mice to cats, with a large supply of rabbit hutches and bird cages also for sale.[95]

Regulating animal dealers

The sights and sounds of the bird market were almost unbelievable, according to James Greenwood, who visited Great St Andrew Street in St Giles in 1867:

> [The birds were] fiercely yelling out their music, as though they had all gone stark mad. Perhaps they had. I almost hope so. Bird music is so intimately associated with hedges, and orchards, and cornfields – the little feathered songsters have credit for such elevated sentiments – that to discover, after all, that a lark will sing as well in a fried-fish shop as when sailing in the sun over a clover-meadow would be unpleasant. No! The birds of St Andrew's must be insane, every lark and finch of them.[96]

As hinted at in the account, Greenwood, and other middle-class agitators, found the trade in wild birds that were destined to be cooped up in cages absolutely deplorable – because of the cruelty to the birds and the working-class bird sellers who perpetrated the trade.

Some birds were just not suited to being caged, even though many owners persisted with them. The nightingale was one such bird. Nightingales arrived in Middlesex on their migration on about 8 April, and gamekeepers could make plenty of money by selling them during the season; one man sold 180 birds for 18s. a dozen to the London market.[97] Potential owners were advised to buy early as the males

Caged birds for sale in Club Row, Shoreditch, early 20th century.

(which sang) arrived around ten days before the females. But buyers were warned only to buy males that were 'meated off' – that were used to their new captive diet and could feed themselves.[98]

Even if the owner had chosen the right bird, with a beautiful song, the nightingale still had to be treated 'affectionately and lovingly waited on, otherwise they will fall silent – 'their hearts soon broken', advised one journal.[99] They would also stop singing if they saw a cat. In the 1850s more than 1,000 nightingales were sold every spring in London alone, and of those, at least seven-eighths would perish because their owners were ignorant about their requirements.

In 1873 *The Era* wrote of the bird-trapping 'low ruffians from the slums of Whitechapel and St Giles' that wandered Hampstead Heath and the fields of Finchley with their 'nets, and traps, and boxes, and springer on their dirty backs' catching birds before sunrise.[100] The article was written a year after the law had started to protect wild birds: in 1872 the first restrictions on the capture and sale of birds under the Wild Birds' Protection Act stated that bird catchers could not 'kill, wound, or take any wild bird, or shall expose or offer for sale any wild bird' during a closed season from March to August.[101] The nightingale, robin and goldfinch were included in the Act, although other birds, such as the lark, thrush and blackbird, were only included in subsequent legislation almost a decade later.

However, this did not stop some dealers. A letter to *The Times* in 1933 described, in disgust, the skylark the writer had seen for sale in Club Row Bird Fair for 6*s.*, advertised as a 'handsome present for a child':

> He was beating his wings against the steel bars of his prison, no bigger than a mouse-trap. His head was drooping, his eyes were half closed in the agony of terror, one of his tiny feet was almost torn off by the string of the snare . . . When is this ignoble slave traffic of catching and selling wild birds to cease?[102]

The trade in dogs on the London streets was equally questionable, although journalists seemed to be dazzled by the range of dogs on offer and their seeming good health. There was no shortage of animals at Leadenhall, where they were well kept in comfortable cages. In 1861 varieties on offer included Scotch terriers, curly haired poodles, dwarf lap-spaniels, Danish dogs, Russian dogs, Swiss dogs and pups from Newfoundland, as well as 'mixed breeds, born and brought up to pattern . . . some of them small enough to be carried in the pocket, and worth a purseful of money'.[103]

Other dog sellers were found in Club Row where they would line the road, each carrying a dog under the arm. The kerb would be filled with baskets of puppies. The range of dogs on offer in 1905 had increased from those listed at Leadenhall: 'mastiffs, retrievers, greyhounds, pugs, terriers of all descriptions, Dalmatians, Borzois, sheep-dogs, Blenheims, and some splendid specimens of the dog for which

Bethnal Green was long famous, the toy bull-terrier. One man one dog is the general rule.'[104]

Fifty years later and the Club Row market was the last street market in London to sell dogs. An account of the market in Kaye Webb and Ronald Searle's *Looking at London and People Worth Meeting* (1953) highlighted the notorious practices which once blighted its reputation:

> The sales technique of the owners is almost as varied as the ware and almost always accompanied by much affectionate handling of the dogs . . . RSPCA interference is needed less often now. The days are gone when sores were covered with boot polish; when doubtful dogs were dyed with permanganate of potash; when, as tradition has it, you could enter the market at one end leading a dog, lose it half way, and buy it back at the other end.[105]

The live animal market in Club Row was finally closed down in 1983, after years of campaigning against the alleged animal cruelty that took place at the market. In 1981 nineteen animal lovers chained themselves together in protest at the market, but for their efforts they were fined £200 for obstruction.[106]

Animals of the Fancy

Many of the animal sellers belonged to a social group known as the Fancy. They not only bred animals for sale as pets, but also indulged their own love of animal sports and competition by owning their own animals. The Bird Fair in Club Row, with birdcages hanging from the roofs to the pavement in almost every house,[107] was one place to view these men at their leisure. Bird fanciers would meet there every Sunday at noon to sell and buy birds and also to meet and compare their birds. The *Strand Magazine* inspected them:

There you see everywhere little groups of men, each with a bird in a small cage tied up in a blue bird's-eye pocket-handkerchief. The tying is all to one pattern. One side of the cage is open to the light, and the bird within is being eagerly examined by quiet connoisseurs. The fanciers, who bring their own birds to the fair and compare notes with acquaintances, do not say very much and are not very demonstrative. There is a reserved, almost melancholy, look on their faces. They suggest the patient listeners rather than the eager talkers. Most of them spend their leisure listening to their own birds or other people's.[108]

These working-class men were more than likely pondering the merits of their chaffinches. Towards the end of the nineteenth century, champion chaffinches had a cult following and singing matches were arranged in many London pubs. But before the fanciers could train their birds they needed to catch them, using a 'pegging' chaffinch – one that had been trained to sing under any circumstances. The catcher would also need a stuffed chaffinch in a cage, which would act as a 'threat' to the wild chaffinch. The cage was spiked into a tree in the vicinity of the victim. Above and below this cage would be some slips of whalebone, sticking out like branches from the tree, covered in sticky birdlime. The pegging chaffinch would be placed at the bottom of the tree, covered in grass, and would begin to reply in song to the victim's threatening calls once it had spied the stuffed bird. The victim would then move in to attack the enemy and would get stuck to the platforms. As many as twenty prime singing chaffinches could be captured this way in a single morning.[109]

Once the birds were trained to sing in captivity, by imitating either a trained bird or a barrel organ, pairs of chaffinches would be brought together in matches lasting fifteen minutes. The victor was the bird

A singing match for birds in a public house in the East End, 1903. The birds are in little cages on the back wall.

that sang the most complete tunes during that time. One famous pair was Shoreditch Bobby and Kingsland Roarer, which met in the 1890s at the Cock and Bottle pub in the East End. At 8 pm their cages were hung side by side on the wall, then the covers over the cages were removed. As they were unable to see each other and did not feel threatened enough to flee – either the cage sides were boarded, or they had had their eyes put out by red-hot needles – they sang relentlessly in a territorial dispute. Two men chalked up every complete 'stophe' or 'limb' sung, and there was strictly no encouraging shouting or whistling allowed. Two minutes from the end the Roarer, who was twenty points ahead, stopped singing and started to feed and have a drink. The owner pulled out a red handkerchief to mop his brow, which was obviously a signal to the chaffinch, and he hopped back onto his perch and won the competition.[110]

One of the other caged birds beloved of the London bird fancier was not a wild-caught bird, but the canary. These were not the expensive green canaries that were once imported into London. By the nineteenth century the canary had been selectively bred to be the now-familiar yellow colour and was mainly bred domestically in Norfolk and Yorkshire, as well as being imported from Germany. The birds were cheap enough for the working classes to buy and thousands upon thousands were brought into London during the Christmas holidays. One journalist described how they were sent to 'rejoice the hearts of us dwellers in cities' with their 'sprightly movements' and their 'joyous and irrepressible notes of ecstasy'.[111]

However, the fanciers did not buy them as Christmas presents and they usually bred their own canaries. By the 1830s there were twenty varieties of canary, including the London Fancy, which was a beautiful bird, deep orange-yellow with jet-black wings and tail – sadly, the breed became extinct during the First World War.[112] These canaries were exhibited at shows, alongside native and exotic birds, such as the Cage-Birds Show at the Crystal Palace or Alexandra Palace (from 1878). At the Crystal Palace event of 1873, *The Times* correspondent reported that the canaries made up 35 out of the 77 classes at the show.[113] He went on to explain the intricacies of canary markings and colours:

It takes many generations to produce the finer tints and markings, and the fanciers sometimes try to steal a march on nature, as we gather from a stringent rule against 'clipped, drawn, trimmed, painted, or coloured plumage'...One peculiarity much sought after by breeders is a

certain dark feather-line around the eye, which is supposed to soften the beaded look of the tiny point of sight, and when perfect will throw a fancier into such raptures as a lover might fall into over the long lashes of his mistress's eyelid.[114]

The canaries were soon rivalled in popularity by the Australian budgerigar – the parakeet known as the fortune-telling bird[115] – at the National Exhibition of Cage Birds and Aquaria at Olympia in 1956. The correspondent for *The Times* believed that caged birds in general were becoming more popular as pets because of people living in flats or rooms where they were not allowed to keep dogs.[116]

Other fowl and fur

One other bird was beloved of the fancy: the domestic pigeon. In the nineteenth century, during the month of May, Leadenhall and Club Row were the scenes of frenzied buying by pigeon fanciers. They came to buy new stock for the season and also to see what was new in the art of pigeon breeding. An uninitiated writer from the *Leisure Hour* explained the different pigeons on offer and the bewildering manner in which the fanciers carried on their purchases:

That thing in the cage, there, which looks like a snow-ball stuck on a pair of legs, and having the smallest possible head adhering to it accidentally, is a Pouter – a fellow who is nothing but crop; that saucy grey fellow above, with the sharp eyes, is a carrier, who will bear a message a hundred miles for you if you like; and next to him there are a couple of tumblers, whose delight it is to amuse themselves with experiments in gravitation, tumbling headlong through the clouds by way of pastime . . . here is a man fenced round by boards in a small inclosure

'Poultry, Pigeon and Rabbit Show at the Crystal Palace', from the *Illustrated Sporting and Dramatic News*, 1891.

[sic], and literally standing up to his middle in young birds rifled from the dovecote, little more than half fledged, and of course not strong enough to fly. Crowding round him, and leaning over the fence, are a swarm of the pigeon-fanciers of the metropolis and suburbs – men who do business among the chimney-pots and circulate their capital amid the clouds ... as they plunge their hands into the struggling mass of downy feathers, pulling forth one specimen after another, you hear them discourse in a mysterious language, and pronounce oracularly upon this fledgling or the other, in terms which, whether they be slangy or scientific, it puzzles you to tell.[117]

The pigeon was traditionally associated with the working classes, who would keep their beloved birds on their roofs and fly them for sport or just for pleasure. Charles Darwin mentioned the Spitalfields weavers – mainly French Huguenots – as being great pigeon fanciers, and pigeons, according to B. P. Brent (a pigeon breeder who corresponded with Darwin), were associated with 'Costermongers, Pugilists, Rat-catchers and Dog-stealers, and for no other reason that we can discern than that the majority of Pigeon Fanciers were artisans – men who lived in the courts, alleys, and other by-places of the metropolis'.[118] Basically, pigeons were cheap to keep and easy to breed. But pigeons also became the hobby of wealthier men in London. The fancier Robert

Fulton, who wrote *The Illustrated Book of Pigeons* (*c.* 1880), believed that the birds provided these men with a way to escape their pressured daily existence.[119]

Darwin immersed himself in the London fanciers' world for three years while researching *On the Origin of Species* (1859), and joined the upper-class pigeon clubs: the original Columbarian Society founded in 1750 (but more probably the Southwark Columbarian Society) and the Philoperisteron Society, which met in the Freemason's Tavern, Great Queen Street. These men, with plenty of money to spend, were more likely to enter their prize birds into the pigeon classes at Crystal Palace. They were also the type who took over the exhibition of fancy rabbits, which had elevated the rabbit from a pelted, edible species of livestock to a valued pet. The most influential rabbit club was the Metropolitan Rabbit Club, which was established in 1829. The club's aim, according to *The Era* newspaper, was to 'rescue the animal from improper treatment' and 'to improve them without pain'.[120] The length of the rabbit's ears was probably the most sought-after breeding trait and in the late 1830s it was common for rabbits to have 13-inch-long ears. However, by the Club Show of 1844, ears were nearly 19 inches long and the Chairman stated that 'it would be his greatest ambition when they could produce rabbits with ears twenty inches long, to present a specimen to Prince Albert.'[121] *The Era* newspaper covered the Club Show of 1847 at the British Hotel in Cockspur Street and was overwhelmed by the emphasis placed on the rabbits' ears: 'The "ears have it" with the fancy conies, and all thoughts of pies, and puddings, and roastings are set aside for ears and "carriage of ears".'[122]

Dog shows

Rabbit shows were commonplace before formal dog and cat shows became popular in London. The fancy bred and kept toy dogs for commercial reasons, and

there were toy spaniel shows held in 1834 at a pub in the Elephant and Castle, and in 1851 at the Eight Bells in Fulham.[123] Greenwood described one of these dog shows at the Duck in Bethnal Green almost with disbelief, as the 'rough men' came not only with their ratting and fighting dogs, but also with their toy dogs:

> Every man possessed at last one dog, and as he sat at the table the animal was squatted by the side of his pot or glass, with his arm around it. These, however, were the 'toy' dogs, marvels of shape and size – so small, some of them, that their weight is reckoned by ounces, and with limbs but little thicker than the stem of a tobacco-pipe, with beautifully-formed heads, and eyes full of intelligence. One could not help reflecting, after gazing first at the dog, then on its keeper, what a pity it was that the former should be tied to such a low-bred companion![124]

By the mid-nineteenth century these pure-bred dogs were being exhibited in several large specialist dog shows which were established in London. Instead of male working-class owners, London ladies could now take their turn in the show ring and could nurture the 'darling ambition of many a feminine soul . . . to possess what is termed "a flyer".'[125]

A newspaper report covering the Great National Dog Show at Crystal Palace in 1874 noted with disgust the outrageous way the female owners doted on their dogs:

> Many a poor, stunted, neglected infant, might have rejoiced to be so washed, combed, stroked, and patted as were some of these domestic pets, who were freshened up with delicate perfumes from fair hands . . . A satin couch for an ugly little monster whose paws were cased in velvet was scarcely a pleasurable sight, while the distracting endearments of the lady owners were

R. Marshall, *A Jemmy Shaw Canine Meeting*, 1855, oil on canvas. A 'canine meeting' at the Queen's Head tavern in the Haymarket.

rather a hindrance to those who sought to make studies in natural history.[126]

The first really large dog show that included pet breeds was held in March 1863 at Ashburnham Hall, next to Cremorne Gardens, in Chelsea. The inaugural International Dog Show also took place in London, at the Agricultural Hall, Islington, two months later. The Chelsea show was praised for its accommodation for the toy dogs, a draught-free wooden building kept at a constant temperature, which 'prevented these pets from being afflicted with any other ailments peculiar to their race'. The toy dogs which excited the most curiosity were housed in 'a mahogany and gilt cage' and were 'two Lilliputian white terriers, named Albert and Alexandra, and

which, although not so large as rats, were exquisitely shaped, and reposed in a blue and scarlet mattress'.[127]

The International Dog Show in Islington was an extraordinary event for Londoners to witness as there were 1,678 adult dogs entered, comprising sporting and non-sporting breeds. The newspapers breathlessly reported that 'Two steam boilers were erected for boiling the food of the animals daily, and the dog biscuit has been laid in by the ton.'[128]

Alongside the Great National Dog Show at Crystal Palace, the other huge dog show in London was Cruft's Dog Show, first held in 1891 at the Agricultural Hall, Islington. Charles Cruft (1852–1938), a salesman with Holborn-based Spratt's dog cakes, established and privately ran this show until his death, after which, in 1948, his widow sold the show

All shapes and sizes; 'The Kennel Club Dog Show at the Crystal Palace', 1883.

to the Kennel Club and it moved to Olympia. Its other London home from 1979 was Earls Court, until it moved in 1991 to Birmingham's NEC. These shows raised the value of pure-bred dogs and Charles Rotherham, the vet to Queen Victoria's dogs – collies, Skye terriers, Pomeranians and a dachshund – attributed the rise in London's dog population between 1865 to 1887 to this phenomenon, as more people began to see their dogs as commodities.[129]

But despite the huge numbers of Londoners who attended dog shows in the nineteenth century, there was much disquiet about the way dogs were seen to be being abused to create fashionable new varieties – much like the recent concerns that have led to the removal of Crufts coverage from the BBC network. One letter writer to the *Reynolds's Newspaper* in 1896 commented on the way breeders 'pander[ed] to stupid fashions' by hacking their dogs' ears into bizarre shapes and removing tail joints to increase the 'perkiness' of the tail carriage. The remedy, he claimed, was for the promoters of the dog shows to 'absolutely refuse to allow a mutilated dog to be shown on their benches'.[130] Other commentators questioned the way in which dogs originally bred to serve a useful purpose had been turned into pets and were losing their natural instincts and skills: for example, the dachshunds that were bred to draw a badger from its set had been turned into 'long-bodied, long-nosed waddlers who disfigure the Brompton Road'.[131]

While there was great variety in the dog world, cats had little to distinguish between them apart from the colour of their coats, and this was why cats were an appendage to rabbit or guinea-pig exhibitions up until July 1871, when the first specialist cat show took place at the Crystal Palace.[132] By this time, imported cat varieties, such as the Persian, Madagascan and other exotics, had swollen the valuable London cat population and enthusiasts sought to promote cat shows as a way to improve the size, form and colour of the much neglected domestic cat.[133] It

'Prize cats at the Crystal Palace Cat Show', from the *Illustrated London News*, 1871.

was also hoped that cats – often seen as 'moveable mousetraps' – would be treated more kindly if their owners saw the 'latent possibilities of their pets' as valuable showing commodities.[134]

General strays

London pets, whoever they were owned by, were the lucky ones compared with the stray cats and dogs that have always been part of city life. In 1387 an edict stated that 'dogs shall not wander in the City at large', so the distinction between wild and wandering dogs and pets was established early.[135] But whereas today strays are collected by wardens and taken to homes, in the past they would have been caught and destroyed, adopted by kind souls or left to freely roam.

As evidence of strays being rounded up and killed, the first attempt to control the Great Plague was a clampdown on the movement of cats and dogs – even before human movement. They were believed to be the most likely animal carriers of the disease, above rats and mice. In June 1665 the Lord Mayor proclaimed that all owners should kill their dogs and cats. Negligent owners would be prosecuted, if they could be found.[136] An official executioner dealt with strays. Pages from the St Margaret's Church-warden Plague Accounts for several weeks in July 1665 show payments to a dog killer for burying 500 dogs.[137] But Daniel Defoe reckoned that 40,000 dogs and perhaps five times as many cats were killed during the Plague.[138]

Strays were often the targets of cruel abuse, as shown in Hogarth's *The Four Stages of Cruelty*, in which boys are tying a bone to a dog's tail, burning out the eyes of a bird, stringing up kittens from a signpost and stuffing an arrow into the anus of a terrified dog. London youths were still up to these cruel antics in 1864 (and probably still are today), as shown in an RSPCA-brought case against a boy under the age of fourteen who was prosecuted for throwing a cat 15 feet into the air in York Court East near Portman Street, Marylebone, presumably testing the theory that cats always land on their feet. It landed with a broken back,

and was found moving its head and forepaws, but was unable to get up. The cat was eventually killed to put it out of its misery and the boy was sent to the House of Correction for one month, with hard labour.[139]

Stray dogs were also lured by the dog snatcher to sell on the streets, to be skinned or sold on to the vivisector. Back in the mid-seventeenth century, these dogs and cats may have landed in the hands of the early London 'scientists' of the Royal Society who used stray animals to experiment on at their head-quarters in Gresham College – on the site of the former NatWest Tower. An anonymous poem of 1662 called 'The Ballad of Gresham Colledge' ridiculed the experiments of Robert Boyle, one of the Society's founders, especially his air-pump studies, in which he looked at the behaviour of various animals in an air-free glass vessel. The following extract from the poem mocks the 'entertainment' on show to John Evelyn in 1661, when he took the Dutch ambassador to see Boyle in action:

To the Danish Agent late was showne
That where noe Ayre is, there's noe breath.
A glasse this secret did make knowne
Where[in] a Catt was put to death.
Out of the glasse the Ayre being screwed,
Pusse dyed and ne're so much as mewed.[140]

Childish entertainment: hanging a dog for fun, from Thomas Bewick's *History of Quadrupeds* (1790), wood engraving.

The poet did not seem to worry about the animal's suffering, but rather concentrated on the seemingly useless and absurd experiment. However, during the course of the eighteenth century, literary responses to vivisection dealt mainly with the abuse of animals. For example, Samuel Johnson wrote in 1758 in *The Idler*,

> Among the inferiour professors of medical knowledge, is a race of wretches, whose lives are only varied by varieties of cruelty; whose favourite amusement is to nail dogs to tables and open them alive; to try how long life may be continued in various degrees of mutilation, or with the excision or laceration of the vital parts; to examine whether burning irons are felt more acutely by the bone or tendon; and whether the more lasting agonies are produced by poison forced into the mouth or injected into the veins.[141]

Under growing public pressure in the nineteenth century, a Royal Commission was set up in 1875 to consider ways of regulating, rather than banning, experiments on animals. One lecturer from St Bartholomew's Hospital stated that stolen cats still ended up in his laboratory. Even after the Cruelty to Animals Act of 1876 instituted a licensing procedure and general inspection criteria for animal experimenters, the practice of using London's strays, or stolen pets, for vivisection was still an issue in the early twentieth century, when University College London's use of a mongrel dog in repeated live surgery over a two-month period during medical lectures in 1903 sparked off a huge controversy which is today commemorated by the statue of a bronze terrier dog in Battersea Park's Woodland Walk, near the Old English Garden. This is not an original statue, but a revised design of the original *Brown Dog* drinking fountain erected in 1906 by anti-vivisectionists in memory of the mongrel.

The plight of strays who met with the vivisectors, in 'Victor Horsley: The Defeated Vivisector', from an issue of the *Anti-Vivisection Review*, 1910–11.

The events and repercussions of the Brown Dog Affair of 1903–10 are well documented elsewhere,[142] but it heralded the way for the protection of the humble stray animal against its use in vivisection.

Once the strays of London were dead, they were generally left in the alleys and ditches of the city. John Stow even suggested that the City ditch which ran from Aldgate northwest to Bishopsgate was called 'Houndes ditch' because of the number of dead dogs that were dumped into it in earlier times. Even by the 1850s and '60s, the once grand address of Leicester Square

was simply a disgrace to the metropolis. Overgrown with rank and fetid vegetation, it was a public nuisance, both in an aesthetic and in a sanitary point of view; covered with the *débris* of tin pots and kettles, cast-off shoes, old clothes, and dead cats and dogs, it was an eye-sore to every one forced to pass by it.[143]

Dead cats and dogs had their uses, however. According to the Swiss aristocrat Horace-Bénédict de Saussure (1740–1799), it was common for the 'vulgar populace' to behave in a generally insolent and rowdy manner on Lord Mayor's Day (until 1959, this was 9 November). It was likely that any well-dressed foreigner would be jeered at, and have mud thrown at him, Saussure reported, but also 'dead dogs and cats will be thrown at him, for the mob makes a provision before hand of these playthings, so that they may amuse themselves with them on the great day'.[144] *Cobbett's Weekly Political Register* also reported in 1812 that people guilty of 'unnatural offences' who stood in the pillory were, 'almost instantly rendered indistinguishable by the peltings in mud, blood, addled egg, guts, garbage, dead dogs and cats, and every species of filth, while the air was filled with hootings and execrations'.[145]

Some scavenging types looked for dead dogs in order to sell on their skins. In 1749 the *Penny London Post* reported that the body of a young lad had been found in the Fleet Ditch, where he had been drowned by the rising tide while searching for dead dogs to skin.[146] Stray dogs, when alive, also provided another trade with a living. Mayhew identified the 'pure-finders' who wandered the streets looking for dog dung, known for its cleaning and purifying properties, to sell onto the Bermondsey tanyards for 8*d.* to 10*d.* and sometimes 1*s.* and 1*s.* 2*d.* per bucket, according to its quality.[147] Poorer quality 'pure' was often found in dog kennels, because the fancy would give their dogs anything cheap to eat, so the best was found in the open streets where other owned dogs wandered freely.[148]

Help for stray dogs

Although stray dogs had been part of London life for centuries, it was not until the mid-nineteenth century that serious efforts were made to relieve the suffering of the homeless animals. For example, there were pleas for funds to set up low-level drinking fountains in London for the use of street dogs, after newspaper reports in 1861 of dogs going mad with thirst. They were sometimes mistaken for rabid dogs and killed on official orders: 'All the dogs want is – water. But as this is denied them, they go mad. Every parish ought to be held responsible for the consequences of neglect in this matter. The evil would then soon cure itself.'[149] The Metropolitan Drinking Fountain and Cattle Trough Association was soon providing such drinking fountains throughout London.

The idea of a refuge for stray dogs, where dogs could be claimed by their owners or sold on if appropriate, was first proposed in September 1860. *The Standard* published a letter by 'A Friend to all Dumb Animals' – Mrs Mary Tealby, from Holloway – appealing for London ladies to send subscriptions for a Home for Lost Dogs to show their humanity for the 'poor little animals in the streets that can scarcely walk from weakness caused by gradual starvation, and ending in a most painful and lingering death'.[150]

The initial response from the public and the press was not welcoming and the idea of a dogs' home was outwardly ridiculed. *The Times* wrote:

> From the sublime to the ridiculous sentimentalism – there is but a single step … When we hear of a 'Home for Dogs', we venture to doubt if the originators and supporters of such an institution have not taken leave of their sober senses.[151]

The *Belfast News-letter* sarcastically protested against the 'exclusive character of the asylum', arguing that there should also be shelters set up for kittens and, possibly, a humane lady could even suggest a home for 'the poor, starving, ragged, destitute, uncared-for little children who pass their days and nights in the streets'.[152]

However, Charles Dickens supported the 'humane effort' of the institution.[153] He wrote of the dichotomy that existed in the world of the London dog: at one end of Islington Road were the pampered pooches of the wealthy being exhibited at the Islington Dog Show, while at the other end was the Home for Lost Dogs, which tried to rehome the desperate and scavenging stray dogs found on the streets.

In October 1860 the home opened in a stable behind houses in Hollingsworth Street, St James's Road, Holloway. The ultimate aim of the charity was to rehome dogs, and within a period of four months around 170 dogs had been taken in, of which 100 were rehomed, reclaimed by the owners or died naturally. Most were 'rough dogs', Scotch terriers, mongrel 'tykes' and a few old fighting dogs.[154] However, because of a lack of space, some dogs had to be destroyed if they were either valueless or dangerous. They were rejected if they were not likely to be sold on and would only eat their 'heads off', or given up as incurable if they had a serious disease or disorder. There was no open-air exercise area as there were no funds to buy any land in, or near, London, and the manager acted as the veterinary surgeon.[155] It was a rather humble beginning for an institution which would later grow into Battersea Dogs and Cats Home.

Although Mrs Tealby died in 1865, a committee carried on her work and, despite still being ridiculed by the press and the public, the Temporary Home for Lost and Starving Dogs (as it became known by 1863) was admitting an average of 850 dogs a month, with about 200 kept there at any one time.[156] Rather predictably, the noise of the dogs' barking prompted plenty of complaints from the neighbours, and in 1871 the home moved to more suitable premises in Lower Wandsworth Road, Battersea (now Battersea Park Road).

However, the new Battersea site had its teething problems, as one letter writer to the *Daily News* highlighted in 1872 after she had visited the home. The main concern was the lack of water troughs for the animals, but also the crowded, institutional nature of the kennels:

> Clean and well kept as the refuge is, it is an awful place for a dog who has been used to a good and affectionate home. Only the strongest can survive its horrors many days.[157]

In response, the home's treasurer attempted to soften the view of the 'horrors' of the refuge. He explained that it was so busy because all unmuzzled dogs, under the Metropolitan Streets Act of 1867, were brought into the home, as well as those sent in by 'the individual efforts of benevolent persons'. The dogs were kept for several days, with all the food and water they required, and if they were weak or sickly they had access to the hospital within the building.[158]

During 1874, 1,486 dogs were restored to their owners and 1,751 sold on to new homes.[159] However, these figures take no account of the other thousands of dogs which were brought into the home. In 1895 nearly 24,000 dogs passed through the Institution, but only about 15 per cent were claimed.[160] Most dogs were put down if they were unclaimed or unsold. There was no alternative because of the pressure on space – although if they were valuable or useful working dogs they were kept a while longer.

Before 1884 dogs were killed by orally dosing them with hydrocyanic acid (prussic acid), but this was distressing, expensive and labour intensive. The solution was the Lethal Chamber, which provided a painless way of death using a narcotic vapour. This chamber could kill 100 dogs at a time. They were taken into the chamber in large cages with several tiers during the night and left for six or seven minutes, during which time the air filled with carbonic acid gas (carbon dioxide) and a spray of chloroform to provide the 'death sleep'. After their on-site cremation, the dogs' bones were taken away by soap makers.[161]

Rabies panics

The Temporary Home for Lost and Starving Dogs, and in particular the Lethal Chamber, became particularly overcrowded during the rabies/hydrophobia panics which broke out in London during the later nineteenth century – stray dogs were regarded as dangerous during the panics as they were potential rabies carriers. The rabies virus would invade a person's central nervous system via a dog's bite and after an incubation period would make the victim begin to feel paranoid and suffer from insomnia. Gradually this anxiety would turn into delirium and sufferers would begin to salivate, their eyes would run and they would be unable to swallow properly, making them frightened of drinking water – the so-called terror of hydrophobia. This was usually recorded as the cause of death, although the actual cause was respiratory failure due to paralysis.[162]

Rabies outbreaks had been horrifying Londoners before the 1800s. In Georgian London there were particularly bad outbreaks throughout the 1750s, beginning in St James's in 1752 and peaking in 1759, when rewards were given for shooting dogs found roaming in the streets, whether rabid or not.[163] The preventative measure was almost as crude as the 'treatment' for hydrophobia, as shown in the case of Lord and Lady Erskine in 1792, who knocked at the door of the surgeon John Hunter in panic after their pet dog had bitten them. Their fear was hydrophobia, although it was highly unlikely that the pampered pet dog would have been suffering from the disease. At their insistence, Hunter treated them immediately by cutting away the flesh

around the bite marks. Neither, in the end, suffered any ill effects from the bite.[164]

The Metropolitan Streets Act of 1867 sought to identify possibly rabid dogs – stray dogs, in other words – by ordering that all unled dogs should be muzzled when out in public.[165] The muzzles had to be made of wire or strong leather to prevent dogs biting each other or the Londoners around them. There were concerns raised about the cruelty of ill-fitting muzzles that irritated the dogs' skins and the fact that muzzled dogs were unable to drink, but the fear of rabies contagion outweighed any welfare issues.[166] Not only were unmuzzled dogs rounded up by plainclothes policemen and taken to Battersea to be put to death, but in times of great panic as in 1877 or 1885, when there were 26 rabies deaths in London, dogs were often beaten to death on the streets using the reinforced police truncheon or were hounded by the public if they were seen to be suffering from a fit, making them look rabid-mad.[167]

It was actually rare to find a rabid dog on the London streets: over 17,500 dogs were brought into the Home during the first three months of a Muzzling Order in 1896, only one of which was found to be suffering from rabies.[168] However, the secretary of the Home stated its positive role in stopping the previous panic in 1886 by 'ultimately disposing of' 40,158 dogs that were received from the police during the period from 10 December 1885 to 20 December 1886.[169]

The dogs brought in by the police mainly came from the roughest areas of London where the owners were too poor to buy a muzzle, or the dogs were, according to the *Pall Mall Gazette*,

> starvelings and mongrels of no value, and fit for nothing but painless extinction ... poor wastrels without a definite owner or visible means of subsistence. The muzzling order is their death-warrant, and the executioner is the Dog's Home, 'supported entirely by voluntary contributions.'[170]

During the Home's history, strays were also put down for a host of other reasons. Large numbers of dogs were traditionally received at the New Year when the dog licences became due (required by law from 1796 until 1987), with intakes in 1905 averaging 171 dogs per day.[171] The Second World War saw panicked owners bringing their dogs in to be put down – 400,000 in 1939 – and in the 1970s, dogs were brought in by their owners who could not keep them any more as they had moved into new council housing in high-rise flats where dogs were not allowed. Most recently 'status' dogs have been abandoned, especially Staffies, and families under financial stress have often had to let such luxuries as the family pet go.[172] The Battersea crematorium has also been used to burn dead dogs found in the streets after they had

been hit by cars: from 1934 to 1935, 233 dogs were killed in the streets of North London.[173]

The Battersea Dogs and Cats Home, renamed in 2002, has over 150 years of good work to its credit, including its role in mopping up the dogs left behind by London's irresponsible, and sometimes hard-pressed, pet owners.

Stray cats

The story of London's stray cats is similar to that of the dogs. Some individuals were moved to help the stray cats, as described by Mayhew in the 1840s. One of the cats' and dogs' meat dealers, or carriers as they called themselves, told Mayhew of a 'coloured' woman who bought as much as 16*d.* worth of horsemeat a day.

The rabies scare of 1886 in a cartoon from *Punch*; beware unmuzzled dogs in the street.

THE DOG SCARE.

THE POLICEMAN AS HE OUGHT TO BE (PROPERLY PROTECTED) OUTSIDE THE SIX-MILE METROPOLITAN RADIUS.

Much to the annoyance of her neighbours, she would get out onto the roof of the house between 10 and 11 am and throw the meat onto the tiles for the hundreds of wailing stray cats in the neighbourhood.[174]

The concern over stray cats seems to have begun gnawing at Londoners' conscience since the late 1870s, when the RSPCA highlighted the 'West-end scandal' of deserting domestic cats in July and August after the season was over. In a letter to *The Times* in 1877, John Colam, Secretary of the RSPCA, stated that during one evening's walk of less than an hour he met 22 cats,

> whose appeals for help were very distressing, not only to myself, but to other persons who stopped, looked on, expressed words of sympathy, and asked each other what could be done to alleviate the sufferers and prevent similar acts of inhumanity.[175]

Colam suggested that to feed all of the cats would be impractical, and this would not strike out the root of the problem: that feeding dependent cats was not included in servant's 'board wages' (reduced pay when the owners were away), that cats were kicked out of the house when the owners left, and that servants and housemaids kept cats' food for themselves, or forgot to feed it to them. It was impossible to prosecute their owners as they were difficult to find and question, and there was no statutory law to remove or kill the starving cats, as the police could do with stray dogs. Colam went on to say that a stray home for cats would probably only encourage owners to turn their cats out.[176]

A home would also be impractical because of the huge numbers of cats that needed housing, and cats do not like to be imprisoned in cages. Colam concluded that an appeal to housekeepers, ladies and servants to prevent this 'annually-recurring abuse' was the only course of action available. The appeal seems to have fallen on deaf ears, though, as the numbers of cats left homeless by their wealthy owners in 1900 was estimated to be between 80,000 to 100,000 cats, out of three-quarters of a million in London.[177]

Despite Colam's fears, and (possibly) inadvertently the reason for the continued high number of abandoned cats in the West End, several homes for stray cats were established to try and deal with the situation. The Dogs' Home in Battersea started accepting starving cats from the West End in 1885 and fed them on mik, fish and horsemeat for a week. Cats that were not found a new home in that time were killed. The Animals' Institute in Kinnerton Street took in starving cats from 1888, and the London Institution for Lost and Starving Cats (LILSC) was opened in 1896 at 80 Park Hill Road, Hampstead, 'rescuing' 10,146 cats in a little over two years.[178] One of the objectives of the LILSC was to 'mercifully and painlessly despatch' any cat in a lethal chamber for the small cost of 18*d.*, and in August 1900 between 50 and 60 cats were being brought into the Institution every day. One newspaper responded with an appeal for more 'tender-hearted women' to take pity on the 'wretched starveling' cats in the streets and pay for them to be killed.[179]

By this time the LILSC had moved from Hampstead to 38 Ferdinand Street, Camden Town.[180] Also in the early 1900s, Our Dumb Friends' League set up Cats' Shelters, which included lethal chambers, in Spitalfields, Tottenham, Chelsea, Fulham, Ealing and Richmond, each dealing with an average of 15,000 cats per year.[181] The homes were particularly busy when slum areas were cleared and people moved to new tenement dwellings, leaving their cats behind, such as in 1937 when as many as 250 cats could be collected in a single day.[182] In 2010 the stray cat population of London was estimated to make up half of the million cats in the city, with shelters such as the Celia Hammond Animal Trust only able to take in emergency cases.[183]

It seems that life for London's strays is still a struggle. They eke out an existence on the debris of the city, while London's scavenging wildlife is booming because the same debris provides a bountiful supply of food. Unlike the strays, they have chosen to make London their home.

The elaborate ceremony known as swan-upping continues today – its purpose is to determine ownership of the swans on the Thames and to give them a health check.

seven

London Wildlife:
The Persecuted and the Celebrated

Londoners and the built environment of the city have been, in equal measure, a curse and a pot of gold to numerous species of wildlife over history: birds, vermin, fish and mammals have been killed by pistols, pollution and poison, yet have regarded London as an ideal place to feed, live and breed. Certain animals, such as the rat, swan and pigeon, have earned their places in London's history because of their interaction with the city, and it is these particular animals that are highlighted in this chapter.

Scavengers in London

The group of wildlife that lives, and has lived, most closely to Londoners is the scavengers. These animals, large and small, were and are attracted to the detritus of human living.

Before street cleaning and regular rubbish collection, the streets of London were filthy and unhygienic: filled with kitchen refuse, manure, dead cats and dogs and so on. As already mentioned, despite commands to the contrary, butchers killed and butchered animals in the City so that blood and offal spilled in the streets and was left to 'putrefy' the air and watercourses. All of London's waste attracted scavenging animals, some of which were made quite welcome.

During Roman times it has been suggested that London was home to many ravens, which lived in a semi-domestic state.[1] By the early medieval period it was a capital offence to kill a raven or kite. The disbelieving secretary to the Venetian ambassador wrote in 1496–7:

> Nor do they [Londoners] dislike what we so much abominate, i.e., crows, rooks and jackdaws; and the raven may croak at his pleasure for no one cares for the omen; there is even a penalty attached to destroying them, as they say that they keep the streets of the town free from all filth. It is the same case with the kites, which are so tame, that they often take out of the hands of little children, the bread smeared with butter . . . given to them by their mothers.[2]

Kites stayed in London in large numbers, warranting Shakespeare's description of London as a 'city of kites and crows'. Autolycus the conman in *The Winter's Tale* warns 'When the kite builds, look to lesser linen', alluding to the kites' preference for clothing on washing lines, which they took to line their nests. The kites stayed in the City until their protected status was reversed and they became quite rare by the eighteenth century, although 'innumerable' kites still nested in the treetops of Gray's Inn Gardens in 1711–12.[3] In 1777 the last kite's nest was pulled down from the trees, and the young birds were dissected, in the interests of science, to see what they had eaten.[4] The last kite seen in inner London was flying over Piccadilly on 24 June 1859.[5]

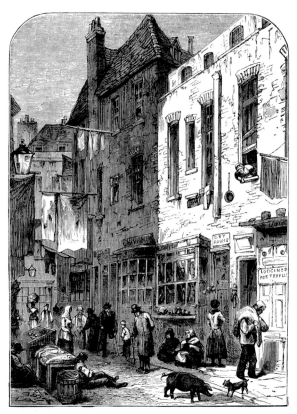

Pigs were often found scavenging in the streets. The Rookery, St Giles, 1850.

Along with the carrion birds, semi-domesticated pigs also 'revelled unmolested in the gutters' to help clear up medieval London streets.[6] Initially they were welcomed as waste-disposal units, but as London grew and standards of living increased, their scavenging tendencies became unwelcome, particularly when they entered houses. In 1292 all wandering pigs were killed.[7] But the monks of St Anthony pleaded the case for their pigs to continue scavenging, as long as they wore bells around their necks.

Rats

However, a most unwelcome scavenger made an appearance to feed off London's waste: the black rat. Excavations in Fenchurch Street and Crosswall, EC3,

in 1983 found rat bones dating from the Roman period, providing evidence of a well-established population of black rats by the third and fourth centuries AD.[8] As probable Mediterranean immigrants they brought with them the Oriental or bubonic plague: the Black Death, as it commonly became known in medieval London. Although the rats were the carriers of the bacteria, it was actually their fleas that passed the plague to Londoners: when a rat died, the fleas had to find another source of blood so they latched onto humans. It is unknown whether Roman London was hit by the plague, but London was certainly affected from November 1348, when, according to medieval records, between 17,000 and 50,000 Londoners died of the disease.[9] The black rats were certainly not blamed at the time for the plague; rather it was thought to be caused by God's anger at human sinfulness and/or astrological misalignments, and to be passed through contagion – touching the body, clothes or goods of the victim.

The black rat's fleas continued to cause devastation in London, culminating in the Great Plague of 1665–6, which killed 15 per cent of the population. The plague started outside the City's walls in St Giles-in-the-Fields, but soon spread as the rats swarmed into the City, searching out the refuse in the streets. It was the last disastrous plague to hit London, but historians disagree about why it petered out. Perhaps the rats became immune to the disease and did not die; therefore their fleas did not have to find new hosts. Some claim that the rats were killed by the Great Fire which swept through the City in 1666, but others argue that not all the slum areas in the City were burnt. Others suggest that it was the bitter winter of 1665–6 that halted the plague. Probably it was a mix of all these factors.

Even though the plague faltered, Stuart London still teemed with rats and wealthier inhabitants employed rat catchers to rid their properties of the thieving creatures. The rat catchers would sing as they wandered the streets in search of work:

> Rats or Mice! Ha'ye any rats, mice, polecats
>   or weasels?
> Or ha'ye any old sows sick of the measles?
> I can kill them, and I can kill moles,
> And I can kill vermin that creepeth up and
>   down and peepeth in holes.[10]

However, the reign of the black rat in London was due to end within a century, as the marauding Norway rat or brown rat entered the country in the first half of the eighteenth century. But black rats could still be found in the old houses of London, around the Isle of Dogs, and in the large warehouses and cellars of the docks. They were also found when the slums of St Giles's were pulled down to make way for New Oxford Street in the 1840s, and black rats had colonized the 'wretched tenements, driven up from the sewers by the victorious browns'.[11] In some areas the two species lived side by side, such as in several London breweries and distilleries, and as late as 1941–2, when 1,020 rats were killed in the docks as part of an anti-rat campaign, just over 80 per cent were found to be black.[12]

However, the 'ratopolis' of London was the common sewers, especially, according to Henry Mayhew, around the slaughterhouses of Newgate Market, Whitechapel, Clare Market and the areas next to Smithfield, where offal was swept into the drains.[13] The brown rats were able to come up from the sewers through house drains and enter the basements of old tenement buildings, even when the new mains drainage sewer was installed in the 1860s.[14] These scavengers made life a misery for many already hungry Londoners and one pamphlet, with the exaggerated title of *Rat!!! Rat!!! Rat!!!*, stated in terms strong enough to scare the populace why the rats were such a problem:

One pair of rats with their progeny, will produce in three years no less a number than six hundred and forty-six thousand eight hundred and eight rats! which will consume, day by day, as much food as sixty-four thousand six hundred and eighty men; leaving eight rats to starve.[15]

The sewers were still infested with rats in the winter of 1943–4, when 650,000 brown rats were killed in the ratopolis during an intensive rat-killing campaign.[16] They are still a huge problem, according to the National Pest Technicians Association, which quoted a total overall increase of 39 per cent in brown rat numbers from 1998 to 2005 because of fortnightly rubbish collections, street litter, use of composting bins and birdfeeders, and poor maintenance of sewage pipes.[17] In 2007 Londoners were never more than 14 metres away from a rat;[18] and this distance is on track to reduce as local authorities scale back their spending on pest control.

In Victorian times brown rats were not only branded as thieves, but as dangerous. Their ferocity was spoken about in almost mythical terms, as seen in the following essay from *The Examiner* in the early 1830s:

It is stated that a few years ago, four prisoners in Newgate, under sentence of death, managed to descend from the water-closet into a sewer, having formed the daring project of proceeding along it until they got to the Thames; but by the time they got as far as Fleet-market, they were beset by such legions of rats, who furiously set upon them to revenge the invasion of their dominions, that the unhappy men were compelled in their agony to scream for assistance, and people having heard them, opened the gratings and hoisted them up; when they were conducted back to the place from whence they came.[19]

The rat catcher at work in the sewers, from Henry Mayhew's *London Labour and the London Poor* (1851).

Henry Mayhew in 1851 also told of the rats being 'numerous and formidable' in the sewers, and of stories he had been told by the sewer men of cornered rats attacking both lone men and sometimes men in groups 'with such fury'. The attacks were so ferocious that 'the people have escaped from them with difficulty'.[20]

Later newspaper reports showed that the rats had not lost their desperation when they were hungry. In the early 1870s there was a coroner's inquest following a rat attack on two children who were left in their beds at home while their mother and father were out. The scene of the attack was an old but respectable house between Highgate and Hornsey, which had become infested with rats. On returning from her errand, the mother found

> the bed stained with blood; one child had wounds in the head and under the eyelids, and a hole eaten through the cheek; she died three days afterwards; [and] an elder child was bitten in the throat.[21]

Similar wounds on children were seen by Jack Black, rat and mole destroyer to Queen Victoria, when he visited a doctor's house in Hampstead: 'The rats had gnawed the hands and feet of the little children, their nightgowns were covered with blood, as if their throats had been cut'. Black unearthed the rats and caught them in his bare hands; he found them to be the 'blood-rat species' – the black rat – which he described as 'dreadful spiteful fellers ... snake-headed, and [which] infest dwellings'.[22] It was not just children that these rats attacked. Black also removed 32 rats from a hole on the island in Regent's Park and found in it fish, birds and lots of eggs (duck and every kind). He even removed rats from a mews where they had attacked 'a pair of beautiful chestnut horses, by gnawing away their hoofs, and had nearly driven them mad'.[23]

The occupation of rat catcher and rat killer, before London's old buildings and slums were demolished, was full-time work for professional men. The damage rats did to homes is made clear in one rat catcher's account:

> I have ketched two hundred in a clergyman's house in Portland Place. They had underpinioned the stables and underminded the oven, so that they could neither bile nor bake. They had pretty well let down every stone in the premises. I had to creep under a leaden cistern, which was underminded so that I thought it would fall down upon me.[24]

If they could, rat catchers would sell on the rats to make more money – mainly to sporting men of the rat-baiting fraternity. At the height of the sport's popularity in the early nineteenth century, rats were worth 6*d*. each, but one catcher in 1870 recorded reduced prices of 2*d*. to 3*d*.[25] Selling of rats was still in evidence on Sunday mornings in Bethnal Green in 1905; the tailboard of one seller's trap was packed with cages of rats which he sold to the 'doggy men' at four for a shilling. According to the *Strand Magazine*, his method of 'serving' the rats was as follows: 'He takes a stout paper bag, opens it, and holds it in one hand. He thrusts the other hand into the cage, grips a rat by the tail, pulls it out swiftly, swings it round, and drops it into the bag. He swings the rat round to prevent it biting him.'[26] The catchers would also skin any dead rats, as their warm and handsome skins could be sold on to the furriers.[27]

Rat killers would use poisons to kill the rats, such as arsenic or *nux vomica* (poison nut of the strychnine tree) powdered up and put in traps scented with oil of rhodium to entice the rats. However, one catcher explained that poisoning was not any good as the rats went away and hid, and then rotted.[28]

Jack Black, Her Majesty's rat catcher and bug destroyer, from Mayhew's *London Labour and the London Poor* (1851).

Other, equally torturous methods were used to kill them. One involved mixing coarse sugar (to tempt the rats) and quick lime, which would 'burn them like arsenic in the stomach'. Another was to have small pieces of cork boiled up in tallow, which when swallowed would make the rats excessively thirsty; after drinking water the cork would swell up and burst their intestines.[29]

Cats were also employed in commercial premises to catch the rats, as they were in domestic houses. They prowled St Katharine Docks in the late 1830s to destroy the rats which had 'previously reeked havoc with the cargoes of sugars'. The scheme cost £104 a year, because two men were employed to look after the cats, and feed them twice a day with meat brought in by the cat's-meat man. How many rats they caught after being fed twice a day is not recorded!'[30] Cats were also employed in the Post Office Headquarters, St Martin's Le Grand, to rid the mailbag rooms of rodents until June 1984, when the last in the line of postie cats, Blackie, died.[31]

Bugs

Rat catchers like Jack Black were also employed to deal with London scavengers of a smaller kind. Like the invading rats, plagues of immigrant bugs thrived in Londoners' homes. They were supposed to have arrived from overseas into the docks.[32]

The cockroach from the West Indies quickly came to infest houses near the River Thames. Robert Southey speaks of these cockroaches in 1808 and also informs his readers that: 'The king of England has a regular bug-destroyer in his household!'[33] Queen Victoria employed a London bug destroyer – a Mr Tiffin & Son. He was of the opinion that the first bugs came into England shortly after the Great Fire of London, in some timber that was imported to rebuild the city. It was about 30 years after the fire that Mr Tiffin's ancestor discovered the first colony of bugs in his house. Tiffin & Son only worked for the upper classes, usually undertaking annual checks to see that servants and visitors had not brought in pests during the year. Many houses had been on the business' books for over 350 years.[34]

One common pest was the bed bug. They were first recorded in the UK in 1583, 'causing alarm among the higher class ladies of Mortlake'. Tiffin remembered one particular case of a bed bug that hid in an immense room and would every night move about 30–40 feet to visit the old lady in bed and bite her. The bug eluded him for so long because it was hidden near the window, which 'bothered' Tiffin as 'a bug never by choice faces the light'. After eventually catching the bug, and giving it an 'extra nip, by way of punishment', Tiffin found out that the old lady did not get up until 3 pm, and, as the curtains were always closed, there was never any light in the room, which explained the bug's hiding place.[35]

Jack Black also exterminated other bugs. He was called in by a Mrs Bat of the William IV public house in Hampstead to destroy ants which were infesting her children's clothes, and he had to destroy 'black beedles' for bakers, and also in cellars, 'where they'd gnaw the paper off the bottles of Champagne and French wine'.[36] But Black reserved his strongest feelings for cockroaches, which he described as 'dreadful nasty things, and equal to Spanish flies for blistering'.[37]

Thomas Moufet first mentioned these beasts in his *Insectorum Theatrum* (1634), when they were probably confined to London and a few other ports. By 1860 they were still mainly confined to the docks. A correspondent for the *Leisure Hour* watched cockroaches flying and crawling near the ships. He stated that they were killed off by the cold, and that he believed this would prevent them from getting into London kitchens, which he said would be an awful outcome as they would be 'gnawing holes as big as mouse-holes, and eating whole basinfuls of sugar at a time. We should have to enlarge our beetle-traps, and the cats would sit watching for them, thinking they were a new kind of mouse.'[38]

However, several of the four species of cockroach found in London had already found their way into the kitchens. The first type was the oriental cockroach or 'housemaid's horror', which was known before the nineteenth century by the belittling title of 'black beetle'. The other was the monstrous 'drummer' cockroach, which made its home beneath the paving stones near Moorgate Street in the late nineteenth century. These bugs ate away the 'plaster', causing the partial collapse of 2 square yards of masonry.[39]

Mosquitoes were another pest which Londoners fell victim to; but this time contact could be fatal. With medieval London being close to the marshy lands bordering the south side of the Thames, in warmer weather the mosquitoes would breed and swarm, causing many bouts of the ague, marsh fever or intermittent fever – known from the nineteenth century as malaria. They must have left the built-up City, because by the second half of the nineteenth century it appears that mosquitoes were regarded as a new immigrant. In 1874 Westminster Palace and the cloisters of the Abbey were inundated with mosquitoes, and the response from the newspapers was to whimsically advise precautions that other countries took against 'these troublesome visitors':

The bodies of the inhabitants of Westminster should be at once smeared with oil, and at night covered over with sand three or four inches deep, the head only protruding, and this should be protected by a handkerchief. These precautions will make them comfortable for the moment, and, in the meantime, as mosquitoes are readily attracted to a lamp, the lime-light in the clock tower would probably prove most useful in the present emergency.[40]

A few weeks later, just up the road in Hyde Park, two mosquitoes were captured by a doctor when they were 'just commencing digging operations' on his hand.[41] A sudden rise in temperature and the unloading of foreign corn were connected with the appearance of mosquitoes between the docks and Pimlico in 1877, and in 1891 it was imported exotic plants that were blamed for bringing mosquitoes into west London.[42] By 1897 mosquitoes were 'inflicting great torture' in Hackney, Stoke Newington and some parts of Stamford Hill.[43] However, even by the beginning of the twentieth century there were still Londoners who did not believe that there were mosquitoes in London – until they were bitten. Similar disbelief hit Londoners during the Blitz when 'London Underground Mosquitoes' were identified as a different species from the above-ground mosquitoes.

Today it is bed bugs that are hitting the headlines as they have made a recent resurgence after being nearly eradicated from 1939 onwards following the introduction of residual insecticides. Nearly four million people in Greater London were suffering a bed-bug infestation by 1939, and since 2009 bed bugs have begun to infest smart hotels in Westminster. This spread has been blamed on the warmer climate, and the bugs hitching a lift with international travellers.[44] In 2012 London was described as a 'bed bug hotspot', with infested properties causing misery to many Londoners. It is enough to make your skin creep![45]

Foxes

It is not just small mammals and bugs that scavenge off Londoners. Foxes have lived for so many generations in London that they are regularly classed as a different type from their country-living cousins. The urban fox is extremely comfortable in the city and lives side by side with humans, relying on them as its principal food providers.

However, the history of foxes in London (excluding hunted foxes) begins with them being imported from the Continent or from Scotland and Wales. These foxes were known as 'bagmen' and were brought for sale at Leadenhall Market where huntsmen/ landowners short of foxes to hunt would buy them in bulk.[46] In 1834 a Mr Drax from the Exeter/ Bristol area bought £500 worth of foxes in London; the local newspaper reported that 'he is making a great many covers'.[47]

One captive fox went down in history as being remarkably unlucky as he was taken up to London in a venison cart four times, having been captured each time in the Duke of Grafton's Whittlebury Forest, in south Northamptonshire. The morning after he arrived in London, he was taken in a hamper by coach to Croydon and when released, was pursued by the Duke's hounds. It was definitely the same fox which kept being caught, because on his third capture his lip was cut, one ear was slit and several holes were punched through the other to mark him. He was eventually caught by the hounds and killed,

but this was unfair, proclaimed *Chambers's Edinburgh Journal*: '[this continued evasion] ought to have entitled him to the privilege formerly granted to a stag who had been fortunate enough to escape from his royal pursuers.'[48]

Wild foxes had first come into the South London suburbs of their own free will by the 1940s. According to a seven-year study by the amateur naturalist W. G. Teagle, the foxes had followed the newly opened up electric railways and roads into built-up areas, where they found excellent food supplies and convenient places to build their earths. Teagle then prophesied that foxes could become as much of the London suburban scene as the blackbird and grey squirrel.[49] How right he was! In 2006 there were over 10,000 foxes roaming London, or sixteen for every square mile.[50]

There were attempts to stop the early fox invaders by trapping them and dumping them back in the countryside. But this was not only cruel to the urban foxes which were unable to survive in the wild, but

Foxes seem to have no fear of the London streets.

also did not work (and still does not work, despite some pest-control companies' methods) as foxes are territorial and when one is removed, another takes its place: the official practice was abandoned in the 1970s.

Londoners now live with their urban foxes, with mixed emotions. Foxes are either fed and encouraged to visit gardens, or disliked for all sorts of antisocial behaviours: emptying the contents of bins, causing disturbances at night by calling and barking, making holes and scenting/defecating in gardens, threatening smaller household pets (or killing them), stealing and gnawing shoes and toys left outdoors, and passing on mange to dogs. They have become so used to their human neighbours that they sometimes enter houses, very rarely with negative consequences. In June 2010 twin girls were allegedly attacked by a fox, and suffered facial injuries, as they slept in their cots upstairs in their Hackney home. The fox had entered the house through an open door. More recently a four-week-old baby in Bromley, southeast London, suffered a similar attack when he had his finger bitten by a fox. The media coverage of both attacks provoked public concern about the London foxes' apparent bravado, with Boris Johnson, the current mayor of London, calling foxes 'a pest and a menace' and demanding a quick solution to the problem. But naturalists and politicians were at pains to point out that it was a very rare occurrence for a fox to attack, so it had probably felt threatened, or had had a blow to the head that had made it act out of character. However, similar attacks had been reported in 2003 in Islington, Dartford and Sidcup.[51] Whether foxes will eventually be either tolerated or destroyed, like past London scavengers, remains to be seen.

Birds

The wild birds that are most associated with London are, and were, also scavengers of a type, as they mainly forged a relationship with the city's inhabitants based on scraps of food. However, while being welcomed into London parks and open spaces, the birds around London had to be wary as they were also at the mercy of people requiring a meal, a pet or a sporting target.

In Tudor times many birds were caught for the pot. The menu from a 'principall feeste' of 1512 shows what was consumed: cranes, redshanks, pheasants, spoonbills, knots, bustards, great birds, curlews, wigeons, dotterels, terns and small birds. All of these birds were found in and around the London Wall, in the marshes lining the Thames or on the wild heaths, such as Hounslow. Even spoonbills were known to be nesting in the old trees at the Bishop's Palace in Fulham during Henry VIII's reign.[52]

If a wild bird was not to be eaten, then it almost certainly provided sport. As already mentioned, carrion birds and kites lived as scavengers in the city while they were protected, but were driven away as their use diminished and open season was once again declared on them. Unfortunately Londoners loved to take potshots at birds that ventured near, and by the mid-nineteenth century the suburbs of London were almost denuded of small birds. One author claimed that even in the 1890s,

> Englishmen are prone to shoot every bit of fur or feather with a gun. Not in the streets of London [where they are protected], but in the big district, or 'fatal cordon' that encircles the City. No birds bigger than sparrows ever manage to get past the guns.[53]

The blasé attitude to killing birds is highlighted in an anecdote told to the ornithologist W. H. Hudson (1841–1922). One Sunday morning a young sportsman on the Hackney Marshes shot down a homing pigeon that was flying towards London. When the bird was picked up it had a card attached to its

Shooting rooks, 1840 (before bird protection laws).

wing – 'Mother is dead'. Apparently the sportsman was 'proud of his achievement', and suffered no guilty conscience.[54]

If birds did manage to arrive in London by the nineteenth century, they were protected on the London streets and in the parks, although on many roofs in the lower neighbourhoods there were still bird traps and snares, and in some of the parks 'veiled bird-catching' was permitted and predatory cats – the chief destroyers of birds – were allowed in.[55] The nesting birds in Crystal Palace, however, were lucky as the wardens 'are obliged to protect the open-air artists who patronise their handsome shrubberies by stringent enactments and bills of pains and penalties'.[56] Seabirds were also protected during their breeding season (April to August) by the Sea Birds' Preservation Act of 1869 and a gentleman who shot 'sea-fowl' in Battersea Park in 1869 'got quite a temporary reputation for the deed'.[57]

Gulls

Once the conditions for bird life improved in the city, many birds took advantage of the food and nesting sites available to them. Black-headed gulls were first sighted in London at London Bridge in 1881 when they arrived, along with lumps of ice that were coming upstream on the flood tide.[58] They were looking for protection from the severe winter which made life on the sea particularly difficult. They flocked in large numbers again during the winters of the early 1890s. Newspapers reported their presence at Blackfriars Bridge in 1892 as an evil omen.[59] Some Londoners even took to taking potshots at the gulls from the bridges for sport. But, as Hudson noted, the 1892–3 season was the last time that the gulls were shot as 'this pastime [was] put a stop to by the police magistrates, who fined the sportsmen for the offence of discharging firearms to the public danger.'[60]

By 1894 black-headed gulls were becoming part of the London animal scene and the public enjoyed the sight of the birds on bleak wintry days. At London Bridge one magazine writer saw

enthusiastic people ... throwing bits of bread for them; and I heard of one City man who was so charmed with the sight that he, though as regular in his hours at office as if he had had clockwork dominating his limbs, even he got so excited that he turned back from his regular course, and, retracing his steps, went to a bakers he knew of, and bought Sally Lunns [a kind of bun], which he then threw to the gulls, and so spent a full half-hour on London Bridge – a thing he had never done in his life before.[61]

The gulls became regular winter visitors to London from October until March; on the Thames and also, by 1897, in St James's Park. They came in such large numbers to St James's that the eastern half of the lake was almost hidden by their bodies. It was even noted that if their number kept increasing, then measures would be needed to ensure that the clumsier ducks, geese and swans which were fighting for titbits were fed sufficiently.[62] In 1909 the gulls' habits were recorded in *The Times*:

Every winter evening at sunset their troops can be seen high in the air over St. James's Park and Belgrave Square, drifting westward to the eyots up the river, where they sleep, in a formation more loose and vagrant than that of the winter rooks in their country roosting-places, but with equal punctuality of habit.[63]

In 1896 the Wild Birds Protection Act was finally passed, to the benefit of all feathered creatures.[64] This provided year-round protection for 80 species of bird, and allowed an unusual influx of rural birds into the city. One bird that did well was the house martin, despite the repeated efforts of irritated landlords to drive it away by destroying its 'ingenious little mud cells', which the birds built under the eaves of the modern terraced houses.[65]

Black-headed gulls on Victoria Embankment.

Starlings

Starlings also began to come into London to roost for the night, while still foraging for food in the countryside during the day. The built environment provided them with perfect nesting places and they built their 'slovenly' nests among the 'thick clustering chimneys' of the 'towering mansions' that had replaced the slum areas of Westminster.[66] The sight of a murmuration of starlings to a jaded City type could be magically restorative, as described by Aldous Huxley in his *Antic Hay* (1923). The following scene is based on Huxley's own experience in Westbourne Square, Bayswater, before 1914. His character Mr Gumbril would sit out on his balcony at sunset waiting for the starlings to roost in the fourteen plane trees in his garden,

> and just at sunset, when the sky was most golden, there would be a twittering overhead, and the black, innumerable flocks of starlings would come sweeping across on their way from their daily haunts [in the suburbs] to their roosting-places …They sat and chattered till the sun went down and twilight was past, with intervals every now and then of silence that fell suddenly and inexplicably on all the birds at once, lasted through a few seconds of thrilling suspense, to end as suddenly and senselessly in an outburst of the same loud and simultaneous conversation.[67]

Starling numbers continued to grow in London until the birds became a nuisance. During the 1970s there were 100,000 starlings roosting in Leicester Square every night; 'they used to wheel, chattering, over queuing London cinema-goers'.[68] In 1949 starlings even stopped the hands on Big Ben when many birds landed on them at the same time. Even an episode of *The Goon Show* (1954) was devoted to the greatly exaggerated Trafalgar Square starling

menace being obliterated by 'Operation Explodable Bird Mixture'.[69] But during the late 1970s and early '80s the starlings disappeared from central London, probably because of a drop in insect numbers.[70]

Sparrows

Another bird on the list for year-round protection was the sparrow, which struck most people, especially gardeners, as unnecessary. It seemed to a correspondent at *The Standard* that the sparrow was the only London bird to have 'the infinite cunning requisite for its self-preservation from the prowling poacher [cat]', which was killing off a great number and variety of birds in the city.[71]

But sparrows were once victimized, as they made tasty morsels for wealthy Londoners from the sixteenth century. Archaeologists have found plenty of evidence for ceramic nesting pots that were once attached to the sides of mansions and other houses of the well-heeled, purely for the reception of sparrows.[72] Some were placed there for benevolent reasons, but, as Samuel Johnson noted in the eighteenth century, they were frequently used for darker purposes.

> The sparrows, not knowing the character of the man with whom they had to do, built their nests in his pots. It was disgusting to hear the fellow express his delight at the prospect of making pies of their young.[73]

Once they were on the protected list, numbers increased rapidly. Some naturalists thought that the sparrow was pushing out other birds from the city because it was 'bellicose and pugnacious in this attitude towards all strangers as is the London street boy'. The remedy, thought this writer, was to destroy the sparrows' nests as quickly as they built them to drive them away.[74]

Feeding sparrows by hand in a London park.

ubiquitous. He is in the busy street under the very feet of the horses, on the deck of the floating wharves on the Thames, in the gardens of the private houses, and at the back door waiting like a mendicant for a crust of bread, in the Zoo catching morsels out of the lips of leopards and lions, venturing without fear into the claws of eagles, and sitting on the coal-tender of locomotives at Kings' Cross and Euston.[75]

Sparrows were, and still are, held with affection in the hearts of many Londoners. Crowds would gather in Battersea Park just before dusk on a February evening to attend the sparrows' chapel, 'hundreds of birds congregating in some large tree to chirrup and chatter an evensong exhilarating and not inharmonious'.[76] Another such chapel was found in a Mr Broom's plane tree in Stationers' Hall Court, just off Ludgate Hill.[77] The sparrow feeders were particularly enamoured – W. H. Hudson saw a succession of unlikely candidates feeding the sparrows in The Dell in Hyde Park in 1898.

But the sparrows remained, despite their detractors. They were everywhere, as described by the bird enthusiast Revd R. C. Cowell in 1893:

[The sparrow] simply swarms in London. He is as reckless and audacious as the urchins of the city. He will perch on the turrets of Windsor Castle without leave, build his nest in the mouth of bronze lions, in the right hand of the statues of great dukes, in the cannon's jaws. He rears his brood in the shelter of stately architectural piles dedicated to art and law and science, and even in venerable sanctuaries like St Paul's and Westminster Abbey; so that still it is true 'the sparrow hath found an house ... for herself, where she may lay her young, even Thine altars'. He is

'I call these my chickens, and I'm obliged to come every day to feed them,' said a paralytic-looking, white-haired old man in the shabbiest clothes, one evening as I stood there; then, taking some fragments of stale bread from his pockets, he began feeding the sparrows, and while doing so he chuckled with delight, and looked round from time to time, to see if the others were enjoying the spectacle. To him succeeded two sedate-looking labourers, big, strong men, with tired, dusty faces, on their way home from work. Each produced from his coat-pocket a little store of fragments of bread and meat, saved from the midday meal, carefully wrapped up in a piece of newspaper. After bestowing their scraps on the little brown-coated crowd, one spoke: 'Come on, mate, they've had it all, and now let's go home and see what the missus has got for *our* tea'; and home they trudged across the park, with hearts refreshed and lightened, no doubt, to be succeeded by others and still others, London workmen and their wives and children, until the sun had set and the birds were all gone.[78]

The sparrows in St James's Park, on the bridge over the lake, would sit on feeders' hands to eat; no doubt because generations of sparrow feeders at the park, stretching back to Charles II, had made them very confident. Stalwart feeders came every day and disliked Sundays and bank holidays, when 50 or 60 'amateur interlopers invade[d] the bridge' and ruined their peaceful routine.[79]

However, sparrow numbers, like those of starlings, have recently plummeted in London with a fall of 66 per cent from 1994 to 2003. They seem to have disappeared even from St James's Park. It seems that now the cockney 'sparrer' needs protecting, as from 2005 it was added to the Red List of British Birds, which details the birds of highest conservation concern (starlings were also added). There are plenty of reasons put forward to explain their disappearance: the loss of small insects on which very young chicks feed, the break-up of sparrow colonies when they fall below a certain number, tidier gardens and houses, predation by cats, magpies and sparrowhawks, pollution and emissions from mobile-phone masts.[80]

Rooks

Another sad loss to London were the rooks that used to frequent many green areas in the City. In the early eighteenth century there was a rookery in the Temple Gardens that had been established by a well-known lawyer of the period, using his own rooks from his estate at Epsom. He transplanted a tree bough with a nest containing two young birds in it from his home, taking it in an open wagon to the Temple Gardens, where he fixed it in a tree. The adult rooks followed their young and fed them, and old and young remained to colonize the gardens.[81] According to the critic and poet Leigh Hunt (1784–1859), it was apt that the rook should be associated with the law courts, it being 'a grave legal bird, both in his coat and habits'.[82] But by 1893, one Revd Cowell was lamenting the fact that the rookeries were 'fast disappearing', with colonies only left at Gray's Inn Gardens (though these rooks were being harassed by crows trying to drive them out) and a few nests in the northwest corner of Kensington Gardens. In 1836 the latter rookery had consisted of nearly 100 nests, and stretched from the Broad Walk near the Palace to the Serpentine. But it was destroyed in October 1880 when the grove of 700 trees was cut down. W. H. Hudson was irate about the act when he remembered the rookery in its former glory:

> As I advanced farther into this wooded space the dull sounds of traffic became fainter, while ahead the continuous noise of many cawing rooks grew louder and louder. I was soon under the rookery listening to and watching the birds as they wrangled with one another, and passed in and out among the trees or soared above their tops. How intensely black they looked amidst the fresh brilliant green of the sunlit foliage! What wonderfully tall trees were these where the rookery was placed! . . . Recalling the sensations of delight I experienced then, I can now feel nothing but horror at the thought of the unspeakable barbarity the park authorities were guilty of in destroying this noble grove.[83]

Ravens

Another 'grave' black bird that lived in London in large numbers, only to disappear, was the raven: these birds last nested in the wild in Hyde Park in 1826. Today they still inhabit the Tower of London and are probably the one 'wild' animal that tourists associate with the city. A visit to the Tower is not complete without seeing the seven ravens which saunter around the grounds, keeping a beady eye on the visitors and waiting for someone to ignore the 'WARNING: RAVENS BITE' sign.

Legend has it that the ravens, traditionally considered an evil omen, were introduced to the Tower by Charles II; it is not clear why he did this, but he was more than willing to kill them off when the Astronomer Royal complained that the birds were interfering with his star-gazing activities in a turret of the White Tower. However, when Charles gave the order to dispatch the ravens, someone informed him of a prophecy that said that if the ravens left the Tower, the White Tower would collapse and a great disaster would befall the kingdom. Charles took the prophecy so seriously that he ordered the observatory to move to Greenwich, and that at least six ravens should be kept at the Tower to prevent any catastrophe.

However, Geoffrey Parnell, the official Tower of London historian, recently scoured records dating back 1,000 years and found no reference to the raven prophecy until an article in 1949 reporting feral cats attacking the Tower ravens. But the lore of the prophecy must have been known before this, as during the Second World War the ravens were all killed or pined away during the air raids, and their deaths were not made public. When the Tower reopened in 1946, there was a full complement of six ravens.

Parnell also found no reference to resident ravens at the Tower before an article of 1895 in the RSPCA journal the *Animal World*, where an Edith Hawthorn referred to the Tower's pet cat being tormented by the ravens, Jenny and a nameless mate. However, this author has found a 'factional' piece in *The Star* newspaper in 1888 which tells of a country girl visiting the Tower of London for the first time: 'She puts up

her *pince-nez* and looks down at the Tower raven, that is peering down at the brass plate that marks the old place of execution.'[84] Presumably there was a raven at the Tower at this time and W. H. Hudson wrote in 1898 of two or three ravens being kept at the Tower 'for many years past'.[85] Either way, Purnell believes that the presence of the ravens only dates back to the late Victorian period, and the raven prophecy to the last century. He concludes that the story of the ravens 'says much about the effectiveness of the machinery at the Tower for manufacturing legends'.[86]

The Raven Master (one of the Yeomen Warders, also known as Beefeaters) looks after the welfare of the seven ravens (six plus a spare), and Raven Masters obviously become close to their cheeky charges. In an interview in 2009, Derrick Coyle, one of the most recent Raven Masters, gave a glowing account of a raven called Thor, who was 'a great talker, he even has the same County Durham accent as me, after mimicking me for all these years'. Thor also said 'Good Morning' to Vladimir Putin and to all of his entourage when they walked up the steps to the White Tower – Thor was perched on the top step – and Putin was 'rather taken aback'. The ravens are fed on lamb hearts, liver, quails, rats and (their favourite) rabbit, some of which is bought in bulk from Smithfield Market once a month, all washed down with bird biscuits soaked in blook.[87] The bodies of dead ravens are kept within the Tower walls in the Raven Cemetery, where their names are added to the Raven Memorial Headstone that has recorded interments since 1956.

Pigeons

The bird with possibly the longest association with London is the pigeon. St Paul's Cathedral is home to one of the oldest colonies; in 1385 the Bishop of London complained about the menace of those with 'a malignant spirit' throwing stones, arrows and darts

A pleasant pastime: feeding the pigeons in the Guildhall Yard, 1877.

at the pigeons (and crows, and other birds) nesting and sitting on the cathedral walls and openings. The missiles were instead hitting the glass windows and stone images of the cathedral, causing damage.[88] These pigeons were probably initially tame.

Centuries later, the colony at the British Museum was established when pigeons at the Meux's Horse-shoe Brewery in Tottenham Court Road ran short of grain to feed on and moved to the Museum. In the early 1880s they were looked after and fed by a gardener who was also a pigeon fancier, but he got into trouble with the bosses for supposed 'wanton cruelty' when an elderly neighbour saw him dispatching two elderly cock birds with a broom – his way

of managing numbers. A later Museum employee (legally) tried to thin their numbers by making the pigeons drunk on grain soaked in whisky, so he could catch and kill them; but the spirit burnt their throats and they flew up onto the roofs and 'perished miserably'.[89] But visitors liked them, and not many other efforts were made to thin numbers. By the time the motorcar had pushed out the horse transport from London – and, more importantly, the horses' nosebags – the pigeons would often go hungry, especially on winter Sundays. One employee felt so sorry for the 120–60 pigeons that he would feed them with four bushels of maize a day – which was difficult to find during the First World War.[90]

Other large pigeon colonies lived at the Law Courts, Temple Gardens and Westminster Palace. The latter colony was 'a recognised institution' according to *Once a Week* magazine, and the birds were 'so tame that you can do anything with them short of catching them with the hand'.[91]

The article continued with some of the best-known pigeons: those of the Guildhall colony, which may have started as a tame collection that moved when its owner died. The 'feathered gentry' here became so numerous in the mid-nineteenth century that 'an incredible number of savoury pies was the result'.[92] But this killing of the Guildhall pigeons was uncommon, according to one newspaper, as the pigeons were as sacred to Londoners as storks were to the Dutch.[93] In addition to these sentimental reasons, under the Larceny Act of 1861 anyone killing any 'stray homers' (tame pigeons) would be fined. In 1920 the slaughterman Reuben Chandler was charged with killing pigeons at the back of the Borough Market, even though he believed they were rock pigeons, and therefore wild. But they were actually, according to expert witnesses, 'stray homers, and possibly worth anything up to £100 apiece'. Chandler was fined £2 and ordered to pay further damages and costs.[94]

However, a campaign reported in detail by *The Times* began in 1926 to officially limit the number of pigeons in London after the powers that be became incensed by the 'filthy' mess that the pigeons created while perching on the Memorial to the London Troops outside the Royal Exchange, Cornhill.[95] There were calls by the Medical Officer of Health for the City of London to discuss the nuisance – in particular the air contamination from the excreta – arising from the presence of about 6,000 pigeons in London, especially in Leadenhall Market. At this site, 'it is not necessary to describe the effect of overhead pigeons on the stalls beneath'.[96] At that time, because of the Larceny Act, stallholders could only destroy pigeon nests and wire over the open spaces in the roof. The Medical Officer called for local authorities to be able to make their own decision to slaughter pigeons to restrict numbers in London by about 2,000. But he shied off from proposing a total cull, as they were still a tourist attraction; 'every one would regret the total disappearance of these birds from our midst'.[97] A clause was duly added allowing the Corporation of London and the Metropolitan borough councils to 'seize and destroy or sell or otherwise dispose of any house doves or pigeons, and take such other steps as may be necessary and reasonably practicable to abate such nuisance or prevent such damage'.[98]

While efforts to remove pigeons have mainly been done quietly, without public outcry, there have been several incidents that have upset many Londoners. The first case was in 1957 when on the forecourt of Victoria station, during Friday rush hour, two young men were seen by 'a crowd of obviously indignant people' catching pigeons with their bare hands. One spectator wrote about their method in disgust to the town clerk of Westminster: 'As a bird was grasped, it was stuffed into a trouser pocket or jacket pocket or gripped tightly in the hand, and feathers were flying about.'[99] It turned out that the men had been employed by British Railways to remove the pigeons that were causing the pavements to become dangerous in wet weather. Their methods caused the 'distress of many people'.[100]

But the greatest furore was reserved for the then Mayor of London Ken Livingstone in 2000 when he stopped Bernard (Bernie) Rayner the pigeon-food seller from selling grain to tourists and Londoners in Trafalgar Square. Livingstone called the 4,000 semi-domesticated pigeons 'rats with wings' and wanted them to move away from the London landmark. But the Pigeon Alliance was mobilized. This group claimed that the pigeons were reliant on humans and would starve if they were not fed, so volunteers supplied them with six 25-kilogram sacks of grain a day. Livingstone responded by using vacuuming machines and industrial hoses to remove the grain and employed several Harris hawks to patrol Trafalgar Square several times a day to scare the pigeons away. The late MP Tony Banks and the TV writer Carla Lane stepped up the campaign by presenting their cases for the pigeons to stay. Banks argued that the pigeons were 'part of the London scene enjoyed by citizens and visitors alike', and Lane added, 'If a pigeon lands on a child's shoulder it will paint a good picture in their mind and show them all animals are worth caring for.'[101] The GLA eventually backed down and accepted a reduction in numbers by reducing the feed over several years. Today Trafalgar Square is almost pigeon free. But there have been questions raised over the cost to the taxpayer of employing the Harris hawks. From 2003 to 2006, although they were just supposed to scare the pigeons away, they actually killed 121 birds, though there was in 2006 still a diehard group of 1,000 pigeons that would not budge. The hawks had cost £226,000 over the three years and had scared away 2,500 pigeons at a cost of more than £90 a bird.[102]

The presence of pigeons in London attracted predators, most notably kestrels, which quite happily adapted to life in central London. In 1871 a pair of kestrels nested on top of Nelson's Column, but the birds later disappeared. It was not until 1942 that *The Times* noted the kestrel returning – a pair roosting on the Houses of Parliament and feeding on the pigeons in the early morning. One observer said, 'It has been a thrill to single out from the undistinguished mob of London pigeons the lithe, athletic form of this little falcon.'[103] Other Londoners were less observant of the kestrels which hovered over Horse Guards Parade, according to the naturalist R.S.R. Fitter, probably because 'gazing upwards . . . [is] a dangerous occupation in London's traffic-laden streets'.[104] One man who did observe a kestrel wrote a letter to *The Times* saying that he feared the kestrel he saw was dead, as it fluttered down into the street in front of his hotel – he was obviously not a keen naturalist.[105] Today it is

the peregrine falcons on the Tate Modern chimney that are after the pigeons.

Other bird life

Writing to the London newspapers and periodicals with wildlife observations became popular in the 1820s to '60s, when the study of natural history became an important pastime for many Victorians.[106] Amateurs shared their observations of London bird life, particularly if rare birds ventured into London. A migratory woodcock, exhausted and stupefied, was found one morning by a milkman huddled up to a lamp post in Albermarle Street, Piccadilly.[107] This was not the only sighting of this rare visitor. A litany of earlier woodcock adventures had ended in disaster: one flew against a telegraph wire in the Strand and died, another was shot in Junction Road, Holloway, one dashed itself to death against a window of the South Kensington Museum and two were found collapsed with exhaustion in St John's Wood Road and upon Ludgate Hill.[108] A storm-petrel flew blindly against a man's face, then dropped down dead at his feet in the Edgware Road, Paddington, and a snipe was found fluttering about in the gutter by the roadside in the busy Strand.[109]

Londoners also, it seems, were and are quite enamoured with the nesting exploits of London's ducks. In 1853 the ducks in Kensington Gardens were singled out for building their nests in the trees. One duck, reported in the *Magazine of Art*, laid her eggs 12 feet up a horse chestnut tree; how the ducklings got to the ground remains a mystery.[110]

In 1959 the St James's Park rangers and the police co-engineered a passage for a family of mallards that had nested in the tulips around the Victoria Memorial, all the way up Constitution Hill, across Hyde Park Corner (where the traffic was held up), until they reached the Serpentine.[111] And in 1992 the head bird keeper of Regent's Park was called to a rooftop garden in nearby Baker Street where a broody duck kept laying her eggs.

When the ducklings hatched, the ranger collected them to save them from having to jump off the ten-storey building and waddle across Marylebone Road in their family quest to get to the nearest water.[112]

Swans

The waterbird with the most historical attachment to London is probably the mute swan of the Thames.[113] Today it is the ancient tradition of swan-upping – a ceremonial census of all the swans on the Thames, to decide ownership of the new season's cygnets – which gives Londoners an idea of the past importance of these birds.

There is no evidence to suggest which king actually claimed ownership of unmarked Thames swans, but the earliest mention of a swan being a royal bird dates from 1186. Crown swans, and all the other swans, would have elaborate nicks made in their beaks, which were their owners' unique identification patterns. Ownership of swans was highly desirable as they were ideal meat for banquets and feasts – real showstoppers. The first reference to swans as a food source was in 1249, and in the reign of Edward III the price of a swan was nearly ten times that of a goose or mallard, and three or four times that of a pheasant.[114] It was not until 1984 that swan was removed from the menu at livery banquets, which was not a bad thing, according to one former Prime Warden of the Worshipful Company of Dyers, who said that it tasted like 'fishy goose'.[115]

By the end of the Middle Ages there were thousands of swans on the Thames; the secretary to the

Swans were once a common sight in central London, as here at Old Whitehall Palace.

Venetian ambassador wrote in 1496–7: 'it is truly a beautiful thing to behold one or two thousand tame swans upon the river Thames, as I, and also your Magnificence have seen'.[116] Aside from the Crown, hundreds of other individuals/families claimed ownership of these swans (some being given the right by the kings themselves) and this did not please Edward IV (r. 1461–70). In the second year of his reign a special Act was passed ordering no person, except for the king's sons, to have a swan mark or be allowed to own a 'game' of swans, unless he owned a freehold property with the yearly value of 5 marks.[117] But even after these restrictions, between 1450 and 1600 there were 630 marks of swan ownership in circulation.[118]

Since the eighteenth century there have only been three swan owners: the Crown, the Vintners livery company (wine merchants) and the Dyers livery company (cloth dyers). The Vintners marked their birds with a notch on either side of the beak – hence the coaching inn called Swan with Two Necks (Nicks) – and the Dyers used a single notch. Previous to these simple notches, the patterns were much more ornate. But they were simplified after the RSPCA brought a case in 1878 against three swan-uppers at Eton, accusing them of torturing four birds when they notched their beaks (and plucked out their feathers – see below).[119] The RSPCA went further by suggesting an alternative method of identification used in Holland on the royal swans – an ivory ring around the neck.[120] They acquired a Dutch royal swan, ringed it and presented it to the Zoological Gardens in Regent's Park. However, after a time Frank Buckland inspected the bird and found it to be

> nothing but skin and bones – a mere skeleton, in fact. The ivory ring with the letters SPCA on it, had acted as a permanent garotting apparatus, which had caused the greatest misery and discomfort, and semi-starvation of the bird.[121]

It was not until 1998 that leg rings were used for identification.[122] The other cruelty practised on the cygnets during the traditional swan-upping was a procedure to make them flightless when they reached maturity. Joints were removed from their wings and/or their flight feathers were pulled out. As already seen, the RSPCA took exception to this pinioning, and naturalists called it 'ancient and time-honoured brutality'. It was also cruel because the swans could not escape the ice in the winter to find food; several flightless swans starved to death in 1902.[123] The practice was stopped in 1978 after pressure from the media and animal-rights groups.[124]

Today the swan-upping, or swan-hopping, as it was corrupted to in the later nineteenth century, takes place on the third Monday in July and lasts for five days.[125] It is done then because the adult swans are in moult so they cannot fly, and the cygnets are too small to fly. The swans are monitored over 79 miles, from Sunbury-on-Thames, Middlesex, to Abingdon, Oxfordshire. The ceremonial route has changed over the years, but the ceremony itself has not.

The Queen's Swan Marker, who decides how to allocate the broods depending on the parent bird's ownership, and the swan-uppers travel in six skiffs (rowing boats) until they see a group of swans.[126] They shout: 'All up!' and encircle the swans with their boats until they can be caught. The swans' legs are tied with hemp twine and then, when ashore (nowadays), they are weighed, ringed and checked over by the Queen's Swan Warden – a professor of ornithology at Oxford University's Zoology Department. The ceremony today is purely for monitoring swan populations, checking the swans' health and disentangling them from fishing tackle or plastic bags, if required.

Since the time when thousands of swans glided about the Thames, their numbers have fluctuated. In 1841, before the pollution of the Great Stink, the Queen had 232 swans, the Dyers 105 and the

Vintners 100.[127] By 1888 this number had fallen to 343 swans in total. Of those, 47 were found living between London Bridge and Thames Ditton, Surrey – mostly off in the tributaries.[128] Larger fluctuations in swan numbers were seen in the last century, with about 700 swans counted in 1914, which had risen to 1,300 birds in the mid-1960s only to come crashing down by 1985 to seven pairs with cygnets.[129] This severe reduction in numbers was mainly due to lead poisoning after the birds had eaten lead fishing weights. After these were banned in the late 1980s, numbers slowly increased to 28 pairs with cygnets in 2006.[130]

Lead poisoning may be a thing of the past, but swan deaths in 2011–12 show that the swans are still at the mercy of human activity – rather depressingly so. Apart from the swans suffering from duck virus enteritis (resulting in a loss of many breeding pairs) and flooding of nests, David Barber, the current Queen's Swan Marker, puts many swan deaths down to vandalism: they are shot at with air rifles and catapults, nests are destroyed and the cygnets are attacked. There are also the usual fishing tackle injuries and swans which are attacked by youths and dogs.[131] In times gone by culprits would have been sentenced to seven years' transportation for unlawfully killing a swan, and even up to 1895 the punishment was seven years' hard labour.[132] During the reign of Henry VII anyone caught stealing even a swan's egg would be imprisoned for a year and fined according to the king's will, and heavier penalties were reserved for the stealing, snaring or driving of the swans themselves.[133]

Thames swans have also been subjected to other unnatural deaths at the hands of their human London neighbours. In 1769 a fire broke out at an oil warehouse on St Paul's Wharf (east of Blackfriars Bridge, on the north bank) and blazing oil flowed into the Thames, causing it to look as though it too was on fire. One unfortunate consequence of the fire was that it 'caused a mortality among the swans, destroying

a prodigious number'.[134] Then, in 1811, 'a Jew' living in Oxford Street stole six royal swans from the Serpentine in Hyde Park. Their bodies were found tied to trees without their skins or feathers. The culprit was found out when he sent the feathers to a feather dresser. It is not clear what penalty the man suffered, although he was held at the Public Office in Bow Street for examination.[135]

It was lucky for the 'Jew' that he did not try to steal one of the ancestors of a notorious 70-year-old swan called Jack who lived in St James's Park in the eighteenth century. Jack had quite a reputation for killing many dogs that worried him, and he once nearly drowned a boy who baited him. In 1768, when the moat around Duck Island was filled in, he was moved to the canal, but his attacks on any passing bird caused his eventual downfall when a pack of Polish geese pecked him to death. But in death, Jack's fearsome reputation grew so that future generations regarded him almost as a deity.[136]

Swans, like sparrows, pigeons and starlings, are not seen within the Thames bounds of inner London as they used to be. Londoners once delighted in seeing the sight of swans in the City, as an account from as late as 1893 shows:

[Swans are found] in front of the Houses of Parliament, hurrying, perhaps, out of the way of some noisy steamer, or stemming the turbulent water that rushes foam-crested astern from the paddle-wheels. You are more likely to see them coming close in to the Surrey side to seize the sweet morsels cast adrift by saunterers on the river-rim, or, in the winter, feeding in the shallows. You may catch a delightful view of them sailing up with the tide, and leaving far behind some lumbering barge – a vision of purity and tranquillity, as they cleave the dark water with their snowy breasts and move calmly on.[137]

The story is the same under the waters of the Thames: the fish of London once used to shoal in vast numbers in the tidal waters of the City, but do so no longer.

Thames fish

William Fitzstephen, when describing the setting of the City in the twelfth century, tells of 'that greatest of rivers, the Thames, which teems with fish'.[138] A century later fishermen earned a good living from the Thames and sold their catches on 'fish days' in the Stokes or Stocks Market, situated where the Mansion House now stands.[139] Eating fish on Fridays, during Lent (except Sundays) and, later, on Wednesdays and Saturdays was required by Christian doctrine and the Thames provided about a half of London's fish supplies. John Stow says of the Thames in 1598:

> What should I speak of the fat and sweet salmons daily taken in this stream, and that in such plenty (after the time of the smelt is past) as no river in Europe is able to exceed it? But what store also of barbels, trouts, chevens, perches, smelts, breams, roaches, daces, gudgeons, flounders, shrimps, eels, &c., are commonly to be had therein, I refer me to them that know by experience better than I, by reason of their daily trade of fishing in the same. And albeit it seemeth from time to time to be, as it were, defrauded in sundry wise of these, her large commodities, by the insatiable avarice of fishermen; yet this famous river complaineth commonly of no want, but the more it loseth at one time it gaineth at another.[140]

Stow recognized the pressure on the Thames fishery, but there was already a set of elaborate codes of regulation preventing overfishing – closed seasons and netting restrictions – with the punishments seeming to fit the crime. In March 1561 a woman accused of illegally landing small fry of all kinds rode around Cheapside and London with 'a garland apon her head with strings of small fishes'.[141] Stow also tells of a great many fish in the City ditch that were once caught and eaten; but by his time, the ditch was reduced to a rubbish dump.[142]

Fishing regulations must have prevented a collapse in supplies, but by the early nineteenth century fresh- and saltwater fish were soon to leave the Thames in shoals. In a parliamentary report dated 1828 Mr Goldham, the Clerk of Billingsgate Market, stated that at the beginning of the century there were about 400 London fishermen earning a good livelihood from fishing between Deptford and London. In about 1810 he knew of as many as ten salmon and 3,000 smelts being taken up in one haul near Wandsworth, and of 50,000 Thames salmon being caught in one season.[143] Some of the boats earned £6 a week, and a salmon was sold at three to four shillings a pound.[144]

Fishing on the Thames has been a common recreation for centuries, as this woodcut from 1663, *The Royal Recreation of Joviall Anglers*, testifies.

The 'Silent Highway'-Man. 'Your Money or your Life!', cartoon from *Punch.* During the 'Great Stink' of 1858, dead wildlife and strays added to the general contamination of the Thames.

By 1820, however, evidence from fishermen stated that there were no flounders, eels, roach, smelts, salmon or other fish in the Thames from Woolwich to Putney.[145]

Fish had apparently been disappearing from the London river for many reasons. The Thames had always been used as a receptacle for Londoners' 'filth' and *The Examiner* in 1828 noted its content. It was

> perpetually contaminated by the foulest animal matter arising from putrid vegetable substances, dead fish, dead dogs, dead cats – the drainings from numerous soap, gas, and other such manufactories – and (O monstrous!) the outpourings of not less than one hundred and forty-five common-sewers – in a word, from that river Thames, 'into which,' said the *Medico-Chirurgical Review,* – 'one hundred thousand cloacae [latrines/sewers], containing every species of filth and all unutterable things, are daily disgorging their hideous and abominable contents?'[146]

The fish were obviously put off from swimming through the noxious soup in the Thames. The gases contaminating the Thames were blamed for causing more damage to fish stocks than the city's sewage, according to one Billingsgate salesman. He blamed the Phoenix Gas Works, south of the river near Vauxhall Bridge, which turned coal into gas for lighting, for killing off millions of freshwater fish when its factory started to empty its 'gas water' into the river in the early 1830s.[147] Other commentators thought the fish were also being frightened away by the steamboats that were then plying the river.[148]

The pollution became intolerable to Londoners themselves in the hot summer of 1858. The smell coming off the Thames, known as the Great Stink, was so ghastly that the caretakers at the House of Commons had to put up canvas moistened with a weak solution of chloride of zinc and lime at the riverside windows to try and purify the foul air. Four or five bargeloads of lime were also spread over the mudbanks on the shore outside the building.[149]

Members of Parliament questioned the Chief Commissioner of Works about the state of the Thames; he stated that he knew of whole cartloads of fish being taken out of the river dead, having been killed by 'the noxious element by which they were surrounded'.[150]

Flounders and trout

Stocks of the most famous of London fish were decimated in this period. The Thames flounder was the best example of the species; it was sold in the big provision stores in London and served on the best ships. These 'jolly little flatfish' once swarmed in the Thames and, according to William Makepeace Thackeray (1811–1863), 'no epicure ever grew tired of flounder souchet [soup] and brown bread'.[151] They were caught between London Bridge and Westminster in the seventeenth century, at Battersea Bridge and London Bridge, and occasionally off Westminster Bridge in later centuries.[152] But they disappeared from the Thames for eight years because of water pollution. It was stated that flounders would climb up onto bundles of floating weed for a moment's fresh air before they left the river.[153]

The famous Thames trout, which frequently weighed 10–15 pounds, also disappeared. It had been larger than normal because of the abundant food in the river, rather than being a distinct species, as many anglers had thought.[154] The London Thames had also afforded 'the largest and fullest' roach in the nation, according to Izaak Walton in his *The Compleat Angler* (1653).[155] In the mid-eighteenth century there were reports of a waterman called John Reeves taking anglers out in his punt to fish the greatest shoals of roach that appeared around old London Bridge. Business must have been brisk because there were many fishing-tackle shops in Crooked Lane, which led to the bridge.[156] But the roach disappeared too, along with its freshwater cousin, the dace (although both have since returned).

Salmon and eels

Probably the two most famous London fish were the salmon and the eel; the polluted river also decimated these. The Billingsgate salesmen knew the Thames salmon as the 'red fish'. In medieval times tens of thousands of salmon ran the river every year and the lucky abbot of St Peter's, Westminster, received the tithe of all the salmon caught within the jurisdiction of the Lord Mayor from Yantlett Creek (which runs from the River Medway to the Thames) to the City Stone at Staines. Catches were recorded and the Churchwarden's *Book of Wandsworth* (1580) stated: 'in this somer the fysshers of Wandesworthe tooke betweene Monday and Saturday seven score salmons in the same fishings, to the great honor of God.'[157] Izaak Walton refered to the Thames salmon as the best in the kingdom. Stock did not seem to dwindle in Walton's time, with 130 Thames salmon being sent to Billingsgate on one day in July 1766: 'There never was known a greater plenty of salmon in the river Thames', said a contemporary record.[158]

However, by 1821 the salmon had been steadily choked by pollution and were so scarce in the Thames that when a salmon was wanted for the coronation dinner of George IV, even a reward of 30s. per pound could not make one appear from the Thames – although two were caught the day after the event between Blackwall Reach and Woolwich Reach.[159] The last migratory salmon was fished out of the Thames in 1833, and the species did not reappear for 140 years, when on 13 November 1974 a single stray salmon from another river was found dead.

Five years later the Thames Water Authority and others came up with a restocking plan; but this had been tried before, most notably by the Piscicultural Society and the Thames Salmon Association during the later nineteenth century, to little avail. Many commentators at that time noted that not only did the salmon have to contend with manufacturing waste, but there were also 'numerous insuperable obstacles they met with, in the shape of locks, weirs, &c.', which stopped their migration upriver.[160] Despite millions of pounds being spent on reintroducing salmon to the Thames, there has not been any real sign of their return.

The sorry tale of the Thames salmon is sadly similar to that of a delicacy from Domesday time: the Thames silver eel – silver because it gleamed. These eels were the fare of royalty and the wealthy. One commentator stated that 'There is no more delicious, wholesome, or nourishing fish than a Thames eel.'[161] The eel larvae travelled all the way from the Sargasso Sea in the Atlantic Ocean, where they spawned, and drifted thousands of miles to enter the fresh water of the Thames (and other European rivers). They would hatch in the mud and sand at the mouth of the Thames, then migrate as very small elvers upstream during the month of May. This passage was known to Londoners as the Eel Fare, as they moved through London in their millions along the banks of the Thames, creating the appearance of a broad black border. One Dr William Roots, who lived in Kingston in 1832, calculated that between 1,600 and 1,800 eels passed by a certain point in one minute.[162] The Fare lasted for several days, as the eels passed through locks and weirs until they found a patch of water in which to rest and grow.

On their way back downstream in the autumn, when they weighed about 3 pounds, they would be caught by dedicated eel catchers in numerous eel bucks. These were traps laid across the currents of the river (obstructing the passage of boats), such as those at the Isle of Dogs in the fourteenth century. Further eels were caught in grig weels, long baskets with funnel necks (similar to lobster pots) that were baited with

Eel bucks on the Thames', 1875, wood engraving.

animal remains and laid under waterweed. An eel spear or fork was used to pin the eels down when removing them from the baskets.

In 1736 there was evidence of a closed season for catching eels from December to the end of February, when the fish 'was not accounted wholesome . . . nor fit for eating'.[163] However, by 1792 the head chef at the London Tavern declared that the Thames eels were good all year round, except during the hot summer months, and that they were the best type of the species – the worst were those eels brought over by the Dutch and sold at Billingsgate Market.[164]

But the silver eels were damaged by the 'foul state of the river at London' and disappeared altogether from 1848 until 1866, when the Thames cleaned up its act.[165] During the nineteenth century eels were difficult to come by and were rarely offered for sale, and if they were, often they had not been fished from the Thames at all. In 1827, during the excavations of the north side of the canal in St James's Park, a remarkably large eel weighing 7–8 pounds was found in the shallow water, reported the *Morning Post*:

> After considerable scrambling . . . it was captured by one of the excavators . . . [and] was immediately purchased by a gentleman present for five shillings, the fortunate captor seeming well pleased with the transfer.[166]

But this specimen paled into insignificance next to the 63-pound eel found in the City Canal at Limehouse in 1840. It took three boys a long time to tussle into submission 'the monarch of the eel tribe', and they were covered in mud from where the eel beat the muddy creek with its tail. The newspaper reports told of a creature about 15 feet long with the thickness of a man's thigh. Eventually the boys sold the eel to a gentleman who bought it for 32*s*. with the intention of exhibiting it.[167] Thames eels were even found in the main pipes under London streets – 'sometimes large

enough entirely to stop the passage of water to the houses' – which had wound their way from Shoreditch up to the Fleet Market in the water drains.[168]

The dwindling stock of Thames eels created an excellent trade in cheaper and lower quality Dutch eels. Since Elizabethan times these eels had been brought into Billingsgate alive in skoots – vessels with perforated tanks in their hulls that held the eels. The Queen gave these boats mooring privilege and each boat had to wait to be relieved because if it left its moorings empty, the privilege would be lost.[169] However, by the early nineteenth century the pollution in the Thames was causing problems not only for the Thames eels, but also for these Dutch ones. They did not mind the sea water on their journey across from Holland, but they had a real objection to the Thames water, which was 'too highly flavoured with sewage matter to agree with their delicate constitutions'.[170] So the skoots had to be moored lower down the Thames, initially at Gallions' Reach, below Woolwich, then at Erith, and by 1859, at Gravesend. Every morning a rowing boat would take a load of eels from the skoot, in a holey box chained to the boat, to set up shop as a floating fish stall opposite Billingsgate. Street salesmen would buy 'a great lump of eels, twined and intertwined in so many Gordian knots, and all alive and writhing', and would either cover them in sand or put them in baskets lined with cabbage leaves to keep them from slithering away – they stayed alive for many hours, and even days, out of water if they were put in a damp place.[171] It was estimated that in 1852 an average of 1,166,830 pounds of eels a year were bought by these salesmen.[172]

Dutch eels were destined mainly to be stewed – a favourite fare of the poor. One periodical described the enormous trade in stewed eels in 1852:

> London, from one end to the other, teems and steams with eels, alive and stewed; turn where you will, 'hot eels' still smoke away, with all the

fragrant condiments at hand to make what is in itself palatable more savory still; and at so low a rate, too, that for one halfpenny a man of the million ... may fill his stomach with six or seven long pieces, and wash them down with a cup full of the glutinous liquor in which they have been stewed. This traffic throughout London is so great, that twenty thousand pounds sterling is annually turned from the sale of this single sweet luxury.[173]

More recently London, especially the East End, was well known for its eel, pie and mash shops, many of which displayed tanks of live eels in their windows. They still exist today, just, and malt or chilli vinegar is sprinkled onto jellied or stewed eels. Eels are still sold at Billingsgate by Mick Jenrick of Mick's Eel Supplies. In business since the 1960s, Mick buys from eel farms in Holland and Northern Ireland. The eels are held in lakes in East London before being brought to the market and sold in holding trays with a capacity of 2 tonnes.

Although the Thames eel returned in 1886, its fortunes have not improved and a study in 2010 calculated that since 2005 the population of the Thames eel had fallen by 98 per cent, from 1,500 to just 50 in 2009. Scientists are unsure of the cause, but it is probably the result of a combination of changes in oceanic currents due to climate change, man-made structures such as dams, and the presence of diseases and parasites.[174] This news upset many Londoners, especially Dagenham lightweight boxer Kevin Mitchell, who swore off jellied eels before a fight, preferring to stick to pie and mash to help save the eels – a slightly misplaced sentiment (as the eels he ate were probably from Ireland), but one that highlighted the plight of one of the finest Thames fish.[175]

Fish in the Thames have still to contend with pollution. As recently as 2011 storm water laden with sewage was released into the Thames to prevent it

from flooding homes, and this incident killed many fish, which were found floating dead on the surface.[176] However, at least the water quality has generally improved since 1957, when a 12-mile stretch of the Thames was declared by Natural History Museum researchers to be biologically dead – completely devoid of oxygen. Subsequent government measures to improve sewage-waste treatment, and the banning of industry from discharging pollutants into its water, have led to revived life in the Thames. Even though the river looks brown and dirty, because it is a tidal river carrying a large amount of sediment, it now supports 120 species of fish, seals in Docklands and dolphins as far inland as between Westminster Bridge and Tower Bridge. Mammals are admired and welcomed into the river today, but in times past, mammals which strayed into the Thames were only welcomed for their carcasses.

Thames large fish and mammals

The earliest records of rogue mammals in the Port of London date back to 1240, when a whale was chased up river to Mortlake,[177] where it was butchered, and in 1457 when four 'great fysshes' were caught between London and Erith. They were actually two whales, a 'sword-fish' (probably a narwhal) and a walrus. But rather than being a curiosity, as they would have become if they had arrived later in history, they were merely carved up and eaten at a feast.[178]

John Evelyn provided a more gruesome, yet detailed, description of a rare mammal in Thames water in June 1658 when a large 'true' or Greenland true whale (a plankton feeder) was caught off Greenwich:

A large whale was taken, twixt my Land butting on the Thames & Greenewich, which drew an infinite Concourse to see it, by water, horse, coach, on foote from Lond, & all parts: It appeared first below Greenewich at low-water, for at high water, it would have destroyed all the boates, after a long Conflict it was killed with the harping yrons, & struck in the head, out of which spouted blood & water, by two tunnels like Smoake from a chimney: & after an horrid grone it ran quite on shore & died: The length was 58 foote: 16 in height; black-skin'd like Coach-leather, very small eyes, greate taile, small finns & but 2: a piked snout, & a mouth so wide & divers men might have stood upright in it: No teeth at all, but sucked the slime onely as thro a grate made of that bone which we call Whale bone: The throate [yet] so narrow, as would not have admitted the least of fishes.[179]

An archway was made of the whalebone, and this monument stood on what is now Whalebone Lane in Dagenham. The whale had arrived during a storm and was seen as an augury of the demise of Oliver Cromwell, who died the following day. The whalebone was re-erected at the Valence House Museum, Dagenham.

London itself became a whaling port in 1725, with the Southeastern Docks (now Greenland Dock) at Rotherhithe home to 120 whaling ships sailing for Greenland. There were processing plants for the whale carcasses outside the city, but the business premises of these whaling ships were in the Elephant and Castle. Further rendering (blubber boiling) was done around the looping bend of the river on what is now the site of the O_2 arena (formerly the Millennium Dome). Whale oil became increasingly important to Londoners since by the 1740s, London's 5,000 street lamps were burning whale oil. It was not until 1836 that the whalers left London for good.[180]

The value of whale oil made the mammals an important capture if they happened to venture into the Thames. In September 1781 a fisherman captured a bottle-nosed whale beyond London Bridge. The carcass, measuring almost 26 feet long, was bought by an 'oil-man' for the large sum of £70.[181] The man

helped to recoup the cost of buying the whale by exhibiting it to the public at London Bridge,[182] before the 'stinking' remains were sent for rendering. However, the anatomist John Hunter persuaded the owner to allow him to dissect the whale; helped by his assistants, he stood on the animal and started to wield his knives.[183] It was reported that one of Hunter's assistants slipped into its 'cavernous mouth during inspection, and nearly died of suffocation'.[184] The newspapers also reported on the whale's anatomical features, including the great vein (or vena cava), which was 'so large as to be capable of containing a child of a year old'.[185]

Mammals which became disorientated and swam up to London ultimately faced their end. This was either because of their commercial value, as above, or because of curiosity, fear for river traffic or wanton cruelty. In 1869 a couple of seals were seen below London Bridge and one of them was driven by the tide up to Battersea Bridge. The *London Reader* reported that one seal was shot in the neck and sank, never to be recovered.[186] And in May 1918 a bottle-nosed dolphin ventured up to Battersea and was shot at. It was also wounded by people throwing missiles at it; so much so that it became stranded and died.[187]

One earlier Thames visitor also met its end, but its death unravelled the most fantastical tale. On New Year's Day 1787 some fishermen caught, with great difficulty, the largest shark ever seen in London, off Poplar. It was alive, but apparently very sickly. When it was taken on shore and its carcass (which was over 9 feet long) was opened, they found in its stomach a silver watch, a metal chain, a carnelian seal and some fragments of gold lace – the undigested remains of a human being. It was thought that these obstructions were the causes of the shark's sickness. The watch had a London maker's mark on it, and after investigation it was found that it had been sold to a Mr Ephraim Thompson of Whitechapel as a present to his son, who was going on his first voyage on board

No mercy for a whale caught off Deptford pier in 1842, as depicted in the *Illustrated London News*.

the ship *Polly*, bound for foreign climes. *Polly* had hit a squall three leagues off Falmouth in Cornwall and the young Thompson had fallen overboard and was not seen again. His family never believed that one day they would, by extraordinary chance, find the last remains of their son in a shark captured in their home city. His father bought the shark, not because he wanted to bury it on consecrated ground, but to preserve it as a memorial to the amazing coincidence.[188]

In the twenty-first century another Thames visitor was also preserved after death, but instead of deliberately killing the mammal, Londoners were more 'humane' and tried to save the 15-foot northern bottle-nosed whale calf, nicknamed Willy (although he was a she), that swam upriver past the Houses of Parliament in 2006. Thousands of whale watchers lined the banks and bridges of the Thames and TV news channels ran continuous coverage of the two-day rescue attempt by a twelve-strong team from the British Divers Marine Life Rescue Group. Willy was very disorientated and river traffic was reduced to protect her, and boats, from harm. She was finally allowed to beach at low tide close to Battersea Bridge and was put into a cradle and hoisted by crane on to a London Port Authority barge and taken down the Thames estuary. However, she died en route and many tears were shed for her.[189] Despite the attempts to save her, it may well have been kinder to have killed her – as most definitely would have been done in any other century – because, as one whale lover stated, she had

a pathetic death, deafened and assailed by traffic, trains, boats and people, frightened by those who sought to save it, starving and therefore suffering terrible thirst, trying futilely to follow a dead-end river to the western ocean.[190]

The whale's skeleton is now in the archives of the Natural History Museum. It is labelled as SW 2006/40 – SW standing for Stranded Whale.

It is probably too far-fetched to imagine an inner London devoid of wildlife, with museum exhibits of past London inhabitants lining the shelves: ravens, pigeons, rooks, sparrows, starlings, salmon, eels, swans and so on. But aside from the scavengers, which are increasing in rather alarming numbers, Londoners are realizing that they need to make changes to the monotony and harshness of the man-made environment to encourage wildlife back into their lives. Projects such as the Cockney Sparrow Initiative and Camley Street Natural Park (in the middle of King's Cross) aim to reconnect communities with wildlife and create green havens. Let us hope that old and new species of wildlife are just waiting to fly, swim or walk into London, when conditions allow – let us not make the same mistakes as our ancestors.

Final Thoughts: An Apology and a Pardon

It is sad to think that animals will no longer play a major role in shaping London's history, or provide solace to Londoners when city life becomes too harsh; but, if one asked the past animal inhabitants if they would return to city life, they would most likely refuse – the exploitation they were subjected to, and the unnatural urban conditions they had to cope with, would linger in the memory. It seems that Londoners must be content to share the city experience with their pets and scavenging wildlife, and view the few remaining animals from afar – behind bars at the zoo or police horses drifting by.

It may be that some animals, like Jumbo, Chunee, Sefton and Willy, will make an impact on Londoners' lives again – precisely because animals are a rarity in the city. Perhaps Londoners can see something of themselves in these animals – placed in an alien environment and struggling to cope; they feel an empathy with them. Animals lighten the city; make it more humane, a flash of life against the man-made. Take Polly the parrot, who lived at Ye Olde Cheshire Cheese in Fleet Street for 40 years until her death in 1926. She, or he (there are varying reports), came from the west coast of Africa and was famous for

> possessing an extensive vocabulary, good and bad, the latter predominating, the bird is a great favourite in Fleet street; but its caustic remarks are sometimes embarrassing, especially if ladies are within earshot.[1]

News of Polly's illness in August 1926 was reported around the world, with the *New York Times* stating that London Zoo specialists diagnosed her as having pneumonia.[2] She had become such a force of nature, and so greatly loved, that when she died on 30 October, many obituaries appeared in the newspapers. One in *The Observer* concluded: 'She could talk fairly well, could imitate the drawing of a cork, and the pouring of wine, and always had one answer to make when asked what she would have to drink – "Scotch".'[3]

Well, cheers to Polly, and to all the other animals mentioned in *Beastly London*. Here's hoping that their histories have enlightened readers about the part they have played in shaping London. Very belatedly, I would like to make a heartfelt apology to them with thanks for their forbearance, and to issue a pardon for those animals that turned and bit the hands that fed them!

References

Introduction: Revealing the Beasts

1 The book will concentrate on animal histories found within the inner London boroughs – so, for example, there is no mention of the Ham Polo Club (or, as it is alternatively known, the London Polo Club) because it is in Richmond, or the horse auction at Southall Market, which survived until 2007.

2 Alfred Rosling Bennett, *London and Londoners in the Eighteen-fifties and Sixties* (London, 1924), p. 100.

3 Ibid., pp. 100–01.

4 Keith Thomas, *Man and the Natural World: Changing Attitudes in England, 1500–1800* (London, 1984), p. 78.

5 Ibid., p. 17.

6 From the strong Protestant and Puritan voices of the Elizabethan and early Stuart period, to the Quakers, Dissenters and Latitudinarians of the later seventeenth century, to the Evangelicals and Methodists of the eighteenth century, who took up the cause. See Thomas, *Man and the Natural World*, pp. 153–9.

7 Ibid., p. 173.

8 Ibid., p. 60.

9 Ibid., p. 129.

10 Ibid., p. 159.

11 Ibid., pp. 253, 182.

12 Ibid., p. 185.

13 Frances Maria Thompson, 'To the Editor . . .', *Voice of Humanity: For the Communication and Discussion of All Subjects Relative to the Conduct of Man Towards the Inferior Animal Creation*, I (August 1830), p. 37.

14 Cited in Hilda Kean, *Animal Rights: Political and Social Change in Britain since 1800* (London, 1998), p. 36.

15 Lewis Gompertz, a founder and secretary of the SPCA, went on to found the Animal Friends' Society after he was expelled from the SPCA for alleged anti-Christian views.

ONE
Livestock: Londoners' Nuisance Neighbours

1 Richard Tames, *Feeding London: A Taste of History* (London, 2003), p. 10.

2 Ibid., p. 11.

3 Ibid., pp. 12–13. The enforced meatless days continued up until the Civil War (1642–1651).

4 Cited in Ben Rogers, *Beef and Liberty: Roast Beef, John Bull and the English Nation* (London, 2004), p. 11.

5 Ibid., pp. 17–18.

6 London Commissariat, 'Report of the Commissioners Appointed to Make Inquiries Relating to Smithfield Market, and the Markets in the City of London for the Sale of Meat, 1850', *Quarterly Review*, CXC (September 1854), p. 289.

7 Ian Maclachlan, 'A Bloody Offal Nuisance: The Persistence of Private Slaughter-houses in 19th Century London' *Urban History*, XXXIV/2 (August 2007), p. 228.

8 Alec Forshaw and Theo Bergström, *Smithfield: Past and Present* (London, 1980), p. 36.

9 Napoleon had rid Paris of its livestock market and butchers at the beginning of the nineteenth century; other animal markets, such as one at Knightsbridge, were held in suburban towns. Knightsbridge Market was held every Thursday until the early nineteenth century. Maclachlan, 'A Bloody Offal Nuisance', p. 229.

10 W. J. Gordon, *The Horse-world of London* (London, 1893), p. 110.

11 Translation of William Fitzstephen in Henry Thomas Riley, ed., *Liber Custumarum*, from the Rolls Series, xii/2 (1860), pp. 2–15.

12 'The Markets of London', *Chambers's Edinburgh Journal*, 19 April 1834, p. 92.

13 Cited in Forshaw and Bergström, *Smithfield*, pp. 35–6.

14 Ibid., p. 36.

15 Ibid.

16 Two half-moon slips per cloven hoof; Shirley Toulson, *The Drovers* (Aylesbury, 1980), p. 18.

17 Ibid., pp. 15–16.

18 Ibid., p. 24.

19 Ibid.

20 Ibid., p. 19.

21 Ibid., p. 20.

22 Daniel Defoe, *A Tour Thro' the Whole Island of Great Britain, Divided into Circuits or Journies* (London, 1927), vol. 1, Letter 1, Part 2. Michaelmas Day was on 29 September, the festival of St Michael.

23 Toulson, *The Drovers*, p. 20.

24 Turkeys had been introduced to Britain in the 1520s, but at that point only graced the tables of the wealthiest Londoners.

25 Toulson, *The Drovers*, p. 3.

26 London Commissariat, 'Report of the Commissioners . . . relating to Smithfield Market', pp. 271–308.

27 Ibid., pp. 305–6.

28 'The Food Supply of London', *Contemporary Review*, October 1868, p. 271.

29 'Transit of Cattle', *Chambers's Edinburgh Journal*, 5 December 1846, p. 362.

30 London Commissariat, 'Report of the Commissioners . . . relating to Smithfield Market', p. 286.

31 Ibid., p. 282.

32 George Dodd, *The Food of London: A Sketch of the Chief Varieties, Sources of Supply, etc.* (London, 1856), p. 244.

33 'Smithfield', *Chambers's Edinburgh Journal*, 9 August 1851, pp. 90–93.

34 Dickens wrote a tongue-in-cheek short story called *A Monument of French Folly* in 1850, setting out the 'stupidity' of the French for moving their livestock market and abattoirs out from Paris to Poissy, 13 miles away, and Sceaux, 5 miles away, compared with the 'blessings' of Smithfield.

35 By the author of *Random Recollections, The Great Metropolis*, etc., 'London Markets: No. ii – Smithfield Market', *London Saturday Journal*, 6 March 1841, pp. 111–13.

36 An early usage of the phrase 'nuisance of Smithfield' seen in *Oracle and Daily Advertiser*, 9 October 1799.

37 Charles i had made the first attempt in 1627 to stop drovers from moving animals on the 'Lord's Day'. 'Parliamentary Compendium: Smithfield', *Liverpool Mercury*, 20 March 1835, p. 94.

38 Maclachlan, 'A Bloody Offal Nuisance', p. 231.

39 Richard Perren, *The Meat Trade in Britain, 1840–1914* (London, 1978), p. 33.

40 Excerpts taken from *Voice of Humanity*, iii (15 February 1831), p. 84.

41 London Commissariat, 'Report of the Commissioners . . . relating to Smithfield Market', p. 284.

42 'Editorial: Smithfield to the Rescue', *Daily News*, 8 September 1852.

43 Cited in Maclachlan, 'A Bloody Offal Nuisance', p. 234.

44 'Smithfield Cattle-market, and its Speedy Abolition', *The Era*, 4 February 1849.

45 'Smithfield Market', *Morning Chronicle*, 9 October 1850.

46 Editorial column, *Morning Chronicle*, 18 December 1850.

47 'Riots and Outrages in Bethnal-green', *The Times*, 19 September 1826, p. 3.

48 'Smithfield', *Leisure Hour*, 9 March 1854, p. 153.

49 Cited in Forshaw and Bergström, *Smithfield*, p. 56.

50 London Commissariat, 'Report of the Commissioners . . . relating to Smithfield Market', p. 284.

51 A lairage is a resting point or temporary accommodation for animals. 'Smithfield', *Leisure Hour*, p. 153.

52 London Commissariat, 'Report of the Commissioners . . . relating to Smithfield Market', p. 283.

53 'The Heart of Mid-London', *Household Words*, 4 May 1850, p. 122.

54 At this time the term 'cattle' referred not just to bovines, but all domesticated animals.

55 Cited in Hilda Kean, *Animal Rights: Political and Social Change in Britain since 1800* (London, 1998), p. 36.

56 'Law and Police: Southwark: The Smithfield Market Nuisance', *The Era*, 1 July 1849.

57 'Imperial Parliament: Islington Cattle Market', *Morning Chronicle*, 21 March 1834.

58 'Country-killed' meat came from livestock that was slaughtered in rural areas and transported to London as carcasses on the railways. 'Smithfield', *Chambers's Edinburgh Journal*, p. 92.

59 'Removal of Smithfield Cattle Market', *The Era*, 21 January 1849.

60 'Smithfield', *Chambers's Edinburgh Journal*, p. 92.

61 'Review: The New Cattle Market at Islington', *Northern Star and National Trades' Journal*, 6 March 1847.

62 'The Last Days of an Old Acquaintance', *Chambers's Journal of Popular Literature, Science and Arts*, 2 December 1854, p. 363.

63 Ibid.

64 'The new Cattle-market of London', *Chambers's Journal of Popular Literature, Science and Arts*, 24 November 1855, p. 327.

65 'Regulations respecting landing, &c, of Foreign Animals': Hansard House of Commons debate, CLXXXIX (12 August 1867), ref. c. 1427.

66 'Smithfield', *Chambers's Edinburgh Journal*, pp. 92–3.

67 'The New Cattle-market of London', *Chambers's Journal*, p. 328.

68 Quoted from a letter written to the *Daily News* by the secretary of MDFCTA announcing the name change, 20 May 1867.

69 'Occasional Notes', *Pall Mall Gazette*, 22 July 1868; 'Metropolitan Drinking Fountain and Cattle Trough Association', *Reynolds's Newspaper*, 15 July 1888.

70 Kean, *Animal Rights*, p. 57.

71 'Spirit of the Journals: The Transit of Cattle', *The Examiner*, 13 November 1869.

72 Thanks to Olivia Hogman of Smithfield Market for this information.

73 Forshaw and Bergström, *Smithfield*, pp. 88–90.

74 Cited in P. J. Atkins. 'London's Intra-urban Milk Supply, c. 1790–1914', *Transactions of the Institute of British Geographers*, n.s., II/3(1997), p. 383.

75 Tames, *Feeding London*, p. 12.

76 John Stow, *A Survey of London* [1598] (London, 2007), p. 195.

77 Keith Thomas, *Man and the Natural World: Changing Attitudes in England, 1500–1800* (London, 1984), p. 95.

78 Peter Mathias, *The Transformation of England: Essays in the Economic and Social History of England in the Eighteenth Century* (London, 1979), p. 256.

79 G. B., 'Death in a London Bog', *Ragged School Union Magazine* (December 1862), p. 282.

80 London Commissariat, 'Report of the Commissioners . . . relating to Smithfield Market', p. 286.

81 Ibid.

82 'The Potteries and the Bramley Road Area and the Rise of the Housing Problem in North Kensington', *Survey of London*: vol. XXXVII: *Northern Kensington* (1973), pp. 340–355, available at www.british-history.ac.uk, accessed 12 November 2012.

83 *Report on the Mortality of Cholera in England, 1848–1849* (London, 1852), p. 166.

84 'The Potteries and the Bramley Road Area and the Rise of the Housing Problem in North Kensington', pp. 340–55.

85 'Notting Hill History Timeline; Chapter 2: Entrance to Hipp (early nineteenth century), available at www.vaguerants.uk, accessed 29 October 2012.

86 'Kensington', available at www.worley.org.uk, accessed 29 October 2012.

87 'Care of Horses in War', *The Times*, 22 May 1939, p. 20.

88 Thomas, *Man and the Natural World*, p. 94.

89 'The Poultry', *Old and New London*: vol. 1 (1878), pp. 416–24, available at www.british-history.ac.uk, accessed 12 November 2012.

90 Thanks to Nick Johnston of Leadenhall Market for this information.

91 'Funeral Extraordinary', *The Times*, 16 April 1835, p. 4.

92 'The Months in London – September', *Leisure Hour*, 3 September 1857, p. 565.

93 W. W., 'The Fauna of London', *The Idler*, November 1910, p. 195.

94 Stow, *A Survey of London*, p. 149.

95 Cited in Atkins, 'London's Intra-urban Milk Supply', p. 384; Tames, *Feeding London*, p. 24.

96 Atkins, 'London's Intra-urban Milk Supply', p. 384.

97 Brewers' grains are the waste barley grains after the infusion with malt during the brewing process.

98 'Chronicles of London Streets: Islington and the New River', *All the Year Round*, 6 July 1872, p. 181.

99 Atkins, 'London's Intra-urban Milk Supply', p. 385; R.S.R. Fitter, *London's Natural History* (London, 1953), p. 187.

100 'Summary of This Morning's News', *Pall Mall Gazette*, 24 November 1873.

101 Cited in Atkins, 'London's Intra-urban Milk Supply', p. 385; London Commissariat, 'Report of the Commissioners . . . relating to Smithfield Market', p. 292.

102 'When Will London Be Purified? – No. III', *The Examiner*, 6 March 1852.

103 The waste 'wash' is left behind after the spirit has been distilled from the infusion.

104 Cited in 'London Milk', *Literary Gazette*, 21 July 1849, pp. 532–3.

105 Alan Jenkins, *Drinka Pinta: Story of Milk* (London, 1970), p. 38.

106 'Literature: Observations on London Milk, &c.', *Lloyd's Weekly Newspaper*, 12 May 1850.

107 'The Food Supply of London', *The Contemporary Review*, p. 267.

108 Cited in Atkins, 'London's Intra-urban Milk Supply', p. 388.

109 'Stoke Newington: Economic History', *A History of the County of Middlesex*: vol. VIII: *Islington and Stoke Newington parishes* (1985), pp. 184–94, available at www.british-history.ac.uk, accessed 12 November 2012.

110 Perren, *The Meat Trade in Britain*, p. 108.

111 Kean, *Animal Rights*, p. 131.

112 Figures from Richard Perren, *Taste, Trade and Technology: The Development of the International Meat Industry since 1840* (London, 2006), p. 82.

113 'Failure of The Foreign Cattle Market', *The Times*, 4 April 1913, p. 12.

114 'Marvels of London's Milk Supply', *New London Journal*, 24 November 1906, p. 88.

115 Cited in Atkins, 'London's Intra-urban Milk Supply', p. 392.

116 Ibid., p. 393.

117 Fitter, *London's Natural History*, p. 187; 'Hackney: Economic History', *A History of the County of Middlesex*: vol. X: *Hackney* (1995), pp. 92–101, available at www.british-history.ac.uk, accessed 12 November 2012.

118 See Gordon, *The Horse-world of London*, pp. 174–5.

119 Framley Steelcroft, 'In the Donkeys' Dairy', *Strand Magazine* (July 1895), p. 329–34.

120 Ibid., p. 334.

121 London Commissariat, 'Report of the Commissioners . . . relating to Smithfield Market', p. 289.

122 'Notes on the Old Ordinances Regulating the Shambles in London', *Athenaeum*, 13 October 1849, p. 1040.

123 'Sketches of Society: Smithfield Market *v.* Islington', *Literary Gazette*, 3 March 1849, p. 155.

124 Ibid.

125 'A Looking-Glass for London – No. xx: Markets – Smithfield and Billingsgate', *Penny Magazine*, 12 August 1837, p. 307.

126 Maclachlan, 'A Bloody Offal Nuisance', p. 238.

127 'Smithfield Market Going', *The Era*, 6 May 1849.

128 Ibid.

129 Maclachlan, 'A Bloody Offal Nuisance', pp. 241–3.

130 'Markets – Smithfield and Billingsgate', *Penny Magazine*, p. 310.

131 James Greenwood, *Unsentimental Journeys; or Byways of the Modern Babylon* (London, 1867), chapter 3, 'Newgate Market', available at www.victorianlondon.org, accessed 12 November 2012.

132 'Smithfield', *Chambers's Edinburgh Journal*, p. 93.

133 Maclachlan, 'A Bloody Offal Nuisance', p. 247.

134 Ibid., p. 248.

135 Ibid., p. 228.

136 Forshaw and Bergström, *Smithfield*, p. 145.

137 Prussian blue is a synthetic paint pigment, a constituent of which is animal oil, prepared from blood. Cited in 'The Smithfield Nuisance', *The Era*, 14 October 1849.

138 Gillian Bebbington, *London Street Names* (London, 1987), p. 63.

139 Charles Knight, ed., *London* (London, 1851), vol. III, chapter 52, p. 26, available at http://hdl.handle.net/10427/53833, accessed 12 November 2012.

140 Ibid., pp. 27–30.

141 From Charles Dickens Jr, *Dickens's Dictionary of London* (London, 1879) under 'Bermondsey Leather Market', available at www.victorianlondon.org, accessed 12 November 2012.

142 'The Food Supply of London', *Contemporary Review*, p. 266.

143 Greenwood, *Unsentimental Journeys*, chapter 15, 'The Leather Market'.

144 Richard Daniel Altick, *The Shows of London* (Cambridge, MA, 1978), p. 39.

145 See Robin Blake, *George Stubbs and the Wide Creation: Animals, People and Places in the Life of George Stubbs, 1724–1806* (London, 2005), pp. 251–3.

146 Guy de la Bédoyère, ed., *The Diary of John Evelyn: First Person Singular* (Suffolk, 1995), p. 86.

147 The Smithfield Club became the official title of the society in 1802. Knight, *London*, vol. II, chapter 45, p. 325.

148 Smithfield Club, *History of the Smithfield Club from 1798 to 1900* (London, 1902), p. 6.

149 Ibid., p. 12.

150 'The Smithfield Club Cattle Show', *Leisure Hour*, 5 December 1863, p. 772.

151 Ibid.

152 'The Choiropotamus and Leucoryx, in the Zoological Society's Gardens, Regent's Park', *Illustrated London News*, 9 October 1852, p. 312.

153 'The Smithfield Club Cattle Show', p. 772.

154 Ibid.

155 Ibid.

156 'The Model Dairy Competition', *British Architect*, 11 October 1895, p. 251.

TWO
Working Animals: Straining Every Muscle

1 'Quickening City Traffic', *The Times*, 19 August 1947, p. 3.

2 Ralph Turvey, 'Horse Traction in Victorian London', *Journal of Transport History*, XXVI/2, p. 164; 'Glanders in London', *The Times*, 12 January, 1894, p. 5.

3 By the author of *Random Recollections*, etc., 'London Vehicles: no. I – Omnibuses', *London Saturday Journal*, 23 January 1841, p. 40.

4 By the author of *Random Recollections*, etc., 'London Vehicles: no. III – Vehicles of Various Kinds', *London Saturday Journal*, 6 February 1841, p. 64.

5 'Van Horses in London', *The Times*, 30 March 1937, p. 7.

6 John Clark, *The Medieval Horse and Its Equipment, c. 1150–c. 1450* (Suffolk, 2004), p. 10.

7 Ibid., pp. 10–13.

8 Ibid., p. 20.

9 Ibid., p. 8.

10 Ibid., p. 98.

11 Ibid., pp. 10, 11. The bridge wardens maintained London Bridge and other rented properties, which supported work on the bridge; 'Shadwell', *The Environs of London*: vol. III: *County of Middlesex* (1795), pp. 383–90, available at www.british-history.ac.uk, accessed 12 November 2012. Horses were replaced in 1750 by a steam engine.

12 Clark, *The Medieval Horse*, p. 11.

13 Ben Weinreb and Christopher Hibbert, eds, *The London Encyclopaedia* (London, 1983), p. 602.

14 Ibid., p. 725.

15 Roy Porter, *London: A Social History* (Cambridge, MA, 1998), p. 143.

16 'The Haymarket, West Side', *Survey of London*: vols XXIX and XXX: *St James Westminster, Part 1* (1960), pp. 210–14, available at www.british-history.ac.uk, accessed 12 November 2012.

17 Harry Hieover, 'Metropolitan Horses', *New Sporting Magazine* (April 1847), pp. 246–8.

18 Henry Mayhew, *London Labour and the London Poor* (London, 2009), p. 358.

19 The only examples of working mews left in London are Bathurst Mews, home of the Hyde Park and Kensington Riding Stables, and Elvaston Mews, home of the Knightsbridge Riding Club. 'London Vehicles: no. III – Vehicles of Various Kinds', p. 62.

20 John Timbs, *Curiosities of London: Exhibiting the Most Rare and Remarkable Objects of Interest in the Metropolis with Nearly Fifty Years' Personal Recollections* (London, 1885), pp. 392–3.

21 C. Douglas Woodward, *The Vanished Coaching Inns of the City of London* (London, 2009), p. 14.

22 Ibid., p. 18.

23 Gordon, *The Horse-world of London*, p. 110.

24 Woodward, *The Vanished Coaching Inns*, p. 21. The rescued Bull and Monk stone sign can be seen in the Museum of London's sunken garden.

25 Gordon, *The Horse-world of London*, p. 108.

26 Harry Hieover, 'Metropolitan Horses', *New Sporting Magazine* (June 1847), p. 451.

27 Harry Hieover, 'Metropolitan Horses', *New Sporting Magazine* (April 1847), p. 252.

28 Harry Hieover, 'Metropolitan Horses', *New Sporting Magazine* (May 1847), p. 339.

29 Weinreb and Hibbert, *The London Encyclopaedia*, p. 401.

30 *London Gazette*, 23 October 1679.

31 'Leicester Fields', *Temple Bar* (June 1874), p. 342.

32 'Dangers of Rotten Row', *The Examiner*, 30 May 1863.

33 'The Chapter of Accidents', *The Examiner*, 11 April 1863.

34 From 'Hyde Park', *Old and New London* (1878), vol. IV, pp. 375–405, available at www.british-history.ac.uk, accessed 12 November 2012.

35 George Cox, 'Horse Tales', *English Illustrated Magazine* (October 1910), p. 4.

36 Mayhew, *London Labour and the London Poor*, p. 35.

37 Gordon, *The Horse-world of London*, p. 105.

38 Ibid., p. 101.

39 Ibid., p. 118.

40 'Home of Rest for Horses', *The Standard*, 11 July 1900.

41 Gordon, *The Horse-world of London*, p. 139.

42 Ibid., p. 145.

43 Ibid., p. 41.

44 Cited in Hilda Kean, *Animal Rights: Political and Social Change in Britain since 1800* (London, 1998), pp. 51–2.

45 Gordon, *The Horse-world of London*, p. 35.

46 Ibid., p. 47.

47 Ibid., p. 34.

48 Ibid., p. 36.

49 Ibid., p. 39.

50 Harry Hieover, 'Metropolitan Horses', *New Sporting Magazine* (June 1847), p. 451.

51 Charles Dickens, *Sketches by Boz* (London, 1836), 'Scenes': chapter 17.

52 Gordon, *The Horse-world of London*, p. 33.

53 G. C. Bompas, *Life of Frank Buckland* (London, 1885), p. 292.

54 Gordon, *The Horse-world of London*, p. 47.

55 Ibid., p. 10.

56 'London Vehicles: no. 1 – Omnibuses', p. 41.

57 Harry Hieover 'Metropolitan Horses', *New Sporting Magazine* (June 1847), p. 454; *Voice of Humanity: For the Communication and Discussion of All Subjects Relative to the Conduct of Man Towards the Inferior Animal Creation*, III, 15 February 1831, p. 102.

58 Turvey, 'Horse Traction in Victorian London', p. 39.

59 Gordon, *The Horse-world of London*, pp. 10, 18; Turvey, 'Horse Traction in Victorian London', p. 45.

60 Gordon, *The Horse-world of London*, p. 16.

61 Ibid., p. 16.

62 Ibid., p. 18.

63 Ibid.

64 Ibid., p. 19.

65 Ibid., p. 21.

66 Ibid., p. 25.

67 Ibid., p. 26.

68 Ibid.

69 'Railways and their Carthorses', *Review of Reviews* (January 1905), p. 64.

70 Gordon, *The Horse-world of London*, p. 49.

71 Ibid., p. 53.

72 Ibid., p. 54.

73 Ibid., p. 56.

74 'Camden Horse Tunnels', available at www.glias.org.uk (Greater London Industrial Archaeology Society) , accessed 12 November 2012, and 'The Drinks Trade: Walter and Alfred Gilbey', available at www.locallocalhistory.co.uk, accessed 12 November 2012.

75 See 'Railway Goods-traffic', *Penny Magazine*, 8 October 1842, for a description of the stables.

76 'Partial Destruction of the Railway Goods Depot at Camden Town', *North Wales Chronicle*, 13 June 1857.

77 Gordon, *The Horse-world of London*, p. 65.

78 Weinreb and Hibbert, *The London Encyclopaedia*, p. 290.

79 Ibid., pp. 495–789.

80 Gordon, *The Horse-world of London*, p. 67.

81 Hieover, 'Metropolitan Horses', *New Sporting Magazine* (June 1847), p. 455.

82 Gordon, *The Horse-world of London*, p. 129.

83 Ibid., p. 130.

84 Ibid., p. 132.

85 Ibid., p. 135.

86 Ibid., p. 134.

87 Ibid., p. 75.

88 Ibid., p. 76.

89 The London Cart Horse Parade and the London Van Horse Parade, established in 1904, amalgamated in the 1960s after entries fell. The London Harness Horse Parade is today held at the South of England Showground, Ardingly, East Sussex.

90 Gordon, *The Horse-world of London*, p. 79.

91 Ibid., p. 80.

92 Ibid., p. 81.

93 Ibid., p. 84.

94 Ibid., p. 85.

95 'The Police Courts: The Traffic in Worn-out Horses', *The Times*, 14 October 1910; Gordon, *The Horse-world of London*, p. 89.

96 Ibid., p. 88.

97 Ibid., p. 113.

98 Ibid., p. 117.

99 Turvey, 'Horse Traction in Victorian London', p. 45; the Board of Works was the precursor to the London County Council; the Salvage Corps worked with the Fire Brigade to salvage goods during fires, and deal with any damaged goods after a fire.

100 Turvey, 'Horse Traction in Victorian London', p. 121.

101 Gordon, *The Horse-world of London*, p. 122.

102 Ibid., p. 70.

103 Ibid.

104 'Animals in the Post Office', pdf, *The British Postal Museum and Archive 2005*, p. 3, available at www.postalheritage.org.uk, accessed 12 November 2012.

105 Gordon, *The Horse-world of London*, pp. 125–6.

106 'The Coming Horseless Fire Brigade', *London Journal*, 30 September 1911.

107 'Horseless Fire Brigade: Last London Pair to be Sold this Week', *The Observer*, 20 November 1921, p. 16.

108 'Ambulances and Fire Brigades', *British Medical Journal*, II/2220 (18 July 1903).

109 'The Metropolitan Asylums Board (MAB)', (n.d.), available at www.workhousesorg.uk, accessed 12 November 2012.

110 'Horse Ambulances', *British Medical Journal*, I/1896 (1 May 1897).

111 Cox, 'Horse Tales', p. 9.

112 Gordon, *The Horse-world of London*, p. 156.

113 'Aldridge's', *All the Year Round*, 18 July 1885, pp. 418–19.

114 James Greenwood, *Unsentimental Journeys; or Byways of the Modern Babylon* (London, 1867), chapter 16, 'The London Horse Market', available at www.victorianlondon.org, accessed 12 November 2012.

115 Weinreb and Hibbert, *The London Encyclopaedia*, p. 757.

116 Translation of Fitzstephen in Henry Thomas Riley, ed. *Liber Custumarum.* Rolls Series, II/12 (1860), pp. 2–15.

117 'A Looking-Glass For London – No. xx; Markets-Smithfield and Billingsgate', *Penny Magazine*, 12 August 1837, p. 309.

118 Cited in Clark, *The Medieval Horse*, p. 8.

119 'A Looking-Glass For London – No. xx; Markets-Smithfield and Billingsgate', p. 309.

120 Greenwood, 'The London Horse Market'.

121 *Bell's Life in London and Sporting Chronicle*, 9 September 1832.

122 'Poor Man's Market', *Once a Week*, 2 September 1878, p. 143.

123 Ibid.

124 Greenwood, 'The London Horse Market'.

125 'Smithfield' *Chambers's Edinburgh Journal*, 9 August 1851, p. 92.

126 'Poor Man's Market', p. 143.

127 Greenwood, 'The London Horse Market'.

128 'The Islington Friday Market', *Leisure Hour*, 20 December 1879, p. 814; 'Poor Man's Market', p. 143.

129 Greenwood, 'The London Horse Market'.

130 Gordon, *The Horse-world of London*, p. 165.

131 Greenwood, 'The London Horse Market'.

132 Mayhew, *London Labour and the London Poor*, p. 29.

133 'An Exhibition of Asses', *All the Year Round*, 10 September 1864, p. 105.

134 'The Food Supply of London', *Contemporary Review* (October 1868), p. 264.

135 'An Exhibition of Asses', p. 106.

136 *The Morning Chronicle*, 21 August 1817.

137 'An Exhibition of Asses', p. 105.

138 Gordon, *The Horse-world of London*, p. 176.

139 Ibid., p. 137.

140 Hieover, 'Metropolitan Horses', *New Sporting Magazine* (June 1847), p. 452.

141 'An Exhibition of Asses', p. 102.

142 *Morning Post*, 8 September 1835.

143 *Voice of Humanity*, II (November 1830), pp. 76–7.

144 *Voice of Humanity*, IV (15 May 1831), p. 156.

145 'Police: Cruelty to Horses', *Morning Chronicle*, 3 December 1832.

146 'Police Intelligence', *Morning Post*, 4 October 1849.

147 'Police Intelligence: Torturing a Cab-horse', *Lloyd's Weekly Newspaper*, 9 August 1863.

148 'Police Intelligence', *Morning Post*, 2 January 1866.

149 'Police', *The Times*, 30 September 1861, p. 9.

150 'Cruelty to Horses, &c.', *Morning Post*, 8 October 1830.

151 Stephen Reynolds, 'A Yokel's Impression of London', *Daily Mail*, 31 August 1907; cited in Christopher Scoble, *Fisherman's Friend: A Life of Stephen Reynolds* (Devon, 2000), p. 187.

152 Ibid.

153 'Cruelty to Animals', *Morning Post*, 16 August 1886.

154 'The Metropolitan Drinking Fountain and Cattle Trough Association', pdf, p. 9, available at www.drinkingfountains.org, accessed 12 November 2012.

155 Ibid., p. 18.

156 Ibid.; J. P. Bacon-Philips, 'Horses in London Streets', *Saturday Review*, 2 August 1930, p. 147.

157 'Repairing Roads with Granite Chips', *Morning Post*, 9 February 1871, p. 3.

158 'Cruelty to Horses', *Morning Post*, 17 September 1887, p. 3.

159 'The Death Traps in the London Streets: How Horses are Caught in Them', *Pall Mall Gazette*, 26 February 1889.

160 Ibid.

161 'The Animals' Institute', *The Observer*, 28 April 1889, p. 5.

162 'Our Dumb Friends' League', *The Times*, 29 November 1900, p. 2.

163 'Ambulance For Injured Horses', *The Times*, 2 May 1910, p. 4.

164 'Our Dumb Friends' League', *The Times*, 14 December 1907, p. 14.

165 'Ambulance for Injured Horses', *The Times*.

166 'News in Brief', *The Times*, 17 January 1936, p. 9.

167 'Proposed Trace Horse for Kingston Hill', *The Times*, 31 July 1912, p. 13.

168 'News in Brief', *The Times*, 19 November 1921, p. 5.

169 'Van Horses in Regent's Park', *The Times*, 7 April 1931, p. 7.

170 'Wimbledon Hill Trace Horse', *The Times*, 28 October 1937, p. 18.

171 Gordon, *The Horse-world of London*, p. 127; Sir Graham Wilson, 'The Brown Animal Sanatory Institution', *Journal of Hygiene*, 82 (1979), p. 157.

172 Clark, *The Medieval Horse*, p. 15.

173 It was not until 1840s that the College branched into the treatment of farm animals.

174 'At the Animals' Hospital', *Strand Magazine*, January 1891, p. 76.

175 Ernest Cotchin, *The Royal Veterinary College London* (London, 1990), p. 95.

176 'A Home of Rest for Weary Horses', *Pall Mall Gazette*, 2 June 1886.

177 'A Home of Rest for Horses', *The Graphic*, 20 August 1887.

178 *Voice of Humanity*, IV (15 May 1831), p. 135.

179 'Cruelty to Horses', *Morning Chronicle*, 14 September 1818.

180 *Voice of Humanity*, IV (15 May 1831), p. 163.

181 'Horrible Cruelty to Horses', *The Era*, 5 November 1843.

182 'Horrible Cruelty to Horses', *Annual Register or A View of the History and Politics of the Year 1843* (London, 1844), pp. 157–8.

183 'Cruelty to Animals Prevention Act', 12 and 13 Vict. Cap. 92. Summary, available at www.animalrightshistory.org, accessed 12 November 2012.

184 Animal dissectors: Gordon, *The Horse-world of London*, pp. 171, 184.

185 In the 1860s Harrison Barber became successors to John 'Jack' Atcheler, who was 'horse-slaughterer to her Majesty'. A carved horse marks Atcheler's grave in Highgate Cemetery.

186 Gordon, *The Horse-world of London*, p. 188.

187 Ibid., pp. 185–6.

188 *Morning Post*, 31 August 1894.

189 Gordon, *The Horse-world of London*, pp. 188–9.

190 Ibid., p. 171.

191 *Morning Chronicle*, 20 August 1806.

192 Gordon, *The Horse-world of London*, p. 151.

193 'Waste of Town Horses', *The Times*, 16 March 1918, p. 8.

194 'Horse-drawn Traffic in London', *The Times*, 18 August 1936, p. 7.

195 'London Horse Traffic', *The Times*, 17 January 1938, p. 20; Ban on Horse-drawn Traffic', *The Times*, 6 February 1937, p. 9.

196 'Van Horses on Parade', *The Times*, 3 April 1934, p. 7.

197 'The Metropolitan Drinking Fountain and Cattle Trough Association', p. 18.

198 'Ban on Horse Traffic Lifted', *The Times*, 4 October 1939, p. 5.

199 'Care of Horses in War', *The Times*, 22 May 1939, p. 20.

200 'Animals' Safety in Air Raids', *The Times*, 28 December 1939, p. 2.

201 'Horses in town-', '-greys and blacks', *The Times*, 25 June 1966, p. 11.

202 Thanks to Sebastian Wormell, Harrods' Archivist, for this information.

203 'Horse-drawn Funerals', available at www.tcribb-horses.co.uk, accessed 12 November 2012.

204 Gordon, *The Horse-world of London*, p. 93.

205 Ibid., p. 91.

206 Cited in John Richardson, *The Annals of London: A Year-by-year Record of a Thousand Years of History* (London, 2000), p. 84.

207 'The Royal Mews: History', at www.royal.gov.uk, accessed 23 March 2013.

208 Duns are sandy yellow to reddish-brown coated horses, with a dark stripe along the middle of their backs; black mane, tail, ear edges and lower legs; 'The Royal Stud', *The Mirror*, 13 March 1841, pp. 171–3.

209 Gordon, *The Horse-world of London*, p. 92.

210 Bays are reddish brown coated horses, with black mane, tail, ear edges and lower legs.

211 'The Work of the Royal Mews', available at www.royal.gov.uk, accessed 12 November 2012.

212 The Household Cavalry Mounted Regiment was established in 1991 when a squadron of the Life Guards amalgamated with a squadron of the Blues and Royals – the rather convoluted history of both of these Regiments is explained at www.army.mod.uk, accessed 12 November 2012.

213 Ceremonial duties include Trooping the Colour on Horse Guards Parade (military parade and march-past on the Sovereign's official birthday), Changing of the Guard at Horse Guards (11 am on weekdays and 10 am on Sundays) and escort duties such as the State Opening of Parliament when the Household Cavalry escorts the Queen's coach, and also the coach carrying the Imperial State Crown.

214 Gordon, *The Horse-world of London*, p. 149.

215 'The Engraving of Camden Goods Yard from the North 1889', available at www.locallocalhistory.co.uk, accessed 12 November 2012.

216 'The Household Cavalry – Horse Guards and Barracks in London and Windsor', available at www.householdcavalry.info, accessed 12 November 2012.

217 'Home of the Queen's Cavalry to be Sold Off', *The Independent*, 10 June 2012.

218 'Mounted Branch: Ceremonial Events', available at www.met.police.uk, accessed 12 November 2012.

219 'Death of the Queen's Trooping Horse', *The Times* obituary, 8 February 1957. Winston joined the Metropolitan Police in 1945 and was stationed at Great Scotland Yard. He slipped and fell, dislocating his back on Thames Ditton High Street when he was enjoying semi-retirement at the Metropolitan Police's training yard at Imber Court.

220 Judith Campbell, *Police Horses* (London, 1967), p. 11.

221 'The Mounted Horse Patrol', *Morning Chronicle*, 9 September 1837.

222 'Our Police System', *Dark Blue*, February 1872, pp. 696–7.

223 Campbell, *Police Horses*, p. 16.

224 'The Trafalgar-Square Demonstration', *The Standard*, 15 November 1887, p. 3.

225 'Police Horse Maimed', *The Times*, 19 October 1931, p. 9.

226 'Maimed Police Horse', *The Times*, 2 November 1931, p. 9.

227 'Maiming of Police Horse', *The Times*, 19 November 1931, p. 9.

228 'Way back when . . .', *The Guardian*, 27 April 1998, p. A6.

229 The People's Dispensary for Sick Animals (PDSA) was founded by Maria Dickin in Whitechapel in 1917, before being established nationwide.

230 'Dickin Medal Horses', available at www.pdsa.org.uk, accessed 12 November 2012.

231 Campbell, *Police Horses*, p. 40.

232 According to Campbell, *Police Horses*, there were 24 stables in London for 201 horses in 1967.

233 'Police Horses Back on Beat as Hyde Park Stables Re-open', *London Evening Standard*, 27 April 2010.

234 Police horses were sent into the troubled Clem Attlee Estate in Fulham in October 2010 as high visibility, but approachable, policing. 'Mounted Police Brought into Fulham Estate in Radical Bid to Cut Crime', *Fulham Chronicle*, 9 November 2010.

235 Duncan Campbell, 'Police Horses May Be Put Out to Grass', *The Guardian*, 4 October 2010.

236 'Dogs and Mounted Unit – History and Overview', available at www.cityoflondon.police.uk, accessed 12 November 2012.

237 'The Whitechapel Murder', *The Times*, 13 November 1888, p. 10.

238 Ibid.

239 'Police Dogs', *The Times*, 15 January 1938, p. 11.

240 'Dickin Medal Dogs', available at www.pdsa.org.uk, accessed 12 November 2012.

241 'Police Dogs' Captures', *The Times*, 15 July 1947, p. 2.

242 'Capture By Police Dog', *The Times* 14 July 1947, p. 4.

243 'Successes in Use of Police Dogs', *The Times*, 17 June 1954, p. 4; 'Police Ready to Use More Dogs', *The Times*, 28 February 1958, p. 4.

244 Ibid.

245 '"Flying Dog Squad" for London', *The Times*, 29 December 1962.

246 C. F. Gordon Cumming, 'Professions for Dogs', *Blackwoods Edinburgh Magazine*, November 1888, p. 694.

247 'London Vehicles; No. III – Vehicles of Various Kinds', *London Saturday Journal*, pp. 63–64.

248 *Voice of Hmanity*, 1 (August 1830), p. 30; 'Dog Carts', *Morning Chronicle*, 25 August 1838.

249 'Coroners' Inquests: Lamentable Death of A Gentleman', *Morning Post*, 16 May 1838, p. 7.

THREE

Sporting Animals:
Natural Instincts Exploited

1 'Living in Roman London: In-depth Analysis: Amphitheatre', available at www.museumoflondon.org.uk, accessed 12 November 2012.

2 'British Mastiffs', *The Mirror*, 8 August 1835, p. 85.

3 'The Colosseum', available at www.neronetoursitaly.com, accessed 12 November 2012.

4 'The Games', available at www.roman-empire.net, accessed 12 November 2012.

5 'Roman Gladiatorial Games: Capital Punishment', available at Classics Department: Brooklyn College: www.brooklyn.cuny.edu, accessed 12 November 2012.

6 The wild bulls were also mentioned by the chronicler Matthew Paris (*c.* 1200–1259), but they were eliminated before the sixteenth century in the London area: R.S.R. Fitter, *London's Natural History* (London, 1953), p. 57.

7 Ibid., p. 54.

8 William H. Forsyth, 'The Medieval Stag Hunt', *The Metropolitan Museum of Art Bulletin*, New Series, x/7 (March 1952), pp. 204–6.

9 'Royal Sports in Olden Time', *New Sporting Magazine* (January 1866), p. 22.

10 Keith Thomas, *Man and the Natural World: Changing Attitudes in England, 1500–1800* (London, 1984), p. 145.

11 Fitter, *London's Natural History*, p. 56.

12 Philip L. Armitage and Jonathan Butler, 'Medieval Deerskin Processing Waste at the Moor House Site, London EC2', *London Archaeologist* (Spring 2005), p. 325.

13 'Forestry', *A History of the County of Middlesex*, vol. II: General; Ashford, East Bedfont with Hatton, Feltham, Hampton with Hampton Wick, Hanworth, Laleham, Littleton (1911), pp. 223–51, available at www.british-history.ac.uk, accessed 12 November 2012.

14 Fitter, *London's Natural History*, p. 44.

15 Ibid., p. 90.

16 'Royal Sports in Olden Time', p. 19.

17 Ian Mortimer, *The Time Traveller's Guide to Medieval England* (London, 2009), p. 259.

18 'Royal Sports in Olden Time', p. 18.

19 'Treasury Warrants: January 1702, 16–31', *Calendar of Treasury Books*, vol. XVII: *1702* (1939), pp. 114–35. Charles also created a 'deer harbour' in Green Park.

20 'Westminster: St. James's Park', *Old and New London*, vol. IV (1878), pp. 47–60, available at www.british-history.ac.uk, accessed 12 November 2012.

21 'Hyde Park', *Old and New London*, vol. IV (1878), pp. 375–405, available at www.british-history.ac.uk, accessed 12 November 2012.

22 Neville Braybrooke, *London Green* (London, 1959), p. 150.

23 Thomas, *Man and the Natural World*, p. 29.

24 Fitter, *London's Natural History*, p. 92.

25 Ann Saunders, *Regent's Park: A Study of the Development of the Area from 1086 to the Present Day* (London, 1969), p. 39.

26 David Brandon and Alan Brooke, *Marylebone and Tyburn Past* (London, 2007), p. 42.

27 Saunders, *Regent's Park*, p. 34.

28 Fitter, *London's Natural History*, p. 92.

29 From: 'Chelsea', *Old and New London*, vol. v (1878), pp. 50–70, available at www.british-history.ac.uk, accessed 12 November 2012.

30 John Richardson, *The Annals of London: A Year-by-year Record of a Thousand Years of History* (London, 2000), p. 254.

31 Stow cited in Fitter, *London's Natural History*, p. 91.

32 *General Evening Post*, 10–12 April 1792.

33 *Public Advertiser*, 8 April 1774; 'Vulgar Sports; Epping Hunt', *Morning Post*, 2 April 1793; *Morning Post*, 28 April 1794.

34 *The Standard*, 2 April 1831.

35 'Epping Hunt', *Morning Post*, 24 April 1810.

36 Cited in W. Hone, *The Every Day Book* (1826), vol. ii, pp. 460–64.

37 'Epping Hunt', *Morning Post*, 9 April 1833.

38 'Epping Hunt', *The Era*, 11 April 1847.

39 'Sport, Ancient and Modern: Hunting: Foxhounds', *A History of the County of Middlesex*, vol. ii: General; Ashford, East Bedfont with Hatton, Feltham, Hampton with Hampton Wick, Hanworth, Laleham, Littleton (1911), pp. 259–60, available at www.british-history.ac.uk, accessed 12 November 2012.

40 Fitter, *London's Natural History*, p. 93.

41 Emma Griffin, *Blood Sport: Hunting in Britain since 1066* (New Haven, CT, 2008), p. 187.

42 Fitter, *London's Natural History*, p. 93.

43 Colburn's *Kalendar of Amusements* (1840) cited in 'Sport, Ancient and Modern: Shooting', *A History of the County of Middlesex*, vol. ii (1911), pp. 266–7, available at www.british-history.ac.uk, accessed 12 November 2012.

44 Peter Quennell, ed., *Mayhew's London* (London, 1984), p. 45.

45 Hansard, HC Deb, 7 March 1883, vol. CCLXXVI, cc. 1648–92, available at http://hansard.millbanksystems.com, accessed 12 November 2012.

46 'Topics of the Week', *The Era*, 10 March 1883.

47 'The Hurlingham Club: History: The Club', available at www.hurlinghamclub.org.uk, accessed 12 November 2012.

48 'Bethnal Green: Social and Cultural Activities', *A History of the County of Middlesex*, vol. XI: Stepney, Bethnal Green (1998), pp. 147–55, available at www.british-history.ac.uk, accessed 12 November 2012.

49 'Mayfair', *Old and New London*, vol. IV (1878), pp. 345–59, available at www.british-history.ac.uk, accessed 12 November 2012.

50 Joseph Strutt, *The Sports and Pastimes of the People of England* (London, 1867), p. 285.

51 The Shocking Details of a Fatal Pugilistic Encounter, &c', *Morning Post*, 29 May 1858, p. 4.

52 'Police Intelligence: Bow Street', *Morning Post*, 25 July 1818.

53 Translation of William Fitzstephen in Henry Thomas Riley, ed., *Liber Custumarum*, from the Rolls Series, XII/2 (1860), pp. 2–15.

54 Griffin, *Blood Sport*, p. 42.

55 Felix Parker and Peter Jackson, *Pleasures of London* (London, 2008), p. 14.

56 *London Chronicle*, 13 August 1791.

57 Thomas Bewick, *A General History of Quadrupeds* (reprinted Leicester, 1980), p. 334.

58 Cited in Walter Besant, 'South London', *Pall Mall Magazine* (September 1898), pp. 120–21.

59 Cited in Strutt, *The Sports and Pastimes of the People of England*, p. 208.

60 *London Evening Post*, 1–3 July 1760.

61 *St James's Chronicle*, 8 October 1762.

62 Parker and Jackson, *Pleasures of London*, p. 14.

63 Richard Tames, *The London We Have Lost* (London, 2008), p. 22.

64 Strutt, *The Sports and Pastimes of the People of England*, p. 206.

65 Besant, 'South London', p. 121.

66 Parker and Jackson, *Pleasures of London*, p. 15.

67 William Hone, *The Table Book of Daily Recreation and Information* (London, 1828), vol. i, p. 490.

68 Besant, 'South London', p. 120.

69 Ibid., p. 119.

70 Tames, *The London We Have Lost*, p. 21.

71 Besant, 'South London', p. 122.

72 Cited in Charles T. Prouty, 'George Whetstone and the Sources of Measure for Measure', *Shakespeare Quarterly*, xv/2 (Spring 1964), p. 133.

73 'The Bankside Playhouses and Bear Gardens', *Survey of London*, vol. xxii: Bankside (1950), pp. 66–77, available at www.british-history.ac.uk, accessed 12 November 2012.

74 Parker and Jackson, *Pleasures of London*, p. 15.

75 G. H. Gater and E. P. Wheeler, eds, 'The Tiltyard and the Horse Guards', *Survey of London*, vol. xvi: *St Martin-in-the-Fields i: Charing Cross* (1935), pp. 5–16, available at www.british-history.ac.uk, accessed 12 November 2012.

76 Because the twenty closely spaced arches of London Bridge held up the flow of the tides, during cold snaps the water would freeze to, in 1683–4, a depth of 11 inches, and last for several months. The bridge was rebuilt in the 1820s and so the big freezes ended.

77 Strutt, *The Sports and Pastimes of the People of England*, p. 207.

78 Cited in 'Hockley-in-the-Hole', *Old and New London*, vol. ii (1878), pp. 306–09, available at www.british-history.ac.uk, accessed 12 November 2012.

79 *Morning Chronicle*, 6 August 1772; *Public Advertiser*, 16 July 1791; *Woodfall's Register*, 28 July 1791; *London Chronicle*, 13 August 1791; *London Chronicle*, 6–8 September 1796.

80 Besant, 'South London', p. 121.

81 'Cruelty of English Sports', *Literary Chronicle and Weekly Review*, 13 July 1822, pp. 445–6.

82 Daniel Hahn, *The Tower Menagerie: The Amazing True Story of the Royal Collection of Wild Beasts* (London, 2004), pp. 97–8.

83 'At the Desire of Several Persons of Quality, &c.', *Daily Courant*, 20 May 1717.

84 Broughton's Amphitheatre was previously known as Mr Figg's Great Room. John Timbs, *Curiosities of London* (London, 1855), p. 11.

85 *Daily Advertiser*, 29 January 1747.

86 'Incidents, Marriages, and Deaths in and near London', *Monthly Magazine* (June 1822), p. 466.

87 'Statement of Facts', *Morning Chronicle*, 15 March 1825.

88 Grantley F. Berkeley, *My Life and Recollections* (London, 1865), vol. ii, p. 101.

89 Ibid., p. 103.

90 Thomas, *Man and His Natural World*, p. 153.

91 Ibid., p. 157.

92 'Henry viii: April 1546, 11–20', *Letters and Papers, Foreign and Domestic, Henry viii*, vol. xxi, Part 1: January–August 1546 (1908), pp. 287–305.

93 'Plague', *Analytical Index to the Series of Records Known as the Remembrancia: 1579–1664* (1878), pp. 329–49.

94 Lord William Lennox, 'Here's Sport Indeed!', *New Sporting Magazine* (March 1869), p. 188.

95 'Proceedings in the Commons, 1601: December 1st–5th', *Historical Collections: or, An Exact Account of the Proceedings of the Four Last Parliaments of Q. Elizabeth* (1680), pp. 267–88.

96 'House of Commons Journal, Volume 1: 9 July 1625', *Journal of the House of Commons*: vol. i: 1547–1629 (1802), pp. 807–08.

97 Hahn, *The Tower Menagerie*, pp. 113–14.

98 Guy de la Bédoyère, ed., *The Diary of John Evelyn: First Person Singular* (Suffolk, 1995), 20 August 1667, p. 164. The gallant horse killed all the dogs and eventually had to be run through with swords.

99 Richardson, *The Annals of London*, p. 164; the Clapham Sect was best known for its campaign to abolish slavery.

100 'Political Duels', *The Times*, 22 June 1787, p. 2.

101 'Postscript, London', *St James's Chronicle*, 9 June 1761.

102 The Metropolitan Police Force was not formed until September 1829. 'Police of the Metropolis', *The Times*, 25 August 1834, p. 4.

103 *Bell's Weekly Messenger*, 20 April 1800.

104 *Voice of Humanity*, 1 (August 1830), pp. 25–6.

105 Ibid., p. 27.

106 Strutt, *The Sports and Pastimes of the People of England*, p. 208.

107 *The Times*, 10 November 1838.

108 Cited in Strutt, *The Sports and Pastimes of the People of England*, p. 224.

109 Thomas, *Man and the Natural World*, p. 183.

110 'Cock-fighting', *Time* (February 1880), p. 553.

111 Strutt, *The Sports and Pastimes of the People of England*, p. 225.

112 Folio cxi b. – June 1363, '*Calendar of Letter-books of the City of London: G: 1352–1374* (1905), p. 154.

113 Richardson, *The Annals of London*, p. 84.

114 'Cock fighting', available at www.museumwales.ac.uk, accessed 12 November 2012.

115 Thomas, *Man and the Natural World*, p. 144.

116 'Here's Sport Indeed!', p. 190.

117 Strutt, *The Sports and Pastimes of the People of England*, p. 225.

118 From 'The Cockpit and Kent's Treasury', *Survey of London*, vol. xiv: St Margaret, Westminster, Part iii: Whitehall ii (1931), pp. 23–36, available from www.british-history.ac.uk, accessed 12 November 2012.

119 Ibid.

120 'The Diary of Samuel Pepys', Monday, 21 December 1663, available at www.pepysdiary.com, accessed 12 November 2012.

121 Ibid., 6 April 1668.

122 Cited in Thomas, *Man and the Natural World*, p. 160.

123 'Old Sporting London', *All the Year Round*, 17 September 1887, p. 220.

124 Atticus Police, 'To the Editor . . .', *Public Advertiser*, 19 February 1757.

125 *St James's Chronicle or the British Evening Post*, 19 February 1762.

126 *Whitehall Evening Post*, 9 October 1783.

127 *Weekly Journal*, 12 April 1729; *Weekly Journal*, 1 November 1729; *Morning Chronicle*, 21 August 1776.

128 *Morning Chronicle*, 17 October 1803.

129 W.T.W., 'To the Editor . . .', *Morning Chronicle*, 18 October 1821; the Bill was defeated by 47 Noes

to 18 Ayes because of fears that the traditional blood sports of the upper classes would be prohibited next.

130 'Preventative Policing', *Morning Post*, 28 May 1822.

131 Greenwood, *Unsentimental Journeys*, chapter 4: A Dog Show, available at www.victorianlondon.org, accessed 12 November 2012.

132 Ibid.

133 'Police Intelligence: Southwark', *Lloyd's Weekly Newspaper*, 21 February 1875.

134 Chris Greenwood, 'Police Unit Takes 1,000 Dangerous Dogs Off the Street', *The Independent*, 9 March 2010.

135 'Sporting: A Rat-killing Match', *Morning Post*, 12 December 1844; 'Sporting: Rat-killing Match', *Morning Post*, 6 February 1845.

136 James Greenwood, *The Wilds of London* (London, 1874), 'At the "Turnspit", Quaker's Alley', pp. 275–9, available at www.victorianlondon.org, accessed 12 November 2012.

137 'The Dog Billy and the Berkshire Rat-killer', *Morning Chronicle*, 4 March 1824; 'Specimen of Civilization!!', *Morning Post*, 16 October 1822; 'Westminster Pit', *Morning Chronicle*, 3 March 1825.

138 'Rat-catcher Extraordinary – Dog Billy Surpassed', *Odd Fellow*, 21 December 1839.

139 Mayhew, *London Labour and the London Poor*, vol. iii, p. 2.

140 Ibid., vol. iii, p. 8.

141 Ibid., p. 12.

142 Ibid., p. 11.

143 'Amusements of the Moneyless', *Chambers's Journal*, 19 May 1855, p. 307.

144 'The Games: Chariot Racing', available at www.roman-empire.net, accessed 12 November 2012.

145 Cited in Strutt, *The Sports and Pastimes of the People of England*, pp. 32–3.

146 Ibid.

147 'Sport, Ancient and Modern: Racing', *A History of the County of Middlesex*, vol. ii (1911), pp. 263–5, available at www.british-history.ac.uk, accessed 12 November 2012.

148 'Hyde Park', *Old and New London* (1878), vol. IV, pp. 375–405, available at www.british-history.ac.uk, accessed 12 November 2012.

149 'The Progress of Racing in England', *New Sporting Magazine* (February 1832), p. 281.

150 'Sport, Ancient and Modern: Racing'.

151 'Hornsey, Including Highgate: Social and Cultural Activities', *A History of the County of Middlesex*, vol. VI (1980), pp. 157–62, available at www.british-history.ac.uk, accessed 12 November 2012; *Public Advertiser*, 16 July 1791; 'Peckham and Dulwich', *Old and New London*, vol. VI (1878), pp. 286–303, available at www.british-history.ac.uk, accessed 12 November 2012.

152 Jack Straw's Castle was the highest tavern in London before being turned into a block of luxury flats.

153 See Robin Blake, *George Stubbs and the Wide Creation: Animals, People and Places in the Life of George Stubbs, 1724–1806* (London, 2005), p. 161.

154 Cited in 'Hampstead: The Heath', *Old and New London*, vol. V (1878), pp. 449–62, available at www.british-history.ac.uk, accessed 12 November 2012.

155 Cited in 'Notting Hill and Bayswater', *Old and New London*, vol. V (1878), pp. 177–88, available at www.british-history.ac.uk, accessed 12 November 2012.

156 Cited in 'Racing: Frying Pan Off the Back Burner', *The Independent*, 10 August 1999.

157 Ibid.

158 'The Western Suburbs: Belgravia', *Old and New London*, vol. V (1878), pp. 1–14, available at www.british-history.ac.uk, accessed 12 November 2012.

159 'To be Sold by Auction By Mr Tattersall', *London Evening Post*, 23 March 1771; *Daily Advertiser*, 2 April 1772.

160 'Tattersall's', *London Review*, 31 October 1863, p. 463.

161 'Tattersall's Repository', *The Mirror*, 7 March 1846, p. 146.

162 'The Western Suburbs: Belgravia', *Old and New London*, pp. 1–14.

163 'The Western Suburbs: Knightsbridge', *Old and New London*, vol. V (1878), pp. 15–28, available at www.british-history.ac.uk, accessed 12 November 2012.

164 A. Croxton-Smith *Greyhound Racing and Breeding* (London, 1927), p. 1.

165 Attendance figures from 'Greyhound Racing', *The Times*, 4 August 1927 and 17 August 1927.

166 'Greyhound Racing', *The Times*, 20 June 1927, p. 7.

167 'Greyhound Racing', *The Times*, 21 June 1927, p. 18.

168 'Greyhounds in London Backyard', *The Times*, 6 September 1927 and 27 September 1927.

169 'Sale of Greyhounds', *The Times*, 7 January 1929, p. 4.

170 'Greyhound Racing', *The Times*, 27 October 1927, p. 7.

171 'Greyhound Racing: Training for Young Dogs', *The Times*, 4 November 1927, p. 7.

172 'Notes of the Week', *Saturday Review*, 25 June 1927, p. 963.

173 Geoffrey Wansell, 'Going to the Dogs', *The Times*, 18 September 1971, p. 12.

174 C. A. Knapp, 'Tin-hare Coursing', *Saturday Review*, 24 December 1927, p. 884.

175 On Guard, 'Dog Racing', *Saturday Review*, 31 March 1928, p. 387; 'Bishop on Greyhound Racing', *The Times*, 1 May 1928, p. 18.

176 Cited in Barker and Jackson, *Pleasures of London*, p. 1.

177 Ibid., p. 2.

178 Cited in Riley, translation of Fitzstephen, pp. 2–15.

179 Cited in Barker and Jackson, *Pleasures of London*, p. 10.

180 Mortimer, *The Timetraveller's Guide to Medieval England*, p. 255.

181 To prevent the horses from lethally clashing, a barrier called a 'tilt' separated the opposing riders; hence the tournament area was called the 'tilt yard'.

182 John Clark, *The Medieval Horse and Its Equipment, c. 1150–c. 1450* (Suffolk, 2004), p. 23.

183 Mortimer, *The Timetraveller's Guide to Medieval England*, p. 255.

184 Richardson, *The Annals of London*, p. 45.

185 'Journey through England and Scotland Made by Lupold von Wedel in the Years 1584 and 1585', *Transactions of the Royal Historical Society*, n.s. IX (1895), pp. 258–9.

186 The first polo match played in England was on Hounslow Heath between the 10th Hussars and the 9th Lancers in 1869.

187 'Polo at Lillie Bridge', *The Graphic*, 2 August 1873.

188 'Polo: Hurlingham', *Morning Post*, 8 June 1874, p. 3; 'Polo in Hurlingham Park', *Morning Post*, 29 June 1874, p. 5.

189 One hand equals four inches or 10.16 centimetres; measurement is taken from the ground to the highest point on the horse's shoulder (the wither). In 1895, the height of a pony was raised to 14.2 hh. Today, the 'ponies' are full-grown horses, ranging from 14.2 to 16 hh – the height restrictions were abolished in 1919.

190 'Club Announcements', *The Times*, 4 June 1927, p. 1.

191 'The Gymkhana', *The Graphic*, 14 July 1894.

192 'Polo at Lillie-Bridge', *Morning Post*, 17 July 1874, p. 7.

193 'The Horse Show', *The Times*, 11 June 1878, p. 6.

194 'The Horse Show', *The Times*, 14 June 1878, p. 4.

195 'Great Metropolitan Horse Show', *Daily News*, 27 May 1867.

196 The Horse Show', *Pall Mall Gazette*, 28 May 1867.

197 'The Islington Horse Show', *The Times*, 15 May 1891, p. 12.

198 'The Islington Horse Show', *The Graphic*, 14 June 1890.

199 'London Olympic Course Builder Appointed', *Horse and Hound*, 24 December 2009.

FOUR

Animals as Entertainers:
Performance, Peculiarity and Pressure

1 Thomas Frost, *The Old Showmen, and the Old London Fairs* (London, 1874), p. 170.

2 Felix Parker and Peter Jackson, *Pleasures of London* (London, 2008), pp. 5–6.

3 Ibid.

4 Frost, *The Old Showmen, and the Old London Fairs*, p. 20.

5 Ben Jonson and Suzanne Gossett, *Bartholomew Fair* (Manchester, 2001), p. 176. Hares beating tabors are seen in illustrations from the fifteenth century.

6 *Daily Courant*, 10 May 1707.

7 Guy de la Bédoyère, ed., *The Diary of John Evelyn: First Person Singular* (Suffolk, 1995), 13 September 1660, p. 115.

8 Frost, *The Old Showmen, and the Old London Fairs*, p. 20.

9 Cited in Philip Armitage 'Jawbone of a South American Monkey from Brooks Wharf, City of London', *London Archaeologist*, vols IV–X (1983), p. 266.

10 Frost, *The Old Showmen, and the Old London Fairs*, p. 190.

11 Henry Mayhew, *London Labour and the London Poor* (London, 2009), vol. III, pp. 127–9.

12 Snakes are not slimy, but their skin is dry and cool to the touch; perhaps the snake performer was referring to woodland debris attached to the snakes.

13 Frost, *The Old Showmen, and the Old London Fairs*, p. 170.

14 Mayhew, *London Labour and the London Poor*, vol. III, pp. 80–81.

15 'A Fatal Carriage Accident: Horse Frightened by a Bear', *Pall Mall Gazette*, 20 May 1898.

16 'The Performing Bear Nuisance', *Illustrated Police News etc.*, 10 April 1869.

17 C. J. Cornish, *Life at the Zoo: Notes and Traditions of the Regent's Park Gardens* (London, 1897), p. 224.

18 'Remarkable Scene on the Thames', *Illustrated Police News*, 22 July 1893.

19 Mayhew, *London Labour and the London Poor*, vol. III, pp. 224–5.

20 Ibid., p. 229.

21 'The Pig-faced Lady', *Illustrated Police News etc.*, 7 January 1882.

22 'A Performing Bear', *The Era*, 16 July 1892.

23 'Killed by the "Royal Bear" – The Inquest', *Pall Mall Gazette*, 2 January 1891.

24 Joseph Strutt, *The Sports and Pastimes of the People of England* (London, 1867), p. 195.

25 Mayhew, *London Labour and the London Poor*,

vol. III, pp. 191–2.

26 Frost, *The Old Showmen, and the Old London Fairs*, p. 22.

27 Jonson and Gossett, *Bartholomew Fair*, p. 176.

28 Frost, *The Old Showmen, and the Old London Fairs*, p. 204.

29 Ibid., p. 271.

30 Ibid., p. 292.

31 Ibid., pp. 80–81.

32 Ibid., p. 161.

33 'The Talking Fish', *The Era*, 8 May 1859; David Paton-Williams, *Katterfelto: Prince of Puff* (Leicester, 2008), pp. 81–2.

34 *Morning Herald and Daily Advertiser*, 18 June 1783.

35 Jan Bondeson, *Animal Freaks: The Strange History of Amazing Animals* (London, 2008), pp. 13–28; Frost, *The Old Showmen, and the Old London Fairs*, pp. 23–5.

36 Ibid., p. 23.

37 Cited in Bondeson, *Animal Freaks*, p. 25.

38 *Morning Chronicle and London Advertiser*, 25 April 1785.

39 The pig was previously trained by Bisset of 'Cat's Orchestra' fame – see later in chapter.

40 *Morning Post and Daily Advertiser*, 29 March 1785.

41 Richard Wroughton, 'To the Editor . . .', *Gazetteer and New Daily Advertiser*, 1 August 1785.

42 Placido, Redige, Dupuis and Meunier, 'To the Editor . . .', *Morning Post and Daily Advertiser*, 4 August 1785.

43 Bondeson, *Animal Freaks*, p. 33.

44 Ibid., p. 37.

45 'The Lament of Toby, the Learned Pig', *The Complete Thomas Hood* (Oxford, 1906), Verses 4–5, pp. 348–9.

46 Bondeson, *Animal Freaks*, pp. 47–61.

47 'Performing Animals', *All the Year Round*, 26 January 1867, p. 105.

48 Richard Daniel Altick, *The Shows of London* (Cambridge, MA, 1978), p. 307.

49 *Morning Herald*, 5 September 1785.

50 *Chamber's Book of Days*, vol. I (London, 1869), pp. 293–5.

51 Strutt, *The Sports and Pastimes of the People of England*, pp. 200–01.

52 'A Dog Drama', *The Era*, 5 September 1880.

53 'The Theatres', *The Era*, 2 August 1840; 'Theatres, &c.', *The Era*, 13 July 1851; 'The Theatres', *The Era*, 2 August 1840.

54 'The "Dog-Drama" at The Alhambra', *The Graphic*, 22 October 1898.

55 'Intellectual Fleas', *Household Words*, 5 July 1856, p. 599.

56 'The Industrious Fleas', *The Times*, 13 March 1833, p. 2.

57 'Intellectual Fleas', *Household Words*, p. 600.

58 'The Aquarium', *The Era*, 5 December 1885.

59 'The Westminster Aquarium', *The Era*, 8 June 1879.

60 'Royal Aquarium', *The Graphic*, 31 December 1898.

61 Frost, *The Old Showmen, and the Old London Fairs*, p. 177.

62 A dulcimer is a stringed musical instrument with the strings stretched over a sounding board.

63 Bondeson, *Animal Freaks*, pp. 7–8.

64 'Sights of London: The March of Intellect: Learned Cats', *Literary Gazette*, 21 February 1829, p. 132.

65 Ibid.

66 'Our Weekly Gossip', *Athenaeum*, 16 September 1843, p. 845.

67 John West, 'The Dog Orchestra', *Strand Magazine* (December 1897), p. 729.

68 The word 'circus' comes from Greek *kirkos* 'circle' and Latin *circus* 'ring'.

69 Isaac J. Greenwood, *The Circus, its Origin and Growth Prior to 1835* (New York, 1898), p. 23.

70 Cited in 'The New Holborn Amphitheatre', *The Era*, 26 May 1867.

71 'Activity on Horseback', *Gazetteer and New Daily Advertiser*, 28 April 1768.

72 Many accounts state that this horse was white, but Mr Cooper in a letter to *Once a Week* insisted that he was a dark bay – he should know as he painted him. A.B.R. Cooper, 'Astley's Horse', *Once a Week*, 10 January 1863, p. 82.

73 'Philip Astley', *All Year Round*, 27 January 1872, p. 210; Philippus, 'Astley's Horse', *Once a Week*, 7 March 1863, p. 294.

74 William Pinkerton, 'Astley's', *Once a Week*, 27 December 1862, p. 10.

75 'Philip Astley', *All Year Round*, p. 210.

76 Ibid.

77 Ibid.

78 Ibid.

79 'Old Astley', *Lloyd's Weekly Newspaper*, 17 October 1897.

80 'Horsemanship, with Alterations, &c', *Gazetteer and New Daily Advertiser*, 3 June 1769.

81 *Public Advertiser*, 20 August 1772.

82 'Horsemanship, Westminster Bridge', *Public Advertiser*, 15 July 1773.

83 'Westminster Bridge', *Morning Post and Daily Advertiser*, 12 June 1775.

84 'Philip Astley', *All Year Round*, p. 207.

85 'Astley's', *Oracle and Public Advertiser*, 1 July 1796.

86 'Positively the last night &c.', *Morning Post and Daily Advertiser*, 30 August 1788.

87 Astley's burned down the first time in 1794. It took Astley less than seven months to re-build.

88 'Real Horses', *All the Year Round*, 28 October 1871, p. 511.

89 'Recollections of Astley's', *Chambers's Edinburgh Journal*, 10 January 1835, p. 398.

90 Joseph Ballard, *England in 1815 as seen by a Young Boston Merchant &c.* (Boston, MA, 1913), p. 36.

91 'A Dreadful Accident . .', *Morning Chronicle*, 7 December 1814.

92 John Coleman, 'A Gossip About Astley's', *The Graphic*, 18 March 1893.

93 'Astley's Amphitheatre', *Theatrical Observer*, 20 August 1844, pp. 1–2.

94 'An Unpolite Elephant', *The Examiner*, 7 September 1828.

95 Charles Dickens, *The Old Curiosity Shop* (London, 1841), chapter 39.

96 Wildrake, 'Scenes in the Sporting World, No. VI – Astley's By Daylight', *New Sporting Magazine*, August 1841, p. 92.

97 The Rosemary Branch Equestrian Theatre in Islington Fields was also destroyed by fire in 1853 with the death of seven horses and several performing dogs: 'Destruction of the Rosemary Branch Equestrian Theatre', *The Era*, 31 July 1853.

98 'The Synopsis', *The Era*, 5 May 1844.

99 'Novel Performance on the River', *The Era*, 29 September 1844.

100 'Real Horses', p. 511.

101 'Mirror of Fashion: Covent Garden Theatre', *Morning Chronicle*, 19 February 1811.

102 'Real Horses', p. 512.

103 'The Performing Elephants at Astley's', *London Journal*, 11 February 1854, p. 377.

104 Cited in Thomas Frost, *Circus Life and Circus Celebrities* (London, 1881), p. 49.

105 'Extraordinary Exhibition at Astley's London', *The Belfast News-letter*, 4 September 1838.

106 'Furious Attack on Mr Amburgh . . .', *Freeman's Journal and Daily Commercial Advertiser*, 13 September 1838.

107 'Drury Lane Theatre', *Theatrical Observer*, 26 January 1839, p. 1.

108 'A Man Killed by a Lion', *Reynolds's Newspaper*, 13 January 1861.

109 '"Wolf!"', *Penny Illustrated Paper and Illustrated Times*, 25 February 1888, p. 122.

110 'Lion Happy Family at the Paragon, Mile-end Road', *Penny Illustrated Paper and Illustrated Times*, 10 November 1894, p. 298.

111 William Pinkerton, 'Astley's', *Once a Week*, 27 December 1862, p. 7.

112 'The New Royal Amphitheatre, Holborn', *The Era*, 5 May 1867.

113 'Sanger's Circus', *The Era*, 6 November 1859.

114 The word comes from Greek *hippos*, horse, and *dromos*, race or course. 'Royal Agricultural Hall', *The Era*, 6 December 1863.

115 *Pall Mall Gazette*, 24 June 1880.

116 Ibid.

117 'Astley's Amphitheatre', *Dramatic Notes* (January 1879), p. 72.

118 'Theatres: Sangers' Amphitheatre', *The Graphic*, 3 January 1885.

119 '"Olympia" at Kensington', *Pall Mall Gazette*, 25 September 1886.

120 See the full text of the handbill: J. W. Myers, *Account of the Stables, Great Course for Chariot Races, etc.* (date unknown), available at www.archive.org, accessed 12 November 2012.

121 The Alhambra was open from 1856 to 1936.

122 'Easter Entertainments: The Alhambra', *Daily News*, 6 April 1858.

123 John Glanfield, *Earls Court and Olympia: From Buffalo Bill to the 'Brits'* (Sutton, 2003), pp. 12–13.

124 'The Wild West Show', *The Era*, 14 May 1887.

125 A. F. Wertheim and B. Bair, eds, *The Papers of Will Rogers: Wild West and Vaudeville*, vol. II (Norman, OK, 1995), p. 85.

126 'Arrival of Barnum's Advance Guard', *Illustrated Police News*, 5 October 1889.

127 'Barnum Revisited', *The Era*, 23 November 1889.

128 'Arrival in London of "The Greatest Show on Earth"', *Illustrated Police News*, 4 December 1897.

129 'The Stage Army at Olympia', *Daily News*, 13 January 1898.

130 The London Hippodrome opened in 1900 with circus and variety acts, but was turned into a music hall and variety theatre in 1909.

131 For an account (probably rose-tinted) of the training methods employed for the Noah's Ark show see Hodgetts and Brayley, 'The Training of Performing Animals', *Strand Magazine* (July 1894), pp. 609–16.

132 *Voice of Humanity*, III (15 February 1831), p. 103.

133 'Vauxhall Gardens – Balloon Ascent of Mr. Green on Horseback', *The Standard*, 1 August 1850.

134 S. L. Bensusan, 'The Torture of Trained Animals', *English Illustrated Magazine* (April 1896), pp. 25–30.

135 Walter J. Burnham, 'Performing Animals: To the Editors . . .', *Liverpool Mercury*, 11 November 1899.

136 Ibid.

137 'A Performing Pig,' *Reynolds's Newspaper*, 26 March 1899.

138 'How a Bear was Made to Dance', *Daily News*, 1 March 1899.

139 David A. H. Wilson, 'Politics, Press and the Performing Animals Controversy in Early 20th century Britain', *Anthrozoös*, XXI/4, p. 318.

FIVE

Exotic Animals:
The Allure of the Foreign and the Wild

1 The Gardens of the Zoological Society of London became popularly known as London Zoo after the music-hall song 'Walking to the Zoo' (1867) by Alfred Vance.

2 Daniel Hahn, *The Tower Menagerie: The Amazing True Story of the Royal Collection of Wild Beasts* (London, 2004), p. 18.

3 H. O'Regan et al., 'Medieval Big Cat Remains from the Royal Menagerie at the Tower of London', *International Journal of Osteoarchaeology*, XVI/5, p. 393.

4 'Henry III's Elephant', *New York Times*, 11 June 1882.

5 Hahn, *The Tower Menagerie*, p. 23.

6 'The Medieval Bestiary: Bear', available at www.bestiary.ca, accessed 12 November 2012.

7 O'Regan et al., 'Medieval Big Cat Remains from the Royal Menagerie at the Tower of London', p. 392.

8 Guy de la Bédoyère, ed., *The Diary of John Evelyn: First Person Singular* (Suffolk, 1995), 9 February 1665, p. 143.

9 Ibid., p. 142.

10 Hahn, *The Tower Menagerie*, p. 139.

11 Samuel McKechnie, *Popular Entertainments Through the Ages* (London, 1969), p. 39.

12 *Flying Post*, 11–14 June 1698.

13 Theodore F. M. Newton, 'The Civet-Cats of Newington Green: New Light on Defoe', *Review of English Studies*, 13 (1937), p. 12.

14 Hahn, *The Tower Menagerie*, p. 119.

15 Bédoyère, ed., *John Evelyn*, 13 February 1654, p. 86.

16 Altick, *The Shows of London*, p. 36. .

17 Bédoyère, ed., *John Evelyn*, 22 October 1684, p. 270.

18 Ibid., p. 271.

19 The Royal Society, a learned society for science formerly known as the Royal Society of London for the Improvement of Natural Knowledge, was founded in 1662. William Stukeley, *Of the Spleen, its Description and History, Uses and Diseases . . . To which is Added Some Anatomical Observations in the Dissection of an Elephant* (London, 1722), p. 91.

20 Bengal is a now partly Bangladesh and the states of West Bengal, Tripura, Bihar, Assam and Orissa.

21 *London Evening Post*, 14 June 1739; *Daily Post*, 29 December 1739.

22 'A Letter from Dr Parsons to Martin Folkes, Esq; President of the Royal Society, Containing the Natural History of the Rhinoceros', *Philosophical Transactions*, XLII (1742–43), pp. 528–9.

23 *London Daily Post and General Advertiser*, 13 October 1738.

24 *London Daily Post and General Advertiser*, 23 December 1738.

25 *London Evening Post*, 22 February 1739.

26 *London Daily Post and General Advertiser*, 27 February 1739.

27 Altick, *The Shows of London*, p. 35.

28 Hahn, *The Tower Menagerie*, p. 152.

29 Ibid., p. 153.

30 Ibid., p. 177.

31 Oliver Goldsmith, *An History of the Earth and Animated Nature* (Philadelphia, PA, 1795), vol. II, p. 136.

32 Hahn, *The Tower Menagerie*, pp. 180–81.

33 *London Evening Post*, 3–5 December 1767.

34 *London Evening Post*, 26–28 June 1764.

35 Robin Blake, *George Stubbs and the Wide Creation: Animals, People and Places in the Life of George Stubbs, 1724–1806* (London, 2005), p. 214.

36 *London Evening Post*, 4–6 February 1772; *London Evening Post*, 27–9 February 1772.

37 Goldsmith, *An History of the Earth and Animated Nature*, vol. II, p. 393.

38 Ibid., p. 398.

39 *World*, 22 November 1791.

40 *St James's Chronicle*, 22–4 November 1792.

41 'Exeter 'Change', *The Observer*, 7 July 1793.

42 'The Beautiful and Superb Collection of Nature . . .', *The Times*, 26 August 1801, p. 3.

43 *World*, 15 August 1792.

44 *Gazetteer and New Daily Advertiser*, 5 May 1792.

45 *Morning Post and Daily Advertiser*, 6 November 1777.

46 *Morning Chronicle*, 9 April 1800.

47 Jessie Dobson, 'John Hunter's Animals', *Journal of the History of Medicine and Allied Sciences*, VII/4 (October 1962), p. 482.

48 'Exhibition of Beasts and Birds, in the Great Rooms over Exeter Change', *The Times*, 12 May 1788, p. 4.

49 *World*, 21 September 1791.

50 Ibid.

51 *James's Chronicle or the British Evening Post*, 31 January 1793.

52 *World*, 5 February 1793.

53 *Daily Advertiser*, 4 February 1796.

54 *The Times*, 5 September 1797, p. 4.

55 'Bartholomew Fair', *The Times*, 4 September 1805, p. 3.

56 'News! Great News! From the Royal Menagerie . . .', *The Morning Chronicle*, 1 September 1807.

57 Frost, *Old Showmen, and the Old London Fairs*, p. 91.

58 Ibid., p. 91.

59 Ibid., p. 159.

60 Ibid., pp. 232–3.

61 Ibid., pp. 241–2.

62 *Morning Chronicle*, 25 December 1823.

63 Lord Byron, *The Works of Lord Byron: Letters and Journals*, vol. II: 14 November 1813 – 19 April 1814, p. 319, available at Electronic Text Center, University of Virginia Library.

64 *Morning Chronicle*, 25 February 1818.

65 *Morning Chronicle*, 9 April 1819.

66 Jan Bondeson, *Animal Freaks: The Strange History of Amazing Animals* (London, 2008), pp. 68–70.

67 Musth is a periodical change of behaviour in adult bull elephants caused by rising levels of testosterone, which makes them aggressive and withdrawn. 'Coroners' Inquests', *The Times*, 2 November 1825, p. 3.

68 See W. Hone, *The Every-day Book* (1826), vol. II, pp. 321–36.

69 Charles Dickens, 'Scotland Yard – Sketches by "Boz"', II, n.s., *Morning Chronicle*, 4 October 1836.

70 'Dissection of the Elephant', *The Times*, 8 March 1826, p. 4.

71 'Police: Bow-street', *The Times*, 15 September 1827, p. 3.

72 'Death of a Wolf', *The Times*, 3 March 1820.

73 *Morning Chronicle*, 24 May 1816.

74 'Buffalo Hunt in London', *Morning Chronicle*, 23 December 1820.

75 Thomas Hood, 'The Monkey-martyr', from *Whims and Oddities*, 2nd ser. (1827), lines 53–6 and 75–91.

76 'Feeding the Wild Beasts . . .', *Morning Chronicle*, 30 May 1829.

77 *St James's Chronicle or the British Evening Post*, 9 December 1794.

78 'National Menagerie', *Morning Chronicle*, 9 September 1823.

79 'The Cameleopard', *Morning Chronicle*, 11 August 1827.

80 'The Camelopardalis, or Giraffe', *Literary Gazette*, 553, 25 August 1827, p. 554.

81 'The Royal Menagerie . . .', *Morning Chronicle*, 27 May 1829.

82 'Escape of a Wolf from The Tower', *Derby Mercury*, 30 April 1834.

83 Hahn, *The Tower Menagerie*, p. 238.

84 Ibid., p. 239.

85 Frost, *The Old Showmen, and the Old London Fairs*, p. 259.

86 Ibid., p. 275.

87 *London Chronicle*, 8 September 1828.

88 Frost, *The Old Showmen, and the Old London Fairs*, p. 288.

89 Ibid., p. 303–4.

90 Ibid., p. 260.

91 See Hone, *The Every-day Book*, vol. I, 1826, pp. 978–9.

92 Frost, *The Old Showmen, and the Old London Fairs*, p. 274.

93 Hone, *The Every-day Book*, vol. I, p. 1181.

94 Ibid., pp. 1181–2.

95 Frost, *The Old Showmen, and the Old London Fairs*, pp. 258–9.

96 'Wild Beast Statistics', *Chambers's Edinburgh Journal* (30 August 1834), p. 246.

97 'Multum In Parvo', *The Newcastle Courant*, 1 December 1837.

98 Alfred Selbourne, 'Wombwell Accidents', *New Sporting Magazine*, XVI/24 (1834), pp. 146–9.

99 Frost, *The Old Showmen, and the Old London Fairs*, p. 343.

100 'Death of Mr George Wombwell', *The Times*, 27 November 1850, p. 7.

101 'Sale of Wombwell's Menagerie', *Daily News*, 10 April 1872.

102 *The Era*, 22 June 1889.

103 Ibid.

104 *The Era*, 31 October 1896.

105 'Leadenhall Market', *Leisure Hour*, 22 August 1861, p. 541.

106 'Death of Jamrach, the Naturalist', *Pall Mall Gazette*, 8 September 1891.

107 'Lions and Tigers Wholesale and Retail', *Daily News*, 12 August 1869.

108 Ibid.

109 'Mr Jamrach's Wild Beast Depot, Ratcliff Highway', *The Graphic*, 24 July 1875.

110 'Jamrach's', *Reynolds's Newspaper*, 23 March 1879.

111 Much of the British trade in exotics moved from London to Liverpool in about 1897: A. G. Page, 'Wild Beasts in a Great City', *English Illustrated Magazine* (December 1897), pp. 249–58.

112 C. J. Cornish, *Life at the Zoo: Notes and Traditions of the Regent's Park Gardens* (London, 1897), p. 206.

113 *Daily News*, 17 October 1873.

114 'The Training of Wild Beasts', *Review of Reviews* (September 1893), p. 284.

115 'The Wild Animal Trade', *Leeds Mercury*, 2 January 1886.

116 'Escape of a Tiger in Ratcliff Highway', *Daily News*, 27 October 1857.

117 Ibid.

118 'Law Intelligence: Wade *v.* Jamrach – a Bengal Tiger', *Daily News*, 8 February 1858.

119 Ibid.

120 'An Alligator in the Thames', *Reynolds's Newspaper*, 24 April 1870.

121 Cornish, *Life at the Zoo*, p. 211.

122 'A Bear at Large', *Reynolds's Newspaper*, 29 September 1878.

123 Frank Buckland, *Notes and Jottings From Animal Life* (London, 1886), pp. 21–3.

124 Richard Bell, *My Strange Pets and Other Memories of Country Life* (Whitefish, MO, 2010), p. 68.

125 Bram Stoker, *Dracula* (London, 1897), chapter 11.

126 Henry Scherren, *The Zoological Society of London* (London, 1905), pp. 14–15.

127 Ibid., p. 15.

128 Ibid.

129 Ibid., p. 268.

130 Wendy Moore, *The Knife Man* (London, 2005), p. 354.

131 Ibid., pp. 314–15.

132 Dobson, 'John Hunter's Animals', p. 479; Moore, *The Knife Man*, p. 289.

133 Dobson, 'John Hunter's Animals', p. 481.

134 Moore, *The Knife Man*, p. 288.

135 W. R. Le Fanu, 'John Hunter's Buffaloes', *The British Medical Journal*, 26 September 1931, p. 574.

136 From Everard Home, 'Short Account of the Life of the Author', prefixed to John Hunter, *Treatise on Blood, Inflammation and Gunshot Wounds* (London, 1794).

137 The Pantheon was a place of public entertainment in Oxford Street, built in 1772. The site is now home to Marks & Spencer's Oxford Street Pantheon branch. *The Reminiscences of Henry Angelo* (London, 1828), p. 96.

138 Wilfrid Blunt, *The Ark in the Park: The Zoo in the Nineteenth Century* (London, 1976), p. 32.

139 Frost, *The Old Showmen, and the Old London Fairs*, pp. 275–6.

140 'Zoological Gardens, Regent's Park', *The Athenaeum*, 15 October 1853, p. 1229.

141 'The Zoological Gardens, Regent's Park', *The Times*, 23 November 1831, p. 4.

142 'The Giraffes', *The Examiner*, 29 May 1836, p. 344.

143 Brian Edginton, *Charles Waterton: A Biography* (Cambridge, 1996), p. 178.

144 Ibid.

145 *Pall Mall Gazette*, 4 November 1867.

146 Scherren, *The Zoological Society of London*, pp. 86–7.

147 '"Waking Up": The Cannibal Snake', *The Graphic*, 3 November 1894.

148 Scherren, *The Zoological Society of London*, pp. 215–16.

149 J. Barrington-Johnson, *The Zoo: The Story of London Zoo* (London, 2005), p. 41.

150 'A Howl from the Hippopotamus', *Punch*, XXV (22 October 1853), p. 168.

151 Telam, 'Humanity: To the Editor . . .', *The Times*, 17 May 1869, p. 8.

152 'Public Amusements', *Reynolds's Newspaper*, 29 October 1876.

153 Philip Hoare, *Leviathan, or The Whale* (London, 2008), pp. 13–15.

154 Piers C. Claughton, 'The Dead Whale: To the Editor . . .', *The Times*, 2 October 1877, p. 7.

155 'Public Amusements: Westminster Aquarium', *Lloyd's Weekly Newspaper*, 23 June 1878.

156 Blunt, *The Ark in the Park*, pp. 235–6.

157 'Jumbo: The Paragon of Elephants', *The Times*, 15 February 1929, p. 17.

158 Henry C. Burdett, 'Jumbo: To the Editor . . .', *The Times*, 6 March 1882, p. 7.

159 Scherren, *The Zoological Society of London*, p. 241.

160 Barrington-Johnson, *The Zoo*, p. 81.

161 'Diksie "Could Not be Saved"', *The Times*, 12 September 1967, p. 2.

162 Blunt, *The Ark in the Park*, p. 135.

SIX

Pampered Pets and Sad Strays

1 Cited in a lecture by Angus Trumble, 'Rossetti's Wombat: A Pre-Raphaelite Obsession in Victorian

England' (16 April 2003), available at www.nla.gov.au, accessed 12 November 2012.

2 Theo Holme, 'Rossetti and Tudor House', *The Times*, 1 January 1972, p. 9.

3 George. C. Bompas, *Life of Frank Buckland* (London,1886), pp. 122–3.

4 Ibid., p. 304.

5 Ibid., pp. 209–317.

6 Ibid., p. 284.

7 Keith Thomas, *Man and the Natural World: Changing Attitudes in England, 1500–1800* (London, 1984), p. 110.

8 'Mr Jamrach's College for Young Beasts', *Leisure Hour*, 17 June 1858, p. 378.

9 C. J. Cornish, *Life at the Zoo: Notes and Traditions of the Regent's Park Gardens* (London, 1897), pp. 313–14.

10 A Lady Vet, 'Humours of a Pets' Hospital', *Quiver* (September 1922), p. 973.

11 Guy de la Bédoyère, ed., *The Diary of John Evelyn: First Person Singular* (Suffolk, 1995), 11 November 1683, p. 265.

12 Robin Blake, *George Stubbs and the Wide Creation: Animals, People and Places in the Life of George Stubbs, 1724–1806* (London, 2005), p. 208.

13 'Outlandish Pets', *The Saturday Review*, 5 April 1890, p. 281.

14 Ibid.

15 'Mr Jamrach's College for Young Beasts', *Leisure Hour*, p. 379.

16 Cornish, *Life at the Zoo*, p. 312.

17 Ibid., p. 313.

18 'Outlandish Pets', *Saturday Review*, p. 405.

19 Ibid.

20 'Novel Domestic Pets', *Review of Reviews*, April 1909, p. 347.

21 A Lady Vet, 'Humours of a Pets' Hospital', p. 973.

22 For Christian's story see Anthony Bourke and John Rendall, *A Lion Called Christian* (London, 2009).

23 Thanks to Harrods' archivist Sebastian Wormell for this information.

24 See 'Exotic Species in the Wild', available at www.met.police.uk within 'Wildlife Crime Unit: Protecting British Wildlife', accessed 12 November 2012.

25 Many thanks to John Clark of the Museum of London for this reference.

26 'English Usage of Beasts', *Gentleman's Magazine*, 13 May 1732, p. 747.

27 Thomas, *Man and the Natural World*, p. 118.

28 Luttrell Psalter: folio 181 verso, folio 33.

29 Thomas, *Man and the Natural World*, p. 110.

30 William Kidd, 'Domestic Pets – The Squirrel', *National Magazine* (February 1857), pp. 254–5.

31 Ibid., p. 254.

32 'Rare Birds in London', *Aberdeen Weekly Journal*, 21 May 1885.

33 Harriet Ritvo, *The Animal Estate* (Cambridge, MA, 1989), p. 85.

34 'English Usage of Beasts', *Gentleman's Magazine*, p. 747.

35 Cited in Thomas, *Man and the Natural World*, pp. 107–08.

36 Bédoyère, ed., *The Diary of John Evelyn*, 6 February 1685, p. 275.

37 Ritvo, *The Animal Estate*, p. 86.

38 'Our Ladies' Pets, and What They Cost', *Tait's Edinburgh Magazine* (May 1856), p. 272.

39 'The Death Rate at Jamrach's', *Pall Mall Gazette*, 13 January 1898.

40 Ritvo, *The Animal Estate*, p. 86.

41 'Social Nuisances', *New Monthly Magazine and Humorist* (April 1844), p. 512.

42 Ignatius Phayre, 'A Change in Pets', *Quiver* (July 1922), p. 809.

43 A Lady Vet, 'Humours of a Pets' Hospital', p. 975.

44 Ignatius Phayre, 'A Change in Pets', p. 809.

45 'Fashionable Honour', *E. Johnson's British Gazette and Sunday Monitor*, 10 April 1803.

46 'The Pets of Authors', *All the Year Round*, 11 July 1885, p. 405.

47 Cited in Andreas-Holger Maehle, 'Literary Responses to Animal Experimentation in 17th and 18th Century Britain', *Medical History*, 34 (1990), p. 46.

48 For a full list of London animal memorials, see Jan Toms, *Animal Graves and Memorials* (Princes Risborough, 2006).

49 'A Cemetery for Dogs', *Strand Magazine* (July 1893), p. 630.

50 Topper was one among many dogs, cats, birds, goats, calves, bears and monkeys which were pets in fire stations and barracks within London. See W. W., 'The Fauna of London: Part II On the Kerb and in the Doorway', *The Idler* (November 1910), p. 196.

51 Cited in Braybrooke, *London Green*, p. 84.

52 'A Cemetery for Dogs', *Strand Magazine*, p. 630.

53 Quoted in *Notes and Queries*, 7th ser., vii.26.

54 Cited at 'London's Lost Dogs', 25 November 2009, available at www.georgianlondon.com, accessed 12 November 2012.

55 'The Fate of Pets', *Good Words* (January 1872), p. 819.

56 Margaret Forster, *Elizabeth Barrett Browning: A Biography* (London, 1988), pp. 117–19, pp. 136–7, 176.

57 'The Fate of Pets', *Good Words*, p. 820.

58 'A Dog Fancier and Pugilist Punished', *Reynolds's Newspaper*, 22 October 1893.

59 *Voice of Humanity*, IV (15 May 1831), pp. 156–7.

60 *Voice of Humanity*, III (15 February 1831), pp. 97–8.

61 Ibid.

62 Ibid.

63 Ibid., p. 99.

64 *Voice of Humanity*, II (November 1830), p. 62.

65 Alfred Rosling Bennett, *London and Londoners in the Eighteen-fifties and Sixties* (London, 1924), pp. 39–40.

66 Thomas, *Man and the Natural World*, p. 109.

67 Daniel Defoe, *A Journal of the Plague Year* (London, 1943), p. 161.

68 The cat statue was added to the Whittington Stone in April 1964. The stone marks the spot where Whittington heard the sound of Bow Bells chiming 'Turn again, Whittington, thrice Lord Mayor of London': Thomas, *Man and the Natural World*, p. 109.

69 Antony Clayton, *The Folklore of London: Legends, Ceremonies and Celebrations Past and Present* (London, 2008), p. 170.

70 W. W., 'The Fauna of London', p. 192.

71 'Leadenhall Market', *Leisure Hour*, p. 541.

72 Many thanks to John Clark of the Museum of London for this reference.

73 See Tim Birkhead, *The Red Canary: The Story of the First Genetically Engineered Animal* (London, 2003), pp. 88–9.

74 Randall moved his business to the Porter's Lodge at the Mews Gate, Charing Cross, in 1717.

75 *Post Man and the Historical Account*, 13 May 1707 and 5 April 1709.

76 Hill's 'Bird Fancyer's Delight', available at www.flageolets.com, accessed 12 November 2012.

77 Peter Quennell, ed., *Mayhew's London* (London, 1984), pp. 248–9.

78 Ibid., p. 243.

79 Ibid.

80 Ibid., p. 248.

81 'Some Notes of a Naturalist in London', *Preston Guardian*, 26 November 1853.

82 T. Sparrow, 'Poverty's Pets', *Quiver* (January 1900), p. 280.

83 Ibid., p. 279.

84 Ibid., pp. 279–80.

85 'Prison Pets', *Chambers's Journal*, 7 July 1883, p. 422.

86 'At the Animals' Hospital', *Strand Magazine*, p. 75.

87 Frederick Hobday, 'Pets and Quacks', *The Saturday Review*, 15 June 1935, p. 747.

88 The Institute was set up after Thomas Brown left over £20,000 in his will to the London University to provide a hospital for diseased animals, and their treatment free of charge (except for their keep), within a mile of Westminster or Southward, but land there was too expensive.

89 James Paget Granville and Richard Quain, 'The Brown Institution: To the Editor . . .', *The Times*, 18 July 1890, p. 13.

90 R.J.M. Franklin, 'The Brown Animal Sanatory Institution – Historical Lessons for the Present?', *Veterinary Journal*, CLIX/3 (May 2000), p. 233.

91 'Retail Therapy: An Overview of Shopping in Georgian London', 1 January 2010, available at www.georgianlondon.com, accessed 12 November 2012.

92 W. W. 'The Fauna of London', pp. 192–4.

93 'A Morning's Ramble near The Seven Dials', *Leisure Hour*, 24 March 1859, pp. 182–4.

94 'Leadenhall Market', *Leisure Hour*, p. 541.

95 'Club Row', *Leisure Hour*, 12 December 1861, p. 795.

96 Greenwood, *Unsentimental Journeys*, chapter 18: 'The Song-bird Market'.

97 Fitter, *London's Natural History*, p. 210.

98 William Kidd, 'Domestic Pets – The Nightingale', *National Magazine* (April 1857), p. 416.

99 Ibid.

100 'Our Omnibus', *The Era*, 20 July 1873.

101 'Wild Birds' Protection Act', *Western Mail*, 9 April 1873.

102 Axel Munthe, 'To Those Who Love Birds: To the Editor . . .', *The Times*, 27 January 1933. Even in 2005 a police raid on a pub in Bethnal Green, in conjunction with the RSPCA, involved the arrest of a group of men engaged in the illegal trade of wild birds.

103 'Leadenhall Market', *Leisure Hour*, p. 541.

104 'Trips About Town: Bethnal Green', *Strand Magazine* (April 1905), p. 465.

105 Cited in 'Dog Days at Club Row Market', 27 April 2010, available at www.spitalfieldslife.com, accessed 12 November 2012.

106 'Fined for Obstruction', *The Times*, 3 June 1981.

107 'Trips about town: Bethnal Green', *Strand Magazine*, p. 463.

108 Ibid., pp. 463–4.

109 James Greenwood, *The Wilds of London* (London, 1874), pp. 273–4.

110 Birkhead, *The Red Canary*, pp. 48–9.

111 William Kidd, 'The Canary – Our Household Bird', *National Magazine* (January 1857), p. 206.

112 Birkhead, *The Red Canary*, p. 105.

113 Foreign birds included Java sparrows from Africa, Chilean starlings and Australian grass parakeets; English birds included black and russet bullfinches, goldfinches, linnets, siskins, redpoles, skylarks, thrushes, nightingales and bearded tits.

114 'The Bird Show at the Crystal Palace', *The Times*, 17 February 1873, p. 7.

115 'Outlandish Pets', *Saturday Review*, p. 405.

116 'Quiet Interlude in Cage Bird Show', *The Times*, 13 January 1956, p. 10.

117 'Leadenhall Market', *Leisure Hour*, pp. 540–41.

118 James A. Second, 'Nature's Fancy: Charles Darwin and the Breeding of Pigeons', *Isis*, LXXII/2 (June 1981), pp. 178, 173.

119 Ibid., p. 170.

120 'Metropolitan Fancy Rabbit Club', *The Era*, 24 December 1843.

121 'Metropolitan Fancy Rabbit Club Show', *Morning Post*, 21 December 1844.

122 'The Metropolitan Rabbit Club', *The Era*, 19 December 1847.

123 Harriet Ritvo, *The Animal Estate* (Cambridge, MA, 1989), p. 100.

124 Greenwood, *Unsentimental Journeys*, chapter 4: 'A Dog Show'.

125 Glenavon, 'Valuable Pets', *Ludgate* (January 1900), p. 215.

126 'Dog Show at the Crystal Palace', *The Era*, 14 June 1874.

127 'The Cremorne Dog Show', *Reynolds's Newspaper*, 29 March 1863.

128 'The International Dog Show', *Lloyd's Weekly Newspaper*, 24 May 1863.

129 Ritvo, *The Animal Estate*, p. 87.

130 Northumbrian, 'Our Brutal Instincts: To the Editor . . .', *Reynolds's Newspaper*, 15 November 1896.

131 'Pet Animals', *Badminton Magazine of Sports and Pastimes* (July 1898), p. 51.

132 Ritvo, *The Animal Estate*, pp. 115–16.

133 'Cat Shows', *Orchestra*, 22 September 1871, p. 396.

134 Glenavon, 'Valuable Pets', p. 216.

135 Cited in Peter Ackroyd, *London: The Biography* (London, 2000), p. 419.

136 A. Lloyd Moote and Dorothy C. Moote, *The Great Plague: The Story of London's Most Deadly Year* (Baltimore, MD, 2006), pp. 115–16.

137 Ibid., p. 121.

138 Defoe, *A Journal of the Plague Year*, p. 161.

139 'Police: Marylebone', *The Times*, 3 October 1864, p. 9.

140 Maehle, 'Literary Responses to Animal Experimentation', p. 29.

141 Ibid., p. 44.

142 See Peter Mason, *The Brown Dog Affair* (London, 1997).

143 'Leicester Square', *Old and New London*, vol. III (1878), pp. 160–73, available at www.british-history.ac.uk, accessed 12 November 2012.

144 Roy Porter, *London: A Social History* (London, 1995), p. 182.

145 *Cobbett's Weekly Political Register*, 13 June 1812.

146 *Penny London Post*, 20 December, 1749.

147 Quennell, *Mayhew's London*, p. 306.

148 Ibid., pp. 308–9.

149 'The Home for Lost Dogs', *Leisure Hour*, 5 September 1861, p. 565.

150 A Friend to All Dumb Animals, 'Something New: To the Editor . . .', *The Standard*, 11 September 1860, p. 4.

151 *The Times*, 18 October 1860, p. 8.

152 'London Correspondence', *The Belfast News-letter*, 2 October 1860.

153 'Two Dog-shows', *All the Year Round*, 2 August 1862, pp. 496–7.

154 *Morning Post*, 27 February 1861, p. 4.

155 Ibid.

156 'Islington: Growth: Holloway and Tollington', *A History of the County of Middlesex*, vol. VIII: *Islington and Stoke Newington Parishes* (1985), pp. 29–37, available at www.british-history.ac.uk, accessed 12 November 2012.

157 'The Home for Lost Dogs', *Daily News*, 20 July 1872.

158 The Treasurer [of], 'The Home for Lost Dogs: To the Editor . . .', *Daily News*, 1 August 1872.

159 'Home for Lost Dogs', *Pall Mall Gazette*, 4 December 1875.

160 'The Dogs' Christmas', *Lloyd's Weekly Newspaper*, 22 December 1895.

161 'The Home for Lost Dogs', *Strand Magazine* (January 1891), p. 653.

162 'For the Bite of a Mad Dog', 20 December 2009, available at www.georgianlondon.com, accessed 12 November 2012.

163 Ibid.

164 Moore, *The Knife Man*, pp. 509–10.

165 Rabies outbreaks also occurred in the first half of the nineteenth century and the Metropolitan Police Act 1833 gave police the right to destroy any animal suspected to be in a rabid state, or one that had been bitten by a suspected rabies carrier.

166 Ritvo, *The Animal Estate*, p. 192.

167 'Hydrophobia', *The Standard*, 2 January 1886, p. 3; Ritvo, *The Animal Estate*, p. 192.

168 Julia Andrews, 'The Dog's Home: To the Editor . . .', *Morning Post*, 15 May 1896, p. 3: a total of 42,500 dogs were received during 1896 – still an unbroken record for the Home.

169 J. Charles Colam, 'Home For Lost Dogs: To the Editor . . .', *The Standard*, 24 December 1886. Through a policy of killing stray dogs and quarantining dogs imported into the country, the UK was officially declared clear of rabies in 1902.

170 'Occasional Notes', *Pall Mall Gazette*, 19 February 1896.

171 Henry J. Ward and Louis Wain, 'Dogs' Home at Battersea: To the Editor . . .', *The Times*, 20 January 1905, p. 14.

172 Holly Williams, 'Creature Comfort: Why London's First Dogs' Home was Met With Howls of Derision', *The Independent*, 13 August 2010.

173 E. Keith Robinson, 'Dogs Killed on the Road: Points from Letters', *The Times*, 9 April 1936, p. 10.

174 Quennell, *Mayhew's London*, pp. 128–9.

175 John Colam, '"Not on Board Wages": To the Editor . . .', *The Times*, 14 September 1877, p. 4.

176 Ibid.

177 'Cats in London', *Huddersfield Chronicle and West Yorkshire Advertiser*, 25 August 1900, p. 3.

178 'Starving Cats', *Morning Post*, 29 August 1888, p. 2; *Morning Post*, 7 July 1898, p. 1.

179 'Cats in London', *Huddersfield Chronicle*, p. 3.

180 *Morning Post*, 9 May 1900, p. 1.
181 Arthur J. Coke, 'Shelters for Stray Cats', *The Times*, 8 June 1910, p. 22.
182 'No Pets in New Tenements', *The Times*, 2 January 1937, p. 7.
183 See *Wonderland: Mad Cats and Englishwomen*, documentary shown on BBC 2 (27 October 2010).

SEVEN
London Wildlife:
The Persecuted and the Celebrated

1 R.S.R. Fitter, *London's Natural History* (London, 1953), p. 31.
2 Ibid., p. 52.
3 'London Birds', *The Speaker*, 16 July 1898, p. 83.
4 W. H. Hudson, *Birds in London* (London, 1898), pp. 121–2.
5 Fitter, *London's Natural History*, p. 87. In 2006 a red kite was spotted in a back garden in Hackney, but this sighting appeared to be an isolated case.
6 'Streets in the Middle Ages', *Chambers's Edinburgh Journal*, 18 January 1851, p. 48.
7 Fitter, *London's Natural History*, p. 51.
8 Philip Armitage, Barbara West and Ken Steedman, 'New Evidence of Black Rat in Roman London', *London Archaeologist*, IV/14 (1984), p. 375.
9 But these numbers are pure estimates as the City's population at the time was about 50,000.
10 A. Lloyd Moote and Dorothy C. Moote, *The Great Plague: The Story of London's Most Deadly Year* (Baltimore, MD, 2006), p. 115.
11 'Rats', *All the Year Round*, 19 September 1874, p. 532.
12 Fitter, *London's Natural History*, p. 153.
13 Peter Quennell, ed., *Mayhew's London* (London, 1984), p. 379.
14 'Rats', p. 536.
15 Cited in 'A Rat! A Rat! – Dead for a Ducat', *Household Words*, 23 November 1850, p. 214.
16 Fitter, *London's Natural History*, p. 176.
17 'NPTA National Rodent Survey Report 2006' (January 2007), available at www.npta.org.uk, accessed 12 November 2012.
18 'Rat Number Surge is "Health Risk"', 5 January 2007, available at www.bbc.co.uk.
19 'On Animal and Vegetable Life in the City of London', *The Examiner*, 22 May 1831, p. 327.
20 Quennell, *Mayhew's London*, p. 328.
21 'Rats', p. 533.
22 'Bohemian London No. II', *St James's Magazine* (October 1870), p. 236.
23 Ibid., p. 237.
24 Ibid., p. 236.
25 Ibid., p. 232.
26 George R. Sims, 'Trips About Town', *Strand Magazine* (April 1905), p. 465.
27 'Bohemian London II', *St James's Magazine*, p. 232.
28 Ibid.
29 'On Animal and Vegetable Life in the City of London', *The Examiner*, p. 327.
30 'Cats and Rats at St Katherine's Docks', *The Mirror*, 16 November 1839, p. 328.
31 'Animals in the Post Office', *The British Postal Museum and Archive* (2005), p. 1, available at www.postalheritage.org.uk, accessed 12 November 2012.
32 Revd Cowell, 'London Insects', *Wesleyan-Methodist Magazine* (November 1893), p. 826.
33 Robert Southey, *Letters from England* (London, 1836), p. 49.
34 'Bohemian London II', pp. 226–7.
35 Ibid., p. 226.
36 Ibid, p. 236.
37 Ibid.
38 The author of *Curiosities of Natural History*, 'What I saw at the London Docks', *Leisure Hour*, 28 June 1860, p. 412.
39 W. W. and L.R.B, 'The Fauna of London: Under Ground', *The Idler* (March 1911), p. 577.
40 'Mosquitoes in Westminster Palace', *York Herald*, 26 August 1874, p. 3.
41 'Mosquitoes in London', *Hampshire Advertiser*, 2 September 1874, p. 4.
42 'Mosquitoes in London', *Berrow's Worcester Journal*, 23 June 1877, p. 6; 'Gnats and Mosquitoes', *Bow Bells*, 3 July 1891, p. 10.

43 'Mosquitoes in London', *Aberdeen Weekly Journal*, 6 August 1897.

44 *Bed Bug Manual*, p. 7; published by Killgerm, www.killgerm.com, accessed 12 November 2012; Nick Collins, 'Rise in Bedbugs Prompts "Pandemic" Fears', *The Telegraph*, 9 March 2009.

45 Victoria Gill, 'Bed Bugs Boom Tracked Using DNA Fingerprinting', www.bbc.co.uk/nature, accessed 28 March 2013.

46 'Attitudes to Foxes: Common Myths', available at www.thefoxwebsite.org, accessed 12 November 2012.

47 'Hunting', *Trewman's Exeter Flying Post*, 23 October 1834.

48 'Natural History: The Fox', *Chambers's Edinburgh Journal*, 10 August 1833, p. 221.

49 'Foxes Move Into London', *The Times*, 22 August 1967, p. 10.

50 James Owen, '10,000 Foxes Roam London', *National Geographic News*, 15 May 2006.

51 Richard Osley, 'Fox Attacked Baby Boy in Cot, Say Police', *The Independent*, 10 February 2013; Adam Fresco, 'A Summer Night, an Open Door, and a Fox Attacks Sleeping Girl', *The Times*, 5 September 2003, p. 3.

52 Fitter, *London's Natural History*, p. 80.

53 'Wild Nature in London', *Magazine of Art* (January 1894), p. 247.

54 Hudson, *Birds in London*, p. 208.

55 'Birds in London', *The Graphic*, 20 March 1875; Hudson, *Birds in London*, pp. 275–6, 302.

56 'Protection against Bird Murder', *Bradford Observer*, 16 September 1869.

57 Ibid.

58 'Sea Gulls at London Bridge', *The Standard*, 20 January 1881, p. 2.

59 'Our London Letter', *Liverpool Mercury*, 18 January 1892.

60 Cited in Fitter, *London's Natural History*, p. 204.

61 'Wild Nature in London', p. 247.

62 'The Increase of Wild Birds In London', *Pall Mall Gazette*, 2 December 1897.

63 'Wild Birds in London', *The Times*, 27 March 1909, p. 7.

64 There was a series of Wild Birds' Protection Acts from 1872 to 1896.

65 'The Increase of Wild Birds In London', *Pall Mall Gazette*, 2 December 1897.

66 Ibid.

67 Cited in Fitter, *London's Natural History*, pp. 127–8.

68 Michael McCarthy, 'Are Starlings Going the Way of the Sparrows?', *The Independent*, 13 November 2000.

69 *The Goon Show*, 'The Starlings', Series 4, Special Episode.

70 McCarthy, 'Are Starlings Going the Way of the Sparrows?'.

71 'The Birds of London', *The Standard*, 26 May 1898, p. 8.

72 Don Cooper, 'Sparrow-pie, Anyone?', *London Archaeologist* (Summer 2004), pp. 245–8.

73 'On Animal and Vegetable Life in the City of London', *The Examiner*, p. 328.

74 'Rare Birds in London', *Aberdeen Weekly Journal*, 21 May 1885.

75 Revd Cowell, 'London Birds', *Wesleyan-Methodist Magazine* (October 1893), p. 750.

76 'London Birds', *The Speaker*, p. 83.

77 'Bird Life of the Streets', *Manchester Times*, 4 September 1875.

78 Hudson, *Birds in London*, pp. 15–16.

79 Philip Howard, 'A Bird on the Hand is Worth Two on the Bench', *The Times*, 30 June 1971, p. 5.

80 Michael McCarthy, 'After Years of Decline, the Sparrow Wins Protection', *The Independent*, 14 October 2004.

81 Hudson, *Birds in London*, p. 307. Hudson writes about the debate surrounding the actual date when rooks came to the Temple.

82 'Birds in London', *The Graphic*, 20 March 1875.

83 Hudson, *Birds in London*, pp. 78–9.

84 'The Modern Country Cousin', *The Star*, 18 December 1888.

85 Hudson, *Birds in London*, p. 27.

86 Geoffrey Parnell, 'Riddle of the Tower Ravens Almost Resolved', *London Topographical Society Newsletter*, 65 (November 2007), pp. 5–7. Boria Sax

has also come to the same conclusion about the Tower ravens: 'How Ravens Came to the Tower of London', *Society and Animals*, 15 (2007), pp. 269–83.

87 'My Life in Travel: Derrick Coyle, Raven Master at the Tower of London', *The Observer*, 1 February 2009.

88 Cited in Fitter, *London's Natural History*, p. 59.

89 E. A. Wallis Budge, 'London Pigeons: Flocks at the British Museum, To the Editor . . .', *The Times*, 18 August 1933.

90 Ibid.

91 'Birds in London', *Once a Week*, 2 September 1878, p. 79.

92 'Rooks and Pigeons in London', *All the Year Round*, 25 April 1874, p. 30.

93 Cited in 'Bird Life of the Streets', *Manchester Times*.

94 'London Pigeons Not Wild', *The Times*, 12 February 1920, p. 11.

95 'City of London Pigeons: Numbers to be Limited and Reduced', *The Times*, 20 August 1926, p. 13.

96 'The London Pigeons: Medical Officer on a Growing Nuisance', *The Times*, 3 May 1926, p. 24.

97 Ibid.

98 'City of London Pigeons: Numbers to be Limited and Reduced', *The Times*.

99 'Pigeons "Pocketed" at Victoria', *The Times*, 8 March 1957, p. 12.

100 Ibid.

101 'Save the Trafalgar Square Pigeons: Background', available at www.savethepigeons.org, accessed 12 November 2012.

102 Hugh Muir, 'Hawks Do Their Worst But Cost of Pigeon War Is Problem for Mayor', *The Guardian*, 29 September 2006. In 2013 the BBC employed Harris hawks to patrol Broadcasting House to create a 'no fly zone' for pigeons and gulls which are now classed as a 'health and hygiene' risk to both staff and the building.

103 'The Course of Nature: Kestrels at Westminster', *The Times*, 4 August 1942, p. 6.

104 Fitter, *London's Natural History*, p. 200.

105 Ibid.

106 See Lynn Barber, *The Heyday of Natural History* (London, 1980), p. 13.

107 'Wild Nature in London', *Magazine of Art* (January 1894), p. 248.

108 'Rare Birds in London', *Aberdeen Weekly Journal*, 21 May 1885.

109 'Wild Nature in London', pp. 249–50.

110 'Some Notes of a Naturalist in London', *Preston Guardian*, 26 November 1853.

111 Neville Braybrooke, *London Green* (London, 1959), p. 189.

112 *The Independent*, 18 September 1992.

113 Mute swans are not actually mute, but honk and hiss a lot.

114 Fitter, *London's Natural History*, p. 41.

115 Valentine Low, 'Swan Upmanship – Queen is First Monarch to Count Royal Lamentation', *The Times*, 21 July 2009.

116 Cited in Fitter, *London's Natural History*, p. 41.

117 A 'game' of swans means the right to catch, seize, and kill or mark all swans in certain waters. 'Swans on English Rivers', *Belfast News-letter*, 7 February 1878.

118 Fitter, *London's Natural History*, p. 41.

119 'Extraordinary Prosecution for "Swan-upping"', *The Standard*, 24 January 1878, p. 2.

120 'Swan Nicking', *Morning Post*, 14 February 1878, p. 7.

121 'Swan Nicking and Ringing', *Illustrated Police News*, 6 April 1878.

122 Low, 'Swan Upmanship'.

123 C. J. Cornish, *The Naturalist on the Thames* (London, 1902), p. 135.

124 See 'My Ancestors from the Towneley Swan Roll', available at www.goodrick.info, accessed 12 November 2012.

125 Previously the event took place on the first Monday in August and lasted for four days, with a banquet at the end ('Swan-upping on The Thames', *The Graphic*, 11 August 1877).

126 There are many collective nouns for a group of swans: a bank, a bevy, a brood, a team, a herd, a flock, a sownding, a whiting, a herd or a lamentation of swans.

127 'Swans and Swan-Upping', *Penny Magazine,* 16 July 1842, p. 278.

128 'Thames Swan Upping', *Morning Post,* 6 August 1888, p. 2.

129 'Swan "Upping"', *The Times,* 21 July 1914, p. 14; Swan Upping brochure (The Royal Household), p. 7–8; pdf available at www.royal.gov.uk, accessed 12 November 2012.

130 Ibid.

131 'Royal Swan Upping 2012, 20 June 2012', press release available at www.royal.gov.uk, accessed 12 November 2012.

132 Low, 'Swan Upmanship'.

133 'Swan-Upping on the Thames', *The Graphic.*

134 'Swan Gossip', *London Society* (August 1879), p. 189.

135 Ibid., p. 190.

136 Braybrooke, *London Green,* p. 176.

137 R. Corlett Cowell, 'The Swans of the Thames', *Wesleyan-Methodist Magazine,* December 1893, p. 907.

138 Translation of William Fitzstephen in Henry Thomas Riley, ed., *Liber Custumarum,* from the Rolls Series, XII/2 (1860).

139 'The London Fish Trade Six Hundred Years Ago', *London Reader,* 3 October 1874, p. 47.

140 From: 'Lower Thames Street', *Old and New London,* vol. 11 (1878), pp. 41–60, available at www.british-history.ac.uk, accessed 12 November 2012.

141 Fitter, *London's Natural History,* p. 81.

142 From 'Lower Thames Street'.

143 Smelts are small saltwater fish similar in appearance to salmon.

144 Cited in 'The Roach and the Dace', *Penny Magazine,* 5 November 1842, p. 437.

145 Ibid.

146 'Supply of Pure Water', *The Examiner,* 5 October 1828, pp. 643–4.

147 'The Thames and Salmon', *The Standard,* 14 May 1866, p. 5.

148 Cited in 'The Roach and the Dace', p. 437.

149 'The State of the Thames', *The Times,* 19 June 1858, p. 6.

150 'The State of the Thames', *The Standard,* 19 June 1858, p. 2.

151 Cited in C. J. Cornish, 'London Fish and Fish-Shops', *Cornhill Magazine* (February 1898), pp. 184–5.

152 'Occasional Notes', *Pall Mall Gazette,* 10 May 1879.

153 From 'Lower Thames Street'.

154 R. B. Marston, 'Our River, III – Fishers and Fish', *Pall Mall Gazette,* 20 September 1884.

155 Cited in 'The Roach and the Dace', pp. 436–7.

156 Ibid., p. 437.

157 Cited in R. B. Marston, 'The Thames as a Salmon River', *Nineteenth Century: A Monthly Review* (April 1899), p. 579.

158 Ibid., p. 580.

159 'Occasional Notes', *Pall Mall Gazette,* 10 May 1879.

160 T.M., 'The Re-stocking of the Thames: To the Editor . . .', *The Standard,* 11 March 1899.

161 'Eel Fare in The Thames', *Pall Mall Gazette,* 24 May 1866.

162 'Eels and Elvers', *Saturday Review,* 21 November 1885, p. 672.

163 'Eel', *Dictionary of Traded Goods and Commodities, 1550–1820, 1550–1820* (Wolverhampton, 2007), available at www.british-history.ac.uk, accessed 12 November 2012.

164 'Eel' from 'Ebony – Egypt Tow', *Dictionary of Traded Goods and Commodities.*

165 'Eel Fare in the Thames', *Pall Mall Gazette.*

166 'St. Jame's Park', *Morning Post,* 3 September 1827.

167 'A Monster of the Thames', *The Standard,* 31 October 1840.

168 'More Marine Stores', *Fraser's Magazine for Town and Country* (June 1852), p. 645.

169 'Eels and Elvers', *Saturday Review,* p. 673.

170 'A Chapter About Eels', *Leisure Hour,* 1 December 1859, pp. 766–7.

171 Astley H. Baldwin, 'Notes about Eels', *Once a Week,* 14 March 1863, p. 334; 'A Chapter about Eels', *Leisure Hour,* pp. 766–7; Quennell, *Mayhew's London,* p. 107.

172 'More Marine Stores', *Fraser's Magazine,* p. 646.

173 Ibid.

174 'Eel Populations in London's River Thames
    crash by 98%', www.bbc.co.uk, 22 January 2010.

175 Ibid.

176 John Vidal, 'Thousands of Fish Dead After
    Thames Sewerage Overflow', *The Guardian*,
    9 June 2011.

177 'Dolphin's Thames Journey', *The Times*, 19 January
    1965, p. 12.

178 Fitter, *London's Natural History*, p. 47.

179 Guy de la Bédoyère, ed., *The Diary of John Evelyn:
    First Person Singular* (Suffolk, 1995), 2 June 1658,
    pp. 108–9.

180 Philip Hoare, *Leviathan, or The Whale* (London,
    2008), p. 277.

181 Wendy Moore, *The Knife Man* (London, 2005),
    p. 395.

182 Eric Hardy, 'London's Own River', *Saturday
    Review*, 23 November 1935, p. 498.

183 Moore, *The Knife Man*, p. 395.

184 Eric Hardy, 'London's Own River', p. 498.

185 *London Chronicle*, 4–6 September 1781.

186 'A Seal in the Thames', *London Reader*, 9 October
    1869, p. 556.

187 Fitter, *London's Natural History*, p. 204.

188 'London's History: The Fish of the Thames',
    available at www.londononline.co.uk, accessed
    12 November 2012.

189 Olga Craig, James Orr and Roya Nikkhah,
    'Day the World Watched a Battle to Save the
    Whale', *Daily Telegraph*, 22 January 2006.

190 Hoare, *Leviathan or, The Whale*, p. 309.

Final Thoughts: An Apology and a Pardon

1 'London Letter: Polly', *Irish Times*,
    16 August, 1926, p. 4.

2 'Famed London Parrot Ill With Pneumonia',
    New York Times, 15 August 1926, p. 13.

3 'Famous Parrot Dead', *The Observer*,
    31 October 1926, p. 19.

Acknowledgements

The idea for this book evolved through discussions with my agent, Laura Longrigg, back in 2007. It is purely down to her encouragement, and that of Jonathan Burt, that this book has been completed. There were times when we thought the beasts of London would never interact with their public again.

My thanks go to several people who have provided me with information and leads: Christopher Scoble, Olivia Hogman of Smithfield Market, Nick Johnston of Leaden-hall Market, Sebastian Wormell, Harrods' archivist, John Clark of the Museum of London, John Richardson and Helen English.

I would also like to thank my father, Tim Velten, for trawling through drawers of prints and rows of books to help me find appropriate illustrations. Other photographic illustrations have been kindly provided by Mark Sheldon, Duncan Rimmer, Nigel Lomas, Michael Winters, Nick Caro, Alex Pink, Gary Wilson, Ronnie Hackston, Jim Gunnee and Joe McIntyre.

This book is dedicated to my daughter Freya Sherriffs, who kept me company while researching and writing this book – any inaccuracies are due to 'pregnancy brain'.

Photo Acknowledgements

The author and publishers wish to express their thanks to the following sources of illustrative material and/or permission to reproduce it. Some locations, not given in the captions for reasons of brevity, are also supplied here.

From William Harrison Ainsworth, *The Tower of London, a Historical Romance* (London, 1840): p. 147; American Kennel Club collection: p. 203; from *Animals' Friend: or The Progress of Humanity*: pp. 18 (1838), 36 (1840); from Mary Bayly, *Ragged Homes and How to Mend Them* (London, 1860): p. 27; from Thomas Bewick, *A General History of Quadrupeds* (Newcastle upon Tyne, 1807): p. 206; British Library, London: p. 146 (Ms. Cotton Nero D 1); The British Museum, London: pp. 85, 62, 180; photos © Trustees of the British Museum, London: pp. 46, 85, 62, 180; from *The Bystander* (25 October, 1933): p. 113; photo Nick Caro: p. 167; The College of Arms, London: p. 115; from John Dando and Harrie Runt, *Maroccus Extaticus. Or, Bankes Bay Horse in a Trance: A Discourse Set Downe in a Merry Dialogue, Betweene Bankes and His Beast: Anatomizing Some Abuses and Bad Tricks of This Age* (London, 1595): p. 127; from Gustave Doré, *London* (London, 1872): pp. 66, 185; photo The Drinking Fountain Association: p. 69; Duke of Buccleuch Collection: p. 181; from Thomas Foster, *Philozoia; or, Moral Reflections on the Actual Condition of the Animal Kingdom . . .* (Brussels, 1839): p. 189; from *The Graphic* (15 October 1887): p. 6; photo Jim Gunnee: p. 191; photo Ronnie Hackston: p. 9; The Hunterian Museum at the Royal College of Surgeons, London: p. 149; from the *Illustrated London News*: pp. 10 (5 June 1858), 23 (21 July 1849), 40 (13 December 1856), 70 (24 February 1855), 124 (21 February 1852), 138 (2 September 1848), 177 (1 April 1882), 204 (27 January 1883), 205 (22 July 1871), 243 (29 October 1842); from the *Illustrated Sporting and Dramatic News*: pp. 93 (31 March 1888), 201 (28 November 1891); from the *Illustrated Times* (26 May 1886): p. 117; photo D. St C. Laurie: p. 79; photo Nigel Lomas: p. 57; photos Joe McIntyre: pp. 163, 191; photo Paul Martin: p. 122; from Henry Mayhew, *London Labour and the London Poor: a Cyclopaedia of the Conditions and Earnings of those that will Work, those that cannot Work and those that will not Work* (London, 1851–62): pp. 218, 219; Museum of London: pp. 45, 109; National Gallery, London: p. 184; National Maritime Museum, London: p. 44; photo National Railway Museum, York: p. 77; from Matthew Paris, *Liber additamentorum*: p. 146; from G. Holden Pike, *Golden Lane: Quaint Adventures and Life pictures . . .* (London, 1876): p. 65; photo Alex Pink: p. 31; private collections: pp. 121, 190; from *Punch* (10 July 1858): p. 237; from William Henry Pyne, *The Costume of Great Britain* (London, 1808): p. 19; photo Duncan Rimmer: p. 71; The Royal Collection (© Her Majesty the Queen): p. 186; photo Royal Mail Archive: p. 74; photo Mark Sheldon: p. 41; photo Gary Wilson: p. 222; photo Michael Winters: p. 214; Yale Center for British Art, New Haven, Connecticut (Paul Mellon Collection): p. 153.

Index